Germany Since 1945

ALSO AVAILABLE FROM BLOOMSBURY

German Modernities From Wilhelm to Weimar, edited by Geoff Eley, Jennifer L. Jenkins, and Tracie Matysik

A Social History of Early Rock 'n' Roll in Germany, by Julia Sneeringer

West German Industrialists and the Making of the Economic Miracle, by Armin Grünbacher

Germany Since 1945

Politics, Culture, and Society

Peter C. Caldwell and
Karrin Hanshew

BLOOMSBURY ACADEMIC
LONDON • NEW YORK • OXFORD • NEW DELHI • SYDNEY

BLOOMSBURY ACADEMIC
Bloomsbury Publishing Plc
50 Bedford Square, London, WC1B 3DP, UK
29 Earlsfort Terrace, Dublin 2, Ireland

BLOOMSBURY, BLOOMSBURY ACADEMIC and the Diana logo are trademarks of
Bloomsbury Publishing Plc

First published in Great Britain 2018
Reprinted 2021

ISBN: HB: 978-1-4742-6242-2
PB: 978-1-4742-6241-5
ePDF: 978-1-4742-6243-9
eBook: 978-1-4742-6244-6

Typeset by Deanta Global Publishing Services, Chennai, India
Printed and bound in India

To find out more about our authors and books visit www.bloomsbury.com and
sign up for our newsletters.

CONTENTS

LIST OF FIGURES, MAPS, AND CHARTS

LIST OF TEXT EXCERPTS

ACKNOWLEDGMENTS

The original idea for this book was the product of two separate events. We thank Stephen Milder for organizing and Konrad H. Jarausch for chairing the stimulating panel discussion that convinced us to take on the project, and we thank Rhodri Mogford for proposing such a book for Bloomsbury and for supporting us on the way. We also thank the following scholars who read or discussed aspects of this book with us: Sean Forner, Larry Frohman, Alfred Mierzejewski, Maria Mitchell, Astrid Oesmann, Katrin Voelkner, Lora Wildenthal, and the anonymous reviewers for the press—whom we expressly thank for their detailed and precise criticisms and suggestions. The participants in a special workshop on writing textbooks at Rice University helped to clarify what we were seeking to do: thanks to Julie Fette, Sayuri Guthrie Shimizu, and Jean-François Brière in particular. Wright Kennedy took time out from his dissertation to produce our maps. Our students read sections of the manuscript and offered excellent suggestions on both content and style. We would like to thank in particular Gary Dreyer, Nicolai Hood, Jungbin Lim, and David Ratnoff. Special thanks are due to Brian Van Wyck at Michigan State University and Clair Hopper and Darren Pomida at Rice University, who read the entire manuscript; Clair and Darren additionally helped compile materials for the pedagogical supplement. Special thanks, too, to our native informants, including Jürgen and Felicia Kübler in Konstanz, Ulf Lietzsch and Guida Nogueira in Berlin, Frank Boberg and Jürgen Beckmann in Bielefeld, and Tanya and Saskia Bodendorf in Cologne, who did not know that they were helping with this project.

LIST OF ABBREVIATIONS

AfD	Alternative für Deutschland, Alternative for Germany
APO	Ausserparlamentarische Opposition, Extra-Parliamentary Opposition
CDU	Christlich-Demokratische Union, Christian Democratic Union
CFSP	Common Foreign and Security Policy
CMEA	Council for Mutual Economic Assistance
CSU	Christlich-Soziale Union, Christian Social Union
DKP	Deutsche Kommunistische Partei, German Communist Party (founded 1968)
DM	Deutsche Mark, currency of West Germany, 1948–2002
EC	European Community
ECB	European Central Bank
EEU	Eurasian Economic Union
EU	European Union
FDJ	Freie Deutsche Jugend, Free German Youth: SED youth organization
FDP	Freidemokratische Partei Deutschlands, Free Democratic Party of Germany
FRG	Federal Republic of Germany, West Germany
GDR	German Democratic Republic, East Germany
JUSOS	Jungsozialisten, Young Socialists: SPD youth organization
KPD	Kommunistische Partei Deutschlands, Communist Party of Germany (1918–1956)
LAND, LÄNDER	federal state/states

NATO	North Atlantic Treaty Organization
NÖSPL	Neue Ökonomische System der Planung und Leitung, New Economic System of Planning and Management
NPD	National Democratic Party
OPEC	Organization of Petroleum Exporting Countries
PEGIDA	Patriotische Europäer gegen die Islamisierung des Abendlands, Patriotic European Against the Islamization of the West
SED	Sozialistische Einheitspartei, Socialist Unity Party
SPD	Sozialdemokratische Partei Deutschlands, Social Democratic Party of Germany
STASI	Ministerium für Staatssicherheit, Ministry for State Security
UN	United Nations
WASG	Wahlalternative—Arbeit und soziale Gerechtigkeit, Voting Alternative—Labor and Social Justice

Introduction: Total defeat

FIGURE 0.1 *A bust of Adolf Hitler amid the ruins of the Chancellery in Berlin, July 6, 1945. (Fox Photos/Reg Speller/Getty Images)*

By early summer 1945, the National Socialist regime had been smashed, and the German state had all but ceased to exist as the Allied forces occupied Germany. For the German citizens who sought to reorganize and rebuild the country, 1945 seemed to be a "zero hour," a qualitative break with the past. But individuals in the Communist, Social Democrat, Christian Democrat, and liberal camps developed models of social political order colored by their experiences and their understanding of German history. How did Germany reach the point of dictatorship, genocide, and total defeat in 1945? Was Nazism the result of mass society or modern culture? Was it the result of capitalism's failure and the political vacuum that resulted? Or was it the result of longer-term failures in German history, dating at the latest from Bismarck but perhaps already from Luther's view of the state?

Unconditional surrender

On May 7, 1945, Admiral Karl Dönitz, Germany's head of state, gave the order for his generals to sign a declaration of unconditional surrender to the Allied forces, valid on May 8. Just over a week before, Adolf Hitler had shot himself; his new wife Eva Braun had taken cyanide at the same time. After just twelve years, the "Thousand Year Reign" of the German Third Reich (1933–45) was over.

Hitler wanted a fight to the bitter end rather than a surrender. In the last days of the war, he called up boys younger than sixteen and men over 50 to defend Berlin—expecting that all would die. Dönitz had a different agenda. Like Hermann Göring, Dönitz hoped to negotiate a surrender with the Western Allies in order to continue the battle with the Red Army in the east. But the Western Allies, despite their distrust of Stalin, demanded unconditional surrender.

First, they did not want history to repeat itself. At the end of the First World War, Britain, France, and the United States—the anti-German "Entente"— had not demanded unconditional surrender, and indeed had not pursued the German army back into Germany. From these events was born the myth that the German army had not really lost—that it had been "stabbed in the back" by disloyal socialists, weak pacifists, and deceitful Jews. Circulated in Germany among disgruntled army veterans and given credence by none other than (former) Chief of High Command Erich von Ludendorff, this myth energized nationalist and radical right groups like the Nazis, who promised to revise the hated peace treaty of Versailles and to overthrow the democratic government that signed it. This time around, there would be no doubt among Germans that Germany had been defeated. Second, and more important: the differences among the Allies were enormous. For Stalin fascism *was* capitalism in its most aggressive, imperialist form. Denying distinctions among capitalist states, he had been willing to enter into an alliance with Nazi Germany in 1939. The Soviets' distrust of the United States and Britain remained three years later; they feared that Germany would seek a separate peace with the West in order to continue its battle against Communism in the east.

For these reasons, the three Allied powers had prepared since 1943 for what would happen after the victory. At the Tehran Conference, which lasted from November 28 to December 1, 1943, Franklin Delano Roosevelt, Winston Churchill, and Joseph Stalin agreed in principle to the joint occupation and military rule of Germany. By the time of the Yalta Conference of February 4–11, 1945, the Red Army stood just outside of Warsaw and the Western leaders were ready to endorse Stalin's demands that the Soviet Union retain the section of Poland that it had annexed following the Hitler-Stalin Pact, and that Poland in compensation receive extensive German territory. The area ceded to Poland was not only predominantly German in ethnic composition, but also an important industrial base. It was at Yalta, too, that the three Allies agreed to the principle of unconditional surrender. After the military victory, the three powers ratified these decisions at the Potsdam Conference of July 17–August 2, 1945. Germany would be divided into four zones of administration, under the control of the United States, the Soviet Union, Great Britain, and France—a newcomer, whose zone was essentially cut out of the ones earlier assigned to the United States and Britain.

The defeated

With unconditional surrender, Germany as a sovereign state effectively ceased to exist. Total war was thus replaced by total defeat, which meant the complete end of the military and of government, at all levels. In a few places, anti-fascist committees had taken over, made up of Germans eager to contribute to their country's liberation. The Allies brushed them aside. The Allies made clear that the Germans would play no part in determining their immediate fate. The occupiers filled the power vacuum that had been the Third Reich.

The 8th of May 1945 represented Germans' moral as well as political and military defeat. The National Socialists had posed as an all-embracing party, a popular movement of national redemption. They proclaimed a new and homogenous "national" or "racial" community (in German, a *Volksgemeinschaft* with the term *Volk*, or people, implying both race and nation), in which all those deemed to be ethnic German were bound together by blood and a common destiny. The ideology of the national community claimed to resolve the political, religious, regional, ethnic, and socioeconomic conflicts that had historically divided the German nation, and to redeem it from its humiliating defeat in the First World War. In its efforts to realize this idealized national community, the Nazi dictatorship ended democracy, created a network of concentration camps for political dissenters and social "misfits," and eventually murdered hundreds of thousands of its own citizens at the same time it drove hundreds of thousands more into exile. Primary among the regime's many victims were German citizens of Jewish descent, who were marginalized, expropriated, and humiliated. About half successfully fled the country. The vast majority of those remaining were first deported and then murdered in the killing fields and camps of eastern Europe. Then, of course, there was the war itself: an aggressive and intentionally brutal war, aimed at stealing everything from bread to oil to art from the occupied lands, and at the systematic murder of millions, all in the name of securing and providing for the national community.

National Socialism strived to create a European empire organized along racial lines. In this re-imagining of the continent, western and eastern Europe were relegated to the colonial "periphery," exploited for the good of the Germanic core. Occupation in France, Belgium, and Holland meant the systematic pillaging of goods, military rule, forced labor, and atrocities against civilians. In the east, occupation meant the end of nation-states entirely, from Poland and Czechoslovakia to large swaths of the Soviet Union. Even more, it meant a vicious effort to erase the cultures of eastern Europe from human memory (what the Jewish Polish lawyer Raphael Lemkin first referred to as "ethnocide"). It meant, too, the forced deportations of millions, the systematic use of forced labor, and a planned policy of starvation—the use of famine as a genocidal weapon—with the goal of opening up territory for German settlers. Nazi occupation also meant the mass murder of Jews, Roma-Sinti, the physically and mentally disabled, and other "biological enemies" before firing squads and at gigantic centers of industrialized killing like Treblinka and Auschwitz.

Carried out in the name of the German people, these crimes were exposed to an international public at war's end. The victorious Allies publicized photographs of what the Red Army found in Auschwitz, while Hollywood greats like Frank Capra, Billy Wilder, and John Huston accompanied the US Army to provide undeniable documentation of Nazi atrocities as the GIs uncovered them. And, indeed, the regime's moral bankruptcy was irrefutable. Seemingly overnight, National Socialism became discredited (even though many of its anti-foreigner, anti-Semitic, and anti-Communist ideologies persisted). What is more, the images captured by the photographers and filmmakers present at liberation became iconic representations of the camps—and powerful condemnations of Nazi barbarism.

The war was brutal for those fighting on the eastern front and for those struggling to survive German occupation. But the final years of war were also brutal for Germans at home. If never immune to the loss of loved ones on the battlefield, those Germans who were not targeted by the regime for racial, sexual, physical, or political deviance experienced the first years of war in relative comfort. They were, as German historian Götz Aly baldly put it, "Hitler's beneficiaries." As the war progressed, however, they quickly felt themselves to be its victims—and indeed were. As the Swedish journalist Stig Dagerman noted, "Deserved suffering is just as heavy to bear as undeserved suffering." From 1943 on, the effects of the war were palpable. In an effort to maintain wartime morale in the face of mounting losses, the Gestapo clamped down on the population, relying on denunciations to root out defeatist or anti-Nazi statements, or to find those listening to BBC or Radio Moscow broadcasts. For these and other treasonous acts, the People's Courts (*Volksgerichte*) pronounced ever harsher verdicts; the number of death penalties it imposed rose nearly twentyfold from 1941 (102) to 1944 (2022).

As US and British bombers penetrated German defenses, city dwellers, particularly those living in the western part of the country, began to experience war first hand. In some cases, the Allies' targets were strictly military: the destruction of industrial plants in the Rhineland, for example. But in others, as in the infamous firebombing of Dresden on February 13–15, 1945, Allied bombers attacked civilian targets. In a separate round of attacks, they targeted the fire engines trying to contain the fires. The aims were military, to target the city's armament industries and position as a transportation hub, but the massive attacks targeted the entire city, including its cultural center and civilian districts. The result was a massive firestorm that sucked the very oxygen out of the air. Around 25,000 people died in the fire, which destroyed nearly half of the residential houses in the town and about a quarter of the industrial buildings. Not content with reality, Nazi propaganda magnified the number of victims by almost ten times and insisted that the main goal was not military targets but civilian deaths. That many believed—and still believe—civilian deaths to have been the primary goal speaks both to the horrors of the fire and the more general importance of the air raids for Germans' sense of victimhood. In fact, modern war, especially air war, tends to blur the lines between military and civilian targets; cities, as places where workers produce stuff for the entire economy and where roads, rivers, and rail lines intersect, are central to the conduct of modern warfare. By the last months of the war, many German cities were flattened by aerial bombings. Allied bombs destroyed more than half of major cities like Cologne, Dusseldorf, Frankfurt, and Stuttgart, and did major damage to dozens more.

In the east, the Red Army advanced steadily back over the territories it had lost some two years before and as it did so it encountered the ghostly landscapes of the recently vacated areas. As the Germans retreated, they laid waste to towns, burned fields, blew up bridges, and murdered or captured civilians for forced labor. Most of the Red Army soldiers must have lost someone during this war; a conservative estimate places the total Soviet combat and civilian deaths at 27 million—far above the causality rates of any other nation. If one looks at just the number of sheer lives lost in the European theater, the Second World War was primarily a conflict between Nazi Germany and the Soviet Union. And revenge undoubtedly accompanied the Red Army on its westward drive. When the soldiers arrived in German cities, they went on rampages of destruction and robbery. They raped an estimated two million women in the areas of Germany that they occupied, including over 100,000 women in Berlin alone. Though few women discussed it at the time, evidence suggests that many of them were raped multiple times, whether in gang rapes or over the course of the war's end and the early days of peace.

Rather than fall into the hands of the Red Army, then, ethnic Germans fled. From Königsberg to the Oder River, millions left the lands which would become part of the Soviet Union and of Poland. Adding to this flood of refugees, the Potsdam Agreement allowed for the Germans' "orderly and humane" removal from Poland and Czechoslovakia as well as the expulsion of ethnic minorities from other eastern European states. Those helping shape the peace thought that ethnically homogenous nation-states would bring stability to central and eastern Europe; and many did not fault Czechoslovak president Edvard Beneš's decision in 1945 to "eliminate the German problem in our republic once and for all." The expulsions were anything but orderly and humane however. Ethnic Germans, whatever their relationship to National Socialism or the German nation, were expropriated and thrown out, crowded into trains or forced to march by foot, suffering under the blows of soldiers and without access to food or water. In the end, about 12.5 million either fled or were expelled from eastern Europe into the new, smaller territories of occupied Germany. At least half a million died in the process.

How did we get here?

As a place on a map and a unified state, Germany had only existed for some seventy-five years. Propelled by the efficiency and power of the Prussian army, a confederation of independent German states beat France in the war of 1870–71 and formed a new German Empire (1871–1918) under Prussian hegemony. The new state combined contradictory elements. Delegates to the new national assembly, the Reichstag, were elected according to the democratic principle of universal manhood suffrage, and male citizens voted in great numbers. The individual states, however, jealously guarded their own, older constitutions and kept unequal systems, differing from state to state, for electing representatives to state assemblies. The democratic Reichstag had the power to pass budgets and laws, but stood against a secretive state apparatus governed by an emperor (or Kaiser) who was also the king of Prussia. The military in particular, dominated by the Prussian General Staff, staunchly protected its independence from the Reichstag. The system lasted nearly fifty years, governing over a period of intense wealth creation, urbanization, and industrialization. And the longer the system lasted, the more difficult it became to ignore demands for actual democracy. With the political support of the masses, the Catholic Center Party and the Social Democratic Party (the largest Marxist party in the world) controlled over half of the Reichstag. Even the military found itself increasingly forced to play the game of democratic politics.

Despite these rumblings from below, the German Empire was not at risk before the First World War. Losing the Great War, however, meant the end of the empire. The Revolution of 1918–19 created united Germany's first democracy, the Weimar Republic (1919–33). Founded in defeat and consolidated by force against insurgents from right and left, Weimar was under attack from the start. Despite the harsh terms of the Treaty of Versailles, despite the domestic chaos and the uncertain economic conditions after the war, the republic managed to find a degree of stability during the mid-1920s—only to face the Great Depression in 1929. As mass unemployment loomed and benefits for the unemployed dried up, growing numbers of Germans turned their anger on the Weimar Republic and its defenders. Communists peeled voters from the Social Democrats; National Socialists attracted voters from conservative and liberal parties; both brought new voters, protest voters, to the polls. In September 1930, the Nazi Party jumped from political insignificance to become a serious presence in the Reichstag with 18.25 percent of the vote. As unemployment hit six million (roughly 25 percent of the working population) in 1932, the Nazis replaced the Social Democrats as the largest party in parliament, though they never gained an absolute majority of the vote in a free election. With the Reichstag paralyzed and their own parties nearing extinction, right-wing politicians decided to risk bringing radicals into power. President Paul von Hindenburg and the Westphalian noble Franz von Papen conspired in January 1933 to appoint Adolf Hitler as chancellor.

Hitler took the opportunity to suspend rights, to clamp down on opponents and open concentration camps for his enemies, and to mobilize Germans behind his national revolution through the introduction of mass organizations, new social and welfare policies, and a rearmament drive that brought jobs—as well as the promise of war. Over the 1930s, the National Socialists took measures to marginalize Jews, to remove their rights as citizens, to expropriate them and force them into emigration. In 1939, Hitler began a war against Poland and intensified attacks on the Jews; Germans overran France in spring 1940. By late 1941, not only was Germany involved in a drive to conquer Europe, with a massive attack on the Soviet Union, it was also beginning the process of murdering European Jews. And so, in 1945, Germany had become known as the nation of dictatorship and concentration camps, of forced labor and murderous occupation policies, of death camps and the Holocaust.

Amid the destruction, Germans tried to make sense of what had happened and how they, as a nation, had gotten to this dark moment in history. Intellectuals, some of whom had fled Germany and others who had lived in "inner" exile, as they called it, offered up their own explanations. Struck by the images of Hitler at his mass rallies, those like the old historian Friedrich Meinecke placed the blame for Nazism squarely on modern mass society. The danger arose when politics became a matter for the masses—for the people as a whole, rather than a qualified few—and because of this, open to all their elemental drives. As Meinecke and other conservative critics described them, the masses were superficial seekers of consumer goods and cheap satisfaction. They moved in groups rather than thinking for themselves, were attuned to the ephemeral communications of radio and television rather than great works, and gave themselves over to populist leaders. Meinecke understood Nazism as the product of this new irrational and unstable politics, essentially a problem of mass democracy not unique to Germans, even if Germany, with Prussian militarism and Protestant ideals of self-discipline thrown into the mix, had shown where this new world could lead. The nationalistic and conservative military historian Gerhard Ritter, himself involved with the conspiracy to assassinate Hitler in 1944, went even

---

THE HISTORIAN FRIEDRICH MEINECKE ON MACHIAVELLISM

The basic dynamic force of the past century and a half [of the arrival of the "era of the masses and of whole peoples awakened to self-consciousness"], the enormous increase in population which by its pressure has called forth wholly new historical phenomena, here again comes to light. Politics is now no longer the affair of the few; ever larger classes, pushing up from below, want to take a hand in it. And this widening of the circle of politically active people multiplies the keys to the chest of poisons in which lie the essences of Machiavellism [i.e. of the notion that "reason of state" may permit a broad range of illegal and violent activities]. From being an aristocratic affair, Machiavellism became a bourgeois affair, and finally became mass Machiavellism. It had already arrived in the age of imperialism before the First World War. Every political leader . . . could appear very noble and great if he took up the really frightful phrase, "my country, right or wrong," and acted accordingly.

No, the Machiavellian, amoral element in the Germans of Hitler's day was not limited to Germany alone but was part of the general fermentation in a monstrous process, whether of the decline or of the transformation of the West into new forms of life. "There is none who doeth good, no, not one," can be thrown back in answer to those who accuse the German people of disturbing the peace of nations by its amoral, intoxicated craze for power.

The truth, however, ought not to be a justification for us Germans. . . . For in the end may not the accusation of our opponents be correct to the extent that, though we were not the only ones, we have produced in the shape of the Germans of the Third Reich the mass Machiavellism which is perhaps the most dangerous for the world?

Source: Friedrich Meinecke, The German Catastrophe, trans. Sidney B. Fay (Boston: Beacon, 1950), 52–53.

THE HISTORIAN GERHARD RITTER ON THE DEMOCRATIC-COLLECTIVIST STATE

Thus, the democratic-collectivist state, deriving logically from Rousseau's premises, turns out to be the most unlimited of despotisms. Under the supposedly "absolute" leader of the monarchist age there always existed the possibility of an appeal to old chartered rights and time-honored traditions. . . . But the collectivist, egalitarian nation-state, creature of the Revolution and hence not bound to any tradition, is a different entity. Its head is, in theory, not omnipotent, being merely the functionary of the popular will, mere deputy. But the popular will is omnipotent—and therewith the state. There is no appeal from the popular will; the nation, being sovereign, is in fact infallible. It acknowledges no judge above itself, is answerable to no one; its freedom is without restraint. It itself is the source of all law; who, then, would or could limit its will? . . . The firm ground of European political traditions was shaken, not by some event in German history but by the French Revolution; the Revolution, likewise, shaped the concepts and slogans with whose aid the modern national dictatorships were established.

Source: Gerhard Ritter, "Revolution in the West: The Principle of the Total Nation-State," in The German Problem *(Columbus, OH: Ohio State University Press, 1965), 46–47, 50. Reprinted with the permission of the Ohio State University Press.*

further than Meinecke. He blamed the traditions of the French Revolution for both Nazism and Communism, claiming that radical democracy had an inborn tendency toward total political control over society.

Others connected the rise of National Socialism to the particular fate of liberalism in Germany. Writing from his self-imposed exile in Switzerland, the neoliberal economist Wilhelm Röpke, for example, read German history as a series of failures or wrong turns: instead of free trade, Germans had tariffs, cartels, and monopolies, fostered by the state; in place of free men, the proletarianized masses; in place of the limited (i.e., constitutional) state, bureaucratic administration. A republic could not succeed, he argued, if its citizens were in a massive revolt against individual responsibility. In his and similar tellings, Germany had veered from the political and economic model established by Britain and France. When exactly it had done so was open to debate, but scholars of various political persuasions agreed: Nazism was the culmination of longer-term failures in German history that started at the latest with Bismarck and perhaps went as far back as Martin Luther.

If conservative intellectuals understood the problem to be mass democracy, their more liberal counterparts concluded the opposite. Germans'

THE ECONOMIST WILHELM RÖPKE ON GERMANY'S TURN FROM LIBERALISM

The actual deep dividing line came in 1879, when Germany passed from Free Trade to Protection and Bismarck began, with cynical openness, to turn the whole of home politics into a struggle between "pressure groups" and to transform the old ideological parties into parties representing interests. It was the year in which the conditions were first created for the growth of cartels and syndicates, of the neo-German monopoly capitalism and the imperialism bound up with it. . . . Thanks to this neo-Prussian economic policy, and thanks also to the unexampled increase in population, there began now the colossal growth of industry, of transport, of the great towns, of the great stores, of the industrial districts; of the mass parties, of State care for mass welfare; of monopolies, trade union federations, and banks—and the old Germany began to disappear and to give place to a Greater Prussia drunk with success. . . . The Greater Prussian economic system meant not only State intervention in industry, monopolies, and subsidies, and political control of economic affairs, but also hierarchical organization and centralization.

Source: Wilhelm Röpke, The German Question, *trans. E. W. Dickes (London: Georg Allen and Unwin, 1946), 168–69.*

failure to rise up against Hitler's dictatorship was seen as simply the last in a long line of failed revolutions, evidence of what Heinrich Mann had already identified—and satirized—as a peculiarly German submissiveness to authority in his 1914 novel, *Der Untertan* (The Loyal Subject). The Communist Alexander Abusch, who evaded Nazi capture by fleeing first to France and then to Mexico, described this condition as one of "corpse-like obedience," a metaphor that journalists Eugon Kogon and Walter Dirks also took up from a Catholic, socialist perspective. The Nazis so easily toppled the Weimar Republic because Germans lacked civic courage, the will to jealously guard and if need be to defend their freedom that only came from critically engaging the world around them.

Finally, there were socialists and Communists who argued that Nazism was not the culmination of Germany's particular history but rather that of capitalism itself. Socialists held that capitalism was a system that exploited working people and was inherently unfair. And they had long argued that nationalism was nothing more than a tool of the upper classes, one that filled their pockets (war and new markets bringing a tidy profit) and protected their status (by preventing the working classes from uniting across national lines). Now they looked at the Third Reich's close ties to industry, its hideous system of slave labor, and its expansionist wars, and saw capitalism—its logic and therefore injustices—followed to its radical conclusion. Then, too,

THE CATHOLIC JOURNALIST EUGEN KOGON ON
THE GERMAN NATION'S SUBSERVIENCE
TO HITLER

At 5 A.M. on Sept. 1, 1939, when Adolf Hitler ordered the German people to march, it marched. Not enthusiastically, to be sure, but obediently.

Not enthusiastic, but obedient: that [is the] formula [that] captures the relationship of the people to the regime just before the war. The attentive and careful observer could perceive that almost everywhere in Germany, aside from the steadfast and radical opponents of the regime, there were few Germans who were not in agreement with one or another of National Socialism's points, but even fewer who would not have disagreed on many more points. "What all would come of this," pretty much nobody knew. They also perhaps did not really want to know; they were sick and tired of "the eternal politics."

The German people happily gave up the rest of normal civilian life for uniforms. For the fact is that of all the clothes that a person can wear, it is the uniform that Germans most fervently covet. To be sure, it became a bit much for some of them when everything, even work clothes . . . were to become uniforms. But for a time, around 1937–38, a large part of the nation went around in uniforms.

When the Führer of this uniformed collective began to make international demands and, even before the echoes of his threatening voice had faded, to realize them on his own, with absolute authority, a feeling of power seized most people, a feeling older people knew well from the days of former glory, which became stronger and stronger until finally it vanquished all faint-heartedness. . . .The sense of empowerment bestowed by the uniform, cast a spell over political reason.

Source: Eugen Kogon, "Das deutsche Volk und der Nationalsozialismus," essay from 1946, repr. in Ideologie und Praxis der Unmenschlichkeit: Erfahrungen mit dem Nationalsozialismus *(Berlin: Quadriga, 1995), 104, 105, 106. Reprinted with the permission of Michael Kogon.*

the Nazis' success was the result of capitalism's inevitable crisis and the political vacuum that resulted. Kurt Schumacher, who would become the leader of the postwar West German Social Democrats, saw, like Röpke, the ultimate source of Nazism in the belief in raw power as the main means of politics. In his explanation, militarists from the old feudal elite joined with heavy industry and the armaments industry to foment a nationalist hysteria against enemies both internal and external, in a mass "mobilization of stupidity."

SOCIAL DEMOCRATIC LEADER KURT SCHUMACHER ON NATIONAL SOCIALISM AS COUNTERREVOLUTIONARY

Things first changed when those who despised the masses began to court the favor of the masses by all available means, when the counterrevolution appeared in the cloak of revolution, when it began to lure the little man and the worker, and above all socially open-minded but indiscriminating young people, to the National Socialist German Workers' Party. This name has shamefully sullied the idea of socialism. . . Nothing distinguishes this odd "workers' party" better than the words of Adolf Hitler, claiming that employers were elevated to their role as masters by virtue of their superior race. This dependence on the old owners of wealth and social status is also apparent in the Nazis' domestic and foreign policy ideas. They are the same methods of political swindle that unified the old and new enemies of freedom and peace: the undermining of the republic, heaping scorn on its core values, and the undeniable will to play the master, cost what it may. . . . Hitler gathered around him the apolitical, the victims and the scraps from the class struggles and great economic crisis. The measures he used were . . . the shameless misuse of the national idea; all the tried and true lying methods of the Pan-Germans, militarists, and imperialists; the appeal to all cloudy and base instincts; character assassination.

Source: Kurt Schumacher, speech of May 6, 1945, in Hanover, from Reden-Schriften-Korrespondenzen, 1945-1952 (Berlin: Dietz, 1985), 208–10. Reprinted with the Permission of Verlag J. H. W. Dietz Nachf. GmbH. The press has not been able to locate a person to whom the rights to the text have been transferred.

Some of the language used especially on the Communist left—the pat references to monopoly capitalism citing the official definition of fascism developed by the Bulgarian leader Georgi Dimitrov, and the catechism-like citation of Stalin—may seem stilted. But underneath it was an attempt to connect capitalism and fascism that echoed analyses voiced on the liberal right, as the Röpke example showed, and by Catholic critics. Fred Oelssner, who joined the German Communist Party in 1920 and became a Soviet citizen in 1940, returned to Germany in 1945 with a well-worked out critique of monopoly capitalism, Prussian militarism, and the state-centered German philosophical tradition. It was this combination, he argued, that had brought the "fateful demon" of violent arrogance and destructive tendencies to the German people.

COMMUNIST PARTY LEADER FRED OELSSNER ON MONOPOLY CAPITAL AND IMPERIALISM

Monopolies are the first and decisive characteristic of imperialism. . . . Monopoly industrial capital and monopoly bank capital grow together, and finance capital appears . . . , i.e. the rule of a small group of powerful masters of firms and finance, who control billions. . . . The development of monopoly coalitions does not stop at borders. Great international organizations of monopoly capitalists arise, who profitably divide up the world between themselves into raw materials, export markets, spheres of influence, and so on. . . . With the economic development of imperialism, an ideological transformation of its agents takes place. Old fashioned liberalism is thrown overboard, while monopoly capital strives to erect reactionary dictatorships. . . . In 1939, German imperialists could for the second time attempt to achieve world domination.

Source: Fred Oelssner, "Der Imperialismus," Neues Deutschland, January 31, 1947, p. 3. Reprinted with the permission of Neues Deutschland Druckerei und Verlag GmbH.

German narratives of Germany since 1945

For all those engaged in the debate, May 8, 1945, seemed to be a "zero hour," a qualitative break in time. How they understood Germany's history influenced what they recommended as a response. It has also shaped later historians' narrative of Germany after 1945, encouraging them to examine those same problems or "peculiarities" of German history first diagnosed in the midst of the destruction as well as to look for new answers. Historian Heinrich August Winkler was of the generation too young to be saddled with responsibility for National Socialism but old enough to remember the dictatorship; he entered the university in the late 1950s, and his work is wrapped up with the postwar attempt to describe what went wrong with Germany, what led it as a nation to National Socialism. Germany, he argued, followed a special path of development that led it away from the "West," and thus away from notions of rights, parliamentary democracy, and modernity. Postwar political as well as cultural history involved the gradual acceptance of all that had previously been rejected, namely ideas of individualism and rights, of democracy and pluralism. With the end of the East German dictatorship, a German nation founded on the notion of freedom developed. By breaking with ethnic nationalism and committing to European integration, Germany had, as he put it, completed its "long road west."[1]

Ulrich Herbert paints a similar success story, but with reservations related to an uncertain future. Part of the generation of leftists reaching intellectual maturity in the 1970s, Herbert describes the surprising turns since 1945 that led Germans to face the world with unprecedented optimism by the second decade of the twenty-first century. Germany had become a rich nation, a model democratic nation, a nation respected for its work coming to terms with the National Socialist past. He also, however, documented the many moments when Germans deviated from this script, including the strong anti-foreigner sentiment in united Germany. Included here, too, were the risks Herbert associated with the Cold War, moments that led to citizens' ambivalence about West Germany's pro-western course in the face of the threat of nuclear war. In the end, he asks whether the very industrial society responsible for the new Germany's prosperity contains major risks as well, indeed dangers that could call German democracy into question. The victorious road to the West of the older generation of democratic historians like Winkler is less clear on Herbert's account.[2]

Hans-Ulrich Wehler offers a third interpretation. Like Winkler, he viewed the history of postwar Germany as traveling two paths, a narrative of escape, in West Germany, from the "special conditions" that previously hindered development on Western lines, and the continuity of those same, older traditions in the oriental despotism (he uses the word "satrap") of East Germany. But the "ingeniously conceptualized" neoliberal doctrine of the Social market economy, which combined market capitalism with social policies to take the edge off of inequality, brought an "element of discontinuity" into the story as well, with an "excessively overreaching" welfare state that "repressed individual responsibility for shaping one's own life." Wehler also feared that mass immigration would create "a new ethnic subproletariat" living in ghettos, resistant to education and assimilation, and open to the influence of "fundamentalist Islamism," which threatened to be a worse danger than the "red threat" of the nineteenth century. A conservative reading, in other words, saw dangers in the very formula of the country's success: its market economy moderated by social policy and its openness to other cultures.[3]

As you move through the chapters of this book it is worth keeping these and other possible framings in mind. What would the period from 1945 to 2017 look like, for example, if viewed from the perspective of popular culture? Or if we told postwar German history as one of migration—of Germans and non-Germans moving east and west as well as in and out of the country? If we placed religion and the process of secularization at the center of our study, how might we complicate current narratives? History is ultimately a series of debates and contingencies and not a foregone conclusion. And historians' interpretations of that history differ and change with the times. How else might we approach the story of Germany's recent past?

PART ONE

Dividing Germany, 1945–70

1

Germany's "Zero Hour"

FIGURE 1.1 *Cologne, March 1945. (The LIFE Picture Collection/John Floreal/*
Getty Images)

*By late spring 1945, Germany's economy was wrecked, its political
system destroyed, and its society under extreme strain due to the effects of
dictatorship, war, and the waves of refugees arriving from the east. The Allied
occupying powers divided Germany and Berlin into four zones, and aimed to
rule Berlin together. The four Allies initially also pursued the "denazification"
of German society through legal proceedings, including the Nuremberg
Trials, and the direct purge of Nazis from positions of economic and social
power. Tensions between the Soviets and the Western Allies emerged quickly,
however, leading to a growing division between East and West. In 1946–47, the
economic divisions became clear, as the United States and Britain established
a combined economic zone (the "Bizone") and the Soviets established an
office for centralized economic planning. In 1948, the currency reform of the
western zones led to the First Berlin Crisis, during which the Soviet Union
closed the borders between Berlin and the zones of the Western Allies. The
Allies responded with the Berlin Airlift. By 1949, hopes for a unified postwar
Germany dwindled, as the Federal Republic of Germany formed in the west
and the German Democratic Republic in the east.*

Germans, non-Germans, and those Germans who had been declared non-
German during the dictatorship—all experienced the defeat in myriad
different ways. One nearly universal condition, however, was dislocation,
both forced and voluntary. As Allied forces moved into Germany, they
encountered millions of people on the move and clogging the roads,
including former forced laborers, former soldiers, and camp survivors from
every country conquered by Germans or held by their allies. Some half a
million children were separated from parents, whose fate, like many of the
children's identities, was unknown. The forty allied nations, newly constituted
as the United Nations, had formed the UN Relief and Rehabilitation
Administration in 1943; it now worked with military authorities to gain
control of the situation on the ground, the massive flow of refugees as well
as the severe food shortages. Of the seven million "displaced persons" in
Germany that UN relief workers struggled to repatriate in May 1945, only
a million remained by September. Of these, a significant number were Jews,
most of them officially "stateless" and the only one in their family to survive.
Some of them were Germans who wanted to leave, their sense of belonging
forever destroyed; a great many came from Poland and the Soviet Union,
where new waves of anti-Semitic violence barred their return. In a final twist
of fate, then, the largest population of surviving European Jews—upward
of 250,000—lived in Displaced Persons, or DPs, camps within defeated
Germany, where they looked for loved ones, regained their strength, and
waited to emigrate. But as Atina Grossmann has shown, if Jewish survivors
remained in camps and under the control of occupation authorities, many of
them until 1948, they did not wait to resume life. Quite the contrary: Jewish
DPs had sex, got married, and had babies—lots of babies! For Jews and
even the Germans they encountered, there was perhaps no more tangible

evidence of Nazi Germany's defeat and the Jewish community's survival than this.

Germans, too, struggled to make their way home: soldiers from the front; surviving "enemies" of the Reich from concentration camps or exile; mothers, children, and old men from places of temporary refuge. Of course, many soldiers (roughly 3.5 million) never returned. And others, prisoners of war, returned only over the course of many years. The Soviets forced several million German POWs to help rebuild the Soviet Union, not releasing them until the end of the 1940s and 1950; those convicted of war crimes remained until as late as 1955. POWs within Germany found themselves pressed into hard physical labor, clearing rubble alongside former Nazi Party members, women as well as men. The military authorities hoped to impress upon them and the entire German population that Nazism alone was to blame for their current state. Able-bodied labor was also in short supply. In Berlin, women between the ages of 15 and 50 were pressed into helping the clearing and reconstruction of buildings. Bands of so-called rubble women (*Trümmerfrauen*) passing stones and bricks from one to the next were relatively few in number, especially in the western zones where neither the women nor authorities liked the idea of employing women in such a manner. They nonetheless loom large in public memory today, with the rubble woman an iconic figure of Germany's "zero hour"—the Germans' suffering as well as resilience.[1]

Many scholars in fact refer to the final years of war and the first years of peace as the "hour of the woman." This is because in the absence of men, and with the struggle for survival now shifting exclusively to the home front, women took center stage. Aside from the continued dangers posed to their persons by occupying soldiers, with incidents of rape peaking in 1945 but certainly not ending in either the east or west, the greatest threat to them and their families was a lack of food and adequate shelter. This was especially true during the severe winters of 1945 and 1947, when disease and infant mortality reached all-time highs. The Allies allotted Germans ration cards with severely restricted calories. To survive, women supplemented their family's rations in a variety of ways: some joined work crews in order to secure higher rations; most scavenged, picking over the parks and countryside for food and fuel; and everyone bartered goods and services on the black market. Prostitution and, more ambiguously, fraternization with Allied soldiers offered German *Fräuleins*—and the people they cared for—access to goods (canned food, chocolate, cigarettes) they could keep or trade, and sometimes even a physical protector. To prevent what little they had from being spread even thinner, German women also guarded against pregnancy and, when that failed, they sought out abortions. Here they joined the countless rape victims, who preferred to risk the dangers of abortion rather than have their tormentor's child.

Soviet and American soldiers, as well as Allied aid workers, often had a distinctly different impression of Germans' situation at the end of the war. If they were shocked it was not by the devastation but rather the seeming lack of it—and by the Germans' sense of self-pity. Russians, both at the time and later, described Germans living in their "clean undamaged white houses"; German women were both disparaged and admired for their healthy good looks. Impressions of the defeated as relatively well-fed, clothed, and clean were, of course, influenced by their knowledge of the misery dealt to the Third Reich's victims. American GIs, for example, described the shocking juxtaposition between the concentration camps and the towns near them, where inhabitants continued to live in comfort, if not quite as well as before. In the end, war and its aftermath did not affect all Germans equally or in the same way. And conditions on the ground looked quite different depending on the geographic location and the personal sympathies of the observer.

What is to be done?

The Allies won the war. They occupied Germany. But they did not have a single roadmap for what should become of Germany. Some called for a peace that would break up the defeated country into smaller states and thereby eliminate its ability to threaten its neighbors again. Others thought that the only answer was a strong German state and economy, integrated into Europe. Though the path the Allies ultimately pursued more closely resembled the second, the dismemberment of Germany did not at the time seem such an unreasonable idea. Germany, after all, had only been a nation-state since 1871 and even then largely as a result of Prussian military might. That many living in non-Prussian regions felt themselves only loosely tied to Bismarck's state was apparent in their efforts to leave it during the Weimar Republic: in 1918–19, the predominantly Polish areas seceded after a revolutionary civil war; Bavarians on both left and right played with the idea of secession on two separate occasions, under the short-lived council government of Kurt Eisner in 1918–19 and within the conservative Bavarian People's Party in the crisis year of 1923; and even some in the Rhineland had flirted with separatism in 1923. These separatist rumblings continued to be heard after 1945. The differences between a predominately Protestant North and a Catholic South and Catholic Westphalia had not faded with time either. Perhaps a large, unified German state was unnecessary; indeed, perhaps German unity, some thought, destabilized Europe.

One plan to dismantle Germany came from US secretary of the treasury Henry Morgenthau in 1944. He proposed to divide Germany into three parts and to eliminate all heavy industry, turning the area back into an agricultural land. Though popular with the French, such plans ran aground on economic reality. As former US president Herbert Hoover noted in 1947, a country divided up in such a way could not feed its citizens, especially with the influx of refugees and expellees from the east. Hoover's concerns were as much political as humanitarian: In the aftermath of the First World

War, he had warned that famine bred anarchy and Bolshevism, and he was no less convinced of that logic after the Second World War. The fear that hunger would push the Germans into the arms of the Soviets increasingly shaped the Western powers' policies on Germany. At the head of the military government, General Lucius D. Clay described the situation for the average German in deeply pragmatic terms: there was "no choice between being a Communist on 1500 calories a day and a believer in democracy on 1000."

While the Allies were not sure what form the new Germany should take, they knew what of the old needed to go: cartels, militarism, and Nazism. Prewar Germany had been characterized by organized capitalism, or what the Soviets called state-monopoly capitalism. Big corporations, connected by overlapping executive boards, had formed official cartels and colluded to fix prices, raise profit margins, and exclude new competition. Rather than challenge such business arrangements, the German state protected and enforced them to mutual benefit. Corporations like Krupp, a gigantic arms manufacturer in the First World War, and I. G. Farben, a massive chemicals concern, provided Hitler and the Third Reich crucial support and profited immensely for it—not least by their extensive use of slave labor. To break up this collusion of private and public power, the Allies agreed on the principle of *decartelization*, the need to break up the existing concentration of private economic power. All sides agreed as well that Germany had to *demilitarize*. Germany had to lose its army, but more importantly the German people had to give up their militaristic traditions. How this would happen on an individual level was murky but ending cartels—and with them the concentration of power in the heavy-war industries—was understood as important to loosening the military's dominance over civilian life generally. And both decartelization and Germany's demilitarization worked to achieve the Allies' last goal and policy, that of *denazification*. Nazis and known Nazi sympathizers should be removed from all positions of power and influence, in every area of German life. In addition to these three goals, the Allies agreed that Germany should pay reparations. Both the French and the Soviet representatives stressed that their countries needed considerable help rebuilding. The form and amount of the reparations, however, remained unclear.

At Potsdam, the four occupying powers still intended to implement these policies jointly, through the new Allied Control Council. By fall 1945, however, relations between the Western Allies and the Soviet Union were already tense. The Soviets installed a pro-Soviet government in Poland over the course of 1945, deliberately sidelining the Polish government-in-exile that had formed in London during the war, and angering the British. The new US president Harry S. Truman, meanwhile, halted loans to the Soviet Union at the very moment the Soviets faced the daunting task of reconstruction. And though the transition to the Cold War is often marked by the famous "Iron Curtain" speech that Winston Churchill delivered in Fulton, Missouri, on March 5, 1946, the British statesman had begun to speak of an iron curtain dividing eastern from western Europe already in the summer of 1945.

Against this backdrop of rising tensions, the occupying forces began to implement the three "D's" discussed above, as they termed them, as well as a fourth, *democratization*, in each of their respective zones. Democracy can take different forms and the Allies' understandings of it differed greatly. The Soviets, for example, understood democracy as involving direct rule by means of a centralized authority. The Americans, by contrast, imagined democracy as decentralized, with more power for municipalities and the Länder (or federal states). There were also differing positions as far as democracy's scope: whether conscious political will should organize socioeconomic life as well, or whether economic resources and relations should be governed by the "free play" of market forces. How the Allies envisioned democracy (its final form as well as the conditions necessary for its success) influenced how they pursued denazification, decartelization, and even demilitarization.

Denazification

Denazification efforts started before the Allies even reached Germany, in anti-Nazi propaganda campaigns broadcast by Radio Moscow and the BBC. As the invading armies drew closer, they publicly revealed what they found. In Poland, the Soviet Red Army documented the horrors of the death camps, constructed for the efficient murder of Europe's Jews through gassing or hard labor, as was the case at Auschwitz, where Soviet soldiers discovered few survivors in the slave labor camps operating alongside the Birkenau death camp. Not far from the German city of Munich, the US Army liberated the concentration camp at Dachau, where, in addition to some 30,000 survivors in various states of emaciation and severe malnutrition, the GIs discovered train wagons filled with dead and rotting bodies. The soldiers forced Germans living nearby to see the camp, and footage from Dachau, Buchenwald, and other camps was shown to German POWs. But revealing dead bodies was not enough: Some German villagers announced that the bodies they saw were really victims of the Dresden bombing raids, for example, and Allied guards reported that screening the atrocities had a numbing effect on soldiers. In short, propaganda was not enough. Nazis had to be removed from positions of authority, starting with the trial of major war criminals at Nuremberg.

The Nuremberg War Crimes Trial

In popular memory, the Nuremberg Trials form the cornerstone of postwar justice, embodying the decision to lay claim to law rather than simply force at the end of the war. Not everyone wanted a trial, however. Both Stalin and

Churchill are on record at different times calling for the simple execution of the leadership. After all, trials can be messy; independent defenders, prosecutors, and judges can ask embarrassing questions of all sides. And when it came to international relations and war, no side was totally innocent of wrongdoing. Last but not least, the Nazi leaders could use the trial as a podium for political speeches—as Hitler had done in 1924 when on the stand for high treason. A publicized trial ran the risk of harming rather than helping Allied denazification efforts. Nonetheless, those in favor of a trial won out, based on the argument that trials would better serve a lasting peace.

Over the summer of 1945, the Allies established the basic outlines of the trial. The accused were to be tried for four sets of crimes: crimes against the peace; war crimes; crimes against humanity (essentially a subcategory of war crimes); and the general charge of conspiring to commit each of these crimes. From start to finish, all of these charges were controversial.

First, could German leaders be guilty of violating international law that they themselves did not recognize? The validity of international law lies in its general acceptance by major states. Otherwise, it appears to be no more than a strong power's command to a weaker one. Related was the problem of whether an individual leader, rather than the state as a whole, could be held responsible for the violation of international law: Many German officers and National Socialist leaders accused of atrocities stated that they

STATE DEPARTMENT MEMORANDUM OF 1944 ON THE NATURE OF THE NUREMBERG TRIALS

The proceeding will be judicial rather than political. It will rest securely upon traditionally established legal concepts. Not only will the guilty of this generation be brought to justice according to due process of law, but in addition, the conduct of the Axis will have been solemnly condemned by an international adjudication of guilt . . . . The Germans will not be able to claim, as they have been claiming with regard to the Versailles Treaty, that an admission of war guilt was exacted from them under duress.

Source: Draft memorandum from Cordell Hull, Henry Stimson, and James Forrestal to Franklin D. Roosevelt, ca. November 1944, p. 3, available online via the Harry S. Truman Library and Museum, at: https://www.trumanlibrary.org/whistlestop/study_collections/nuremberg/ documents/index.php?documentdate=1944-11-00&documentid=8- 11&pagenumber=1

were only following orders. These remain important issues for international law today.

Second, justice should presumably apply to all parties. If the Allies tried German leaders for deeds that the Allies themselves had committed, then in what sense could the trials produce "justice"? The chief prosecutor for the United States, Robert H. Jackson, was well aware of the thin ice the United States stood on: "We have some regrettable circumstances at times in our own country in which minorities are unfairly treated." Indeed, many actions taken against Jews under Hitler—denying voting rights, segregation, banning sexual relations across "racial" lines and forced labor—had parallels in laws against African Americans in the US South, and governments around the globe condoned compulsory sterilization in their efforts to control unwanted populations at home and abroad. The Soviet Union under Stalin had also clearly committed a good many atrocities against its own people, while Great Britain and France still maintained empires using violence and strict racial hierarchies. And, during the war, the Allies themselves had carried out actions against civilians, from bombing raids to population removals that potentially violated international law as well. Because of the potential for debate, the military judges reserved the procedural right to "rule out irrelevant issues and statements," and made it clear that referring to Allied actions was irrelevant in this sense.

The specific charges were also problematic. Proving conspiracy to commit crimes against the peace assumed that violating the peace was a crime. Prosecutors argued that since Germany had signed the 1928 Kellogg-Briand Treaty, and thereby agreed to resolve disputes by means other than war, the Nazis' aggressive war violated the treaty. But the Nazi leadership argued, first, that their actions were "defensive," and, second, that their government had renounced the League of Nations, so that the treaty could not bind them. Similarly, war crimes charges rested on Germans' violation of the Hague Conventions of 1899 and 1907, which set down the laws of war among the major European powers. The Allies argued that the Hague Conventions covered all "civilized nations" and that Germany was therefore subject to it. The defendants disagreed about whether Nazi Germany had been bound by international law at all.

Crimes against humanity proved problematic, too, if differently so. The court used the charge to prosecute the Nazi leadership for crimes against its own citizens, a significant shift away from the sacrosanct position international law traditionally accorded state sovereignty. The danger lay in implying that all nation-states (not just the Nazi state) were not fully sovereign, that they were not free to treat their own civilians as they saw fit. More to the point, with "humanity" as a legal standard that trumped the laws or conventions promulgated by a sovereign state, the state itself could be criminal. Perhaps for this very reason, the concept of crimes against humanity, however, fuzzy, was quickly taken up in international discussions as a symbol of progress, a path forward and away from a bloody past.

Whatever the law, the evidence presented was damning. The Allies produced documentation, written and visual, of hostage taking and the execution of civilians in German-occupied lands; the deliberate killing of prisoners of war, with numbers into the millions on the eastern front; forced labor; and the concentration camps. The French prosecutors brought seven witnesses to the stand who had been in the death camps, including Auschwitz. Their reports were devastating. Some defendants even removed their headphones to avoid hearing the translations. But even here, problems arose. The Soviets insisted on charging the German defendants with the murder of 22,000 Polish nationals—military officers, police officers, and intellectuals—in and around the Katyn Forest. That strategy proved mistaken when the German defendants brought evidence that the Soviets had, in fact, perpetrated the massacre.

Other false notes sounded: Neither the Soviets nor the French, for example, wanted to focus on the fact that Jews were primary victims. The British and the Americans did, however, ensuring that that part of the story was not lost to the public. Furthermore, Hermann Göring was able to give a speech blaming the Jews in Germany for their own fate. But in the context of the documentation produced, his assertions sounded empty. Especially astounding was the number of defendants claiming not to have known about the Final Solution, at least in its first and deadliest year, 1941–42. Göring, Joachim von Ribbentrop, Baldur von Schirach, Albert Speer, and Ernst Kaltenbrunner, all deeply involved with the regime, denied any knowledge. Given the vast resources devoted to the extermination of European Jewry and the extent to which war and genocide were bound up together, such claims were hard to believe.

The judges, appointed by each of the occupying powers, sentenced twelve defendants to death by hanging, three to life imprisonment, and four to shorter terms. Three, who had not been involved with the war itself, were acquitted. Göring, the highest-ranking Nazi official on trial, and defiant to the end, spared himself the hangman's noose with the help of a well-hidden cyanide tablet.

Lawyers still argue about the legal basis of the trial. Some view it as a legal travesty and an example of victors' vengeance, while even its defenders recognize its problems. Regardless of its particular legal value, the trial succeeded as a public statement and a precedent for war crimes trials in the future. In Germany, the Nuremberg Trials and the twelve further war crimes trials that followed—involving the crimes of doctors and judges, big industries using slave labor, and the Einsatzgruppen—served an essential public function. Between 1945 and 1949, the press in occupied Germany reported extensively on the trials, and through them publicized National Socialism's crimes against humanity. Some themes, like the persecution of the Sinti and Roma and of homosexuals, did not yet become matters for public discussion. Indeed, as we will see, Nazi-era antigay legislation remained on the books in both Germanies for decades to come.

Denazification in the American and Soviet zones

The reports from the Nuremberg Trials formed the backdrop to the denazification proceedings in the different zones of occupation. Denazification meant more than purging institutions of their main Nazi leaders. It meant the systematic investigation of hundreds of thousands of people, a huge undertaking considering that over 8.5 million Germans had been members of the Nazi Party. It also implied a broader reeducation of the German population. The zones proceeded differently, and altered their policies as the tensions between East and West began to increase.

The United States established the model for the western zones, adopting a systematic, case-by-case approach to the problem. The military authorities produced a questionnaire with 131 questions, which it planned to distribute to all adult Germans in order to divide up the population into five categories based on individuals' relationship to Nazism. Depending on their classification, Germans might be imprisoned, fined, restricted in their employment, or declared free and clear. Authorities were quickly overwhelmed, however, especially since many of them were unable even to read German. Substantiating Germans' assertions of innocence or a lack of political conviction was difficult as well. Nonetheless, some 42 percent of those public officials employed under the Third Reich were initially dismissed in 1945–46.

Conservative circles, in particular, disliked the denazification proceedings. Catholic Church leaders contacted the military authorities directly to condemn a process that, they feared, would aid trade union leaders, Social Democrats, and Bolshevism, while excluding from leadership positions churchgoing members of the middle class who had joined the Nazi Party. Public opinion polls in the US Zone of Occupation, meanwhile, showed that while in November 1945 some 50 percent of the population supported denazification, that percentage had shrunk to 34 percent a year later.[2]

Over the course of 1946, the US military turned the process over to a German staff, which was more lenient. They excluded certain groups, for example. Men born after 1919 and who were thus fourteen years old or younger when Hitler became chancellor were assumed to have been brainwashed and thus not responsible for their actions. To get around the difficult and hugely time-consuming task of double-checking a questionnaire's facts, the tribunals also began to accept sworn affidavits from third parties. By 1948, Germans in the western zones mockingly referred to the certificates of denazification as "Persil certificates": those who held them had been washed clean of Nazism as routinely as laundry washed with Persil soap. Others accused the US occupiers of punishing "small fry" and letting "big Nazis" escape. The Germans were not entirely wrong. In the context of increasing tensions with the Soviets, the establishment of a stable, functioning state in the west became a top priority and one that required the help of established professionals and businessmen, almost all of whom had accommodated themselves to Nazism. Both the United States and the Soviet Union snatched up experts—in rocket science, for example—and Nazi intelligence officers for their own security projects.

The Soviets claimed, with some justification, that they were far more effective than the West in purging Germany of its Nazi remnants. Denazification in the Soviet-occupied zone was certainly much harsher and much further-reaching: the authorities removed Nazi members from important positions and put some 120,000 of them into camps under the control of the Soviet secret police (NKVD). The Soviets also used denazification as a tool against their own political opponents. Some Social Democrats, for example, were sent to the former concentration camp at Buchenwald. Distinguishing between "nominal" and "activist" Nazis, they removed the latter from the political and administrative spheres as well as the teaching profession and judiciary. The remaining "small" Nazis—those who were perceived to be disproportionately targeted in the West—were ultimately granted something of an amnesty if they proved willing to help build a new, socialist Germany.

Denazification in the East showed some similarities with the process in the West as well. Especially in rural areas, Germans gradually took over the task of evaluating individual cases. And here, too, the locals were often lenient with the people they were examining. Serious efforts at denazification came to an end by 1948, as focus shifted to forming new states in both East and West Germany. The same was true of the British and the French zones, as well, both of which had applied far looser standards for the denazification process. Faced with the need to integrate former Nazis, both East and West German governments passed laws that limited the effects of denazification after 1949. In 1951, for example, the West German parliament passed the Reinstatement Act permitting a large number of "denazified" public servants to return to the civil service; in 1952, the East German parliament reinstated full citizenship right for some Nazi Party members and former army officers.

Despite the limitations of denazification in both East and West, the program had an effect. For several years, the elites who had run the Nazi regime faced serious uncertainty. Some of the worst of their lot were executed, others put in jail. The press reporting on the Nazi problem in Germany and the legacy of Nazism in Europe was extensive and effective. Even though many teachers active under Nazism returned to schools in both East and West Germany by the late 1940s, across occupied Germany the propaganda-laden textbooks of the Nazis were removed from the classroom.

The Soviet Zone of Occupation

Official Soviet histories explained Nazism as the outcome of an alliance between conservative landowners, industrialists, and military elites. Any attempt to smash fascism therefore had to eliminate these elites' power—

and the social and economic roots of that power. From the very beginning, then, denazification went hand-in-hand with Soviet occupation policy aimed at upending the existing, capitalist system.

The Soviets, like the other occupying powers, initially divided their zone into military districts governed by officers who, straight from the battlefield, were little prepared for an occupation. Moreover, their purpose was at first unclear. If their primary aim was to secure reparations, then the Red Army should secure factories and other valuable goods for the Soviets' later use. If their aim was to lay the foundation for future German self-rule, by contrast, then they needed to take actions to reconstruct the ruined economy. Lacking clear directives and frequently left to their own devices, local officers often built up little fiefdoms on the basis of the armed troops they commanded.

Despite the confusion and decentralized state of things on the ground, the Soviets began to reshape society with the help of German Communists, many of whom returned to Germany with the Red Army. Under the slogan *Junkerland in Bauernhand* (Junkers' Land into Farmers' Hands), for example, the Communists introduced radical land reforms. They confiscated large estates—the seats of some of Germany's oldest families, many already abandoned by occupants fleeing the Red Army—as well as the smaller estates of former Nazis, and redistributed them to hundreds of thousands of "new farmers." Many of the new farmers, including large numbers of refugees from the east, lacked the know-how and the materials to run a farm successfully, and as a result the reforms were only moderately successful. But the land redistributions were nonetheless popular, not least as an example of how to pull up the roots of fascism.

At the same time, the occupiers took over control of big industry—and dismantled it. Between 1945 and 1948, the Red Army conscripted German workers to remove around two-thirds of heavy industry and an estimated 80 percent of auto and aircraft production plants. Though the initial plan was to ship these materials to the Soviet Union as reparations, much of it ended up rusting in the harbor at Rostock or on train tracks. Germany's capacity to wage a future war was doubtless greatly diminished. But without industry there was also no work and the Soviets were clearly to blame. The dismantlement of industry did not constitute a coherent economic plan for creating a stable state or a peaceful society. And it was certainly not popular with the Germans.

On a political level, the Soviet authorities called for a new, German democracy. With this goal in mind, in summer 1945 they approved four parties, three of which had existed in Germany before 1933: the Communist Party, the Social Democrats, the Liberal Democrats, and the new Christian Democrats. By approving four parties, the Soviets indicated their support for pluralism. The German Communists likewise adopted a moderate tone by calling for a broad-based, anti-fascist, popular front. At the same time, however, Walter Ulbricht, who headed the returning group of Communists resident in Moscow during the war, remarked to a comrade that "it must look democratic, but we should have everything in our hands." Others in the same Soviet-based National Committee for a Free Germany, like Anton Ackermann and Wolfgang Leonhard, hoped for a more open democracy, less akin to Stalin's model of one-party control. The lack of unanimity among German Communists mirrored that of their Soviet superiors, who remained uncertain about what "democracy" should look like in Germany, and thus which of the possible courses to promote. Both German Communists returning from Moscow and the Soviet occupation authorities agreed, however, that the Communists should play the leading role in the rebuilding of Germany.

Unsurprisingly, then, the first party to be approved in the Soviet zone was the Communist Party (KPD). On July 11, 1945, it issued a manifesto declaring its intended course. The party's Central Committee called for the establishment of an "anti-fascist democratic regime, a parliamentary democratic republic with all rights and freedoms for the people," including private property rights. The document made no mention of Marxism or even socialism. The party leadership formulated the manifesto following a face-to-face meeting with Stalin in Moscow, who had stressed the need for the Communists to embrace a parliamentary, democratic republic in order to attract support from the other occupied zones as well; he left no doubt, however, that the "hegemony of the working class and its revolutionary party" had to be secured. For Ulbricht, downplaying a commitment to class struggle and Soviet-style Communism made the Communists appear less under the control of the Soviets and more conciliatory.[3] But the Communists' new course was more than mere rhetoric. It also reflected a contingent within the party that sought a peaceful path to socialism. The so-called revisionists, in particular Ackermann, contended that the Second World War and the unconditional surrender of Germany had destroyed the old political and economic power apparatus in the country. As a result, they argued, the Germans were in a unique position to pursue a peaceful path to socialism; they did not have to follow the Stalinist model of encouraging violence against "class enemies" to reach their goal. On this reading, the manifesto and party slogans like the "German road to socialism" and "democracy of a new type" were not Machiavellian attempts to conceal a power grab, but expressed the continuing allure of a German "third way" beyond Soviet Communism and US liberal democracy. Echoes of this "revisionist" approach to political rule would resound at critical moments in East Germany, in 1953, 1956, 1968, and again in the 1980s.

Communist leaders could hold such different visions of Germany's open future largely because the foreign policy of the Soviet Union remained open, in East Germany and across Soviet-controlled Eastern Europe. In the Soviet zone as in Poland, Hungary, and Czechoslovakia, the occupying regime permitted non-Communist parties to form. At the same time, Communists staffed the most important government offices and had the closest connection to the Soviet forces. With this distinct advantage in hand, the Communists pushed for the formation of an anti-fascist bloc of parties, which meant the creation of other, non-Communist parties.

The Communists had, however, a difficult relationship to the other democratic parties, especially the Social Democrats, who posed the biggest threat to them at the polls. Both parties claimed to represent the German worker; they spoke the same language of class struggle and human emancipation; they had similarly strong credentials as anti-fascists. But their political positions had differed sharply during the Weimar Republic and afterwards. The Social Democrats had defended parliamentary democracy and its institutions, while the Communist position had attacked parliamentary democracy as a front for the power of the bourgeoisie and old elites. In 1919 and again in 1920, the Social Democratic leadership had used right-wing paramilitary groups—which themselves rejected both democracy and the socialist tradition—against the Communists, viewing the Communists as the main threat to the republic. In the late 1920s, the Communists declared the Social Democrats to be social fascists and the main enemy of the revolution. From the perspective of many Social Democrats, the Communists had connived with the National Socialists to destroy the republic after 1929. Animosity between the parties remained after the war. Nonetheless, the Social Democratic Party (SPD) was the next party approved in the Soviet occupation zone, on June 15, 1945.

Within both the Communists and the Social Democrats, many blamed the two working-class parties' split for the Nazis' rise to power; they had been fighting each other when they ought to have been fighting the Nazis. With an eye to overcoming past mistakes, the Soviet occupation authorities, the Communists, and some Social Democrats began to talk already in summer 1945 of uniting the Social Democrats and the Communists in the Soviet zone. Initially, the impetus for a unified workers' party came from the Social Democrats, and the Soviet administration rejected it, fearing that the Communists would be overwhelmed by experienced Social Democrats. By fall 1945, however, the Social Democrats in the Soviet zone began to distance themselves from the heavy-handed political tactics of the Communists and the Soviet administration, at the same time that Social Democracy in the western zones, under the leadership of the anti-Communist Kurt Schumacher, rejected any cooperation with Communists. The political parties in the eastern and western zones, in other words, had begun to diverge, signaling already in 1945 the division of German politics. By November 1945, Ulbricht and Stalin had agreed on a change of course, and began to demand a unified workers' party, now with the aim of neutralizing the Social Democrats. In April 1946, the Soviet administration forcibly combined the two parties to create the Socialist Unity Party (SED). No free vote by Social Democratic Party members took place in the Soviet zone; in western Berlin, where such a vote did take place, 82 percent opposed the merger. Those who defended the Social Democratic Party after the merger faced political persecution, some were forced to leave the Soviet zone and some imprisoned in former concentration camps like Buchenwald.

Two other parties formed in summer 1945: the Liberal Democrats (LDP), who represented the defenders of constitutional democracy, the rule of law, and property rights from the Weimar Republic, and a new party formation, the Christian Democrats, which sought to bridge the Catholic-Protestant divide from before 1933. Leaders of both parties agreed to become part of what came to be called the "anti-fascist front." The eastern Christian Democrats defended both Christian values and religious education and, under the influence of the Catholic labor leader and anti-Nazi resistor Jakob Kaiser, far-reaching plans to socialize major industries. Between 1945 and 1947, Soviet occupation authorities forced changes in leadership in the Liberal and Christian Democratic parties. In 1947, they expelled Kaiser, by then increasingly critical of authoritarian occupational policies, from the Soviet zone. Before long, the Liberal Democrats and Christian Democrats became tame "bloc parties" in support of the new state in formation.

Already by the end of 1945, the opening for alternative paths of development in the Soviet zone had narrowed. Not because the Socialist Unity Party had won the hearts and minds of the people. The elections on October 20, 1946, demonstrated the party's limited support. In the Land assemblies of the Soviet zone, the Socialist Unity Party won slightly over 47 percent of the vote, less than the "bourgeois" parties (Liberal Democrats and Christian Democrats) combined. More telling were the election results for Greater Berlin, where all four occupying powers administered the vote, not the Soviet administration alone. The Social Democrats received 48.7 percent of the vote, the Christian Democrats 22.2 percent, the Socialist Unity Party 19.8 percent, and the Liberal Democrats 9.3 percent. In short, free elections did not produce the outcome desired by the Soviet occupation and the Socialist Unity Party. After this election, the Socialist Unity Party shifted to the "unity list" voting system then being imposed in other Eastern Bloc states: Each voter cast a single vote for a single list of candidates drawn from the different parties and mass organizations, determined in advance by the Socialist Unity Party. This list represented "unity" behind the anti-fascist program. The alternative to voting for the unity list was to vote "no," which required a procedure that made a negative vote evident to election observers. Free elections with a truly secret ballot were over.

By the end of 1946, a system of de facto one-party rule was developing in the Soviet zone, based on the power of the occupation. In June 1947, the Soviet occupying authorities created a new institution, the German Economic Commission (discussed further below), which amounted to the first zone-wide bureaucracy in charge of organizing production. Out of the initial disorder, a new order centered on economic control and planning began to develop in the Soviet zone.

The American Zone of Occupation

The US, British, and French zones saw a similar movement from disorder and indecision to the gradual formation of state-like institutions—and an ever-clearer division of Germany. In the American zone, military officers played a major role in the first months after the war, just as they did in the Soviet zone. Often unable to speak German and trained to respect efficiency rather than to think in political terms, they nonetheless banned "political" organizations such as anti-fascist committees with strong socialist and Communist representation. The officers not only distrusted them but had no interest in conferring over economic reconstruction. In this, they were not unlike their Soviet counterparts; occupation authorities called the shots. And, like the Soviets, the Americans supported those Germans whose politics and worldview most resembled theirs. But unlike the Soviet generals, the Americans made decisions based on pragmatism and, if anything, a desire to avoid politics. For this reason, they favored supposedly "unpolitical" and experienced experts and religious leaders to lead municipalities. The problem was, it was precisely the experts who tended to have been involved with Nazism. Only on August 27, 1945, did the Americans permit the official formation of political parties at the district level; nearly a year passed before they permitted the formation of parties across the western zones.

Roughly the same four political groupings developed in the western zones as had in the Soviet zone: the Social Democrats, Communists, Christian Democrats, and a variety of small liberal parties eventually united under the name "Free Democrats." As mentioned above, the western Social Democrats formed under the leadership of Kurt Schumacher, a grim survivor of the Nazi concentration camp system. After 1945, the Social Democrats continued to defend parliamentary democracy and basic rights, but also sought to transform society through labor law, social measures, and what they called "economic democracy." Schumacher called for bringing basic industries like coal and steel producers under state control, first in order to respond to the challenges of rebuilding the economy, and second to deprive their owners, many of whom had collaborated with the Nazis, of economic power. He also denounced the Communists as agents of a foreign power, and refused to work with Social Democrats in the eastern zone.

The Christian Democratic Union (CDU) (or its sister party, the Christian Social Union in Bavaria), by contrast, was a new party in the west (as it was also in the east). Its roots lay in the Catholic Center Party from before 1933. The Center had been a conservative party when it came to questions of morality and the family, but it was also a party that questioned Prussian militarism, supported social legislation, and helped to form Germany's first democracy. The persecution of the church in the 1870s had allowed it to combine a heterogeneous group of voters, some pro-business, some pro-labor. The Center was also opposed to "Marxist" socialism, which it associated with atheism and materialism (although the party was not without a Christian Socialist wing, which sought closer cooperation with the Social Democrats during the Weimar Republic). It distrusted National Socialism as a party with atheistic or materialistic tendencies as well— though this distrust did not stop Center politicians from trying to cooperate with the Nazis before 1933. After 1933, some of the former Center Party leaders actively collaborated with the Nazis, as did members of the church hierarchy itself, in an attempt to protect church institutions and to fight Communism. One reason for the failure of the Center Party to reestablish itself after 1945 lay in the moral failure of these leaders, as some of the Catholics who resisted Hitler and later contributed to founding the new, Christian Democratic Party recognized.

After 1945, both Social Democrats and Christian Democrats sought to expand their party memberships beyond the tight social milieus from which they had gained their members before 1933. The Social Democrats now reached out to non-workers, including followers of organized religion and intellectuals. And the very name of the CDU declared an end to the historic split between German Catholics and Protestants with the party's basis in underlying Christian principles. Anti-Catholic ideas persisted within the Social Democratic milieu, however; despite his attempt to open the party up, for example, even Kurt Schumacher made statements against the Catholic Church in the 1949 electoral campaign, contributing to the Social Democratic loss. At the same time, suspicion of Protestants persisted in some Catholic communities as well. Local communities in Westphalia, for example, responded with hatred to Protestant refugees from the east relocated in their midst. And socialists, especially for the rural Catholics and the Christian Democratic leadership, remained outside of respectability. Until the 1960s, furthermore, the Christian Democrats had close ties with the Catholic Church hierarchy, even appointing priests to parliamentary committees dealing with social issues. When change came, in other words, it came slowly.

Despite their major and deep differences, though, the Social Democrats and the new Christian Democrats both affirmed parliamentary democracy. Both also stressed basic values that stood above nation and state. The Social Democrats called for social justice across international borders; the Christian Democrats appealed to Catholic notions of God-given natural laws that limited actions of the state. Neither subordinated basic values to reasons of state. Both offered a clear alternative to the statist and nationalist traditions that had culminated in National Socialism.

Neither party had a monolithic approach to politics, reflecting their diverse memberships. The Christian Democrats, in particular, combined both a labor and a business wing. The labor wing, connected to Catholic labor unions, approved a unified trade union encompassing both "Christian" and "Free," that is, secular, trade unions, something Catholic leaders had not condoned before 1933. Under the dynamic leadership of Jakob Kaiser, who took over after his expulsion from the Soviet zone in 1947, the labor wing dominated early party discussions. It left a strong impression, for example, on the Ahlen Program approved by the Christian Democrats in British-occupied North Rhine-Westphalia in February 1947. That program called for partial state control of basic industries and the overcoming of both capitalism and Marxism, appealing to a left that might have otherwise voted Social Democratic. On the other side, and initially weaker, was a business wing that came to be associated with Konrad Adenauer. Almost seventy when the war ended, Adenauer had served as the mayor of Cologne before the Nazis came to power. Adenauer quickly made a reputation after 1945 as an anti-Communist and anti-Socialist, and as a figure not tainted by Nazism. His basic viewpoints—a rejection of left-wing experiments with state control of industry but also a call for closer economic union with France and the Benelux countries—would prove winning combinations in the 1950s.

The third major political grouping came together under the slogan of "liberal." Germans use the term "liberal" differently than do Americans. The liberal tradition stood for the rule of law, the free market, and individual rights. But the National Liberals of the German Empire had also supported German unification under Prussian hegemony: they had been nationalistic and at times militaristic. Small left-liberal splinter parties, meanwhile, combined nationalism and social reform. Liberalism remained splintered during the Weimar Republic, and collapsed already before 1933. After 1945, several different liberal groupings reappeared and eventually formed the Free Democratic Party (FDP), which stressed democracy and individual freedom as well as the power of the free market. Despite its new focus, the party retained its internal differences. One part of the party was committed to a respectable, democratic state under the rule of law: men like Theodor Heuss, whose anti-fascism in Weimar was unimpeachable. The party's right wing, by contrast, emphasized free-market policies, individual property, and nationalism. The Free Democrats thus collected together principled defenders of parliamentary democracy and free trade as well as business interests and the German nation, including a disproportionate number of former Nazis. The party's contradictory make-up explains—and allowed for—its future seesawing on social and economic programs and between government allies.

The Communists at first enjoyed significant support in parts of the western zones, based both on their reputation as an anti-fascist force and on earlier support in some urban areas such as Bremen and Hamburg. In 1946 and 1947, the party gained more than 10 percent of the vote in five of the thirteen Länder. Despite remaining distinct in name from the Socialist Unity Party in the East, however, Communist support in the West dissipated with the transition to dictatorship in the Soviet zone and the early 1950s purges of the Communist leadership. By the time of the first elections in the Federal Republic, the Communists received some 5.7 percent of the vote,

FIGURE 1.2 *Election campaign poster for the Free Democratic Party from 1949. It reads: "Put a stop to it! Enough with denazification, loss of rights, infantilization! Enough with second-class citizenship! Whoever wants civil equality, vote FDP." (Friedrich-Naumann-Stiftung für die Freiheit, Archiv des Liberalismus)*

an amount that dwindled away to virtual insignificance by 1956, when the party was banned.

The military governments of the western zones oversaw the formation of political parties, excluding parties that seemed too close to National Socialism. They also influenced developments by favoring those Germans whose politics and cultural affinities best matched theirs. Adenauer, for instance, was an early favorite—and backroom conversation partner—of the US occupation forces, despite his clashes with the British, who removed him as mayor of Cologne in 1945. And many Germans who came to hold key administrative positions returned to Germany from the United States, where they had obtained academic positions and collaborated with American social scientists. In all four zones, the military governments officially encouraged German debate and discussion. German-run newspapers were of course important here but so were political and cultural journals like the *Frankfurter Hefte* and *Die Wandlung* (The Transformation). All such endeavors required paper—a scarce resource—and printing rights, both dependent on the specific occupier's stamp of approval. Consistent with Americans' individualist and psychological approach to denazification, US occupation policy stressed the need to replace Germans' negative associations of democracy with financial ruin and political chaos, and used cultural programs, too, as a way of doing so. The reopening of cinemas and theaters also contributed to Allied efforts at restoring the sort of open public exchange that had ceased to exist in the Third Reich.

The American and British zones opened the way to greater German self-governance in 1946, within limits. All four occupying powers created new federal states, the so-called Länder, and in the process broke up the powerful state of Prussia that had dominated German politics since 1871. Allowing municipal elections in spring 1946, the occupiers called on political and legal experts, including some close to the Communists, to draw up plans for Länder constitutions, so long as they protected both parliamentary democracy and certain basic rights. The constitution writers did not always act as the American forces wanted. The Hessian Constitution of 1946, for example, called for public control (in German, "collective ownership") of heavy industry, the railroad, and utilities like water and energy, and over 70 percent of Hessians approved the plan in a referendum demanded by the Americans. In these instances, the reins of occupation revealed themselves: The American occupying forces refused to implement the plan, both because they opposed public control of the economy—it smacked too much of socialism for their taste and worked against US business interests—and because they wanted to reserve such decisions to a united Germany.

The occupying powers continued to talk of unification. But a dramatic divergence was underway. The political parties representing Germans increasingly operated separately, and by 1947 the rupture was complete. While the Soviet zone moved from early recognition of parties and an initial pluralism to ever less political freedom, the western zones invited German Länder to develop their own constitutions and allowed political parties, though they excluded those on the far right and eventually the far left, and invited German Länder to develop their own constitutions. The diverging political conditions mirrored a much broader global division between American and Soviet power.

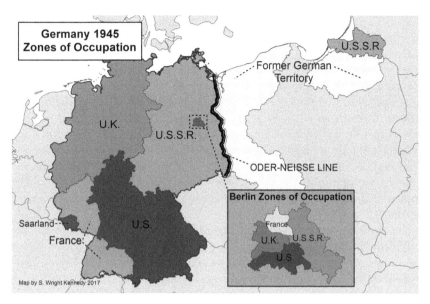

MAP 1.1 *Occupied Germany and Berlin, with zones.*

The Cold War and division

The growing international tensions between the Western Allies and the Soviet Union came to a head in 1947. Bankrupted by war and unable to maintain its overseas empire, Great Britain withdrew its financial support from Greece, in the midst of a bloody civil war between pro-Communist and anti-Communist factions, and Turkey in 1947. Concerned that Greece and Turkey might soon fall into the Soviet orbit, President Truman petitioned Congress for an economic and military aid package designed to stop Communism from spreading to Greece and the rest of the world. The containment policy (or Truman Doctrine, announced by US president Truman on March 12, 1947), which aimed at limiting Soviet influence, defined US international aid and relations from this point forward. And from the American perspective, the world looked dangerously in peril: In 1946, Greece's neighbor Yugoslavia, under Communist leadership since the partisans liberated the country and established a new People's Front government in 1945, moved further into the Soviet orbit amid rising East-West tensions, while the Soviets pressured the Communists at the head of Czechoslovakia's democratically elected government to do the same. Korea divided into a Soviet-dominated North and a US-dominated South. And in western European countries like France and Italy, the Communist Party made important electoral gains. Communism, in short, showed itself an indigenous force with local support—support that German Communists could only envy and that the United States judged with good reason a threat.

Occupation policy in Germany was thus part of a much larger international conflict. Despite statements by Soviet and US foreign ministers in 1946 and 1947 promising a unified Germany, their military governments' actions pointed toward the division of Germany. On January 1, 1947, of the same year, General Clay announced the formation of the Bizone, an economic union of the US and British zones that allowed agricultural and industrial goods to be more easily exchanged. In March 1948 the French agreed to join as well, forming the Trizone (which gradually took shape over the next six months). Thereafter, in June 1947 the German Economic Commission (discussed above) began to plan production in the Soviet zone of occupation. These were not merely economic decisions; they implied different conceptions of social organization in eastern and western Germany.

The growing tensions were the immediate background for General Clay's statement about the importance of calories to the success or failure of Communism in Germany. To promote economic growth, the United States proposed the European Recovery Program in mid-1947, later known as the Marshall Plan for US secretary of state George Marshall. The plan provided funds (some $150 billion in today's dollars) to help rebuild Europe. As in so many other areas, the goal was not to return to the prewar status quo but rather to reorient Europe's economy and financial practices, in this case to bind the various European states into economic and trade relations with each other, and with the capitalist West. The program promoted the return to the free-market policies by removing obstacles such as trade barriers, and supported the modernization of individual firms and factories. The plan took concrete form by summer 1947. The United States offered to extend it to eastern Europe, and both Czechoslovak and Polish leaders indicated their support. Stalin, however, banned all Eastern Bloc countries from participating in the Marshall Plan. The plan, after all, would have linked banks, currency, and production to the system of the West; it would have put international banks in the capitalist world in the position of influencing Soviet planning. In this way, the Marshall Plan seemed to confirm Stalin's conviction that a future conflict with the West was inevitable. Indeed, Stalin viewed the aid package as a sign of American aggression, little more than a cover for capitalist expansion and US imperialism. Although Stalin was undoubtedly security-obsessed to the point of paranoia, in this instance he was not completely wrong. The Marshall Plan, in addition to providing much needed aid to western Europe, was a boon to US companies in need of new markets. In response, the Soviet Union and the areas of Europe under its influence rejected US aid and reinforced its system of centralized economic planning.

The western European states, by contrast, welcomed the plan, even as they chafed at the strings and conditions that came with it. France and Britain were hemorrhaging money and resources in the occupation and in new colonial wars. They wanted relief desperately, and would become the largest recipients of funding. Germany received by contrast a relatively small amount. But the Marshall Plan was not just about money. It was a signal that the United States would stand behind its European allies and not retreat inward, as it had after the First World War.

From Bizone to currency reform in the west

Merging the British, American, and French occupation zones to create the Trizone improved the economies of western Germany. But it could only do so much. The old Reichsmark was still in use. Over the course of their economically disastrous reign, the Nazis had printed more and more of the currency and then, to counter the inflationary pressure all that money created, they had imposed various price controls and rationing. The occupation authorities had issued more of the currency as well. But price controls and rationing could not change the underlying economic conditions: The average German did not go to stores or exchange currency for the goods they needed. Instead, they relied on the black market and bartering, and the only thing that had a stable value was American cigarettes. Germans and foreigners with businesses kept production low; despite some economic growth in 1947, general uncertainty about the future hindered investment, and no one wanted to amass a bunch of money whose value was questionable at best. Any way forward required a major reform.

More specifically, it involved a massive currency reform, planned for 1948. The introduction of a new currency in the western zones meant eliminating many (but not all) price controls and rationing cards and creating a new central bank. Germans of all political persuasions feared that reform would lead to speculation, higher prices, and more suffering for the worse off. As news of the plan spread, Social Democrats and others voiced the additional concern that currency reform would cement the division of Germany. After all, neither the Socialist Unity Party nor the Soviet occupiers would likely accept a new currency under the control of a western central bank.

A vocal group of German economists supported the currency reform, however. This group, loosely associated under the term "ordoliberalism," though they themselves called it "neoliberalism," advocated what they came to call a "social market economy." Their central figure, Walter Eucken, spoke of a capitalist, market-oriented economy that also promoted social order by creating rules to eliminate monopolies, and by guarding against concentrations of economic power either in the hands of private people or the state. Unlike those who came later and who defined what neoliberalism means today, the ordoliberals did not want to return to unregulated, free-market competition: "It is clearly intolerable," Eucken argued, "that the economic system should be left to organize itself." Social market theorists distrusted the market in itself and demanded strong state action to limit its negative effects.

The economist Ludwig Erhard, whose name would become synonymous with the "economic miracle" of the 1950s, picked up the slogan social market economy as he planned for the currency reform, and quickly linked it to the Christian Democrats. First as director of economics or the Bizonal

CHRISTIAN DEMOCRACY ADOPTS THE SOCIAL MARKET ECONOMY

What does the CDU understand by "social market economy"?
The "social market economy" is the socially bound organization of the commercial economy, which brings the achievement of free and industrious people into an order that produces a maximum of economic utility and social justice for all. Both freedom and bonds create this order, which is expressed in the "social market economy" through real competition and independent control over monopolies. Real competition is present when a real competitive order is ensured that, under conditions of equal chances and fair conditions of competition, rewards the better effort. The cooperation of all participants is steered through prices in conformity with the market.

The "social market economy" is sharply opposed to the planned economic system, which we reject whether its management is centralized or decentralized, controlled by the state or by self-administration.

The "social market economy" is also sharply opposed to the so-called "free economy" of liberalism. In order to avoid a relapse into the "free economy," it is necessary to ensure real competition and independent control over monopolies. Because just as little as state or semi-public forms should guide the commercial economy and individual markets, so little should private individuals and private associations take on such tasks. The "social market economy" renounces the planning and guidance of production, the labor force, and sales. It affirms, however, the methodical influence of the economy by the organic means of a comprehensive economic policy based on an elastic adaptation to market observations. Through a sensible combination of monetary, credit, trade, tariff, tax, investment, and social policy . . . , this economic policy fulfills its final goal of serving the welfare and the demands of the entire nation. This fulfillment of demand obviously also includes appropriately provisioning the destitute part of the population.

Source: From the "Düsseldorf Guiding Principles" from the 1949 Congress of the Christian Democratic Union, available from the Konrad Adenauer Foundation at: http://www.kas.de/upload/ACDP/ CDU/Programme_Bundestag/1949_Duesseldorfer-Leitsaetze.pdf

Economic Council in 1948, and then as minister of finance under Adenauer starting in 1949, he was able to put market-oriented policies into place. Against his many opponents—including some from within the Christian Democrats—he argued that a rapid currency reform would free companies to start producing and provide goods better than the state could. On June 20, 1948, the reform went into effect: people exchanged a certain amount of the new Deutsche Marks for their old Reichsmarks, at a 1:1 ratio for wages and pensions, but at a far lower ratio for savings. After all, savings in Reichsmarks were essentially worthless. The value of the currency plunged 90 percent: someone with 1,000 marks in savings was left with around 100 marks. Real goods, like homes and factories, by contrast, remained in the possession of their owners. The coming reform did not aim at equality.

The reform formed a collective experience for all those living in the western zones. With the suspension of rationing, the stores suddenly and quickly filled with goods. Unemployment increased, though economists at the time suggested that the number of employed actually remained the same; the jobs lost were either fake, designed only to get benefits, or part of the black market economy and therefore illegal. Production, meanwhile, increased by some 25 percent in the first two months. Average Germans may have felt their buying power sink and workers complained about greater job insecurity, but the reform succeeded in stabilizing the economy as a whole. The Social Democrats guessed correctly, however, that the currency reform exacerbated the division between East and West Germany. In fact, it contributed to the First Berlin Crisis of 1948–49.

The First Berlin Crisis and the Berlin Airlift

Just like Germany as a whole, Berlin was divided into four sectors, with the crucial difference that for Berlin, the four power Control Council together administered the city. Each power had its own headquarters in the sector under its control, as well as its own military personnel. But many basic services, from power to water to transportation, continued to be administered by the city as a whole; likewise, many workers lived in one sector and worked in another. In other words, the city still largely functioned as one unit. Berlin remained connected to the western zones by way of three roads as well as water, rail, and air connections, ensuring that the Western occupation authorities could maintain their supply lines.

In early 1948, the Soviet occupational authorities walked out of the Allied Control Council that ran Berlin, protesting the increasingly independent policies of the Western occupational authorities. The result was governmental paralysis. Germany itself increasingly appeared to be a divided land. If that were the case, a divided Berlin made little sense, not just for the Soviets but for all the occupying powers. It might have made more sense to give Berlin up and to reduce the number of potential flashpoints in the tense relations between East and West. And indeed, the Soviet occupation authorities began to increase pressure on the other allies in Berlin over the first half of 1948, to make just this point. Against the objections of the Soviet authorities, however, the Western Allies implemented their currency reform in the western zones of Berlin. Now there were two currencies in Berlin, working on very different principles. More important, old Reich marks, worth 10 percent of their original value in western Berlin, still maintained their value in the Soviet sector, leading to a flood of currency from the west to the east—and leaving the Soviet zone with useless currency.

The Soviet occupation authorities sought to resolve the Berlin problem by force. Citing the need for repairs, they closed off rail, road, and canal access to Berlin. They did not publicly state that they were permanently cutting off contact: that would have been a breach of the Potsdam agreements, and a possible cause of war. Nonetheless, they cut the western part of Berlin off from all the other zones—including eastern Berlin. People living in the western part of the city lost their main source of electricity because the generators were in the east, and police and fire departments were split.

To give up Berlin at this point might have signaled a limit to Americans' commitment to their European allies. Consequently, the United States decided, in conjunction with Britain, to fly in food and fuel into the western zones of Berlin. What is today known as the Berlin Airlift was a risky venture and in no way a guaranteed success. Nonetheless, the United States and Great Britain began the enormous project of providing for Berlin's western residents, flying over 200,000 flights from April 1948 to May 1949. The logistics were difficult. The Western Allies developed a complicated system for planes to land, unload, and take off rapidly after dropping their cargo.

The Soviets did not respond to the Berlin Airlift with force. To shoot down civilian planes would have cost them their stake in the institutional organization of Germany and the high moral ground, and violated the four power agreements for the occupation of Germany, and, most importantly, the peace. If the Berlin Airlift did not provoke another war it nonetheless changed the city of Berlin. From now on there were two governments, two city halls, two Berlins—East and West.

The German historian Ulrich Herbert has remarked on the strange transformation that occurred between 1945 and 1948. For the Western Allies, Berlin went from the symbol of Nazi imperialism to the symbol of the "free world." And for the West Berliners and western Germans in general, US and British pilots had made the transformation from bombers to providers.[4] By 1948, Germany, as well as Berlin, was divided into four occupational zones, with the division between East and West recognized (if not necessarily accepted) as the new status quo. It was a division visible across postwar Europe, solidifying in part because neither the United States nor the Soviet Union could risk outright confrontation. Too much was at stake, including the possibility of another major war. But stalemate did not mean paralysis. Already in July 1948, the Western occupying powers called for representatives from the Land-level parliaments in the US, British, and French zones to write a new German constitution. The Soviet zone followed suit somewhat later, blaming the West for dividing Germany.

Further reading

Boehling, Rebecca. *A Question of Priorities: Democratic Reform and Economic Recovery in Postwar Germany*. New York: Berghahn, 1996.

Dagerman, Stig. *German Autumn*. Minneapolis: University of Minnesota Press, 2011.

Douglas, R. M. *Orderly and Humane: The Expulsion of the Germans after the Second World War*. New Haven: Yale University Press, 2012.

Eucken, Walter. *The Foundations of Economics: History and Theory in the Analysis of Economic Reality*. Chicago: University of Chicago, 1951.

Forner, Sean. *German Intellectuals and the Challenge of Democratic Renewal: Culture and Politics after 1945*. Cambridge: Cambridge University Press, 2014.

Frei, Norbert. *Adenauer's Germany and the Nazi Past: The Politics of Amnesty and Integration*. New York: Columbia University Press, 2002.

Grossman, Atina. *Jews, Germans, and Allies: Close Encounters in Occupied Germany*. Princeton: Princeton University Press, 2009.

Lagrou, Pieter. *The Legacy of Nazi Occupation: Patriotic Memory and National Recovery in Western Europe, 1945-1965*. New York: Cambridge University Press, 1999.

Loth, Wilfried. *Stalin's Unwanted Child: The Soviet Union, The German Question, and the Founding of the GDR*. New York: Palgrave Macmillan, 1998.

Marrus, Michael. *The Nuremberg War Crimes Trial*. New York: Bedford, 1997.

Merritt, Richard L. *Democracy Imposed: U.S. Occupation Policy and the German Public, 1945-1949*. New Haven, CT: Yale University Press, 1995.

Merritt, Anna J. and Richard L. Merritt. *Public Opinion in Occupied Germany: The OMGUS Surveys 1945-1949*. Urbana, IL: University of Illinois Press, 1970.

Naimark, Norman. *The Russians in Germany: A History of the Soviet Zone of Occupation, 1945-1949*. Cambridge: Belknap Press, 1997.

Nicholls, A. J. *Freedom with Responsibility: The Social Market Economy in Germany, 1918-1963*. New York: Oxford University Press, 2000.

Roberts, Geoffrey. *Stalin's Wars: From World War to Cold War, 1939–1953*. New Haven, CT: Yale University Press, 2006.

Spilker, Dirk. *The East German Leadership and the Division of Germany: Patriotism and Propaganda, 1945-53*. New York: Oxford University Press, 2006.

Taylor, Frederick. *Exorcising Hitler: The Occupation and Denazification of Germanyh*. London: Bloomsbury, 2011.

Zahra, Tara. *The Lost Children: Reconstructing Europe's Families after World War II*. Cambridge, MA: Harvard University Press, 2011.

2

New states, East and West

FIGURE 2.1 *Steelworks Combine East in Eisenhüttenstadt, East Germany. The sign reads: "Our first iron is proof of the economic rise in our republic," October 1951. (bpk Bildagentur/Herbert Hensky/Art Resource, NY)*

FIGURE 2.2 *The new Coca-Cola plant and distribution center in Bad Godesberg, West Germany, September 1953. (Bundesarchiv, B145 Bild-F000982-009/Rolf Unterberg)*

The Allied occupation and the Cold War determined the shape of both East and West Germany. In neither case can one talk of the result of a completely free decision taken by the German people, and Germans in both East and West tended to view their new constitutional orders as something imposed from without. But that viewpoint obscures the central role played by Germans, especially in the West, in creating their new states. The new Federal Republic, formally under the control of the US, British, and French forces, combined a liberal constitutional model with what was called a "social market economy," essentially a free market supplemented by state regulations and social policy. The new German Democratic Republic, made up of the former Soviet Zone of Occupation, combined party dictatorship with a planned economy. Over the 1950s, two distinct models of politics and society came to exist side by side, opposed but not isolated from each other. One of the many results of this arrangement was a steady stream of skilled and white-collar workers from east to west, sapping East German society of a necessary part of its labor force. The Cold War division of the world thus directly shaped both foreign and domestic policy as well as the culture of divided Germany.

The West German Basic Law: Federalism, basic rights, and "militant democracy"

The process of writing a constitution for a separate West German state began in summer 1948 with the Western Allies' decision to transfer significant state authority to the Germans. On July 1, 1948, they issued the Frankfurt Documents to the heads of the western Länder, establishing the general parameters for the constitution that the Germans themselves were called on to draft. In addition to dictating that the new German state would take the form of a parliamentary democracy, the Allies stipulated that the new constitution should ensure a significant amount of power at the level of the Land while still allowing for a sufficient amount of central authority, as well as provide a clear set of basic rights. The documents went on to stress that a new West German state would not have full sovereignty: the Allies would continue to control aspects of foreign policy and foreign trade. And they reserved to the Allies the special right to declare and take actions to respond to a state of emergency.

Except for the limitations they placed on German sovereignty, the Frankfurt Documents generally matched the desires of German leaders. True, the Social Democrats favored a more centralized state than did the Christian Democrats, who in turn wanted to ensure that Catholic-dominated Länder could retain significant control of education and cultural policy. A particularly heated debate in fact took shape around the Christian Democrats' efforts to protect confessional schools and the Social Democrats' insistence on nationwide secular schooling. Even this could be worked out within the framework of the Allied requirements, however: postwar West German democracy rejected the separation between church and state, while at the same time guaranteeing religious freedom of the individual. The one potential sticking point was the fact that the founding of a West German state meant giving up on a unified Germany. But such was the price Germans paid. To stress the temporary nature of the new system, the West German founders used the term "Basic Law" rather than "constitution," which, they argued, would imply the consent and will of the German people. While annoyed by the political semantics, the Western Allies nonetheless conceded.

Drafting the Basic Law

The Basic Law (as Germany's constitution is still known today) was drafted in two stages. The eleven Länder governments first held a meeting of constitutional experts at the old Herrenchiemsee castle. On an island in Bavaria's largest lake, some forty miles south of Munich near the Austrian border, this initial "working group" remained sequestered for two weeks while it developed a draft constitution, documented the legal arguments behind it, and provided a detailed commentary indicating those points where no consensus existed. The result was a document that stressed the separate identities of the Länder, the "federalist" principle that the Allies had insisted upon, and formed the starting point for the Parliamentary Council.

Länder governments appointed representatives of the major political parties to serve as members of the next phase, the Parliamentary Council. Though all major parties were present (even the uncooperative Communists), the Social Democrats and Christian Democrats dramatically outnumbered the other delegates. Of the 65 members entitled to vote, four were women. Many representatives had been at Herrenchiemsee, and three had even helped draft the Weimar Constitution back in 1919. All of them were preapproved by the Allies, having undergone multiple denazification screenings. This last fact—and delegates' willingness to compromise and adhere to the Allies' repeated interventions—caused observers like the American journalist Theodore White to describe council delegates as powerless marionettes, while at the same time declaring this group of "waifs, strays, victims, outcasts and [anti-Nazi] resisters" to be "more devoted to liberty, republicanism, and democracy even than ourselves." Whatever the Parliamentary Council's faults and very real limitations, the Basic Law was indeed written by the Germans, not by the Allies. It reflected Germans' particular concern to avoid the failures of the Weimar Republic (even if they did not always agree on what those were) and their conviction that the constitution itself was a vital means of preventing history's repetition.

The shape of the West German Basic Law

The recent experience of dictatorship and war shaped the entire Basic Law; in both form and content, the document declared the new state's antithetical relationship to Nazism. The Preamble stressed that the Germans, "conscious of their responsibility before God and men," and desiring to "serve world peace" as an "equal partner in a united Europe," gave themselves a preliminary constitution. This one statement declared the new state's commitment to all that the Third Reich had violated: natural laws standing above human actions (part of the Catholic tradition), human rights (a key part of liberalism and socialism), peace, and European cooperation. Immediately following, Article 1 of the Basic Law stated: "Human dignity is inviolable. To respect and protect it is the duty of all state authority." It was followed by other basic rights: liberty and equality before the law, freedom of conscience and freedom of expression, the value of marriage, family, and education, freedom of association, movement, choice of occupation, rights to property and to political asylum—a right that would become controversial in the 1980s, when immigration became an important issue in political life. The Basic Law furthermore banned the death penalty, after the bloody history of its use under the Third Reich. Christian Democratic and Free Democratic delegates initially resisted including the principle that men and women have equal rights, though gender equality had been protected already under the

1919 Weimar Constitution. In response, one of the few female delegates, Social Democratic member Elisabeth Seibert, organized a massive letter-writing campaign by women across the western zones of occupation, and the Parliamentary Council finally relented: Article 3 declared the equal rights of women and men (although it would be years before ordinary laws were redrafted to reflect this basic right). The placement of values and guaranteed rights before any description of the new government itself rhetorically asserted their preeminence in the constitutional order.

The rest of the document bore this hierarchy out. For example, the Basic Law established the Bundestag (Federal Parliament), a representative legislative assembly elected by the people, as the most powerful constitutional body. But it also stated clearly that the laws it passed could not infringe on the "essence of a basic right" or amend the "basic principles" of the state or human dignity. In other words, the Bundestag stood explicitly under the Basic Law; it could not surreptitiously undermine the constitution's basic principles. To ensure that the Bundestag stayed within constitutional parameters, a new Constitutional Court was created to review complaints brought by citizens against the state. The German Empire had had no high court that could rule on the constitutionality of laws. In the Weimar Republic, a special court could be convened to answer specific constitutional questions, but the handful of times it met, its judgments were controversial. The founders of the Federal Republic thus deliberately broke with tradition, though they left the precise form of the Constitutional Court to be determined at a later date.

The Bundestag itself functioned as a check on the executive—and a corrective to past mistakes. Under the Weimar Republic, the president had been elected directly by the people (unlike members of parliament, who gained their seats according to the number of votes cast for their party, not person). Direct elections gave greater legitimacy to him and his actions, a fact underscored by the president's constitutional power to dissolve the legislative body in cases of deadlock and to rule in its place during national emergencies. Nothing, in fact, better revealed the president's position above parliament—and the Republic's dependence on his democratic disposition—than the extensive emergency powers granted him by Article 48 of the Weimar Constitution and used after 1930 to undermine the Republic. To avoid this problem, the new constitution confirmed that all power, even the executive's, derived from parliament: the Bundestag and Bundesrat together elected the president, whose powers were limited and largely ceremonial.

If the recent past argued against a strong president it also favored the federalist system mandated by the Allies. Many Germans passionately argued that democracy was best protected at the Land level, pointing not only to the Third Reich but also to the Soviet Union for evidence of the authoritarian tendencies of centralized power. Though Social Democrats distrusted the state far less than their Liberal and Christian Democratic colleagues, and in fact argued that local tyrants and provincial bigotry were more to be feared than the central authority, they, too, were interested in allocating power to regional and local governments. The constitution reserved a variety of rights to the eleven Länder, particularly pertaining to the police and cultural matters (education, religion), and again made the Constitutional Court the arbiter of cases involving issues of federal versus Land jurisdiction. Along with the Bundestag, drafters created a second legislative body, the Bundesrat (or Federal Council), to represent the Länder at the national level. The Bundesrat could exercise a limited veto power over laws from the Bundestag, and in some cases had an absolute veto right.

Every (West) German aged 21 and older cast two votes in national elections. The first vote was for a candidate in their voting district, the second for a party. The first vote, then, was for a person, ensuring that strong direct support for a candidate whose party was not popular across the country would translate into a voice in the Bundestag. The second vote, for a party, served to ensure that the number of Bundestag seats each party held after an election was proportional to the total percentage of votes they received—hence the term "proportional representation" to describe the system. Essentially, if a party received 40 percent of the second votes, then direct candidates plus those on a list drawn up by the party would amount to 40 percent of the total party vote in the Bundestag. If a party failed to win 5 percent of the vote, however, it failed to make it "over the hurdle" and into Bundestag—unless at least three of its candidates were elected directly in the vote for a candidate, following a constitutional revision in 1953.[1] The system of proportional representation handed a lot of power to the party leadership, which drew up a list of individuals for the second (party) vote, but balanced that power against the power of individual voting districts to elect specific candidates.

The 5 percent hurdle indicated that the Parliamentary Council understood parties themselves to have played a role in the Weimar Republic's demise. Their sheer number had worked against any one party winning a majority of seats; three, four, or even five parties formed coalition governments, which regularly collapsed under the weight of internal differences and parliamentary stalemate. And at least two parties, the National Socialists and the Communists, had actively sought to overthrow the parliamentary system. After the elections of summer 1932, these parties held the majority of votes in the Reichstag, enabling them to topple any government without having to provide a replacement. The drafters therefore blunted deputies' ability to topple governments. The Basic Law declared that the Bundestag could only initiate a vote of no confidence in a government if it could muster a majority of votes in favor of a new one. In this way deputies were not denied the power to remove an inept government but they were forced to take immediate responsibility for doing so. This "constructive vote of no confidence" effectively increased the stability—and power—of the chancellor and his or her government. The constitution also permitted the prohibition of parties hostile to democracy. All political activity had to work within the framework of what the Basic Law called the "free democratic basic order."

All parties therefore had to agree to respect the principles of democracy. Again, the Constitutional Court had the responsibility of determining a party unconstitutional. In this respect, the new German democracy would be "militant," not passive in response to its challengers.

Lastly, the Basic Law developed explicit procedures for Germany's eventual reunification. Article 23 stated that the Basic Law would come into force in other parts of Germany, including the Saarland then under French control, only when they joined the Federal Republic. Article 146 stated something rather different: that the Basic Law "shall cease to apply on the day on which a constitution freely adopted by the entire German people takes effect." The first implied a process of unification involving the eastern states' absorption into the existing, West German constitutional order. The second underscored the Basic Law's temporary nature, pending a real decision—and constitution—by and for a united nation.

Reception of the Basic Law

In retrospect, the Basic Law did indeed become a lasting legal foundation for postwar West Germany and eventually a united Germany. At the time, however, it came under considerable criticism. Many objected to it as a product of closed deliberations among party elites or, echoing Theodore White, of the Allied powers. Conservative voices bemoaned the loss of a directly elected president outfitted with extensive emergency powers: how could a state survive war or civil unrest without decisive (i.e., independent) executive action? Others feared that proportional voting would result in rule by parties and special interest groups, obscuring the interests of a common national good. And the power granted to the Constitutional Court led many to fear an undermining of popular sovereignty by an overactive judiciary. Finally, socialists and other left-leaning commentators feared that the provisions of "militant democracy" might be used to shut so-called radicals out of public discussion; in seeking to protect democracy, they argued, the drafters in fact threatened to stifle it. These and other criticisms demonstrate the high degree of compromise that went into the Basic Law, so that no one was entirely satisfied. But they also reflect the existence of alternative political visions. A number of Germans in the western zones, for example, agreed with their compatriots in the east that 1945 presented an opportunity for radically new solutions to old problems; others saw in 1945 a moral impetus for German society's re-entrenchment in Western Christian values. These two groups shared many of the drafters' own suspicion that the average German was, at best, politically immature and at worst an unrepentant Nazi.

For those involved, the drafting of the Basic Law was an engrossing process of debate, late night compromises, and even great optimism, occasionally thrown into doubt by the Allies' interventions. But for the vast majority of Germans living in the western zones the Parliamentary Council's labors

CRITICAL RECEPTION OF THE BASIC LAW

The West German Basic Law today enjoys near universal support within Germany. But in the early years of the Federal Republic, many, especially on the right, thought it a document that reflected Germany's loss of sovereignty, that provided so many individual rights that it undermined society, and that ended up destroying any real state authority.

The lawyer Wilhelm Grewe, for example, stated in 1949 that one could "only speak of a limited constitutional autonomy that has been conceded to the German nation" by the military occupation; implicitly he (and others on the right) declared this an imposed constitution.[2]

Ernst Forsthoff noted furthermore in 1955 how the Federal Republic combined a lack of "responsibility for the external and internal security of the republic," since in its early years the country was barred from developing its own army, with the "luxury . . . of freedoms in their most generous form": by implication, the strong basic rights of the new West German state really symbolized a lack of sovereignty and responsibility. By implication as well, they were not really stable and lasting, since at the mercy of external powers. Instead, they created a "freedom that does not bind the individual to the state but rather isolates him in his individual existence," and by extension meant the "disappearance of authentic authority."[3]

And Werner Weber in 1951 attacked the Basic Law for disempowering the executive and delivering the country up to rule by political parties. Elections, he stated, involved "nothing more than opting between already organized political parties and the candidates they present. . . . The people are completely and without exception subordinated to political parties."[4]

Criticism came from the left as well. The left-leaning journalist Dolf Sternberger criticized the Parliamentary Council for having crafted a "dead" rather than "living" constitution, a constitution so fixated on throwing up barriers to its misuse that it reduced democratic politics down to bare numbers and political parties. "What must one do, to avoid the 'mistakes of the past' this time? This question is far more common than the more natural and healthier question: what must one do to make [the constitution] good?" The percent-clause and the proportional voting system—the drafters' "mechanical" and "technical" solutions to parliamentary rule—masked what was, according to Sternberger, an underlying "fear of the majority." This, he argued, was a serious problem. However unpredictable and hard to control majority rule might be, it and a minority, "a right to govern and a right to opposition," were the cornerstones of democratic legitimacy. Answering his own question, Sternberger stated that a good constitution required less fear and more trust, and the *positive use of freedom*. As it was ratified in 1949, however, the Basic Law did not make the move from negative to positive measures as he had hoped, nor did it seem to have replaced fear with "courage," what Sternberger translated "in the language of constitutions" as "freedom."[5]

were of little interest. Although living conditions were improving, Germans were still too close to the "hunger years" of 1943–48 to recognize that the worst was behind them, much less to anticipate the prosperity to come. An immediate consequence of the 1948 currency reform had been a high unemployment of over 10 percent that persisted until 1952: the elimination of the black market forcing large numbers into the legal workforce at the same time the introduction of the new Deutschmark raised the cost of labor. Firms cut their rising expenses by cutting workers. Returning POWs further strained this already tight job market. One immediate answer to the problem of unemployment was to push women from the workplace, a privileging of male heads of households reflected in the pro-family language of the Basic Law itself (see Chapter 3) and the churches' championing of traditional gender roles. But with seven million more women than men in postwar Germany this was no real solution; the spike in female unemployment only added to the misery of the immediate postwar period, severely burdening those families who depended on the incomes of daughters, sisters, widows, and wives.

Even in the best cases, Germans struggled to adjust to their new circumstances: to defeat and occupation, to material deprivation, to the happy but often difficult return of husbands after long absences. And they mourned their loved ones as well as the comfort and happiness, real and imagined, of a previous life. The war, in other words, continued to define Germans' daily lives for years to come and so it is perhaps unsurprising that 73 percent of those polled in March 1949 claimed moderate to complete indifference to the future constitution. The drafters' decision to forgo a popular referendum did more than emphasize the Basic Law's provisional status: it highlighted the distance between the drafters and the people they represented.

The Federal Republic takes form

On August 14, 1949, the first elections took place in the Federal Republic of Germany (FRG). Some 15 parties took part, including the big four: the Social Democrats, the Christian Democrats, the Communists, and the Free Democrats. The outcome was not at all clear: unemployment was over 10 percent, and the Social Democrats criticized the right for supporting a new state that entailed the division of Germany. As it turned out, the Social Democrats received nearly a million more votes than the Christian Democrats alone, without their "union" partner. Together, the two parties would have had an overwhelming majority.

But Adenauer did not want to rule with the Social Democrats, which his party's propaganda—and the majority of CDU/CSU adherents—grouped together with the Communists. He and the Christian Socials therefore pieced together an alliance with the small, conservative German Party and the Free Democrats. He squeaked by: his coalition elected him chancellor by one vote. His decision had two important, and probably unintended, effects.

First, it ensured that there would be a strong, unified opposition party with enough history and smart, experienced people to offer alternatives to the existing party. In this respect, Adenauer's decision helped to consolidate a democratic tradition. Second, Adenauer opened a way to integrate anti-Communist and anti-Socialist groups on the far right, the groups that had undermined the Weimar Republic. In so doing, he undoubtedly contributed to a problematic normalization of German society just a few years after mass murder. He may also, however, have prevented the emergence of a right radical opposition.

The Social Democrats' leader, Schumacher, as a democrat, German nationalist, and victim of the concentration camps, lent his party moral stature. His antifascist credentials did not necessarily endear him to those with ambivalent or compromised relationships to Nazism. And Social Democrats' long history as leaders and representatives of the working class hurt their electoral chances as least as much as it helped. Schumacher spoke to his working-class base in the election, defended the nationalization of industry, and attacked the churches, pushing even those potentially pro-Social Democratic workers who were Catholic (or indeed strong Christians) back toward the predominantly Catholic Christian Democrats. Schumacher died in 1952. He was succeeded by Erich Ollenhauer, a hardworking leader who could not reverse the Social Democrats' position. In 1953, the Social Democrats' focus on organized labor and criticism of integration in the West ran up against the fact of economic success and the resurgence of anti-Communism fueled by events in East Germany. The Social Democrats lost. And over the course of the 1950s, the Christian Democrats gradually increased its hold on the electorate, gaining an absolute majority in 1957 (the only time that happened in the forty-year history of West Germany). By the end of the 1950s, there were only three parties gaining enough votes to enter the Bundestag: the Social Democrats; the Christian Democrats; and the Free Democrats.

The Christian Democrats had support from business against labor; from rural areas, for whom the Social Democrats represented the city; and from Catholic workers distrustful of socialism. They also gained support from the population because of the economic recovery. In its election propaganda, the Union conveyed an image of a peaceful, family-oriented, religious, small town Germany, threatened by Communism and the masses. These images of a restored family life may help to explain the party's appeal to women, who disproportionately voted for Christian Democracy. Women's votes contributed to the Social Democrats' losses throughout the 1950s. Within Bavaria, the Christian Social Union gradually consolidated a loyal clientele, combining anti-socialism with local patriotism and pork barrel politics, leading Bavaria over the next decades to economic modernization and prosperity. The CDU agreed not to campaign in Bavaria and the CSU agreed to stay out of the rest of West Germany. (Because of their tight alliance, this book refers to the two parties together as the "Christian Democrats.")

The Christian Democrats also gained increasing support from the small parties that dropped by the wayside over the 1950s. These were mostly conservative parties of one kind or another. Some of their base went to the Free Democrats; indeed, that party's nationalist bent attracted a hard core of Nazis. Some, however, turned to Christian Democracy, with its strong stance against socialism and Communism and its increasing blind eye to an individual's past under the Third Reich, exemplified by the 1951 Reinstatement Act readmitting many former Nazis to the civil service. The Western Allies thwarted German efforts to further reverse denazification by refusing right-wing lobbyists' demands—and conservative politicians' slightly more subtle arguments—for the inclusion of a general amnesty in the 1952 general treaty formally ending West Germany's status as an occupied territory. But under Adenauer a number of people with questionable pasts held positions of government authority. Hans Globke, who helped write the standard legal interpretation of the 1935 Nuremberg Laws, served as director of the chancellery, for example, and Theodor Oberlaender, Adenauer's Minister for Expellees, was accused of committing atrocities on the eastern front. Oberlaender's case finally became such a distraction that Adenauer removed him from office.

Adenauer liked power and was adept at using it, something which regularly provoked protest and personal attacks from Social Democrats. Adenauer aimed to consolidate the new West German state, to make it more stable, secure, and sovereign—but under his paternal guidance and with a tight connection to the Western Allies. For this reason he is often remembered as an overbearing, even authoritarian, leader disinclined toward democratic discussion. In this, he may have resembled many of his generation: Germans with an anti-Nazi record who continued to distrust the population at large. More interesting than Adenauer's personality, though, is what happened "under the radar screen," as institutions developed that would both provide for stability and for change in West Germany.

The conservatives' fear of a weak state did not materialize. An expanding economy reduced tensions between workers and employers. More importantly, for the constitutional discussion, the principle of the constructive vote of no confidence worked. Removing Adenauer would have required working with the Social Democrats, and the parties in alliance with Adenauer were, if anything, less compatible with the Social Democrats than the Christian Democrats; a positive vote of no confidence was therefore very unlikely. The result was the strengthened power of the chancellorship. Adenauer knew this and played his role well: intervening in special committees and setting the agenda when his ministers failed to reach consensus. By the end of the 1950s, instead of complaining about a weak state, many on the left complained instead about a superpowered executive, a "chancellor democracy."

The Federal Constitutional Court, however, developed in a way that displeased Adenauer. In several instances, the Court's very presence affected government. On the issue of German rearmament, for example ministers were forced to develop constitutional arguments to defend their desired policy. In 1961, when Adenauer sought to exercise more control over public television, the court rebuffed him, reinforcing the rights of the Länder. As Adenauer said about the court's ability to restrain the majority, "That's not something we envisaged."

The Court played a key role in developing the concepts of the Basic Law into workable law. The Court, for example, made the notion of a Free Democratic Basic Order real in its decisions banning certain political parties. The first such decision involved the far right. At issue was the Socialist Reich Party, a radical, anti-Semitic, neo-Nazi party founded in October 1949 after splitting from a small, far right party that had won five seats in the first Bundestag elections. Although the party had only one seat in the Bundestag, it received over 10 percent of the votes in elections to the Lower Saxon assembly in 1951. The Court was clear: any party in the German democracy had to adhere to the basic principles of democracy, the rule of law, individual rights, an independent judiciary, and the rights of other political parties in order to be legal. The court declared the neo-Nazi party illegal. More controversial was the Court's judgment against the Communist Party in 1956, in response to a request from Adenauer's ruling coalition already in 1951. The West German population had clearly expressed its verdict on the Communists at the voting booth; the party, which had drawn significant support in the first years after 1945, had sunk to insignificance by the mid-1950s. The democratic order seemed capable of defending itself, and the party posed no clear threat to West German democracy. Nonetheless, in 1956 the Court banned the Communists, in a lengthy and tortured decision that remains controversial. One did not have to be a Communist to question whether Adenauer pursued the party for political rather than legal reasons; after all, some Communist party members participated in demonstrations against rearmament (discussed further in Chapter 3), while others had connections with the Socialist Unity Party in the east. Notably the Court's willingness to pursue radical parties declined after this decision.

If the banning of the Socialist Reich Party and Communists limited political expression in the Federal Republic, other rulings by the Court expanded political speech. In the Lüth Decision of 1958, the accused had called for a boycott on political grounds against a new film directed by Veit Harlan, who had directed the infamous anti-Semitic film *Jud Süss* under the Nazis. According to West German civil law, boycotts constituted illegal interference in free trade. Instead of simply upholding the anti-boycott rules of civil law, the Constitutional Court argued for the need to balance the principle of the free market with the principle of free expression. It therefore decided in favor of the accused, extending the reach of basic rights and contributing to an expansion of free speech over the next decades.

Initially ignored by most citizens, the Basic Law quickly shaped West German political and indeed social life, through the new institutions it created; the new, legalistic problems it brought forward that limited and balanced state action; and a new approach to politics focused on the principles of the Basic Law itself.

The East German constitution and Socialist Unity Party rule

The birth of the GDR, like that of the FRG, is inseparable from its international context. The occupation in the west set strict limits to the shape of West Germany, pushing it toward integration into Western economic and military systems. The pressure in the east was stronger—not just because the Soviet Union was a dictatorship, but also because the Soviet system relied on conscious and direct commands rather than the "soft power" of the market. Without the Cold War, without the Soviet Union, there was no GDR.

The Soviet occupiers made the Socialist Unity Party's rule possible. They removed anti-Communist leaders (including Social Democrats) from power, and brought pro-Soviet Germans into leadership positions in the administration, from small towns all the way up to the central planning offices. Nationalization of banks and major firms as well as land reform eliminated any threat from leading "class enemies" as well. Of course, the Soviet leadership, like American leaders in the West, pursued its own geopolitical interests. Even as the German Communists in the new Socialist Unity Party gradually transformed the GDR into a state socialist society modeled on the Soviet Union, the Soviet authorities suggested that they might sacrifice the GDR in the interest of Soviet security. Indeed, it was Stalin who kept alive the possibility of a united, neutral, and demilitarized Germany in the center of Europe. His flexible approach to the future of the GDR, combined with the initial exploitative occupation policies discussed in Chapter 1, prompted Wilfried Loth to describe the GDR as "Stalin's unloved child."

At the same time, Germans did play a role in creating the GDR. Historically, Germans had been central in developing Marxism as well as Marxism-Leninism: Karl Marx and Frederick Engels, the movement's spiritual founders, were of course German. The Communist leaders who were flown into the Soviet zone on April 30, 1945, were convinced that they knew the laws of history, and that they had a heroic role to play in implementing them. History was about class struggle; they would, with Soviet help, bring about a revolution of the working class, implement the kind of economic planning that had made the Soviet Union into a strong, socialist land, and lay the foundation for the further spread of socialism. The final goal—for Germany, Europe, and the world—was Communism, the moment when people finally came into possession of their own lives and own societies.

At the center of the Socialist Unity Party stood men (and a handful of women) who knew exactly what they were striving for: a particular kind of socialism, under the control of state authorities and planners, and a state under the control of a vanguard party, what the leader of the Russian Bolsheviks Lenin called a "party of a new type." The party Lenin imagined back in 1902 was essentially a group of professional revolutionaries, which worked with iron discipline on behalf of all those who could not (or would not) devote their lives to politics. The 1917 Russian Revolution ended monarchical rule but not the need for Lenin's vanguard party—quite the contrary, as the Communists understood it. In power, the party was to act as the mouthpiece of the people. Democracy, as Lenin conceptualized it immediately following the revolution, combined local activism with central decision-making. Political leadership rested on a complex root system, starting with the local councils and workers' committees at the lowest level and gradually feeding into a central trunk headed by the party and its chosen leaders—a governing Politburo with a "party secretary" as the head of state. Decisions should be reached by the leaders of the party based on the full input of those below and then implemented by all members of the party. In theory, the party, and the flow of decisions up and down the party "tree," was to bypass the state bureaucracy and representative nature of parliamentary democracy in favor of citizens' more direct participation in their own government. In 1921, however, Lenin banned internal party dissent: anyone who tried to organize in opposition to the party line was potentially building a "faction," and could on that basis be cast out of the party. Intended as a means of protecting the revolution from its many domestic and international enemies, the ban remained in place even after the Soviet Union stabilized and all hopes of counterrevolution were quashed. Indeed, it became the much-loved tool of Lenin's successor, Stalin, who rid himself and the Communist Party of all those who fell under his paranoid gaze.

The German Communists who sought to implement Lenin's brand of socialism in postwar Germany had survived Nazism by fleeing to Moscow. There, they managed to survive the deadly Stalinist purges and gain Soviet support for their resistance efforts. When they returned to Germany in 1945, many of them did so not only with the protection of the Red Army but also having internalized the rules and norms of the Soviet Communist system. The importance of party discipline was the one lesson that many German Communists walked away with after twenty years of fighting fascists in the streets of Weimar and, later, struggling to survive in the underground resistance or in exile. Like many of their counterparts in the west, this same history had taught them to distrust their fellow Germans: if they had brought Hitler to power once, why would they not bring fascism to power again? Thus after the Socialist Unity Party had successfully consolidated power across the Soviet Zone of Occupation, its leaders moved to transform the party along the lines

THE ROLE OF THE PARTY IN EAST GERMANY

The Communist Party in the Leninist tradition—in the GDR under the name Socialist Unity Party—informed the political organization of the state from top to bottom. The party justified its leading role in two ways. First, it claimed to know the dynamic laws of social progress. Second, it claimed to be founded on the enthusiastic support and cooperation of the working masses. Knowledge and direct involvement: these two motifs appear across official declarations, taking different forms at different times, some involving more and some less involvement of the masses, the party, and the party leadership.

The dual—and at times contradictory—notion of party leadership could appear even in party propaganda, as the example of Farmer Arnold from 1960 shows. The pamphlet appeared in the context of Ulbricht's grand push to eliminate private farms in order to control agricultural output, by putting farmers together into an "LPG"—a "Landwirtschaftliche Produktionsgenossenschaft," or collective farm (The full version of this pamphlet is available at the excellent "German Propaganda Archive" maintained by Calvin College.)

Farmer Arnold, the pamphlet stresses, is an exemplary farmer: his farm produces grain and livestock, which he delivers to the state in return for guaranteed good prices. But he assumes that his successes are his own: "All that concerned him was his own desire to wring more from the soil and thus increase his income still more." He did not recognize that his success was based on the GDR's protection against Western capitalists.

When the party called for collectivization, "he became skeptical. He could not accept this transformation in agriculture. He doubted the LPG and behaved toward it like a bachelor who never finds a wife because he always finds something to complain about."

Farmer Arnold, according to the pamphlet, engaged in a kind of "private socialism," failing to connect his own enthusiasm for production with the greater needs articulated by the party: "Farmer Arnold, however, makes a long-outdated argument. The LPG should first set a good example before he, the 'good farmer,' applies to join. If all farmers and all of the working class were so reluctant, finding 1,000 objections to socialist construction, Farmer Arnold himself would not be so prosperous today. Even worse, such an attitude would put the solution to the national problem of the German people in serious jeopardy, and endanger the power of the workers and farmers."

In short, Farmer Arnold's is the wrong sort of socialism, which parts ways with the superior knowledge of the party: "Farmer Arnold wants his 'own socialism.' For him, socialism means remaining an independent farmer, receiving good prices for what he produces, and earning enough so that he can live a comfortable life. . . . For us, building socialism means much more. Socialism should provide a comfortable life for all. . . . There can never be socialism without collective farms, for only large-scale LPG production guarantees that labor productivity constantly increases and that there is a surplus of production. As Lenin says, in the last analysis labor productivity is the decisive factor for the victory of the new social order."

Source: Excerpts taken from: Farmer Arnold and His Relationship to Socialism (1960), available at: http://research.calvin.edu/german-propaganda-archive/arnold.htm.

envisioned by Lenin, a goal captured in the song, "The Party is Always Right," written for the Socialist Unity Party's Third Party Congress of July 1950.

To reach this goal, of course, one needed more than songs. One needed state institutions. Although the path varied considerably in the Soviet zone from that taken in the western zones, they, too, started this process with a constitution. The function of the constitution in the Soviet zone and first decades of the GDR was, however, quite different from its role in the Federal Republic. In the West, the constitution served to organize state power: to determine how power should be assigned, who could hold power, and what the limits were to power. In the East, by contrast, the constitution served in 1949 primarily as a symbol of commitment to German unity and democracy; it was a piece in the public relations battle fought out in Germany between East and West, not a document that organized power. Thus the process of creating the constitution was different. Three different "People's Congresses" convened between 1947 and 1949, claiming to represent all Germans in their common desire for unity. The People's Congress elected a People's Council in 1948; dominated by Socialist Unity Party delegates, the Council essentially rubber stamped a constitutional document already drawn up by the Socialist Unity Party. The process of composing the constitution, in short, was staged, and served primarily propagandistic goals as well as foreign policy goals for the Soviet leadership, which discussed each step with the Socialist Unity Party leadership in advance.

The GDR Constitution appeared to be far more democratic than the Basic Law. Unlike the West German Basic Law, the GDR Constitution made provisions for the direct participation of the people, for example through referenda. It outlawed actions seeking to overthrow the regime (which every legal system does at some level), but proclaimed a set of strong, democratic rights to support the right of the people to engage in direct democracy. It also guaranteed rights of property and assembly. Beyond that, it not only guaranteed the legal equality of men and women (as did the West German Basic Law), it asserted the principle that women should receive equal pay for equal work (not part of the Basic Law). Added to these measures, the constitution also proclaimed a dominant People's Chamber, basically a parliament elected by free, secret elections, which stood opposite a second chamber, representing the Länder. On paper, the constitution stressed the ability of the people to act directly in political life. All of these aspects made the document appear to be a more democratic document than the Basic Law, especially in the eyes of many West German Marxists.

In practice, however, neither chamber included democratically elected members. Voting took place by way of the Unity List, and the latter was constructed and approved by the highest level of the Party. The People's Chamber supposedly introduced and approved laws. In practice, it occasionally came together to approve what the Party demanded. The rights were nice on paper; in practice, the needs of the state could always trump the rights. The party dictatorship recognized rights unless it decided that some exigency required their suspension. The constitution recognized Länder, like in the Federal Republic, but the government eliminated them by decree in 1952 without ever altering the constitution itself. On paper, the People's Chamber formed a special committee to ensure that laws and administrative acts conformed to the constitution. In practice, it did nothing of the sort.

The People's Chamber ultimately served as an unconvincing symbol of democracy. Since elections to it took place by the "unity ballot," those elected were functionaries and intellectuals whom the party leadership assumed would approve what the party asked. The delegates performed honorary functions and gave the appearance of action but real power lay elsewhere, as everyone knew. The East German constitution was in this sense something between a piece of ineffective propaganda and a farce. It failed even to mention the glaringly obvious role of the Socialist Unity Party in running the country.

The party in East German life

Real government took place within the Socialist Unity Party, and the Socialist Unity Party modeled itself on the Communist Party of the Soviet Union, in the specific form that it had assumed under Stalin. The transition to this "party of a new type" took place between 1947 and 1950. A structure emerged that would remain relatively stable for the rest of the GDR. At the top was the First Secretary of the Central Committee, later the General Secretary. Ulbricht maneuvered himself into this job, gradually consolidating authority. Under him was the Politburo, the main site of collective decision-making, loosely equivalent to a government cabinet. In 1950 it consisted of nine voting members and five nonvoting; though these numbers changed over the years, one thing did not: the dominant power of the First Secretary. In moments of crisis (1953, 1956, 1971, and 1989) other members could take the initiative against the First Secretary, but only at great risk. Alongside the Politburo was the Secretariat of the Central Committee, which functioned in conjunction with the large Central Committee. The Secretariat consisted of between 51 and 165 members, as well as some nonvoting members. It met four times a year and, with only partial access to information held by the Politburo, it ultimately had little influence over politics.

Finally, party organizations reached into every neighborhood and social organization. This model of party organization saw many reforms over the years, but the model of top-down party control reaching into the lowest levels of society was a constant of GDR society. Children were expected to join the Young Pioneers and later the Free German Youth (FDJ). Alongside the Socialist Unity Party, several other parties were permitted to exist. Known as "bloc parties" because they were part of the "coalition" under the Socialist Unity Party, parties such as the Christian Democrats or the German Farmer's Party officially embraced "socialism," by which was meant the political system of East Germany. The National Democratic Party was formed in 1948 to give a political place in East Germany for former Nazi party members. Alongside the parties, so-called mass organizations like the union federation and the Democratic Women's Federation sent representatives to the People's Chamber. They also provided cultural programming and discussions oriented toward their constituents. The aim of these and numerous other organizations was to integrate the population into the socialist state.

The party cadre was central to the functioning of the state. It is not surprising, then, that the leadership oversaw regular purges of those who were deemed unable to ensure the correct understanding and execution of the party line. The purges of the early years also reflected, or perhaps mimicked, the paranoid style of late Stalinism. Accusations of "social-democratism," "opportunism," and "reformism," or of espousing the ideas of Stalin's rivals and critics—Leon Trotsky and Yugoslavian leader Josip Tito foremost among them—took aim at those who did not take the Soviet Union as their model. Ideological accusations accompanied charges of sabotage, corruption, and damage to the plan: crimes against the "people's property" became subject to draconian punishments. Identifying wayward comrades and providing state's evidence against them fell to Ministry for State Security, or the Stasi, as the East German secret police was more commonly called. Closely tied to the Soviet KGB, the Stasi proclaimed itself the "sword and shield" of the party. As such, it spied not only on Socialist Unity Party members but on the entire population and came to be one of the most effective and repressive intelligence agencies in history.

Some of the cases that the Stasi helped build took the form of highly publicized show trials, modeled after the ones during Stalin's purges. The state put individuals as well as groups on trial for espionage. Common throughout the new "people's republics" of eastern Europe, these sorts of show trials came to exemplify Soviet-style tyranny for the West. In the GDR, they took on a particularly grotesque form in the 1950–52 campaign against "cosmopolitanism." In this instance, party members who had returned from exile in the West found themselves accused of treasonous anti-Sovietism. Paul Merker, for example, a devoted Communist since the 1920s, had gone into exile in Mexico. There, he had organized aid for other exiled Communists, wrote of Jews' special suffering under Nazism, and advocated for a new Israeli state as a response to Nazi misdeeds. In 1946, Merker returned to Germany and to his place among the inner circle of Communist leaders. His privileged position proved fleeting however. After the establishment of Israel in 1948 and the new country's decision to ally itself with the United States, Merker's earlier statements, including his 1940 condemnation of the Hitler-Stalin pact, became evidence of his anti-Soviet sentiments. When Stalin's paranoia took an anti-Semitic turn in the last years of his life, Merker was hauled before a secret show trial and sentenced to hard labor for his involvement with "Jewish capitalists." Merker survived by outliving Stalin: he was released in 1956, in the wave of amnesties following Stalin's death.

The primary reason for removing Merker was almost certainly the distrust and hostility he inspired in Stalin and Ulbricht (a longtime party rival) respectively. As Jeffrey Herf has noted, however, the case revealed as well what happened to anti-fascism when it went from being a general rejection of fascism to an official ideology explaining the East German state's moral superiority. Official anti-fascism reduced the struggle against fascism to the struggle of the working class, which the party claimed to represent. As a result, the German attack on European Jewry became a marginal issue in official statements; anti-Semitic violence ceased to appear as a crime in itself, and the East German state, as representative of the heroic working class, became absolved of the responsibility for remembering Germans' misdeeds in the Holocaust. While such issues remained important in some intellectual circles, official history ignored them for decades.

The "Economic Miracle" in West Germany

The consolidation of the state and political parties in West Germany took place against the backdrop of the "economic miracle," the sudden shift from scarcity to wealth and to a consumer-oriented culture. The fact that people at the time used this term starting in the early 1950s to describe what they were experiencing captures for us, decades later, West Germans' surprise at their changing lifestyles. Scarcity did not begin for Germans in 1945. World War One had brought scarcity, rationing, hunger. The weak economy of the interwar years meant that workers still earned little, and the Great Depression made their living conditions even worse. Under National Socialism, people had jobs, but their money had little to buy: guns, not butter, were being produced from 1939 on. And then there was the war.[6] In the 1950s for the first time in some two generations, West Germans experienced an expanding economy. It undoubtedly seemed miraculous. An impression made all the stronger by the fact that after 1949 growth was continuous. However novel all this was, West Germans quickly accepted it as the new norm, hoping against hope that trade cycles and bubbles were a thing of the past.

The ordoliberals offered a clear explanation for the economic boom: Germany had finally broken with cartels, had taken measures to make the market a level playing field, and allowed the free market to do its work. But the story is not quite so simple. First, the percentage of GDP dedicated to social spending—meaning state-funded or subsidized programs—steadily increased alongside the expanding economy. Second, the economy was not "free" from one moment to the next; international investment remained tightly regulated and major economies' currencies did not float on the international market, ensuring stability for West German exporters. After all, the West German social market was designed to protect against the uncertainties of the market as much as unwanted intervention by the state. Third, the FRG was not the only booming postwar economy. In fact, except for Great Britain, all of western Europe and Japan saw high growth rates. There can be no doubt that the currency reform and an opening of international markets helped West Germany, but the reasons for the so-called miracle should be sought elsewhere.

A number of different factors came together to produce German growth. US-backing in the form of Marshall aid lent the new Deutschmark legitimacy and encouraged both foreign and domestic investment. Not only did a good deal of industry remain intact despite the war (precision bombing had not been so precise!), but when companies replaced old machines and factories, they were able to purchase the newest technology, increasing productivity even more. Just as important to postwar economic growth: the FRG, like the GDR, had an educated, skilled workforce, whose abilities had been hitherto lost to unemployment or squandered on the war. It was also a cheap workforce; wages remained relatively low throughout the early postwar period—and profits correspondingly high, for several reasons. Labor unions, gutted under National Socialism, remained weak, as did class solidarity, undermined by Nazi racial ideology but also the egalitarianism of wartime destruction and the promise of reconstruction. Workplace militancy was low, too, in part because of the Communists' exclusion from factories and FRG society as a whole (with the exception of a few places such as the Ruhr coal mining districts, for example), and in part because of the moderating force of Catholic workers in the newly unified trade unions. Just as critically, the number of people seeking work continued to exceed the available jobs until the mid-1950s; employers did not need to pay high wages, in other words. In addition to the last of the returning POWs, there were the expellees and refugees from the east. Far from being welcomed, these Germans, officially referred together as *Heimatvertriebene* ("persons driven from their homes"), were treated with suspicion and even racist (often mingled with religious) prejudice, commonly denigrated as "Poles."

Over 80 percent of those forced to leave the former German territories went into agriculture but wherever they ended up, they created a group of disadvantaged and more importantly underpaid workers, depressing wages further and acting as a depressant, again, on unions. Last but not least, a continuous trickle of East Germans made their way to West Berlin and then West Germany between 1949 and 1961. This group of "refugees" (the only Germans to be designated as such by the 1953 Expellee and Refugee Law) was disproportionately made up of young men with professional training. Seeking better work, they contributed to the already tight labor market. The result was relatively high-quality work at relatively low labor costs, capable of being sold on foreign markets.

Low wages relative to profits and the exploitation of expellees point to the "hidden" sources of West Germany's economic miracle. Here, too, women played an important role. As mentioned above, women's involuntary exit from the labor force helped returning soldiers and POWs enter it. But before that—and even the 1948 currency reform—women paved the way for economic recovery, literally and figuratively. Not only did they provide thousands of hours of poorly or uncompensated labor but as Elizabeth Heineman has argued, these women's stories of backbreaking reconstruction work became West Germany's story. Similar to the image of a phoenix rising from the ashes, the Rubble Woman became an important symbol of West German perseverance, hard work, and economic success; like the phoenix, she, too, implied that history began again in 1945. But if Rubble Women were prominently featured in the "rubble films" of the early postwar years—images and memories that live on even today—the women themselves faced growing discrimination, particularly those of "marriageable" age and older, cut out of the labor market in favor of "male breadwinners."

Other "costs" of the economic miracle included the rushed denazification of technical experts and industrial magnates who were useful for the economy. Social Democratic leaders also argued that the FRG's particular path to prosperity came at the expense of German reunification, and possibly sustained peace, given that another source of the recent boom was the country's further economic and military integration with the West. Such arguments were lost, along with any other negative aspects, as recovery became tangible and the last but crucial contributor to the FRG's economic success came into sight: demand. Demand soared, from the Western Allies involved in the Korean War, and just as critically from within the country, as people began to purchase the stuff they hadn't purchased for thirty years: furniture, new clothes, and later also radios, televisions, cars. Only when relative wages and employment rose again and people could buy consumer durables did prosperity go from being a slogan and a hope to becoming a reality for wide swaths of the population.

The constant expansion of production and wealth certainly contributed to the Christian Democrats' success, and to the mystique surrounding Minister of Economics Ludwig Erhard and his slogan "prosperity for all."

But there was another side of the expansion of wealth that didn't sit so well with Erhard: social policy. Unemployment declined over the 1950s, hitting 4 percent in 1956, while wages began to increase, giving working people the gradual sense of a more secure, predictable life; but the condition of the elderly and disabled declined. Private pensions and life insurance had been demolished by Nazi public finance or by the costs of war and currency reform. The FRG's public pension scheme, based on a model set up in the 1880s, was inadequate to say the least, but the Christian Democrats and Free Democrats balked at doing more. In the midst of growing prosperity, however, images of poor people struck a chord. The Social Democrats demanded attention to social security already in the early 1950s. Adenauer's government first responded by citing the need to increase production above all else. Then the Christian Democrats and Social Democrats together approved a bill transferring funds to those who had suffered from the war. But the problem did not go away and the Social Democrats looked primed to take advantage of the government's inaction at the polls. To prevent just that, Adenauer intervened personally to push through a major pensions reform bill in 1957. The new program provided unemployed, disabled, and retirees with 60 percent or more of their average yearly income, and automatically adjusted this income to current wage levels, guaranteeing that social security recipients' standard of living would not fall behind others. The pensions were funded through deductions from employees' income, with matching payments from employers.

The result of all this was twofold: First, the Christian Democrats and the Christian Socials in Bavaria won the 1957 election handily; they appropriated the Social Democrats' idea for pension reform and ensured support from Catholic workers. Second, by the end of the 1950s, West Germany was becoming a full-fledged European welfare state. Nearly a third of GDP flowed through public hands—despite the dominance of ordoliberal thinkers in government.

East Germany: Decision for socialism and centralized planning

The GDR took a very different path to economic reconstruction. From the start, German Communist leaders aimed to construct "socialism," by which they meant a Soviet-style economic system. There are lots of models of socialism. Some involve worker-run firms, which produce for the market; others involve management of raw materials to reach certain outcomes. The Soviet model of a socialist economy closely correlated to its model of the "party of a new type." In the Soviet Union, a centralized State Planning Commission sought to coordinate inputs and outputs, supply and demand, across the entire economy. Socialism in this sense—comprehensive, centralized planning aimed at specific goals—corresponded to the conception of the Party, as a conscious avant-garde setting the direction for economic development. The Plan both exemplified the Marxist-Leninist model of the Party and dramatically enhanced the power of the Party over society. Ulbricht's faction of the Socialist Unity Party favored implementing this model of socialism.

But Soviet foreign policy limited the Communists. German Communists' plans to create a socialist economy repeatedly bumped up against Soviet self-interest. The Soviet leadership did not want to resolve the "German problem" too quickly, whether this meant committing to a separate Communist Germany or to a united but neutral country in the heartland of Europe. As long as Germany's fate remained open, the Soviets could use it as a negotiating chip in their dealings with the Western Allies. So they waffled and kept German Communists' own aspirations in check. Already in the early years of occupation, for example, those German Communists closely allied with the Soviets helped create the new People's Firms in East Germany. By 1948, these became the basis for centralized planning in the Soviet zone under the German Economic Commission. But even in 1949, as the Socialist Unity Party announced the first Two Year Plan, its leaders were not permitted to announce the "construction of socialism." Though few in London or Washington were interested in a neutral Germany by this late date and even fewer trusted Stalin enough to negotiate, the Soviets continued to hold out.

The GDR meanwhile faced major economic obstacles. Eastern Germany had historically been poorer than western Germany. Furthermore, not only had the war destroyed much industry but the Soviet policy of removing industrial plant or putting it under the control of "Soviet joint stock companies" had also deprived eastern Germany of material, labor, and products that would have aided in reconstruction—hardly a coherent policy if the Soviets were aiming at creating a puppet state from the start. In addition, the growing separation between East and West cut eastern German firms off not only from their historical trading partners but also from their sources for raw materials. The Soviet Union had itself suffered horribly from the war, and was not able to provide either the aid or the capital investment that the western zones of occupation could enjoy.

The economic planners of the German Economic Commission and its successors (the Ministry of Planning, after 1950 the State Planning Commission) grappled with these immense problems of scarcity and limited control of resources. At the same time, even before 1949 they began to develop some of the patterns associated with Stalinist planning, already pushing forward toward the Soviet model of economic organization. The Socialist Unity Party sought to solve problems related to poor planning, scarce resources, or hoarding with activism from below: they called for enthusiasm and initiative on the part of workers now that firms were owned by the people, encouraged competitions between different groups of workers, and offered special rewards for overfulfilling the "labor norm" for certain tasks. In the miner Adolf Hennecke, for example, they found their own version of the Soviet hero of labor Alexey Stakhanov, a miner who busted the labor norm in the Soviet Union in 1935. On October 13, 1948, Hennecke allegedly produced almost four times the amount of coal normally produced in a shift. His success was a well-planned stunt, which served as propaganda for the workers to exert themselves in the interest of the state. When grassroots activism was not enough, the Socialist Unity Party also had a ready-made set of explanations for the economic failures, which corresponded to the purges of the time. Failure did not emanate from the system itself, but from saboteurs, wreckers, and malingerers, all terms derived from the dramatic years of forced industrialization under Stalin.

But even after 1949, as the GDR replaced the Soviet Zone of Occupation, the Socialist Unity Party could not announce its goal of socializing the economy. Only in 1952, after Stalin's diplomacy on Germany finally ran its course, did Ulbricht have the chance to announce the "construction of socialism" in the GDR. It remains a matter of debate to what extent Stalin would have sacrificed control over East Germany in order to gain a demilitarized and neutral united Germany, although most scholars doubt his intentions. The tight connection of GDR developments to the needs of the Soviet state, however, remains indisputable.

In any case, East and West Germany increasingly took on the functions of exemplars for the different economic systems. And here the GDR clearly looked worse. In the best of cases, its economic conditions would not have allowed for the kind of wealth that one could see in the FRG in the early years of the economic miracle. The GDR's first central plan, with its emphasis on heavy industry, allowed even fewer commodity items to appear on the market. As the economic gap between the two economies widened, those younger, more skilled, male workers who could find lucrative jobs in West Germany, did so. Their westward migration only increased the vicious cycle, putting more pressure on the East German economy.

Under these conditions, the Soviets finally allowed the Socialist Unity Party leadership to fully embrace the state socialist project. At the second party conference of June 9–12, 1952, Walter Ulbricht became the General Secretary of the Socialist Unity Party, cementing his position as the Stalin-like leader of East Germany, and the party officially announced the "construction of socialism." From that point on, the GDR joined its fellow "people's republics" in following the model of the Soviet Union. The Socialist Unity Party undertook a campaign to reverse the land redistribution policies of 1945–46, which gave land over to individual farmers, and to collectivize farms. It also began another round of measures to nationalize those firms and small businesses that were still in private hands.

But socialism, like capitalism, is far more than an economic system. Its construction required uprooting the previous class structures and traditions and replacing them with a new Soviet-style society. For this reason, families and schools were just as important as the workplace when it came to teaching East

Germans new—socialist—ways of seeing and being in the world. Contrary to what anti-Communists claimed, the Socialist Unity Party did not seek to destroy marriage (as a largely religious institution) or the family. Instead, the party established marriage and the family as fundamental pillars of socialism, arguing that only under socialism could love and affection—rather than money—provide a basis for either institution. Toward that end, the 1950 Law for the Protection of Mothers and Children and the Rights of Women forbade discrimination between the sexes and between married and unwed mothers. Single mothers and their children could claim the same rights and entitlements as those granted to married women, including eleven weeks of paid maternity leave and child allowances. And, for the first time, married women possessed the same legal and financial rights as their husbands, including finding employment outside of the home. Marriage and legal independence were no longer an either/or; East German women could have both.

The party also launched sweeping education reforms, requiring not only that the principles of Marxism-Leninism be taught at all levels but also declaring the end of two long-standing German traditions: a four-track system separating students into different schools and the role of the official churches in providing education. The first was replaced by a unified, eight-grade school attended by all East Germans—similar to the American system. Getting the churches out of the schools took more work. To give a sense of what German Communists were up against: as late as 1933, 80 percent of German elementary schools were confessional and even the Nazis kept religious instruction. With their organizational networks still largely intact, Catholic leaders quickly reestablished their influence in the western zones. Despite their best efforts, Catholic and Protestant churches failed to do so in the east. Not only was religious instruction eliminated in East Germany's schools but education proved the beginning of the Socialist Unity Party's active campaign against the churches as backward and potentially subversive institutions. The Socialist Unity Party viewed Protestants with particular suspicion in part because Lutheranism was historically the region's dominant confession; 81 percent of East Germans identified as Lutherans in the 1949 consensus. But also because the church retained its all-German institutional structures: East German pastors regularly communicated with their counterparts in the FRG and thus immediately attracted the attention of the Stasi. Jehovah's Witnesses, however, faced the most severe repression. Though originally recognized by the state as "victims of fascism," they were banned in August 1950. In yet another show trial, the state sentenced nine witnesses to harsh prison terms for "systematic agitation against the established order and espionage for an imperialistic power"; hundreds of others were imprisoned by lower courts while those who could went underground.

Last but not least, the Socialist Unity Party undertook new, prestigious projects. In Berlin, the showplace of the East, the regime undertook a massive reconstruction of one of the avenues leading into the center of town, which it renamed Stalinallee. Outside of Berlin, Stalinstadt (Stalin City, changed in 1961 to Iron Foundry City or Eisenhüttenstadt) became the first planned workers' city of the GDR. Designed to provide housing for workers in the new steel mill founded nearby, Stalinstadt offered a model for the ideal socialist city. Three- and four-story apartment blocks contained day care and shopping facilities as well as schools, and boulevards and parks added a grand air. In the end, however, redevelopment projects such as these would prove too time consuming and costly for a society in dramatic need of new housing. But Stalinstadt and Stalinallee nonetheless stood as a symbols of the good life to be found in the socialist city of the future.

Ironically, workers on the Stalinallee posed the first major challenge to the Socialist Unity Party's model of state socialism.

Further reading

Epstein, Catherine. *The Last Revolutionaries: German Communists and their Century*. Cambridge, MA: Harvard University Press, 2003.

Harsch, Donna. *Revenge of the Domestic: Women, the Family, and Communism in the German Democratic Republic*. Princeton: Princeton University Press, 2007.

Heineman, Elizabeth. "The Hour of the Woman: Memories of Germany's 'Crisis Years' and West German National Identity." *American Historical Review* 101 (April 1996), 354–95.

Herf, Jeffrey. "East German Communists and the Jewish Question: The Case of Paul Merker." *Journal of Contemporary History* 29 (1994), 627–61.

Kommers, Donald, and Russell A. Miller. *The Constitutional Jurisprudence of the Federal Republic of Germany*. Third edition. Durham, NC: Duke University Press, 2012.

Leonhard, Wolfgang. *Child of the Revolution*. London: Pluto, 1979.

Loth, Wilfried. *Stalin's Unwanted Child: The German Question and the Foundation of the GDR*. New York: St. Martin's Press, 1998.

Mitchell, Maria. *The Origins of Christian Democracy: Politics and Confession in Modern Germany*. Ann Arbor, MI: University of Michigan Press, 2012.

Moeller, Robert. *War Stories: The Search for a Usable Past in the Federal Republic of Germany*. Berkeley: University of California Press, 2003.

Ruggenthaler, Peter. "The 1952 Stalin Note on German Unification: The Ongoing Debate." *Journal of Cold War Studies* 13, no. 4 (2011), 172–212.

Spevack, Edmund. *Allied Control and German Freedom: American Political and Ideological Influences on the Framing of the West German Basic Law*. Ann Arbor, MI: University of Michigan Press, 2001.

Spilker, Dirk. *The East German Leadership and the Division of Germany: Patriotism and Propaganda 1945-1953*. New York: Oxford, 2006.

Van, Dijk. The 1952 Stalin Note Debate: Myth or Missed Opportunity for German Unification? Working Paper No. 14, Cold War International History Project. Washington, DC: Woodrow Wilson Center, 1996.

White, Theodore. *In Search of History: A Personal Adventure*. New York: Harper & Row, 1978.

3

Stability, consolidation, and dissent in West and East

FIGURE 3.1 *View of the Hansaviertel, September 1960. (ullstein bild/Getty Images)*

FIGURE 3.2 *View of Stalinallee and the Frankfurter Tor, June 10, 1958. (ullstein bild/Probst/Getty Images)*

East and West Germany diverged economically and politically over the 1950s. In the west, the economic miracle led to a rise in West German living standards and an increasingly positive perception of liberal democracy. Both politicians and people sought further stability in the model of a heterosexual, nuclear family with a primary male breadwinner. Konrad Adenauer, the leader of the Christian Democrats and West Germany's first chancellor, pushed for economic and military integration into the anti-Communist West. This did not go unquestioned. In fact, NATO membership, remilitarization, and nuclear armament provoked widespread popular protest at home. Despite ongoing opposition, the CDU won a landslide victory in September 1957; their campaign slogan—"No experiments!"—captured the spirit of the times.

In the east, political and economic stability remained an ongoing battle. Following Stalin's death in March 1953, dissent within the East German government and a mass uprising of East German workers threatened Walter Ulbricht's leadership. With the help of Soviet military force, Ulbricht put down the revolt and his political enemies but he faced an ongoing crisis of legitimacy. Economically, the GDR suffered from labor shortages made worse by the continued loss of manpower to the west, especially through the open border between East and West Berlin. Necessity and ideological commitments thus encouraged women into the workplace in East Germany. Their presence did not, however, put an end to the "brain drain" or the social and political insecurity that it produced. Chapter 3 closes with the

Second Berlin Crisis of 1958–61, which culminated in the construction of the Berlin Wall in August 1961.

Berlin's position as an open but divided city offered the superpowers and their respective German allies an unusual opportunity to perform for the other—anticipating later US-Soviet debates over the material rewards and lifestyles of the competing political systems. In West Berlin, a series of Marshall Plan-sponsored exhibitions culminated in the U.S. State Department's 1952 exhibit "We're Building a Better Life," which sought to introduce the "American way of life" to thousands of East and West Germans. Visitors oohed and aahed over modular single-family homes, with their gleaming appliances and rational floor design, and gawked at the happy housewife as she made use of these innovations to dote on her husband and two children. One year later, East Berlin responded with its own exhibit, "Living Better, Dwelling More Beautifully." In both cases, the home stood in for the "good life" each regime claimed to be building.

Both city governments competed to imprint their particular political values on the buildings and urban landscape they were busily reconstructing. Architectural style was, in fact, a hotly contested question for all those concerned to demonstrate Germany's break with Nazism and the triumph of their particular vision of the future. None of the preferred and disavowed styles held objective value; political meaning had to be read into them. But in the FRG, the classical ornamentation and stone facades favored by nineteenth- and early twentieth-century architects were now associated with authoritarian power structures and not infrequently compared to the monumental architecture favored by the Nazis and the Soviets. Modernist architecture, with its stripped down facades of glass and steel, appeared democratic by virtue of its very transparency and became the officially sanctioned style of the FRG. Planners in the GDR reached the opposite conclusion: East German authorities defended Germany's neoclassical tradition and judged "formalist" or abstract styles alien, divorced from the people and thus undemocratic by nature. Following the tenets of Soviet Socialist Realism, they argued that the architectural style best suited to serve the people's economic and social needs was one that drew on the existing culture and historic fabric. The party declared modernism, as a style devoid of such roots, a product of "rotting capitalism," an architectural style in the service of imperialism and unscrupulous finance.

West Berlin's Hansaviertel and Stalinallee Boulevard in East Berlin captured these different interpretations of "democratic" architecture and the two countries' different political systems. The Hansaviertel consisted of a number of high-rise apartment buildings, each designed by a different modernist architect and positioned in an irregular, or "free," pattern amid an expansive park. In keeping with its "garden-city" ideal, the West German district was purely residential; two traffic arteries provided access to the rest of Berlin. All of this worked together to underscore the FRG's commitment to individualism and the West. In contrast, the six- to seven-story buildings on Stalinallee faced the boulevard itself, their uniform stone facades drawing the eye down the length of East Germany's "first socialist street." If the Hansaviertel was a garden, Stalinallee was densely and unapologetically urban, with shops and restaurants on the ground floor; all the needs of daily life were to be accessible to the residents living above. The apartments also boasted monumental columns and high-quality materials like fine porcelain tile previously reserved for the houses of the wealthy. Such ornamentation proclaimed the workers' privileged status, as well as the regime's desire to "ennoble" everyday life, just as the boulevard itself reflected the GDR's alliance with the Soviet Union.

West Germany: Stability

By the end of the 1950s—just ten years after its founding and fifteen years after Germany's unconditional surrender—the FRG had achieved unquestioned stability. So much so that many West Germans would look back on the 1950s and remember it as a quiescent and unpolitical decade. Such memories probably tell us more about West Germans' sense of turmoil in the decades that came before (1930s and 1940s) and after (1960s and 1970s) than they do life and politics in 1950s FRG—for West German society was neither complacent nor conflict-free. But it is true that continued economic growth, the restoration of traditional gender norms, and anti-Communism, as well as the FRG's full integration into the Western bloc, contributed to West Germans' growing sense of security and well-being.

Stability at home

It is nearly impossible to overestimate the importance of the economic miracle to the short- and long-term success of the FRG. The last chapter discussed its contribution to a specifically West German national identity predicated on the values of hard work and self-sacrifice, and the notion of 1945 as the "zero hour." Whether one embraced or rebelled against this particular version of postwar reconstruction, economic growth acted as something of a cure-all. Wealth did not flow equally but as long as the economy continued to grow, very few were willing to rock the boat. The basic assumption, even among weary labor unions, was that the scale and speed of economic growth was sufficient to ensure that all members of society would benefit—in other words, the pie was presumed big enough for everyone to get a share, even if some pieces would be bigger than others. Then, too, West Germans were eager to put the "hunger years" behind them and to enjoy life. For many, 1955 was the start of a distinctly new, post-postwar era: with the return of the last of the POWs and food widely

MAP 3.1 *Länder of the Federal Republic of Germany*

available, they no longer lived in the shadow of the war. Newspapers and popular magazines talked about a *Freßwelle*, or a feeding frenzy, thanks to improved food supplies and standards of living, tangible by mid-decade. If Germans' average daily calorie intake had tipped below 1,000 in 1945/46, it rose to 3,000 ten years later.

Of course, West Germans did more than just eat. They also shopped. They bought new consumer durables like vacuum cleaners, sewing machines, refrigerators, and washing machines—those very products on display in the touring exhibitions of American model homes. They perused department stores stocked with "ready-to-wear" clothing and fashion accessories. And if Hitler planted the dream of the "people's car," it was American-style credit and payment plans that first made car ownership a reality for middle-class West Germans. Between 1950 and 1960, the number of cars in the FRG rose from just over 500,000 to over four million. The car was in many ways the ultimate purchase: it symbolized prosperity, mobility, and freedom—all that the West promised. Ever larger numbers of West Germans took to the road in search of fun and relaxation. Camping was a particularly popular leisure activity, no doubt because of its affordability. New camping sites opened across the FRG and new models of cars were introduced specifically with the camper-tourist in mind. Whether driving their own Volkswagen T1-Bus or part of an organized group vacation, West Germans quickly developed a reputation as tourists in search of sand and sun. Tourism, like the car, was a symbol of West German recovery and mobility in conscious distinction to the GDR and its citizens' immobility. Traveling outside Germany began slowly and was not always tension-free; more than one West German encountered resentment from locals, as to be German was still—for many Europeans—to be a Nazi. But tourism was also part of West Germans' integration with the West, relevant not only politically, as travel came to be conceived in terms of "friendship tours," but also psychologically and emotionally.

West Germans also enjoyed sports, perhaps as a kind of replacement patriotism. In 1954, the West German soccer team qualified for the World Cup for the first time and went on to win in a close contest against the favored Hungarian team. So unexpected was the win, that it immediately became known as the "Miracle of Bern," the city where the final game was played. As was customary, after the West German victory the band played the national anthem, the *Deutschlandlied*, with its opening line "Deutschland, Deutschland, über alles"—Germany, Germany, over all. Some of the crowd sang it; the West German champions did not, one choosing instead to chew gum. The memories of war were too recent, German nationalism too compromised. Whatever the problems in phrasing, though, there was no denying the sense of euphoria that swept the Federal Republic, and the players were greeted as heroes.

Increased material well-being provided political stability to the FRG. The percentage of West Germans who supported democratic rather than monarchical or Nazi political views grew in close correlation with the average West Germans' weight. The contrast to the early years of the Weimar Republic, Germans' first attempt at democracy, is striking. Democracy, once associated with national humiliation, economic ruin, and political mayhem, was now synonymous with economic success.

Democracy as a concept was linked with the economy in another way as well, through the representation of labor. Labor unions gained recognition from the Christian Democratic government as the legitimate representatives of workers, even if the relationship between the unions and the government was often tense. The presence of a strong Christian workers' movement within the CDU both split the labor vote and ensured that Adenauer's government had to take labor seriously. Adenauer himself, in consultation with his old friend the labor leader Hans Böckler, supported the right of workers in companies over a certain size to elect representatives to a supervisory board of directors, a practice known as codetermination. Codetermination had roots in the Catholic-dominated Christian labor movement of the late nineteenth century, which strove for a harmonious and cooperative relationship between workers and owners, as well as in the 1920s Social Democratic movement for economic democracy. The laws that eventually institutionalized codetermination under Adenauer did not go as far as labor unions wanted but they did serve to open lasting lines of communication between workers and management, further contributing to the country's political and economic stability.

West Germany's reconstruction rested on a third pillar: the nuclear, patriarchal family. One widely shared memory of Nazism—and postwar interpretation of totalitarian regimes generally—was the state's radical intervention in, and ultimate destruction of, the private sphere. For many, overcoming Nazism thus entailed reestablishing traditional relations and power dynamics between the state and the individual on the one hand, and between women and men, children and parents on the other; it meant the re-entrenchment of Christian values and official recognition of a divinely ordained natural order. Even those uninterested in confronting the legacies of Nazism understood the family to be the cornerstone of a strong nation and judged a single-mother family to be as abnormal as the war and occupation. From the very beginning, then, reconstructing Germany meant reconstructing the family—and the reassertion of male authority.

In addition to the millions of women "doomed" to spinsterhood or widowhood, the high divorce rate among recently reunited couples—the number of divorces more than doubled what they were before the war—so alarmed commentators that they began to talk of a wholesale "crisis of the family."[1] The close proximity of East Germany only enflamed such fears as church leaders commonly decried socialism (in their minds akin to Nazism) as the destroyer of families, intent on tearing children from their mothers and sending the latter into the workforce. How to address this problem was a topic of much postwar debate in part because of the unfinished business of the Basic Law: Article 3 established gender equality but the drafters left the question of its implementation to a later date. The adoption of a new civil code revising the marriage and family laws in place since 1900 was a necessary first step, but so contentious was the subject and so strong was the opposition to reforms judged contrary to the needs of the family—protected by Article 6 of the Basic Law—that no reform took place until 1957. In the meantime, Adenauer created the Federal Ministry for Family Affairs (later renamed the Ministry for Family and Youth Affairs) to provide West Germans guidance in these matters. The person appointed to head the new ministry was Franz-Josef Wuermeling, an outspoken defender of marriage based on the "Christian-occidental tradition" with close ties to Catholic lay associations. As the minister for family affairs, Wuermeling rejected the "socialization of the family," which to his mind included any conception of women's equality that threatened the "Christian foundations" of the father's authority. The ideal middle-class family was one in which the husband was the sole breadwinner and the wife cared for the children and household; the family itself was conceived as an inviolable space, free from government intervention.

Measures taken by Wuermeling and the Christian Democrats promoting their vision of domesticity ranged from the relatively commonplace to the highly contested. The FRG offered economic incentives for marriage and children in the form of tax breaks, and, like every other Western country at the time, continued to criminalize abortion and homosexuality. When the Equal Rights Statute was passed in 1957 it bore the ruling party's heavy imprint. The statute made significant strides toward establishing men and women's equal civil status: for the first time married women gained the right to inherit property from their husbands and to manage assets that they brought to the marriage. Women's right to work, however, was permitted only "as far as this can be combined with her duties in marriage and family." In this spirit, outside employment could be held against women in divorce proceedings *and* the male breadwinner became the only legal head of household. A woman could not act on behalf of her children or the family without her husband's approval, and did enjoy equal property rights. As for the children, the law bound them to their father. Few disagreed with the notion that women's primary responsibility was to the family. But the Christian Democrats' protection of paternal privilege, based on a conception of social order connected to Catholic social doctrine, encountered fierce opposition from the Social Democrats, Free Democrats, and even from women within the Christian Democrats, and was ultimately short-lived. Brought before the Constitutional Court in 1959, the court affirmed the statue's general premise that gender difference could justify the sexual division of labor in some areas but it agreed with the opposition that children's welfare was not one of those areas. The Equal Rights Statute was thus partially revised to grant mothers equal rights over their children.

But many West Germans—men and women—desired refuge from recent upheaval and the uncertainties of reconstruction; for them, the nuclear family symbolized a return to "normal life" (or the experience of it for the first time) and required little or no government incentive. This orientation toward security and normality certainly helps to explain the electoral victories of Christian Democracy in the postwar years: the 1957 electoral slogan "No Experiments" struck a chord after so many years of upheaval. Traditional gender roles and heterosexual norms were reinforced in schools and by the stereotypical designation of some jobs as suitable for men and others as suitable for women. It was visible in popular culture—films, television shows, and magazines—and most certainly in advertising, which both implicitly and explicitly argued, for example, that

vacuum cleaners and the right dish soap offered women a better kind
of emancipation than they had perhaps experienced during the war. The
significant attention given to the female consumer was proof, however,
that gender norms were not as static as some hoped. Far from the careless
or insatiable spendthrift previously imagined, the modern, middle-class
housewife was savvy—a cool-headed consumer whose ability to negotiate
the wide array of choices served both her family and German society as
a whole. Discouraged from participating in formal politics, West German
women received a voice as "consumer-citizens." And, despite efforts to
keep married women at home, women entered the workforce in ever
larger numbers, though they did so not as "career women" but as part-
time employees. Because part-time employment did not fit breadwinner or
industrial visions of male labor, and part-time work was therefore seen as
less valuable, it came to be accepted as appropriate for women—even for
housewives who, conservatives reasoned, surely enjoyed the extra pocket
money that part-time work provided.

FIGURE 3.3 *"Saturday, Dad is Mine"—May 1. Poster of the German
Confederation of Unions (DGB) demanding the five-day work week, 1956. (bpk
Bildagentur/Knud Petersen/Art Resource, NY)*

But masculine ideals had changed as well: the West German husband/father was still the king of his castle but he was a properly domesticated one. This was evident simply from the emphasis on men's identity as husbands and fathers; his place in society rested on his being the head of the household—and a civilian—not on his worth as a soldier. The distant authority figure lingered or, perhaps, now lounged in his favorite chair, but as Frank Biess showed in his work on returning POWs, there was a discernible break with the militarized and overtly aggressive masculinities of the previous three decades. In 1956, the German Confederation of Unions used this new ideal to campaign for a five-day work week.

This conservative form of domesticity remained strong into the 1960s, even if theory and reality did not always match up. Consensus on this alone brought a modicum of stability to the FRG but the patriarchal family served to defuse conflict and larger social tensions in ways historians have yet to fully explore. Many men returned from war physically or psychologically broken by what they had seen and done; nearly all stalwartly refused to discuss the experience. Some women rebelled against new or resurrected social constraints but most quickly adjusted to the new circumstances as best they could, many no doubt welcoming what they hoped would mean less work and a greater ability to juggle obligations to family and to work. To understand how the nuclear family helped stabilize West German society is to recognize how the costs as well as the benefits of reconstruction were "privatized." In other words, we must place post-traumatic stress disorders, domestic abuse, limited opportunities for women, and divorce alongside the happier memories of reunion, the baby boom, and material gains.

Stability abroad: Economic and military integration with the West

The alliance between West Germany and the United States is today taken for granted. It was not so in 1945, and not just because of Hitler. A long cultural tradition in Germany viewed what it called "Americanism" as something decadent and destructive of "Western" values: superficial, oriented toward the material rewards of money and markets, privileging pragmatism over deep German philosophy, casting Beethoven aside for modern jazz. Not only the National Socialists had played to these sentiments, condemning the "mongrel culture" of the United States; so had other leading intellectuals, from right to left, from Martin Heidegger to Max Horkheimer and Theodor Adorno. Turning toward the United States was not an obvious move.

Already a year after the war, Konrad Adenauer did not see an alternative to an alliance with the West. By the time he had become chancellor, the new West German state had neither army nor full sovereignty, and was facing, from his view, a culture-destroying Soviet dictatorship. His main challenger, Kurt Schumacher, on the other hand, insisted that taking sides

MAJOR INTERNATIONAL AGREEMENTS OF WEST GERMANY UNDER ADENAUER

1949: *Petersberg Agreement*. International treaty between the Federal Republic and the United States, France, and Britain reduced the industrial dismantlements and permitted West Germany some limited rights while also requiring it remain demilitarized and accept some international control over the Ruhr District.

1951: *Treaty of Paris*. Formed the European Coal and Steel Community, aimed at creating a common market for coal and steel in Western Europe.

1952: *European Defense Community*, based on the membership of the European Coal and Steel Community (never came into being after the French parliament rejected it in 1954).

1952: *Luxembourg Agreement*. West Germany agreed to provide reparations to the Jewish people, including payments to Israel for the costs of resettling Jewish refugees and to the World Jewish Congress.

1953: *London Agreement on German External Debts*. Agreement of the United States, France, and Great Britain to renegotiate German debts related to the Treaty of Versailles (1919) and post-1945 credits extended by the United States. The deal lowered by about 50 percent the total amount owed by Germany, and spread it out over decades, in order to spur West German economic growth.

1954: *London and Paris Agreements*. International treaties between West Germany and the NATO states; allowed West Germany "the full authority of a sovereign state" (although not official sovereignty), ended the occupation, and also permitted West Germany to enter NATO.

1955: *West Germany becomes a member of NATO*.

1957: *Treaty of Rome*. Organized the European Economic Community, the forerunner of the later European Union.

1963: *Elysee Treaty*. Treaty of friendship between West Germany and France, aimed at lasting reconciliation based on stronger economic and cultural ties.

meant dividing Germany. He advocated a neutral Germany, peaceful, democratic, and undivided. Schumacher may have lost the first elections, but his vision was powerful and attracted a broad spectrum of voters— its "national neutralism" appealing even to some conservatives. In the end, of course, Adenauer's vision won out. It is unclear, however, what chance Schumacher's had: neither the French nor the United States would have welcomed a united Germany in the form of a sovereign, neutral, and independent economic powerhouse.

Adenauer favored a broader integration of Europe, imagined as a community of nations with similar values. For Adenauer, the Occident, or "West" rested on Europeans' shared Christian and humanist heritage and stood, if not in opposition, then in sharp contrast to the Orient or "East" (the German word is *Abendland*, which some believed also excluded the United States!). Adenauer hoped to bind Germany to this Western European community—and just as critically, to bind it to Germany. His ultimate ability to do so rested on the fact that his vision for Europe was shared by Christian Democrats across Europe, many of them in equally high positions of power. The Italian prime minister Alcide De Gasperi, for example, was the undisputed head of the Italian Christian Democratic Party and an early champion of European integration. He and Adenauer knew each other, if not well, from having traveled in the same circles in the 1920s, and when the two men met again they found much common ground. They, along with Robert Schuman, statesman and leader of the Christian Democratic Party in France, worked together for a united Europe, a vision of Europe that understood Christianity as a precondition for lasting peace and an essential attribute of the European "cultural family." Their success won them a place in history as the founders of the European Union. And today the institutions and self-understanding of the European Union still betray a spiritual debt to Christian democracy, even if it has been tempered by time and committed secularists, and often overshadowed by economic matters.

The initial impetus for economic union came from France, for primarily defensive reasons. The Monnet Plan of 1946, named after the French civil servant and economist Jean Monnet, sought to put German resources in the Ruhr and Saar regions under French control. The Marshall Plan and the Cold War forced France into a less confrontational position. In this context, Schuman, French foreign minister at the time, proposed a plan in 1950 to put steel and coal in West Germany, France, Italy, and the Benelux countries under a supranational authority. The proposal had economic grounds: the need to organize supplies in the postwar period of reconstruction. Even more important, however, it advanced the idea of European unity, rather than the antagonisms that had led to war. It was a unity, too, based on the principles of democracy in direct opposition to the Soviet Union.

Adenauer declared Schuman's plan a breakthrough. His willingness to work toward union put the two most powerful continental powers on the path toward what they called "the true foundation of an organized Europe." Their declaration was followed by a new institution: the European Coal and Steel Community, established by the Treaty of Paris in 1951. Hindrances still existed to closer cooperation, however, not least French control over the German-speaking Saarland. In 1954–55, France at first tried to create an independent state out of the economically and militarily strategic Saarland; a 1955 referendum in the region rejected that solution, leading the way to the 1956 Saar Treaty, in which France agreed to conditions to return the Saarland to Germany, which took place in 1957. With the resolution of the Saarland issue, a hindrance to further negotiations on Europe was laid aside. In 1957 the Western European countries signed the Treaty of Rome, which laid the foundation for the European Economic Community of the following year. Thirteen years after a divisive and horrible war, the Western European powers had begun the process to create a common market for goods, increased mobility for workers, and standardized duties, tariffs, and regulations. West Germany joined the General Agreement on Tariffs and Trade in 1951 and the International Monetary Fund (IMF) in 1952, as well: Adenauer's Germany was firmly embedded in the Western, capitalist world.

Adenauer's push for reparations for the Holocaust, to be paid to Israel and the Jewish Claims Committee, should be seen in the same context: as a move to assert that West Germany belonged in the community of civilized nations. Despite strong opposition from within his own party and Israel's refusal to recognize the West German state, Adenauer brokered a reparations agreement with Israel in the 1952 Luxembourg Accords. He then pushed the reparations bill through the Bundestag in March 1953 with the full support of the Social Democrats. 3.45 billion German marks were promised to Israel and to the Jewish Claims Conference. Only 24 percent of West Germans, in an opinion poll of the time, supported these reparation payments.

Adenauer's foreign policy drew a line in the Cold War, and also across Germany, cementing the split between East and West, as the Social Democrats repeatedly complained. As noted in the previous chapter, for example, Adenauer refused to consider the Stalin Note of 1952, which suggested a plan for reunifying Germany under conditions of free and fair elections, but requiring it to remain neutral. Whether or not the note was serious, the United States required that free German elections precede any negotiations, a condition that the Soviets refused to accept. Furthermore, Adenauer's government refused to recognize the Oder-Neisse Line as the legitimate border between Germany and Poland. And if that were not enough, the government adopted what it called in 1955 the Hallstein Doctrine: West Germany refused diplomatic recognition to any country that extended diplomatic recognition to East Germany (with the exception of the Soviet Union). The Adenauer government argued that, according to the Basic Law, only the Federal Republic had the mandate to represent Germany, and that East Germany, controlled by the Soviets, was not a freely established and self-governing German state. The GDR, in popular West German and Cold War discourse, was simply referred to as "the Zone."

Adenauer's aim to remilitarize West Germany deepened the divide between East and West. To hold such a position was radical, after the Second World War and the Holocaust. And indeed, Adenauer may not have totally trusted the Germans: his intention was not simply to rearm them, but to bind them to other European countries through an integrated European military. At first, though, his call for rearmament met with heavy opposition. In 1949, the German Bundestag resolved not to rearm. But over the next year, tensions on the Korean peninsula led to a bloody hot war, a conflict in which Chinese forces supported by the Soviet Union clashed with UN forces led by the US Army. With a war between East and West suddenly on the table, Adenauer called for a West German contribution to Western European forces. His call was met with a mass peace movement, supported by university students, intellectuals, trade unionists, church leaders, and even some Christian Democrats. Under the slogan "without me" (*ohne mich*), they gathered more than six million signatures and participated in peaceful demonstrations across the country. The protests included pacifists, Communists, and also some nationalists, who opposed putting German soldiers under foreign (Western) command.

The Korean War gave Adenauer the support he needed; West Germany agreed to create a small defense force in 1952. An attempt to create from this a wider European Defense Community, an idea proposed in 1950 paralleling the European Coal and Steel Community, failed because of French fears of losing control over its own forces. But West German rearmament plans continued. In 1954, the Western Allies increased their military potential across western Europe and included tactical nuclear weapons in their arsenal. In the next year, the FRG entered the North Atlantic Treaty Organization (NATO), though with the understanding that weapons of mass destruction would not be produced on German soil. As part of the agreement, the Western Allies officially recognized limited sovereign rights of the West German state.

By the end of 1955, West Germany created a new army, the Bundeswehr. All sides were aware of how controversial the decision was, especially given that any officer with military experience would have served in the last war. The government therefore promoted the ideal of a citizen-soldier, who would pledge allegiance to the Federal Republic and would study democratic and constitutional values as part of his military training. A 1956 constitutional amendment furthermore only authorized defensive military actions by the army, unless the constitution stated an exception to that rule. In 1956, the Bundestag made one year military service compulsory for men as a way to ensure that the army would reflect the citizenry of a democratic republic. As citizens in uniform, soldiers gained unprecedented rights: they could unionize and were free—even obligated—to refuse to follow commands that violated the Basic Law. Equally unprecedented was the constitutional right to conscientious objector status. Men who objected to military service based on religious conviction or ethical or humanitarian views could not be forced into it; after establishing their credibility before an examination board, conscientious objectors were allowed to perform some alternative form of civilian service. In short, the Bundeswehr very consciously sought to break with German militaristic traditions that reached back into Prussian history.

When the Soviet Red Army invaded Hungary to put down a popular revolt in 1956, the military gained wider acceptance. But never unqualified acceptance. Many continued to protest the draft and a large proportion of nineteen-year-olds required to register did not report. Several legal aid organizations sprang up to provide support and information about conscientious objection to young men, and to advocate for broader grounds on which to object to military service. In 1957, the peace movement appeared again, this time over the stationing of atomic weapons on German soil. Over 1.5 million people participated in mass demonstrations calling to "fight against atomic death" (*Kampf dem Atomtod*)—members of trade unions, Social Democrats, Free Democrats, writers, intellectuals, and housewives, as well as the leadership of the main Protestant church association and some members of the Catholic clergy as well. Even if they did not publicly support these protests, over 80 percent of West Germans polled opposed stationing atomic weapons on German soil. Such impressive consensus did not, however, convince Adenauer's government to change course, or work against the Christian Democrats in that year's election. But these organized, peaceful, democratic protests laid the groundwork for the later protest movements of the 1960s and 1970s.

By the end of the 1950s, the Federal Republic had become an integral economic and military member of NATO and the European Economic Community. Adenauer never stopped paying public lip service to German unification but he ultimately chose Western integration over national unity. Schumacher was not wrong when he argued that the two were incompatible. But the Social Democrats' repeated defeat in national elections indicated that the majority of West Germans favored Adenauer's path all the same, rejecting Schumacher's call for neutrality in foreign policy along with the socialist alternative that the party pursued even after Schumacher's death in 1952. Tired of defeat, a growing number of Social Democrats pushed for change. The articulate and highly intelligent economist Karl Schiller, for example, called for the Social Democrats to reorient their party toward market economics. Socializing industry would not in itself necessarily help workers. Instead, the party should aim at an economy that would grant each individual an equal chance at success, through better educational possibilities, better workplace training, and ensuring jobs for youth through macroeconomic measures to promote full employment. Schiller looked outside of Germany for inspiration: to Keynes, to the ideas for social reform developing in the United States, for example. Most important, he came up with an economic slogan that fit the new, pragmatic age: "As much market as possible, as much state as necessary."

Alongside Schiller was Willy Brandt. The child of an unwed mother, a cashier, Brandt drifted toward the anti-Stalinist left already in the Weimar Republic. During the war, he went into exile and worked in the anti-German resistance. After the war, he returned to Berlin, one of the West Berlin Social Democrats who rejected fusion with the Communists. Over the 1950s he gradually rose in prominence: a great speech giver, a master at seizing political moments. In 1957, he was elected mayor of Berlin just as the Second Berlin Crisis, described below, began. Brandt rejected the Social

Democrats' call for German neutrality, because as a West Berliner, he saw the key role of the United States in guaranteeing West Berlin. At the same time, already in the 1950s he called for dialogue with the East, to reduce the suffering of individuals on both sides.

Schiller and Brandt represented the reformist wing of German Social Democracy. After intense internal debate, they and others from a younger generation of reformers finally reached their goal: in 1959, the Social Democrats adopted the Godesberg Program. For the first time in its history, the party renounced the principle of class struggle; renounced the goal of nationalizing industry; and stated that it planned to work within the framework of capitalism to reach goals of social reform and broader democratic principles. The aim was to form a broad party capable of winning elections, accepting at the same time West Germany's integration into the Western, capitalist economy and participation in NATO. Though the Social Democrats' reorientation at Bad Godesberg was undoubtedly an attempt to save the party from electoral death it was also evidence of the strong consensus that characterized life in 1950s FRG—what younger West Germans increasingly described as the pressure to conform socially, culturally, and politically.

East Germany: Challenges to the construction of socialism

Stability came later to the GDR than it did to the FRG. In fact, it was not until the 1960s that the question of East Germany's continued existence was truly put to rest. The "construction of socialism," officially begun in 1952, meant increasing central control over the economy and cracking down on those private firms and farms that remained. The new measures kept the economy in flux and sowed dissent within society. One of the most tangible signs that recovery remained a goal more than a reality was the continued rationing of everyday necessities (such as meat, butter, and shoes) until 1958. Many East Germans expressed their discontent by voting with their feet. Before 1952, Germans could make their way through fields and forests and cross the German–German border without encountering significant obstacles. After 1952, the only remaining route for would-be emigres was over Berlin; the numbers who poured into West Berlin increased from about 230,000 to over 400,000 between 1952 and 1953.

If the 1950s was a decade of ongoing disruption, the building blocks for later stability were nevertheless laid. Outward migration and the worker uprisings of 1953 disrupted and very clearly influenced socialism's "construction," but they did not stop it. The Socialist Unity Party continued its push to transform East German society and to integrate the GDR fully into the Soviet sphere. The Stasi tracked regime "enemies" and, when all else failed, the regime built an impermeable border to prevent East Germans from "opting out."

The uprising of June 17, 1953

On March 5, 1953, Joseph Stalin died. The Soviet leadership was unprepared; there was no normal process for finding a new general secretary. A triumvirate took over. The course of Soviet policy was unclear. They disagreed about what to do with East Germany, and there is some indication that the sinister Lavrentij Beria, head of the security apparatus, was willing to sacrifice it for other gains. One thing was clear to the new leadership, however: German Communists had been overly zealous in their pursuit of socialism. The Soviet leadership called for a new course at home, freeing many political

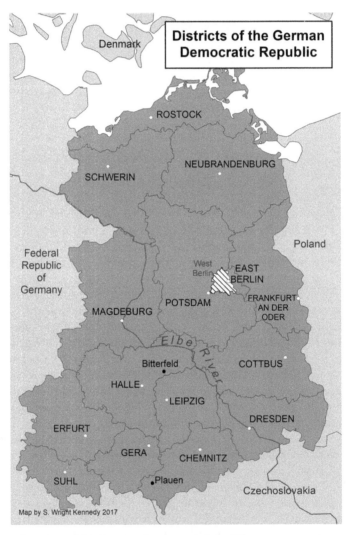

MAP 3.2 *Districts of the German Democratic Republic*

prisoners and shifting resources somewhat more toward consumer goods. It demanded that the Socialist Unity Party adopt the new course as well, in a June 2 missive to the party leadership.

On June 11, the official party newspaper, *Neues Deutschland*, published the Soviet leadership's call for a new course in the Soviet Union. The Socialist Unity Party dutifully reversed some of its previous economic policies but not the decision to increase labor norms by 10 percent in honor of Walter Ulbricht's birthday. That decision was politically short-sighted, even if it was motivated by the fact that the GDR's labor productivity continued to languish behind West Germany's. Its aim was to push workers to take the initiative to overcome this widening gap.

In the week that followed, small demonstrations and confrontations took place at several places in the GDR. And on June 16, a delegation of workers constructing the Stalinallee marched to Berlin-Mitte, the center of power, to present its complaints to the trade union leadership. Finding nobody to talk to, they next marched to the main building of the regime in East Berlin, where they shouted down Party representatives. Party leaders themselves appeared unsure what to do. In the face of this apparent loss of will, some in the crowd began to call for free elections and a new government.

On the next morning, June 17, 1953, the workers at Stalinallee—workers who were held up as heroes of socialism, who received relatively high wages—went on strike. Strikes, protests, and violent confrontations occurred all across East Germany as well, with more than a million participants in

FIGURE 3.4 *East German workers with a banner demanding lower work quotas on June 16, 1953. (ullstein bild/Getty Images)*

some seven hundred cities and towns. The crisis had become a general strike, a general confrontation with the rulers of the GDR. Masses, predominantly workers, stormed city halls and police stations. The party was powerless. The government fled into the protective arms of the Soviet authorities. The Soviets took over command. As they deployed troops with tanks, the protests gradually came to an end.

The party leadership had an explanation ready: the uprising was an "attempt at a fascist coup," organized by a West German elite that they accused of harboring old Nazis. They could point to the swastikas that some protesters had painted on buildings. But it was not a fascist coup attempt; the protesters, often younger, used the symbol held to represent evil for the "anti-fascists" in power. The uprising of June 17 was in fact a workers' uprising against the very party that claimed to represent the workers.

The Soviets were faced with a dilemma. Walter Ulbricht was hardly a beloved man; his decisions had pushed the GDR to the brink of collapse; his colleagues now called for him to be removed. And he had acted essentially in opposition to the Soviets' own policy after Stalin. But in the face of the GDR's possible collapse, the Soviets supported him. With his neck now safe, Ulbricht removed some of his main opponents at the top level, including the head of the Stasi, and conducted a purge of thousands of party members down to local levels. More than 13,000 individuals were arrested for their role in the general strike, and between 50 and 125 lost their lives either in the uprising or as a result of the trials that followed.

The GDR stabilized, but the leaders of the Socialist Unity Party never forgot the lesson of June 17, 1953. Until its dissolution in 1989, they feared that a workers' revolt, caused by a lack of consumer goods and too much pressure by the government, could threaten the GDR's existence. Leaders of the FRG did not forget, either. They named June 17 the "Day of German Unity," and this became West Germany's one national holiday before 1989.

Moving forward from June 17

With the uprising in mind, the party redirected its attention to the ongoing process of reconstruction. It scaled back labor quotas and temporarily focused on light industry—manufacturing clothes, home appliances, and furniture—in an effort to provide more consumer goods to the workers. The task was lightened by the Soviet Union, which relieved the GDR of its responsibility for delivering reparations.

East and West ultimately promised their populations the same thing: "the good life." And though the good life frequently translated into access to consumer goods in a contest that the West was winning, this was not the only arena in which the two systems competed for superiority in the hearts and minds of their respective populations. The Socialist Unity Party trumpeted socialism's commitment to gender equality and the family, for example, and pointed to the FRG's continued failings in this regard. As East German president Otto Grotewohl put it, "When people say that women's honor is injured by their integration into the production process, then I'd like to say: one can impose nothing more dishonorable on a woman than to expect her to be her husband's unpaid maid." Though the regime fell short of its publicly vaunted ideals, it nonetheless made advances in gender equality. Women had always worked at home; in farming, with its close familial ties; or in light industry. From 1950 to 1955, however, far more women moved rapidly into the wage labor force. Growing numbers of women attended university, though they remained underrepresented in technology and science. Medicine was one occupation, however, which women entered in significant numbers, as was law, causing some to refer to a "feminization" of the East German judiciary. By the end of the decade, women accounted for one-third to a quarter of East Germany's prosecutors, judges, and jurists. Most prominent among them was Hilde Benjamin who stepped into the shoes of a recently purged party member to become minister of justice. A Communist since 1928, Benjamin had proved her value to the East German state during the show trials of 1950–52, when she gained international attention as the harsh "Red Hilde." More commonly, the party appointed women to symbolic positions, such as town mayors and members of the People's Chamber. Whether employed in the factory or by the party, the point was that the women were working. Work gave many women the financial independence to free themselves from unwanted marriages. And in legal proceedings such as divorce, it granted women a status equivalent to men: rather than "housewife," the designation given to all female spouses in the FRG regardless of their occupation, East German women—like all East German men—were identified by their work or profession.

At the same time the state drew women into the workforce, it also encouraged them to have babies. Over the course of the 1950s, the Socialist Unity Party increased paid maternity leave, child allowances, and other monetary incentives. Under Soviet pressure, it also reversed its earlier position on abortion and greatly restricted legal terminations. Though East German women continued to obtain abortions illegally, birthrates climbed. If women were to be mothers and workers—not to mention wives and party members—childcare was a basic necessity but here they got little help. Efforts to create a state childcare system came in spurts and the number of day care and kindergarten facilities fell far short of the need. East German men, like West German men, showed little interest in sharing the burden of housework and childrearing, and indeed traditional notions of femininity—that women wear make-up and exude grace and charm—and women's role in the home remained alive and well. The emphasis placed on heavy industry and, along with it, male labor hardly helped East Germans to re-imagine men as partners in childrearing. But that did not mean that there were no changes in this area. The Socialist Unity Party promoted a "softer" form of masculinity, even in comparison to the FRG. Advice manuals, school curriculum, and counseling centers not only established the ideal man as someone who worked well, served his country and cause, enjoyed sports, and valued friendship, but also instructed the East German man on how to cook, for example, and even the finer points of interior design. From the mid-1950s on, sex education included men in the state's efforts to regulate and reform even the intimate lives of its citizens.

In 1954, the party circulated its proposed Socialist Civil Code, provoking anger from the Lutheran Church over its lenient divorce criteria, the assumption that wives could and should work, and the state's encroachment on parental authority. It was not the first clash between church and state but it did signal a new round in the Socialist Unity Party's efforts to weaken Christianity's hold on the values and worldview of its citizens. That year, the Socialist Unity Party launched a national campaign introducing the *Jugendweihe*, essentially a socialist version of Christian confirmation that celebrated fourteen-year-olds' coming of age in a secular ceremony held every April. Alternatives to Christian christening and burial ceremonies were offered as well, drawing on secular ceremonies from the nineteenth century. Together these amounted to an unabashed attempt by the party to weaken religion's influence and to bind youth to the state, one that required East Germans to choose not only between church and socialism but, as the Socialist Unity Party saw it, between faith and reason, superstition and science. Parents who insisted on the religious ceremony were noted; church ties hindered their and their children's education and career opportunities. Even decades later, when the future German chancellor Angela Merkel went through religious confirmation rather than the secular *Jugendweihe*, she saw fit to join the Communist youth organization to ensure access to higher education. The party's goal was not to destroy religion but rather to relegate it firmly to the private realm. The church had traditionally acted as an intermediary between private and public (family and state); under socialism, schools and youth organizations like the Young Pioneers and the Free German Youth would fulfill that role. And propaganda and political bullying proved effective: if the first *Jugendweihe* ceremonies attracted a tiny percentage of the country's fourteen-year-olds, by the end of the decade the vast majority participated, and Christian confirmations dropped precipitously.

Eastern integration: Warsaw Pact, CMEA

The GDR's integration into the Eastern Bloc ran parallel to the FRG's Western integration. Instead of NATO, there was the Warsaw Pact (known as The Treaty of Friendship, Cooperation, and Mutual Assistance); rather than the European Economic Community, East Germans belonged to the Council for Mutual Economic Assistance, or CMEA. The Warsaw Pact first formed in 1955, as a response to the fears unleashed in Czechoslovakia and Poland by the FRG's remilitarization and as a means for the Soviet Union to maintain control over the militaries of Eastern Europe. The GDR did not yet have an army but on Stalin's instigation, the Socialist Unity Party had created armed units known as the *kasernierte Volkspolizei,* or People's Police in Barracks. This paramilitary-like force now provided the building blocks for East Germany's new army. On March 1, 1956—just six months after the formation of the West German *Bundeswehr*—the Socialist Unity Party created the National People's Army (NVA).

Unlike the Bundeswehr, the NVA was initially made up of volunteers. So long as the border between East and West Germany remained porous, the state avoided requiring compulsory military service. Universal male conscription was only introduced in 1962, after the building of the Berlin Wall. The NVA also insisted on ideological rigor—the soldiers took an oath to defend the GDR's "socialist achievements"—and strict obedience, not least because the 1953 uprising had shown that soldiers might have to turn their weapons on the GDR's own population. That possibility put intense pressure on NVA soldiers, especially in crisis moments such as 1961, when they helped to protect the construction of the Berlin Wall against an alleged threat from the West but were in fact facing their own population, and during the 1989 Revolution. Conscientious objector status was not recognized but the law allowed those not willing to serve in the main army to serve as "construction soldiers" (*Bausoldaten*), engaging in heavy labor.

One significant obstacle still existed to the GDR's Eastern integration, and to the "construction of socialism" more generally: East Germans' continued feelings of animosity toward their state. The war cast a long shadow on individual lives and on people's attitudes toward Russians: The mass rapes lived long not only in women's memories but in the thousands of "*Russenkinder*" (children with Russian fathers) who were born and grew up in the GDR. The thousands of Germans deported to the Soviet Union after the war as forced laborers in addition to the 3.2 million POWs held much longer on average by the Soviets than by the British and Americans were also not soon forgotten—or forgiven. But the Socialist Unity Party did what it could to mend fences and promote international solidarity. Most notably, the party pursued the same sort of cultural programs that West Germans used to improve relations with western Europe and the United States: student and "friendship" exchanges, Russian language instruction, and musical and theatrical tour companies.

Criticism and dissent in the GDR

One group was notably missing from the 1953 crisis in the GDR: the intellectuals. In West Germany, some intellectuals were in the forefront of the peace protests; in East Germany, they stayed on the sidelines as the workers took to the streets. The playwright Bertolt Brecht could write a sarcastic poem about how the regime should vote out the people and elect a new one; that was quite different from taking the side of the workers.

Critical of the German state and military, intellectuals wanted a break with the past and called for a new, better world. This was true after the First World War, when many—most famously the artist Käthe Kollwitz—turned to pacifism and Communism, and it was true for still others after the Second World War. The Red Army had made the heaviest sacrifices in the war. The language of the Soviet Union was one of anti-fascism: a strong language, which, along with the project of building a new, socialist Germany, proved very compelling to many intellectuals on the left. Two examples—Ernst Bloch and Anna Seghers—show the complex motivations of the Marxist, indeed Marxist-Leninist, intellectual in the GDR.

The philosopher Ernst Bloch was delighted to be invited to the University of Leipzig in 1948, and to join in the anti-fascist state. A thinker deeply marked by the German classics, which he soaked up in his youth, he had also been exposed as an upper-middle-class German-Jewish child to the workers' movement in his hometown of Ludwigshafen. The First World War radicalized him, and he sympathized with the revolution of 1918–19. He read it, however through the lens of his study of religious movements for political redemption, like the Anabaptists of the early sixteenth century, radical reformists who sought to break with Catholicism and usher in a new world. Over the 1930s, Bloch connected his study of the "philosophy of the future" with Marx, and then with Stalin, whom he defended to the hilt. Bloch returned from exile in the United States to be a star of Marxist philosophy at the University of Leipzig.

There, however, Bloch had to face the dogmatism and paranoia of the party, which ran up against his more radical approaches to teaching and thinking about philosophy. He defended, for example, a humanistic, open, lively form of teaching; the party supported rote memorization. As he defended open discussion, the party wanted stock phrases. A conflict was bound to appear—even as Bloch tied himself in knots defending the party. The crisis came after 1956, in the context of "destalinization" (discussed below), when Bloch's students—people like the young Gerhard Zwerenz from Leipzig—refused to limit their speech. Their approach to philosophy undermined the claims of the party to know everything. Zwerenz left East Germany in 1957, just ahead of an arrest warrant; other Bloch students did as well. Bloch remained dedicated to the GDR, and tried not to betray it.

Anna Seghers serves as a second example. She joined the Communist Party in 1928, wanting a more radical response to National Socialism. Also a German Jew, Seghers was lucky to escape to Mexico. Her experiences inspired her brilliant novel about the fate of those refugees caught as the Nazis extended their reach across Europe. Her most famous work, *The Seventh Cross*, was one of the few works about concentration camps to appear during the war, and was made into an American movie in 1944.

Seghers returned to the Soviet zone with some hesitation, but became wrapped up in the project of constructing a new society. Not only her work, also her speeches and her actions show her desire to build new, anti-fascist institutions: from writers' associations to the new playhouses. She knew all the leading East German intellectuals, from Bertolt Brecht to the ex-Expressionist poet Johannes Becher. Committed, energetic, and smart, Seghers sincerely believed in the party, in the construction of socialism. For her, the uprising of June 17, 1953, was a misguided attempt to deliver socialism up to the hands of the capitalists—an interpretation born, perhaps, out of a deeper distrust of mass popular movements following her experience of Nazism.

The Socialist Unity Party recognized the importance of intellectuals for its own legitimacy, and provided them with special provisions, access to scarce housing, and freedoms that ordinary people could not enjoy. In exchange (conscious or not), intellectuals' presence allowed the regime to present itself as a center of German culture. But the relationship proved a two-edged sword. To be intellectuals, they had to have some freedom—limited in the 1950s, but always present, and always with a potential edge.

That edge showed itself in the next crisis of Ulbricht's leadership, in 1956–57. Once again, changes in the Soviet Union had a direct effect on East Germany. On February 25, 1956, the First Secretary of the Communist Party, Nikita Khrushchev, gave a secret speech to an unofficial, closed session of the Twentieth Party Congress; GDR delegates were not in attendance. In that speech, he described the "errors" and "crimes" committed under Stalin's rule, and accused him of having a "capricious and despotic character" and developing a "cult of personality" ultimately damaging to collegial party work. The GDR delegation was informed of the speech. But upon returning to Germany, Ulbricht avoided informing other party leaders of the content of the speech. The party leadership here, as so often, sought to avoid any discussion of any possible mistakes in the past; Ulbricht may also have recognized that his own pattern of aggrandizing power and controlling information even within the Politburo sounded perilously close to what Khrushchev described in Stalin.

The "Secret Speech" eventually made its way into the public realm, after having been published first in the West. The effect on Eastern Europe was electrifying. The so-called People's Republics like Poland, Czechoslovakia, Hungary, and of course (East) Germany had existed as countries prior to the Soviet-sponsored takeovers by Communist parties in the late 1940s and had their own political traditions; the condemnation of Stalin opened up the possibility of a more independent approach to socialism. In Hungary in particular, both workers and intellectuals moved to reform the existing system. In the GDR, the Socialist Unity Party attempted to contain discussion of the speech within the party as a whole but criticism surfaced quickly nonetheless: Politburo member Fred Oelssner, a man with an long record of work in Moscow and with German Communist leaders, accused Ulbricht in July 1956 of authoritarianism and a cult of personality; Karl Schirdewan, another Politburo member with a long history in the Communist movement, joined others in calling for a reversal of Ulbricht's decisions, as did several other leading members of the planning apparatus. These discussions amounted to an attack on Ulbricht's position as head of the party.

More dangerously, philosophers, economists, and writers, especially younger party cadres, echoed the discussions taking place in Hungary and called for a socialism that included free, critical culture. These so-called "revisionists" were committed to Marxism-Leninism and the special role of the party. They were also committed to their specific areas of knowledge, and felt suddenly free to criticize the philosophical dogmatism, the economic rigidity, and the lack of respect for law that they saw as undermining the regime. As they built up their cases—not connected with each other, not presenting a frontal assault on the GDR—their logic again and again bumped up against the sacred place of the party in the GDR. It was the party's representatives who declared philosophical truth, hindering creative thought; who asserted how a socialist economy should be organized, rejecting reforms that could make it function more effectively but would remove power from the party; who asserted the right of the party to intervene and alter law when it declared such actions necessary.

In Hungary, the critical discussion veered off into a dramatic revolt against Soviet hegemony in November 1956, especially as the Hungarian leadership announced that Hungary was leaving the Warsaw Pact. The Red Army put down the revolt by force. Once again, a crisis changed the balance of forces in Ulbricht's favor. The Soviets could not risk further political unrest and so they threw their weight behind Ulbricht—who quickly moved against his critics in the party elite; Oelssner, Schirdewan, and Ernst Wollweber, the head of the Stasi, lost their positions of power in 1958. Ulbricht also led the "ideological offensive" against the critics, whom he called "revisionists" seeking to undermine the established truths of Marxism-Leninism, undertaking campaigns especially in law and economics. And the government went after those who had clearly gone too far in opposing the general secretary. Wolfgang Harich, for example, a young, up-and-coming, and faithful Communist professor of philosophy in Berlin, had tried to put these reformist ideas into action. He and several associates drew up a "Platform for a Special German Path to Socialism," which involved toppling Ulbricht and creating a united Germany; he naively passed the platform to the Soviet Embassy. Ulbricht made of Harich an example by way of a show trial, where he was forced to confess his crimes and ask the Stasi for forgiveness, and a punishment of ten years in prison (he was released early in 1964). Rather than constantly monitor his own public statements under this oppressive regime, Bloch left the GDR for the FRG in 1961, where he became a leading figure in the German New Left of the 1960s and 1970s, critical of both East and West, but remaining within a Marxist paradigm. Harich, by contrast, apparently accepted and internalized his punishment. He became a minor figure who policed the margins of intellectual discourse, working within the bounds of official GDR ideology. Seghers, finally, watched in silence in 1957 when her friend Walter Janka, head of the important GDR publishing house Aufbau, was sentenced to prison for counterrevolutionary activities. Despite severe misgivings, expressed in writings not published during the GDR, she opted for the regime.

1953 had sent a message to workers, who were abandoned by the intellectuals: do your work, and we will provide more consumer goods. 1957 sent a message to intellectuals, whose fate was apparently irrelevant to the workers: follow the party line and we will continue to grant you privileges. The intellectuals were not necessarily convinced, but Ulbricht's actions revealed to them the limits of their freedom of expression and power in the Marxist-Leninist state. Destalinization in East Germany was a flop.

Culture and politics in West Germany in the 1950s

Critical intellectuals in the FRG found West German society oppressive and stultifying as well. Wolfgang Abendroth, for example, a professor of political science and judge in Hesse, felt that the Godesberg Program had betrayed socialism. He and his fellow Marxists in West Germany were certainly anti-Soviet: they had had enough of dictatorship. But they had a radically different notion of what the Federal Republic had wrought. On their account, West Germany was not a venture into democracy; it was the restoration of capitalism that entailed the restoration of the very social (as well as economic) conditions and power relations that had brought Hitler to power. The trade unions, they argued, had been pushed into a corner. The potential for radical criticism had been silenced with the Constitutional Court's decision to ban the Communist Party. The result was a stiflingly quiescent society.

Abendroth's student Juergen Habermas described the historical process of "restoration" as a problem for the West as a whole, not just the FRG, and argued that the "public sphere" had to be rehabilitated. The "pluralism" defended by Cold War intellectuals like former exile Ernst Fraenkel had come to mean that interest groups, not reasoned public debate, ran politics, and contestation and protest were viewed as potentially subversive of the democratic order rather than an intrinsic part of it. Habermas and others like him believed that students could—and would—lead the way toward the republic's sweeping reform, one that challenged all parties, including the Social Democrats, in its demand for more democracy, everywhere, from the workplace to the family to the schools.

These radical intellectuals protested against the efforts to normalize and de-radicalize German culture, and could find many examples of such tendencies around them. About 20 percent of all West German films in the decade, for example, were the so-called Heimat or homeland films. These were schmaltzy and clichéd movies, usually set in idyllic surroundings with no hint of industry, modern tensions, or the racist horrors of the recent past. In fact, they brought in elements of the recent past—but in a way that neutralized them. In *The Heath is Green* of 1951, for example, the beautiful girl Helga falls in love with Walter, a young forest ranger whose job is to stop poachers. Unfortunately, Helga's father, an expellee and once proud owner of a large estate, is one such poacher. With an ending that happily resolves this conflict—and returns the lovers to one another's arms—the movie describes in part adaptation to a new *Heimat*; the particular experiences and even cultural distinctiveness of expellees are overcome by Helga's (presumed) marriage to Walter. The chaste relations between the lovers, the natural landscape of trees and wild animals, the reconciliation of people to place: all of these contributed to a sense of normalization. And that was probably the source of the movie's popularity, to provide a depoliticized space, a space where German victimhood was central and life took place within the comfortable confines of the family.

But one movie should not be taken as representative for culture as a whole. Earlier that same year, the director Willi Forst premiered his film, *The Sinner*. The main character, the "sinner," is Marina, a woman who turns to prostitution when her old life is destroyed by the war. She is redeemed through her love for an alcoholic artist but then, after brief happiness, she is tested again: Alexander, the painter, is suffering from incurable brain cancer. Marina prostitutes herself to pay for an operation, which fails, and then helps him to commit suicide before killing herself.

The character survived because of prostitution; euthanasia or mercy killing was presented as a real problem; and if all that were not enough to raise the church's hackles, the main character, a beautiful woman with whom the audience could sympathize, commits suicide, a mortal sin. Representatives of both Protestant and Catholic churches on the film censorship boards opposed the release of the film, but were outvoted—a fact that shows just how deeply churches were involved with cultural politics in the early Federal Republic. When the film appeared, representatives of the Catholic Church called for a boycott; protests against the film began almost immediately, and in some cities took violent forms. Following massive boycotts, the film disappeared from the cinemas. But before it did, millions had seen it.

Within literature, as well, the 1950s was certainly more than a decade of schmaltz and normalization—although certainly escapist romances and adventure novels were on offer here, too. This was the decade when a new generation of German writers burst onto the scene and made a name for itself in the literary salon run by Hans Werner Richter known as Group '47. The most intriguing figures of the time were introspective, fascinated with what cannot be said. The poet Ingeborg Bachmann, for example, started with the existential philosophy of Martin Heidegger, whose work (with its depictions of nature sometimes resonating with the mood of Heimat films) explored the nothingness underlying existence and the possibility of something beyond; she turned away from him, to find instead in the crisp thinking of the analytical philosopher Wittgenstein entry into the division between what can be said and what cannot be said, implying a non-present presence of God. Her work was obscure, suggestive, and utterly transformative—but only for the small elite that would read her. Other writers found a way into a broader public.

Two novelists in particular, Heinrich Böll and Günter Grass, brought new German literature to an international public. Böll came from the Catholic milieu in Cologne, from a family that disliked Hitler. After the war, he began publishing, mostly on war-related themes, and by the end of the 1950s had made a name for himself as one of the leading authors of West Germany. *Billiards at Half Past Nine* appeared in 1959 to great acclaim: here was a novel written in a modernist style—fragmented perspective, going back and forth between present and past in order finally to explain the present. The main character, Robert, is an architect, who has put his skills to use for the German army at the end of the war, as they destroyed infrastructure to hinder the advance of the Allied troops. Robert uses his power to destroy monuments of German civilization, including a famous abbey—apparently a reference to the Maria Laach abbey, a rallying point for anti-democratic monks before 1933, whose abbot supported National Socialism early on. In this way Böll, himself from a Catholic family, extended his critique of German society to the Catholic Church. The architect destroys, instead of preserving, in protest against the hypocrisy of the Germans. In Böll there is a hint of nihilism mingled with a critical take on Germany's past. But there is also a clear distinction between the good and the evil—between what Böll calls the Lambs, apparently referring to the pacifists of the Seventh Day Adventists who were persecuted under Hitler, and the others.

Günter Grass offered a rather different world. Grass's *Tin Drum*, also published in 1959, starts with an unreliable narrator, Oskar, who writes from an insane asylum. Oskar's parentage is unclear—was his father a Polish nationalist or a Nazi?—as is his age: he decides at three years of age to stop growing. But he plays his drum, both with and against the Nazis. The novel develops in a complex, indeed overly complex, way, which undermines any attempt to provide a stable story—and certainly undermines the kind of racial stability Nazism prized, given how Grass interweaves German with Polish culture. His characters are odd, at times grotesque; his work includes explicit sex and explicit violence. Despite the grotesque characters, Grass's writing is realistic: so realistic, so unsymbolic, that it was especially disturbing to his critics—of whom there were many. Grass was judged an anti-German intellectual. And indeed, his assessment of German society in the 1950s was anything but kind: there is, for example, a bar in postwar Germany known as the "Onion Cellar," where people go to make themselves act like they are crying. In other words, as the psychoanalysts Alexander and Margarete Mitscherlich would write in a famous book several years later, the Germans were unable to mourn. And this point links the authors: a critique of a culture that is unable to get away from its own obsessions to take responsibility for what it has done.

The paragraphs above give the impression of a Germany obsessed with its relationship to the recent, violent, and dictatorial past. But not all West German culture took such a serious, introspective tone. And a good deal of anxiety sprang not from past events but from a quickly unfolding present in which American jazz and then rock 'n' roll swept the country and overturned social conventions as they went. Although this new music was initially condemned as un-German (the conservative intellectual Wilhelm Röpke oddly saw jazz as the same as Nazi marching music, merely sexualized culture), youth lapped it up. With money they earned or received from their parents, teenagers bought records and imitated the "rocker" fashions of Marlon Brando and James Dean; they hung out in groups, on street corners and at the movies; and they defied convention in "wild" dances that frequently involved jumps, flips, and what older commentators described as "vulgar and erotically expressive movement." In short, they panicked their elders. Parents expressed particular concern for the "hysteria" Elvis Presley unleashed among teenage girls, and for the blue jean- and leather jacket-wearing *Halbstarken* (hooligans), with their coifed hairstyles and devil-may-care attitudes. Though fears of a delinquent or rampaging youth were real, they also expressed general unease, not only over the pitfalls of consumer society but, more specifically, over the "Americanization" of German culture. As Uta Poiger has pointed out, however, the Cold War eased the way for rock 'n' roll's acceptance; while the East German establishment continued to condemn the transgressions of rock 'n' roll, they gradually became points of pride for liberal democracies in the Cold War.

The Second Berlin Crisis and the stabilization of the GDR

In October 1957, the Soviets were able to send the first man-made satellite, Sputnik, into orbit around the Earth. The effect on world opinion was huge: the Soviet Union, regarded by the West as a backward country, had jumped ahead of the United States in technology. Khrushchev, now at the height of his power, saw proof of the long-term superiority of the Soviet model of centralized planning: it could focus resources and expertise on the most important parts of the economy and produce surprising outcomes. He predicted that within twenty years, the Soviet Union would overtake and surpass the United States in productivity.

Ulbricht went one step further. By 1961, he declared in July 1958, "socialism will win" and the GDR would "overtake and surpass" the FRG in per capita consumption. He based his claims on what his experts said. In 1956 and 1957, the East German economy was expanding dramatically; in the same years, the West German economy saw a momentary drop from over 10 percent to around 6 percent growth, and the rate was even lower in 1958. Convinced that the inherent contradictions of capitalism were revealing themselves and that the inherent advantages of socialism were finally coming into place, Ulbricht made his bold claim.

Once again, the GDR took measures to complete the collectivization of farms, with a massive barrage of actions and propaganda in 1959–60. And once again, the farmers voted with their feet, traveling to East Berlin and from there to the West. A poor harvest in 1961 exacerbated the problem. Along with lower agricultural production, the East German economy faced other challenges: the GDR economy remained dependent on imports of raw materials and advanced machinery from Poland and Czechoslovakia but also from West Germany, and these supplies were constantly at risk. (Indeed, despite the appearance of a total break between East and West, one cannot understand the East German economy without taking into account its trade connections with West Germany, an issue to which we shall return.) The other planned economies of the East at times failed to deliver due to their own crises. And Western economies demanded Western currency for their goods, which was notably scarce in the East.

The economy also suffered for reasons noted by the "revisionists" whom Ulbricht had silenced. The system was heavily centralized; the plan had become a fetish. The centralized planning system tended to focus on big numbers, to represent the economy in the aggregate, which said little about quality and "fit." When goods were not right, the planners had to respond somehow; civil courts were overwhelmed with complaints about quality, quantity, and delivery time of goods. Within this system, customers and socialist firms alike had an incentive to hoard goods as well as labor, since neither suppliers nor the planners were reliable: better to have things for barter than to be left with nothing at the end of the day! The entire system seemed oriented against efficiency.

By 1960, the Seven Year Plan proclaimed in 1958 was dead. Debt increased to the West and the supply of consumer goods plummeted. In the first half of 1961, emigration from East to West Germany reached record levels. Those who left were disproportionately young and skilled; doctors and skilled professionals, for example, whose chances of finding employment in the West were strong. In total, some 2.75 million Germans migrated from east to west between 1950 and 1961.[2]

This was the immediate context for the construction of the Berlin Wall. Ulbricht used the economic emergency of 1960–61 to stress to the Soviets the problems West Berlin posed for the GDR. But the Soviets had few good options for how to proceed. On November 27, 1958, Khrushchev had issued an ultimatum calling for a demilitarized city of West Berlin within six months, a gambit that suddenly made Berlin the center of tensions—including nuclear tensions between the major powers of the Cold War. His aim was to force the West to negotiate with the Soviet Union over Berlin, and to open a wider range of issues, hoping for peaceful diplomacy and concessions. But Khrushchev did not hold to his ultimatum. He delayed it multiple times for a series of reasons—and the United States did not budge on its guarantee of West Berlin.

Under these conditions, Khrushchev decided on the minimal option: to build a wall. The Warsaw Pact countries, sick of subsidizing East Germany and losing their own citizens through West Berlin, agreed. In early July, the Soviets sent a secret message to Ulbricht to start preparing. Now the East Germans could build a wall. In this sense, the decision was clearly that of the Soviet Union.

The GDR leadership had in fact already developed secret plans for walling off the city in 1952; by summer 1961, Ulbricht had extensive operational, economic, and tactical plans in hand. He was ready to go. He had been accumulating barbed wire, he knew what day of the week it should happen (early Sunday), and he had plans for Soviet reinforcements and for what to do with the subways. The Soviets made the final decision, but the East Germans succeeded in maneuvering them toward their second most favored outcome (the first being GDR sovereignty and control over all of Berlin).

Ulbricht put Erich Honecker in charge. Honecker had joined the Communists at eighteen years old, and had worked to organize a Communist resistance under the Nazis. He was arrested in 1935, and spent the rest of the Nazi years in jail. In 1946, he founded the Free German Youth and gained increasingly in power as he stood by Ulbricht in 1953 and again in 1956. Just under fifty years old, Honecker was one of the young ones in the Politburo, and since 1958 in charge of military matters.

The plan for building the Wall was given the code name "Mission Rose," and set for the morning of Sunday, August 13. The previous evening at 10:00 PM, Ulbricht invited state leaders to his dacha (the Russian word for summer house) north of Berlin; there they were informed that actions would be taken against the "hostile activities of the revanchist and militarist forces of West Germany and West Berlin," taking the form of securing borders as any "sovereign state" would. On that morning, Soviet forces took up position some distance away from the borders with West Berlin, so as not to be visible, and East German forces gathered near the border. In short order dozens of kilometers of barbed wire were rolled out.

It took days for the border to be completely sealed off, since many houses were situated right at the border itself. But already on August 29, East German border guards engaged in the first deadly shooting of a person trying to cross the border. Clearly, an order had been given to shoot-to-kill, though no copy of that original order has ever been found. Over the next months, the barbed wire was gradually replaced by a cement wall with barbed wire on top, a "death strip" that was often mined, and then a second, interior wall.

The GDR leadership declared the new boundary an "anti-fascist protective wall." But all the heroic language in the world could not alter the facts, obvious to everyone: the East German government had built a wall to keep its population from leaving, from voting with its feet. The Wall was not a triumph, it was a grand defeat. East Germany did not control the access to and from West Berlin, it still did not have full sovereignty.

Behind closed doors, US political leaders may have breathed a sigh of relief at the removal of a potential flashpoint in the Cold War. As President John F. Kennedy said in private, "A wall is a hell of a lot better than a war." Two years later, Kennedy came to Schöeneberg in West Berlin, to speak before a huge crowd of West Berliners: the Wall now came to exemplify the East German system for the West. In his famous "Ich bin ein Berliner" speech of June 26,

1963, the American president noted that "freedom has many difficulties and democracy is not perfect. But we have never had to put a wall up to keep our people in." The GDR now owned a permanent symbol of the system's weak legitimacy. But at the same time, the Berlin Wall contributed to a sense of stability in East Germany, the precondition for socialist development.

Further reading

Betts, Paul. *Within Walls: Private Life in the German Democratic Republic.* Oxford: Oxford University Press, 2010.

Biess, Frank. *Homecomings: Returning POWs and the Legacies of Defeat in Postwar Germany.* Princeton: Princeton University Press, 2006.

Bruce, Gary. *Resistance with the People: Repression and Resistance in Eastern Germany, 1945–1955.* Lanham, MD: Rowman and Littlefield, 2005.

Castillo, Greg. *Cold War on the Home Front: The Soft Power of Midcentury Design.* Minneapolis: University of Minnesota Press, 2010.

Connelly, John. *Captive University: The Sovietization of East German, Czech, and Polish Higher Education, 1945–1956.* Chapel Hill, NC: University of North Carolina Press, 2000.

Harrison, Hope. *Driving the Soviets Up the Wall: Soviet-East German Relations, 1953–1961.* Princeton, NJ: Princeton University Press, 2003.

Harsch, Donna. *Revenge of the Domestic: Women, the Family, and Communism in the German Democratic Republic.* Princeton: Princeton University Press, 2007.

Howell-Ardila, Deborah. "Berlin's Search for a 'Democratic' Architecture: Post-World War II and Post-Unification." *German Politics & Society* 16 (Fall 1998), 62–85.

Klemperer, Victor. *The Lesser Evil: The Diaries of Victor Klemperer, 1945–59.* Translated by Martin Chalmers. London: Weidenfeld and Nicolson, 2003.

Large, David Clay. *Germans to the Front: West German Rearmament in the Adenauer Era.* Chapel Hill: University of North Carolina Press, 1996.

Mitcherlich, Alexander and Margarete. *The Inability to Mourn: Principles of Collective Behavior.* Translated by Beverley R. Placzek. Boston: Grove Press, 1975.

Moeller, Robert. *Protecting Motherhood: Women and the Family in the Politics of Postwar West Germany.* Berkeley: University of California Press, 1993.

Osterman, Christian, and Charles Maier. *Uprising in East Germany 1953: The Cold War, the German Question, and the First Major Upheaval Behind the Iron Curtain.* Budapest: Central European University Press, 2001.

Patch, William. *Christian Democratic Workers and the Forging of West Germany, 1920–1980.* New York: Cambridge University Press, 2018.

Poiger, Uta. *Jazz, Rock, and Rebels: Cold War Politics and American Culture in a Divided Germany.* Berkeley: University of California Press, 2000.

Thomaneck, J. K. A. "Anna Seghers and the Janka Trial: A Case Study in Intellectual Obfuscation." *German Life and Letters* 46 (1993), 156–61.

Willke, Manfred. *The Path to the Berlin Wall: Critical Stages in the History of Divided Germany.* New York: Berghahn, 2014.

4

Politics and generational change in 1960s West Germany

FIGURE 4.1 *Café Kranzler at Kurfürstendamm and Joachimsthaler Strasse, West Berlin, 1965. (ullstein bild/Sobotta/Getty Images)*

The 1960s saw not only a political shift in West Germany, as Adenauer and others of the older generation left the stage and the Social Democrats began to gather more support, but also significant social changes. After the Berlin Wall closed off labor migration from East Germany, West Germany began to recruit workers from the economically depressed countries of southern Europe. The so-called guest worker program inadvertently laid the foundations for a more diverse and consciously multicultural society. By decade's end, two million foreigners lived in West Germany. The Holocaust also gained new attention with the trials of Adolf Eichmann in Jerusalem and the Auschwitz Trials in Frankfurt. The public discussion of Nazi war crimes proved especially important for younger West Germans, increasingly critical of postwar society. By the late 1960s, West German students and older leftists participated in protests against imperialism, the Vietnam War, and the constraints of Cold War consumer society. The fatal shooting of student Benno Ohnesorg in June 1967, the passage of the Emergency Laws in 1968, and the increasingly violent confrontations between police and demonstrators raised real questions about the future of German democracy, as both defenders of the new system and its critics accused each other of "fascist" tendencies.

West German culture in the 1950s has been described as quiescent and unpolitical. As the previous chapter demonstrated, that account does not encompass the times. While movies and magazines gave a picture of a quiet "normalizing" society avoiding the past, the decade saw anti-Communism, the reorganization of Social Democracy, mass peace protests concerning remilitarization and atomic weapons, and the first hints of student unrest. In addition, some changes that seemed to herald an era of normalization in fact reflected important changes. Radio news in the Nazi period, for example, was marked by high propaganda in heated tones; news anchors in 1950s West Germany, by contrast, used a matter of fact, reasoned, dispassionate, analytical tone in their broadcast. They aimed at a responsible journalism for a responsible democracy. Far from being unpolitical, these broadcasts pointed the way toward a different, more critical relationship between media and politics. All of these changes—in politics, between generations, and within the media—paved the way for the developments of the 1960s.

West Germans increasingly expected job security and a decent standard of living, the kind of comfortable affluence that welcomed guests under the red-and-white awnings of Café Kranzler on Kurfürstendamm, West Berlin's busiest shopping boulevard. Younger West Germans also expected the sorts of political and social freedoms associated most powerfully with the United States. When governments fell short of those expectations, many protested. Students, yes, but also workers, artists, intellectuals, and those we might describe simply as "average citizens" scrutinized the gap between society's professed values and lived experience—and demanded more. It was a consciously bottom-up revolt and immensely creative: participants aimed not only to overturn old authorities and social mores but to replace them with alternative ways of living, seeing, and being in the world. There was not one single cause but rather a number of different flashpoints. What activists shared in common was a desire to break through the constraints placed on everyday life and politics by both Cold War anti-Communism and postwar amnesia. For them, Café Kranzler and Kurfürstendamm were not evidence of the Western world's superiority but rather of the complacent, consumer society they sought to escape—and to upend. The revolt of the 1960s was both a global revolt and one tied to a specifically postwar German commitment to resist Nazism. If those involved ultimately made up only a fraction of the population, their actions and the questions they raised reverberated widely so that few in West Germany could be said to have been unaffected.

From Adenauer to the Great Coalition:
Politics as usual?

If change was in the air by the 1960s, a *lack* of change marked high politics. Adenauer was now in his mid-eighties and still chancellor. Although his party won the elections of 1961, the results were sobering. The Social Democrats gained slightly but the real threat for the Christian Democrats was the Free Democrats' upward surge thanks to former Christian Democratic supporters looking for a political change. The Free Democrats demanded that Adenauer leave his post before the end of the next term as a condition for their joining the coalition.

It was not a slow downward slide in the polls, however, that finally brought Adenauer's reign to an end. Rather, it was a media scandal of his own making. On October 10, 1962, the weekly newsmagazine *Der Spiegel* published an article detailing how woefully unprepared the West German

---

KONRAD ADENAUER SPEAKS ON
THE SPIEGEL AFFAIR, 1962

‟ Now, ladies and gentlemen . . .”

[Ongoing shouts from the Social Democrats]

“We have . . .”

[Continuing shouts from the Social Democrats]

“a chasm of treason in our land”

. . .

For, ladies and gentlemen,

[shout from Walter Seuffert (SPD)]

when a journal, which has a circulation of 500,000 copies, systematically engages in treason to earn money . . .”

[Excited shouts from the Social Democrats: Pfui! Whistling and ongoing shouts . . .]

Source: Konrad Adenauer, speech to Bundestag on November 7, 1962, from Deutscher Bundestag 4. Wahlperiode, 45. Sitzung, p. 1984.

army was for a military attack. In response, the defense minister and leader of the Bavarian Christian Social Union, Franz Josef Strauss, ordered the arrest of the magazine's editors and an illegal search of their offices. Strauss even went so far as to place a call to the German military attaché in Spain, requesting that the author of the article—then vacationing in Spain—be arrested. It was, in short, a blatant attempt to muzzle the press, which quickly became a media spectacle. Not only were Strauss's methods of dealing with political enemies displayed to the world, but, Adenauer, who backed Strauss in private, was himself drawn in after he referred to the event as "an abyss of treason."

The Spiegel Affair was in many ways a perfect storm, one that had been building since the late 1950s. It announced the ascendancy of a new generation of journalists who no longer saw their job as one of consensus-building and dispassionate reporting. Instead, they embraced Anglo-American practices of investigative journalism and proved all too willing to scrutinize the claims of authority. It also drew strength from a growing public discussion not only of German guilt and history, but also of the nature of democracy. Prominent academics like Habermas and writers like Grass participated in protests against the Adenauer government; even conservative newspapers criticized what the government had done in the name of democracy. The Free Democrats resigned from the coalition and refused to join a new government unless Strauss was removed. Adenauer resisted calls for his own resignation until October 1963; even then he showed no signs of understanding that his actions had amounted to an attack on the new understanding of democracy in West Germany.

Adenauer's resignation did not usher in a completely new era. The Christian Democrats remained, for a time, the leading party in politics. The new chancellor, Ludwig Erhard, in many ways embodied the spirit of the economic miracle; voters continued to affirm the Christian Democratic economic accomplishments of the previous decade. But there were changes. Erhard, like Adenauer, favored embedding Germany in the Western alliance, but he privileged the transatlantic alliance with the United States, whereas Adenauer had focused on a tight alliance with Catholic France. And, notably, Erhard was Protestant not Catholic. Though the Christian Democratic Party remained predominately Catholic, Erhard signaled its successful move away from the closed milieu of the old Center Party.

Indeed, starting in the 1960s the close connection between Catholic Church hierarchy and Christian Democrats became looser, and Catholic doctrine played an ever lesser role in party politics. This distance operated on both political and religious levels. On a political level, a new generation of Catholic intellectuals began to question the hierarchy's narrative of its persecuted role under National Socialism. In a series of 1957–62, for example, the later Constitutional Court justice Ernst-Wolfgang Böckenförde (born 1930) showed how many heroes of the Catholic resistance in fact greeted the end of democracy in 1933, basing his arguments on the research of his generational comrade Rudolf Morsey. He also echoed more radical

Catholic critics like Walter Dirks in asking whether the church's reliance on an eternal natural law in fact contradicted the logic of democracy. On a theological and religious level, the great debates surrounding the Second Vatican Council (1962–1965) led to church documents calling for more efforts at ecumenical cooperation; and the church finally rejected the notion that Jews were responsible for the death of Jesus. Individual Catholics may have remained strong in their faith but these debates weakened their identification with the Catholic political tradition. On a broader scale, this meant that religion was gradually releasing its hold on German politics, as not only Protestants voted Christian Democrat but ever more Catholics felt free to vote for the Social Democrats.

Nonetheless, the Christian Democrats and Christian Socials continued to win elections in the early 1960s. Erhard's reputation as the "father of the economic miracle" helped him win the election in 1963 and re-election in 1965, but his was anything but an easy chancellorship. Erhard remained resistant to new economic impulses from the Anglo-American world, including Keynesian notions of how to respond to economic crisis. He remained attached to a conservative model of the state based on what he called the "formed society," a society with a strong state that could guide rather than be controlled by interest groups. The problem, as Erhard and many of his generation were slow to recognize, was that West German society was changing fast, and with it the state itself. The 1960s quickly demonstrated that the experiences of the 1950s, far from being the new norm, were, in fact, a never-to-be-repeated anomaly.

A sudden downturn in the economy in 1966 awoke West Germans to the fact that economic growth and full employment were not guaranteed conditions of postwar life. It was the first economic hiccup of the postwar period and, as such, revealed West Germans' deep-seated insecurities; many West Germans feared that political crisis would follow economic crisis, as it had in the Weimar Republic. Their fears were misplaced but Erhard's chosen path to economic security did ultimately lead to his resignation. Determined to avoid an increase in government spending, the chancellor called for a balanced budget, and, in the ensuing conflict over how this would be achieved, his coalition with the Free Democrats collapsed.

Erhard resigned, giving way to the first Grand Coalition in fall 1966: an unlikely alliance of Social Democrats and Christian Democrats under Kurt-Georg Kiesinger. For many Germans on the left, especially younger Germans, the Grand Coalition was a disappointment. Yes, the Social Democrats shared power on the federal level for the first time but in an alliance with the Christian Democrats, ensuring continuity rather than a break. And, yes, a new chancellor was in charge, but Kiesinger was a former Nazi Party member. For some on the far right, meanwhile, the Grand Coalition meant that the Christian Democrats had sold out to the left. As a result, the Grand Coalition may well have contributed to a radicalization of both far left and far right in the late 1960s.

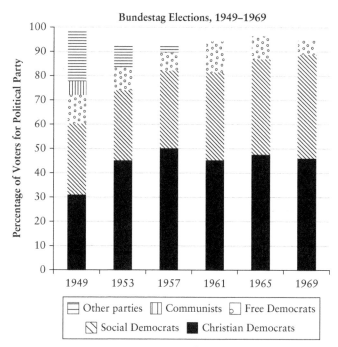

CHART 4.1 *Bundestag Elections, 1949–69*
Note: *Where figures add up to less than 100%, the remaining votes went to parties that failed to fulfill the conditions (in particular the 5% hurdle) required to enter parliament*

Despite this criticism, the Grand Coalition did break with Adenauer's authoritarian style of government and with Erhard's adherence to his policies from the 1950s. The moralizing rhetoric of the ordoliberal economists, those proponents of the free market who so shaped the formation of the Federal Republic, gave way to the "modern" and "modernizing" rhetoric of technocratic control, informed by Keynesianism and American economics. Karl Schiller of the Social Democrats and Strauss of the Christian Social Union, two very different and original politicians from opposite sides of the political spectrum, developed in tandem an economic policy to respond to the downturn. They eased interest rates and boosted investment in basic infrastructure and, at least temporarily, convinced people that the government could manage economic crises, if only the technical experts were allowed to make the right decisions.

People at the top level of government, in the universities, and in the mass media enthusiastically embraced notions of modern planning. New centers sprang up to employ the theoretical framework of cybernetics in order to foresee probable futures, and to recommend policies. In West Germany (and also, as the next chapter explores, in the GDR), economists and politicians assumed that the high rates of economic growth associated

with the economic miracle would continue indefinitely, if only futurology
and economic policy cooperated.[1]

Income, consumption, and opportunity

The mild recession of 1966–67 shocked West Germans because the years
between 1949 and 1965 were ones of amazing growth. The auto industry
in particular boomed. Even as prices of raw materials and labor increased,
the price of cars decreased. Both private and public companies—Daimler-
Benz and Volkswagen—pulled this off through dramatic and steady
improvements in productivity. Despite heavy influence from America,
Volkswagen, for example, followed specific German forms that helped its
growth and survival. In addition to relying on a variety of suppliers, the
German tradition of codetermination (discussed in Chapter 3), brought
workers into the process of improving productivity and, when necessary, of
negotiating the ups and downs of the market. Both multiple suppliers and
codetermination allowed the company to remain flexible in its production
plans and labor agreements, and to emphasize quality. By the end of the
1960s, Volkswagen had managed to break into the US markets, selling over
a fifth of the cars it produced in Germany in the United States.

West Germany's "boom" economy confronted one clear limitation, even
at its height: a labor shortfall. Before August 1961, the FRG benefited
greatly from the incoming flows of well-educated and trained East German
workers. This source of labor ended with the Berlin Wall. But even before
that the need for skilled and semiskilled industrial labor drove the FRG to
sign bilateral labor agreements with the governments of Italy (1955), Spain
and Greece (1960), Turkey (1961), Morocco (1963), Portugal (1964), and
Yugoslavia (1968). In each case, the FRG established temporary, rotating
contracts to secure labor that was both cheap and, because the workers
were young and noncitizens, did not claim welfare resources. The migrants
received one- to two-year nonrenewable work permits, and after the permits
expired, they were expected to rotate out of the system—to return home,
not empty handed but with new skills. Such was the hope of the workers'
governments, whose own goals entailed a trained workforce. The system
put in place was relatively straightforward. Prospective workers applied at
West German extension offices in their home countries and, if they passed
the medical exam, their application went to an agency in the FRG, which
assigned workers to both private and public businesses.

Germans referred to these contract laborers as guest workers, in a deliberate
effort to avoid the term "foreign workers," used to refer to forced laborers
under the Third Reich, as well as "immigrant," which suggested a permanent
relocation and maybe even rights. It did not take long, however, before
both the temporary timeframe and the hospitable reception implied by the

very phrase "guest worker" proved empty: Guest workers lived in cramped dorms near the work sites; effectively isolated from the local population, they lived very much as outsiders. Also, sending the workers back after their "shifts" proved disruptive. Frequent rotation, as originally agreed upon, required constant retraining and thus unexpected costs. For this reason, the Bundestag suspended the provision for temporary, rotating workers, and from 1965 on, work and residence permits could be renewed. Early plans to prevent the workers' families from joining them also fell by the wayside, if for more political than economic reasons. On several occasions, the Federal Ministry of Interior attempted to prohibit or greatly restrict migrant families' reunification. However, concern for the FRG's public image—specifically its image as a liberal, democratic state nothing like the Third Reich or the GDR—forced officials to back down; family reunification was granted to foreigners who could demonstrate proof of adequate housing. By 1969, the total number of foreigners living in West Germany totaled two million, with Italians making up the largest group. The labor shortage was solved. Now immigrants could stay in the FRG for long periods, working menial jobs that few Germans were willing to accept but that were essential to the FRG's economic success. The two-tiered system of German/non-German, citizen/noncitizen allowed German citizens to rise socially.

Nonetheless, many equated economic prosperity with an increasingly democratic society. The West German sociologist Helmut Schelsky asserted that the FRG was a classless, or "leveled," society. Clearly class differences remained, as did differences of opportunity based on race and gender. But it is true that West German society as a whole became wealthier. Wages remained relatively stagnant in the 1950s but as the economy continued to expand in the 1960s, they increased by almost 80 percent. And with that wealth came more access to entertainment—to rock 'n' roll, as we have seen, but also to modern art and literature, to film, and to sports. Germany's professional soccer league, the Bundesliga, was founded in 1962 not only because the national team lost to Yugoslavia in that year's World Cup quarterfinals and many argued that a national league would improve their game and keep their best players from leaving. The average West German now also had time and money to attend professional matches. Similarly, generous labor laws, passed against the will of Erhard, provided two weeks or more of paid vacation days. Growing numbers of West Germans could and did travel abroad, to Austria and Italy, then further afield to Spain and Majorca, until they became the globetrotters we know today.

This same consumer affluence drove the so-called sexual revolution. The introduction of the Pill in 1961 freed men and women in the FRG, and elsewhere, from the fear of unwanted pregnancy. From this point forward, traditional attitudes toward sex and marriage faced sustained attack from above and below. A new wave of experts promoted healthy and open sex lives as part of a well-adjusted childhood and happy marriage. Sexologists in particular pointed to the work of Wilhelm Reich, who decades before argued that sexual repression led to psychosis. Others used unfavorable comparisons to the GDR to sway public opinion: mainstream magazines like *Stern* and *Spiegel* ran articles describing how East Germans, particularly women and adolescents, were less sexually repressed than they. Expert opinion received support not only from the eager libidos of West German youth but also from entrepreneurs like Beate Uhse, who started out selling advice and contraception to desperate couples, primarily by mail, before establishing her now famous sex-shop empire. The marketing of sex manuals, illustrated journals, films, and other materials dedicated to educating West Germans on their sexuality—spurred on by mass demand—led to looser "decency" laws and sex's sudden visual presence. By 1966, people were referring to a "scx wave." Women's nude and partially nude bodies, previously banned from public sight, confronted West Germans at every turn; sex sold itself— and pretty much anything else. A consensus on what constituted acceptable or "tasteful" nudity on the one hand and socially harmful nudity did not exist. More importantly, it could not be legally determined: in 1969, the courts legalized pornography. "Liberation" in this sense seemed to mean the objectification of women, unaccompanied by legal reforms to protect women against sexual discrimination. It is not surprising, then, that 1968– 69 also saw the formation of a new women's movement.

That same year the Bundestag also reformed Paragraph 175 of the penal code. Penned in 1871 and notoriously expanded under the Third Reich, Paragraph 175 criminalized homosexuality. The law remained in force in the early FRG; Adenauer's government gave little consideration to reforming it beyond cleansing it of Nazi amendments. Male homosexuals, imprisoned in Nazi concentration camps, were not officially recognized as victims, and worse: after liberation, some were rounded up and forced to carry out the remainder of their prison sentence. But after persecuting 44,000 men between 1949 and 1962, the same liberalizing trends discussed above propelled change in this arena, too. By mid-century, expert consensus—lawyers as well as sexologists—favored liberalization of antigay laws, as did Social Democrat Gustav Heinemann's appointment as justice minister in 1966. It took three more years, however, and the election of Willy Brandt as chancellor, before homosexual acts for men over twenty-one were decriminalized. The reform of Paragraph 175 did not end homophobia or mean homosexuality was now accepted by the mainstream. But it was a crucial step toward those two ends and the emergence of a gay public sphere in the 1970s.

As the sexual revolution and expansion of gay rights suggests, greater security and wealth affected consumption and also West Germans' expectations from life. Within a generation, upward social mobility became a possibility for many more than before. And as the economy grew, it demanded more educated people, as well: more engineers, more scientists, more people able to think critically and communicate. But the universities remained by and large unchanged. They were relatively small and still dominated by professors and students from the upper middle classes. In the early 1960s, social scientists began to predict an "education catastrophe," noting the failure of the West German educational system to prepare the country's youth for the modern economy. The liberal social scientist and politician Ralf Dahrendorf went further, proclaiming education a basic right in any developed society, and one that required state support and a reorganization of the university system.

Confronting the past

Despite its later reputation, the 1950s had not been a decade of utter silence about the Nazi past. As discussed above, the atrocities of the war and the Holocaust appeared repeatedly in West German culture, from the novels of Böll and Grass and the iconoclastic Wolfgang Koeppen, to films like *Roses for the State Attorney*, to the translation of the *Diary of Anne Frank*, performed in countless schools in both Germanys. That discussion remained part of society, but not the focal point of political life. Around 1960, the relative political silence on Nazi war crimes was broken. In the city of Ulm a special court set up to pursue National Socialist crimes tried several former members of *Einsatzgruppen*, the mobile killing units that followed behind the German Army, murdering Jews and other "biological enemies" starting in 1941. The trials drew a good deal of attention and resulted in sentences of up to fifteen years. That an individual could murder thousands of civilians and receive such a light sentence appears, from today's vantage point, unjust. But that they were tried and found guilty proved times had changed: fifteen to twenty years after the war, West Germans were more willing to confront the past.

More important for raising not just German but international consciousness was the trial against Adolf Eichmann. Captured in Argentina by the Israeli secret service, Eichmann was sent to Israel to stand trial for his role in organizing the Final Solution. In the trial, he portrayed himself as a simple civil servant with the aim of doing things efficiently; he denied any direct role in the Jewish genocide and denied that he wanted the genocide to take place. The evidence suggested otherwise. The prosecution submitted thousands of documents, proving Eichmann's deep involvement as well as the involvement of huge numbers of ethnic Germans. The true revelations, however, came from survivors. Absent at Nuremberg, their testimony helped build the case against Eichmann, while the trial itself—televised and reported on around the world—publically honored and legitimated that testimony for the first time. In the end, Eichmann may not have personally killed anyone but he was shown to have helped organize the transports and the death camps that did. The Israelis executed him on June 1, 1962.

The same man who informed Israel's secret service about Eichmann's whereabouts in Argentina, judge and prosecutor Fritz Bauer, also initiated the Auschwitz Trials, a series of trials charging twenty-two camp officials and guards for their roles in the Holocaust. German, Jewish, and homosexual, Bauer had himself experienced the inside of a concentration camp—arrested along with Kurt Schumacher and other Social Democrats in 1933. Released after nine months, he fled to Denmark and, later, to Sweden. Unlike many German Jews who survived, Bauer returned to Germany in 1949, and to the civil service. But he kept both his Jewish and sexual identity secret; homosexuality, after all, was a criminal offense and Bauer was all too aware of postwar Germans' unabated anti-Semitism, not least because he worked alongside former Nazis who, like him, had returned to their jobs as judges and public officials. To say that Bauer's investigation of Nazi criminals and his success in bringing them to trial provoked controversy is to put it mildly. Bauer himself received numerous death threats. But from 1964 until his untimely death in 1968, his actions kept the activities of leading Germans in the spotlight, particularly ex-Nazis who had found their way into the Christian Democrats and Free Democrats. Both parties, not coincidentally, sought a statute of limitations that would have set an end to war crimes trials after a certain number of years. Intense public scrutiny and dissent within their own ranks, however, forced them to extend that statute, until finally giving up on it entirely. Participants in the murderous crimes of the Third Reich could not escape prosecution by arguing that too much time had passed.

The West German media followed the trial in depth and, unlike ten years before, the debate surrounding it led to a change in Germany itself. The schools began to incorporate a history of Nazism and the Holocaust into their curricula for the first time. A new generation of historians began investigating the collapse of the Weimar Republic and Nazism's rise. More immediately, the trials showed how well mass murderers had managed to integrate themselves into West German society. The GDR happily contributed to this process of consciousness-raising by publishing so-called "Brown Books," containing the biographies of other leading Nazis living comfortably in West Germany. Suddenly, the history of the Federal Republic took on a brown hue. The Holocaust remained a peripheral concern: it would take another decade before West Germans as a whole focused on the Jewish victims of Nazism. But the trials provoked a sustained and emotionally wrenching unmasking of perpetrators.

Student protest and radicalization

Born in 1936, the young law student Peter Gente stumbled across the work of the philosopher Theodor Adorno, one of the crucial inspirations for the student movement, in 1957. Of Jewish descent and a Marxist, Adorno had spent the war years in the United States, and had returned to teach at Frankfurt University in 1949. In essays and radio addresses, he took up the question of German guilt and the legacy of fascism and Auschwitz on German culture. When Gente, filled with enthusiasm for his new intellectual hero, described Adorno's thoughts to his mother, she dismissed it as "Jewish subversion"; as Gente's biographer puts it, his mother "had preserved her sense for racial distinctions beyond the war." Gente quit his legal studies and turned instead to philosophy and sociology, eventually working with Adorno and founding his own leftist publishing house, Merve.[2]

Gente was one of many student activists and former radicals who cited the failure of their parents' generation to confront their Nazi past as crucial to their eventual politicization. Students exposed professors, accused fathers, and felt themselves responsible for preventing fascism's return. Though rebellion famously rocked societies around the world in the 1960s, not only in Western Europe and the United States but also in Mexico, China, and Eastern Europe, it took a particular, radicalized form in the FRG.

Germany's position on the frontlines of the Cold War also played an important role. It was no accident, for example, that the Free University (or FU) in West Berlin was an early site of radicalization. Founded in 1948 on the principles of free speech and student co-representation, the university granted its students unprecedented freedoms. The product of the Cold War, they served to distinguish the "free world" in the West from universities and life in the East. But administrators got more than they bargained for when students took them at their word and proved especially active and critical of the West German government. Already in the late 1950s, for example, Berlin students organized protests against atomic weapons in the Federal Republic.

West German remilitarization brought radical youth to West Berlin, where they were exempted from military service. Meanwhile, the Berlin Wall brought a string of smart, critical East Germans to the West. One of these was Rudi Dutschke, who, along with many other East Germans, attended the Free University, moving freely between home and university in East and West Berlin until the Wall ended such arrangements. The Soviet suppression of the Hungarian uprising in 1956 made Dutschke an early critic of the GDR; though it cost him friends and family, he decided to stay in the West and at the Free University, where he continued to study philosophy and social theory. And he began to organize politically. His decision to make a life for himself in the FRG did not mean that Dutschke had rejected socialism. He remained convinced that capitalism did more to undermine than promote social and political equality. But Dutschke was an antiauthoritarian socialist, critical of the bureaucracy and party domination characteristic of Soviet state socialism. He found there were many others like him living in the FRG: critical of both sides in the Cold War and, in the West, of the way anti-Communism was used to enforce political and social consensus by shutting down all discussion of political alternatives. This included members of the Socialist Students' Federation (SDS), the Social Democrats' "youth" organization for those under thirty-five, whom the party expelled for refusing to disavow Marxism and adopt the Godesberg Program. It also included artists and intellectuals who pushed the limits of both art and politics in the hopes of revolutionizing society as a whole.

Feeling themselves shut out of West German parliamentary politics, many began to explore other, often international contexts for radical action.

Anti-colonial struggles took center stage in world politics from the mid-1950s onward. They offer one example of how international politics and domestic politics fused in the 1960s. The same imperialist powers that fought Nazi tyranny in the name of democratic freedom turned to squashing rebellion in their colonies immediately after the war. The governments of France and Great Britain as well as Belgium and the Netherlands used violence, even extensive military force against populations who now demanded independence. Student exchange programs designed to promote international relations and West Germans' further Western integration brought West Germans in contact with students in North America and western Europe but also students whose countries were embroiled in this conflict. Whether writing for student papers or in groups like the African Student League and the Latin American Student League, they helped bring the anti-colonial struggle to West German campuses and, from there, to the streets of the FRG.

But why would West Germans, young or old, understand this to be their fight? There were at least two reasons. First, one legacy of the Nazi past was that many felt duty-bound to oppose imperialism as Germans. One could dispute Nazism's ties to capitalism—the "why" behind its expansionist aims—but not that the Third Reich was an empire; part of "never again" entailed, for anti-imperialists, ending the subjugation of foreign populations not just in Europe but everywhere. And their own recent experience of occupation only encouraged solidarity with colonized peoples. The second reason had to do with the FRG's particular relationship to the United States. The United States was the FRG's greatest ally and chief defender against Communism, and more than two hundred thousand American soldiers lived on West German military bases. What the superpower did, even outside of Europe, concerned West Germans greatly. And though officially anti-imperialist, the United States supported the suppression of national liberation movements that threatened to bring Communists to power; for similar reasons, they armed and protected authoritarian leaders in jeopardy of being ousted by left, popular revolt. As the United States began its campaign in Vietnam in 1965, the international media was filled with pictures of Americans dropping carpet bombs and napalm on civilian and military targets alike (because in a guerrilla war there is no clear distinction between civilians and soldiers)—in support of a corrupt, authoritarian regime. Germans' response to US foreign policy was mixed: Erhard and other members of the political establishment officially supported its intervention in Vietnam and threw state dinners for US-backed dictators like Moïse Tshombe and the shah of Iran. The SDS joined foreign students and other student groups in protest. It is hard to overstate the sense of betrayal and the disillusionment that many younger West Germans experienced, having grown up admiring the United States not only as a land of rock 'n' roll and Coca-Cola but also of freedom and democracy.

FIGURE 4.2 *Anti-Vietnam Demonstration in Frankfurt am Main, with people carrying flags and posters against the USA and in support of the Vietcong, April 16, 1968. (ullstein bild/Wolfgang Kunz/GettyImages)*

The working class in Germany, meanwhile, was relatively quiet even though the unions were strong. There were different explanations for workers' lack of political engagement beyond the ballot box. Most famously, the "Frankfurt School" social theorists Theodor Adorno, Max Horkheimer, and Herbert Marcuse put forth the idea that consumer culture deadened working-class resistance. The barrage of popular culture, fashion, and other mass-produced commodities alongside the availability of cheap stuff theoretically numbed workers to the ongoing barbarism of capitalism. Workers' exploitation was now less obvious—migrants rather than Germans worked the worst jobs and received the worst pay—and televisions, cars, and vacations could now be theirs, too. Like the middle classes, they focused on working their way up the existing ladder. For this reason, Franz Fanon, a French Afro-Caribbean and vocal supporter of Algeria's fight for independence, suggested that the struggle against the current system of oppression had shifted from the old urban, industrialized centers to the world's colonial periphery, specifically to the fight against imperialism in the colonized states. In other words, there was a new revolutionary actor: the third world. Europeans or Americans (the "first world") remained necessary in the fight for radical change. But in this new understanding those most able to resist were, like the colonized people of Africa, Asia, and Latin America, on the margins of established society. West German students were not the most obvious candidates to take on this revolutionary task, but a number of them came to view themselves as revolutionary actors. The work of social and political theorist Herbert Marcuse provided language to support this. For Marcuse, only persons in liminal positions (underprivileged because of race, age, poverty, or even their declared mental state) could see the truth of this totalizing society. They could do so precisely because they stood outside it and if they maintained that position—if students refused to be integrated, refused to participate in the existing system—then they might slowly undermine it.[3]

Police broke up initially peaceful student protests with brutal force and arrests. Conservative politicians joined local officials and West Germany's largest media concern, the Springer Press, in painting protesters as "rowdies" and Communist insurgents. Hostile commentators declared that the delinquents should "go back" to where they came from (presumably the GDR); some implied that concentration camps were their proper place. This experience alone convinced students of their marginalized status and the historical significance of their actions. By attempting to draw attention to faraway injustices, they had revealed the limits of democratic tolerance at home. While many older West Germans interpreted mass demonstrations as attacks on the existing democratic order, every confrontation with authority increased students' sense that the FRG remained authoritarian, potentially even fascist, despite its oft-repeated claims of being the democratic, free Germany.

German students, like those in other countries, felt called upon to resist fascism. Now, what was fascism? That was a hard question. But many who came of age during the Eichmann and Auschwitz trials took their duty to resist it seriously. Emotions ran high because the stakes appeared high. Students in the United States, France, and the FRG, for example, denounced the Vietnam War as an imperialist venture but even more crucially, as genocide; to fail to end the war was to repeat events that they (indeed, the international community) had sworn to prevent. And for West Germans at least, prevention was just as important as resistance, whether this meant preventing fascism's resurgence in a previously fascist country or the conditions (authoritarianism, imperialism, capitalism) that they understood produced it. After all, history showed that resisting fascism after it rose to power was futile. Timothy Brown in fact argues that this was about all students learned about anti-fascism in history classes of the early 1960s. Over the course of the decade, however, they discovered a second buried "past": a revolutionary left politics first destroyed by Nazism and then deformed (Communists) and betrayed (Social Democrats) after 1945 by the left-wing parties. It was a past of possibilities and bitter defeat that students reclaimed and, as time went on, fiercely debated. In this process, books banned or out of print in the FRG but available in the East made their way across the German-German border in the traveling backpacks of Western students and the hands of East German visitors to West Berlin. Dutschke and others explored the early, still provocative works by Karl Marx; they read Che Guevara and the "Red Book" of the Chinese Communist leader Mao Zedong. And they analyzed Fanon's *Wretched of the Earth* and Marcuse's *One-Dimensional Man*. In this way American, European, and postcolonial perspectives both informed West German students' understanding of the FRG and included them in a global struggle. Their shared sense of embattlement and perceived high stakes also contributed to a certain militant machoism within the student movement, one that tended to reinforce rather than revise the traditional gender roles of the men and women involved. The absence of women's names among the thinkers and leaders discussed above is no accident; despite the movement's commitment to equality and liberation, it retained the patriarchal values of society at large.

Countercultural revolt

It is difficult to talk about any one aspect of "1968" in isolation because cultural, social, and political acts overlapped. To reject the empty popular music of the 1950s—the so-called "*Heimat Schlager*," or "hits of the homeland"—or even crooner boys' bands of early rock 'n' roll for Jimi Hendrix and the Rolling Stones was to rebel against far more than musical tastes. This was true for self-styled rebels. And it was true for horrified onlookers, the largely older West Germans who understood long hair and loud music as no less dangerous to their way of life than political demonstrations. Adopting British and US youth fashion, rooted in the edgier, more aggressive sounds and styles of working-class culture, defied bourgeois German sensibilities; youth rejected not only a particular German notion of high, educated culture but also an older generation's effort to re-civilize postwar Germans by eliminating, or at least containing, the radicalism, male aggression, and deviance associated with Nazism. The early 1960s witnessed the rise of the "*Gammler*," a label derived from the verb "to bum around" and applied to nonconformist youth of all types, from students and artists to hippies, rockers, and freaks. *Gammler* rejected the so-called achievement society; instead of scrambling to get up the social and economic ladder, they hung out in public squares, experimented with a wide array of drugs, and hitchhiked to places near and far. By the 1970s, a flourishing underground existed of bars, coffee houses, and concert venues; writers' and publishing collectives printed small runs of their own works, local "scene" circulars, and even illegal materials on the cheap. In this and other ways, West Germans undermined—or countered—the mainstream monopoly on media, culture, and even public space.[4]

Visual artists like Joseph Beuys, born in 1921 and a veteran of the Second World War, bridged generations and the worlds of art and performance.

Beuys, like many countercultural artists and musicians, criticized the art world's commercialization and sought various ways to undermine it. His works took aim at the very notion of great art—art that is acclaimed, collected, eternal—by using common, everyday items (most famously fat and felt) in installations that often only lasted a few hours or days. In his 1965 "action," *How to Explain Pictures to a Dead Hare*, Beuys covered his head with gold leaf and honey and wore one shoe wrapped in felt, the other one soled with iron; for two hours he walked around a gallery room before onlookers, explaining the works on display (all his) to the dead rabbit he carried in his arms. Unsettling, yes, and incomprehensible to many, Beuys' work aimed to get people thinking and, ideally, to address bigger social and political issues. Characteristic of the countercultural revolution "from below," Beuys defined art broadly, essentially rejecting art as a profession by declaring everyone an artist and every action a work of art. Understood in this way, art could not be separated from society and politics. If anything, art might act as a guide to a more reflexive, humane way of living.

Art and politics intersected even more explicitly in the person of Dieter Kunzelmann, the "bohemian" of the antiauthoritarian movement who delighted in breaking down the boundaries between fun and politics. He and other members of the notorious West Berlin collective, Commune I, understood the liberation of society to rest on the liberation of individual consciousness and drew directly on developments in the art world to disrupt people's everyday existence. Spectacle and spontaneity, even fantasy, characterized "happenings" and direct actions that purposefully provoked; they counted on their audience's response as much as Beuys. Even failed actions demonstrated the power of such provocations to expose what was otherwise hidden: Two members of Commune I were arrested for planning a bomb attack on US vice president Hubert Humphrey's motorcade. Authorities quickly discovered that the "bomb" was made entirely of pudding but not before the Springer Press gleefully reported on the assassins' arrest and painted the two men as pawns of Communist China. In this instance, the action revealed the blatant disregard for evidence in the newspaper's eagerness to grab headlines and to condemn student activists. Less intentionally, it also demonstrated a penchant among certain activists for pushing the line between humor and open violence.

Commune I is remembered for its provocative actions, its "free love" and drug use, and its network of avant-garde artists and intellectuals. It stands in, however, for many, far less famous countercultural attempts to revolutionize the everyday by eliminating authoritarian behaviors and unequal power structures at home and at school. Experiments in communal living—shared apartments, houses, even farms—sought to free individuals from the patriarchal family, not only by eliminating the traditional head of the household and what many perceived as the sexually repressive mores of bourgeois marriage, but also by distributing the burden of domestic labor.

Reality often fell short. Many of the radical men from West Germany still viewed women as providers of housework and sex. The contradictions became divisive in some of the communes, where women made their demands for equal respect and responsibility clear—and met with a lack of understanding or even open resistance.

Even when they failed on their own terms, the goal was to rethink one's personal relationships—those between men and women as well as parents and children—so that they reflected the same egalitarian values activists sought to realize in society at large. New pedagogies likewise aimed to create an atmosphere that fostered individual exploration and growth. Convinced that rigid discipline and rote memorization encouraged authoritarian personalities, they introduced less structured learning activities designed to promote independent, critical thinking.

The rise and fall of the extra-parliamentary opposition (APO)

Established leftists like Habermas, Protestant theologian Helmut Gollwitzer, and the writer Magnus Enzensberger admired the younger generation for their demonstrated willingness to protest the hypocrisies of the current system and to defend democracy if necessary—to do, in other words, what previous generations of Germans failed to do. They, like many on the left, understood German democracy as an ongoing project, one that students might help push forward. Though they did not always agree on what should be done, recent domestic developments encouraged the sense that the need for action was real. The light shed on Nazis' integration into West German society added weight to earlier left critiques regarding the FRG's failure to break with Nazism, as did police brutality and the vilification of protesters. The new government—the Grand Coalition—did not help in this regard, as noted in the previous chapter. At best, this was seen as a malfunction of representative democracy that left many—not just Marxists!—feeling disenfranchised. Within this context, if not for this reason alone, a number of concerned citizens formed a loose umbrella organization known as the APO (Extra-parliamentary Opposition), which they hoped would provide a counterweight to the ruling coalition. Trade unionists, intellectuals, left Social Democrats, critical Free Democratic supporters, members of confessional organizations, peace activists, and students—radical and otherwise: over time their differences would trump their commonalities. But in the short term, opposition to the East-West binary that threatened to destroy the world, plus a desire for greater democracy and a loosening of traditional social conventions moved these West Germans to coordinated action. Together, they insisted on a third way, a path between Western capitalism and Soviet-style state socialism.

The likely passage of new Emergency Laws was the rallying point for APO, capturing all of the activists' fears regarding the state of West German democracy. The proposed legislation established the protocols to be followed in a state of emergency caused by foreign invasion, civil unrest, or natural disaster. It was the last thing that stood between West Germans and full national sovereignty: without it, the United States and other Western Allies retained the right to intervene militarily as they saw fit. Conservatives had called for the creation of emergency legislation repeatedly since 1949 only to be thwarted each time by the Social Democrats. But when the Social Democrats entered into the Grand Coalition, their opposition to the Emergency Laws ended too. From their point of view, controlling the state in a time of emergency was an appropriate task for a mature representative democracy. It was only a matter of time before the legislation's passage.

THE LAWYER WERNER MAIHOFER ON THE DANGER OF EMERGENCY LAWS

Today, the enemy in our state stands neither left nor right but rather in the middle, with every second democrat and second autocrat from whom, in a future domestic or international crisis, we cannot expect one thing in any case: that they defend the achievements of our free legal and social democracy out of conviction and with determination. . . . Our young, still untested democracy will only survive the dangers and temptations of a future domestic or international crisis without harm, therefore, if . . . the democratic check of parliament and public remains fully effective, so as to avert any temptations to stray toward something "extralegal," be it constitutional, be it international law, up front.

From the executive itself, however, some sort of noteworthy resistance against anti-democratic developments, authoritarian tendencies or totalitarian practices, is not to be looked for, as we learned from the "Spiegel Affair" as well as the phone-hacking scandal.
. . .

In a future crisis, democracy in Germany stands and falls with the ability of parliament and media to act, and with the extraparliamentary opposition within the intelligentsia and workers, the backbone of our country's positive democratization process.

Source: Werner Maihofer, speaking to those gathered at the "Demokratie vor dem Notstand" congress in Bonn on May 30, 1965, published in Wilhelm Bauer and Gunter Wegeleben, eds., Sonderheft: Demokratie vor dem Notstand. Protokoll des Bonner Kongresses gegen die Notstandsgesetze am 30. Mai 1965 (Frankfurt/Main: neue kritik, 1965), p. 11. Reprinted with the permission of Verlag Neue Kritik.

German history, however, provided a different story of emergency powers. It was emergency legislation, passed with the help of the famous Article 48 of the Weimar Constitution, which empowered Hitler and allowed him to eliminate his enemies and consolidate control in 1933. Trade unionists and dissenting Social Democrats also feared the laws' misuse against labor strikes, otherwise protected by the constitution. Tens of thousands of West Germans protested in teach-ins, workers' strikes, conferences, and student groups dedicated to "democracy on the verge" and "democracy in crisis." And in the weeks leading up to the Bundestag vote, some 70,000 people from all over the FRG joined to "march on Bonn." Despite such displays of mass opposition, the Christian Democrats and Social Democrats were not swayed. The Emergency Laws were passed by parliament on May 30, 1968, with only the Free Democrats casting a vote of dissent. Their inability to influence parliament or official government policy left protesters frustrated, disillusioned, exhausted.

The year 1968 is often used as shorthand for the entire period of global revolt, capturing both the height of the protest movement and its radicalization. In the FRG, however, that moment occurred a year earlier, after a West Berlin police officer shot and killed a twenty-six-year-old student named Benno Ohnesorg. One date burns brightest in student radicals' memory (and indeed of many West Germans): that of Ohnesorg's death on June 2, 1967; if there is one image, it is that of a shocked young woman cradling Ohnesorg's bloody head. The day began with demonstrators in front of the Schöneberg City Hall protesting the state visit of the Iranian shah, a key figure in the Western anti-Communist alliance. He was also, as Iranian expellees and West German students did their best to publicize, guilty of human-rights abuses and repressing democratic reform. Inviting the shah to West Germany and to West Berlin legitimated his actions and his dictatorship. The West Berlin authorities responded to the planned demonstration with a major police presence. When shah supporters (mostly agents of the Iranian secret police) attacked the demonstrators, the police did not protect them but instead joined in the assault. Later that day, police brutally broke up demonstrators awaiting the shah's arrival outside the city's opera house. In the course of the ensuing chaos, under circumstances that have yet to be fully explained, Ohnesorg was shot in the head by the plainclothes police officer, Karl-Heinz Kurras (who we now know was a Stasi agent). City authorities refused to acknowledge any wrongdoing and there was no serious investigation of the death. Instead, officials joined the Springer Press in blaming the violence on the students and Kurras was twice exonerated by the courts despite glaring inconsistencies in his and corroborating testimonies.

To understand the fear and anger that Benno Ohnesorg's death sparked within certain segments of the population one must again recall the pervasive presence of former Nazis in West German institutions. Like Kiesinger, the country's president, Heinrich Lübke, was a former member of the Nazi

Party. West Berlin police commander Hans-Ulrich Werner joined the SS in 1939 and later won praise for his role in brutally suppressing "partisans" (i.e., Jews and other designated enemies of the Reich) in Ukraine. Even the city's chief of police, Social Democrat Erich Duensing, was a former career officer in the Wehrmacht known for granting appointments to old army, SS, and Gestapo comrades. For those West Germans already questioning whether civil liberties and the rule of law were safe in these men's hands— hands that, with the passage of the Emergency Laws, could legally suspend the constitutional order—the events of June 2 seemed to provide concrete evidence that they were not. Distrust of the entire West German political system grew. In Hannover, members of SDS and the emerging APO gathered to take stock.

They were not the only ones who felt shut out of the political system. Self-proclaimed patriots on the other side of the political spectrum founded the National Democratic Party (NPD) in 1964, a party that openly held up as its hero Rudolf Hess, Hitler's one-time deputy führer. By 1968, the NPD held seats in seven regional assemblies, winning entrance to four of them in 1967 alone. In 1969 the party received 4.3 percent of the national vote, not enough to pass over the 5 percent hurdle to enter the Bundestag but more than enough to fan fears of fascism's revival. The question, then, that preoccupied those gathered in Hannover and asked by students drawn into politics by Ohnesorg's death was: had the time for (armed) resistance come?

In April 1968, three events occurred in quick succession that, in retrospect, marked the splintering of the protest movement. The first was an arson attack on two Frankfurt department stores by a German literature and pedagogy student, a charismatic high school dropout, a poet, and an aspiring actor. Their attack on the stores, in addition to protesting capitalism and consumer society, aimed to shock West Germans out of their indifference to the Vietnam War. Gudrun Ensslin, the oldest of the four at twenty-eight, defended their act on moral grounds. In a claim implicating the judge—and all established authorities—she explained that her generation had learned "that speech without action is wrong." Just over one week later, a young Munich house painter with a troubled background and a connection to the NPD, Josef Bachmann, shot Rudi Dutschke; Dutschke lived another eleven years, but never fully recovered from the head wounds. Bachmann was probably acting alone; in the climate of fear and increasing paranoia, however, much of the left assumed a wider conspiracy. Specifically, they accused the Springer tabloid, *Bild*, of inciting violence, having urged its readers to "stop the terror of the young reds now!" and "eliminate the troublemakers." Some 2,000 activists descended upon the West Berlin publishing house; riots broke out across the FRG and in cities like Amsterdam and Paris.

Though the weekend's violence was largely limited to the destruction of property, it revealed activists' fundamental disagreement over the way forward. Ulrike Meinhof, a columnist for the popular leftist magazine, *konkret*, praised the Frankfurt arson and the Easter riots for moving beyond protest to actively resist that which protesters no longer wanted to occur; she joined others in describing demonstrators' willingness to hit back—to counter violence with violence—as a therapeutic first step toward Germans' emancipation from their traditionally slavish disposition. The majority of activists, though sympathetic to the frustration and sense of urgency motivating the calls for increased militancy, rejected it. The APO and SDS dissolved. Some redirected their energy and optimism onto Willy Brandt and his election to the chancellorship in 1969. Those too thoroughly disillusioned with parliamentary politics to follow that path pursued others: some chose to "drop out" of politics and society, to turn their energies on fixing themselves; others formed small Communist splinter groups, so-called K-groups, committed to the doctrines of Mao, Trotsky, or Lenin; while students and intellectuals who rejected that path established their own "undogmatic" circles. Lastly, others, the Frankfurt arsonists and Meinhof among them, continued what they saw as the fight against fascism. They went on to terrorize 1970s West Germany in "urban guerrilla movements" such as the Red Army Faction (RAF) and 2nd of June Movement (the latter's name a reference to Ohnesorg's killing).

Other fissures existed within the movement, too, which contributed to the disorganization and disintegration at the end of the decade. Arguably, they also contributed to its lasting legacy in the decades to come. For years, SDS women expressed frustration with the group's male-chauvinist culture; many admitted to feeling silenced, relegated to secondary positions, and cajoled into sex by comrades' accusations of frigidity. Topics like childcare and abortion rights were dismissed as women's issues: the revolution promised to end discrimination and gender inequalities. Women themselves did not necessarily disagree with this; for many who helped birth the autonomous feminist movement of the 1970s, the move from their home in SDS to feminism was painful, if also necessary to finding their voices. Similarly, the gay liberation movement emerged from the left protest circles in the 1960s but would not come into its own until gay activists, too, split from the antiauthoritarian movement to pursue gay liberation outside of class revolution.

Further reading

Brown, Timothy Scott. *West Germany and the Global Sixties: The Anti-Authoritarian Revolt, 1962-78*. New York: Cambridge University Press, 2015.

Connelly, John. *From Enemy to Brother: The Revolution in Catholic Teaching on the Jews, 1933-1945*. Cambridge, MA: Harvard University Press, 2012.

Doering-Manteuffel, Anselm. "Turning to the Atlantic: The Federal Republic's Ideological Reorientation, 1945-1970." *Bulletin of the GHI Washington 25* (1999), 3–21.

Heineman, Elizabeth. *Before Porn Was Legal: The Erotica Empire of Beate Uhse*. Chicago: University of Chicago Press, 2011.

Herzog, Dagmar. *Sex after Fascism: Memory and Morality in Twentieth-Century Germany*. Princeton: Princeton University Press, 2005.

Ruff, Mark Edward. "Clarifying Present and Past: The Reichskonkordat and Drawing Lines between Church and State in the Adenauer Era." *Schweizerische Zeitschrift für Religions- und Kulturgeschichte* 106 (2012), 257–79.

Schildt, Axel and Detlef Siegfried, eds. *Between Marx and Coca-Cola: Youth Culture in Changing European Societies, 1960-1980*. New York: Berghahn Books, 2006.

Seefried, Elke. "Reconfiguring the Future? Politics and Time from the 1960s to the 1980s." *Journal of Modern European History* 13 (2015), 306–16.

Seefried, Elke. "Steering the Future: The Emergence of 'Western' Futures Research and Its Production of Expertise, 1950s to early 1970s." *European Journal of Futures Research* 2 (2013), 15–29.

Slobodian, Quinn. *Foreign Front: Third World Politics in Sixties West Germany*. Durham: Duke University Press, 2012.

Thomas, Nick. *Protest Movement in 1960s West Germany: A Social History of Dissent and Democracy*. Oxford: Berg, 2003.

Varon, Jeremy. *Bringing the War Home: The Weather Underground, the Red Army Faction, and Revolutionary Violence in the 1960s*. Los Angeles: University of California Press, 2004.

Whisnant, Clayton J. *Male Homosexuality in West Germany: Between Persecution and Freedom, 1945-69*. New York: Palgrave Macmillan, 2012.

Wittmann, Rebecca. *Beyond Justice: The Auschwitz Trial*. Cambridge: Harvard University Press, 2005.

5

Behind the Wall: East Germany on a new path

FIGURE 5.1 *Woman looking through a hole in the Berlin Wall, October 1, 1961.*
(The LIFE Images Collection/Robert Lackenbach/Getty Images)

The Berlin Wall defused the city's potential as a site of Cold War conflict at the same time as it consolidated East Germany's claim to be a viable, lasting state. Internally, closing the border also halted the drain of labor to West Germany, and cut off the option of those dissatisfied with the regime to exit the country. After overseeing the construction of the Wall, Ulbricht directed a new wave of economic reforms that sought to stabilize and develop the country's economy, which was accompanied by a short-lived period of openness in the arts. After 1965 and the fall of Soviet premier Nikita Khrushchev, however, conservative leaders in both the GDR and Soviet Union worked to halt the economic reforms and to reinstate ideological conformity. The East German government's support for the Warsaw Pact invasion of Czechoslovakia in August 1968—less than thirty years after the Nazi invasion—made clear the limits to both economic and cultural reform. By the end of the 1960s, East German youth began to emulate the blue jeans, long hair, and rock music of the West, just as the man who would become the Socialist Unity Party's second general secretary and East Germany's second head of state, Erich Honecker, began plans to unseat Ulbricht. He did so with Moscow's help, out of a mutual desire to undo recent reforms and to return centralized planning and control to the GDR.

With the Wall in place, the Socialist Unity Party leadership hoped for stability. Now the country would no longer lose its skilled workers to the West. Now socialism could finally develop on its own foundations. Such was the hope. First, however, the police and Stasi concentrated on quelling any potential unrest due to the construction of the Wall, their expressed goal being to neutralize the "enemies of socialism." Almost 20,000 people were arrested for political crimes in the second half of 1961, some placed in new "labor camps" aimed at "reeducating" the inmates to carry out productive work.[1] The clampdown lasted for only a few months, and met no active protest.

Second, the Wall itself required reinforcement. Over the next few years, the hastily constructed barrier of concrete and barbed wire evolved into an external wall, internal wall, guard towers, and what became known as a "death strip" in the middle. After 1975, the entire system was rebuilt and reinforced, at great cost. Since the Wall went directly through the city, and often through neighborhoods, the process required the removal of people and destruction of houses immediately on the border. The long, 866-mile border between East and West Germany itself saw a similar construction project, already begun in the early 1950s but reinforced starting in the late 1960s. Here, to save labor, mines and anti-personnel explosive devices triggered by tripwires made crossing the border deadly. In the middle of the city, by contrast, armed guards had the task of shooting those seeking to flee the republic. More than 100 people died in the attempt to cross the Berlin Wall, and many hundreds more died on the long border between East and West Germany. The GDR/FRG border cut through existing populations as well. In some cases, entire villages were removed; in others, walls barred settlements from the border itself, and windows facing the border were bricked up. People living near the border experienced additional surveillance and controls.

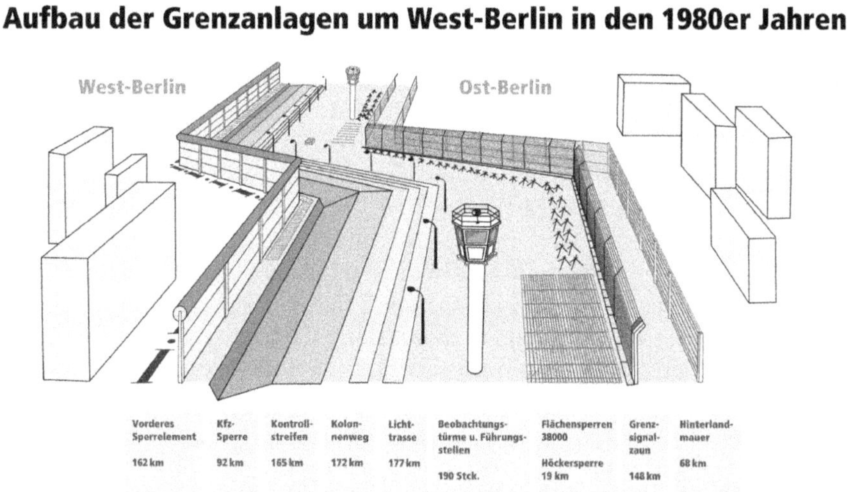

Aufbau der Grenzanlagen um West-Berlin in den 1980er Jahren

Vorderes Sperrelement	Kfz-Sperre	Kontroll-streifen	Kolon-nenweg	Licht-trasse	Beobachtungs-türme u. Führungs-stellen	Flächensperren 38000	Grenz-signal-zaun	Hinterland-mauer
162 km	92 km	165 km	172 km	177 km	190 Stck.	Höckersperre 19 km	148 km	68 km

FIGURE 5.2 *Sketch of the security and surveillance reinforcements made to the (state) border between East and West Berlin. From left to right, the boxes indicate the elements of the security system: (A) Outer barrier wall [facing West Berlin]; (B) Motor vehicle barrier; (C) Supervision strip; (D) Passage for convoys; (E) Floodlights; (F) Observation towers and command posts, 190 units; (G) Surface barrier [Flächensperre; actually a mat of steel spikes, called "asparagus patch" by GDR soldiers and "Stalin grass" by West Berliners] and anti-tank barriers; (H) Signal fence [equipped with electric alarms]; and (I) Interior wall. (Ralf Roletschek/ Wikimedia Commons)*

The Wall, however brutal, successfully stabilized the GDR. Just as West Berlin remained part of the capitalist West because of direct US guarantees of its security, East Germany's system remained predicated on Soviet support. But for the time being, party leaders could breathe a sigh of relief. With the country's existence secured, the labor force stabilized, the never-ending irritation of West Berlin partially removed, they could focus on getting their house in order. The last great era of economic reform in the GDR began in 1963, initially dominated by a new generation of technocratic elites rather than party officials. Alongside the economic reforms, cultural life soon opened up as well—although limits appeared quickly. The entire society, meanwhile, entered into a process of transformation and "normalization"—which brought with it all sorts of new problems for the regime by the end of the decade.

The New Economic System of Planning and Management (NÖSPL): Contradictory reforms

State socialism took different forms at different times. Indeed, the history of the Soviet Union itself included moments of extensive market freedoms within an overall socialist framework such as the New Economic Policy (NEP) of the 1920s, as well as moments of direct state control. Previous East German reformers invoked the NEP in the 1950s, only to be silenced. Now, however, the time had come for a decentralizing socialist reform, one that would shift many decision-making powers to individual firms in order to focus their attention on decreasing costs and increasing efficiency, in East Germany and across Eastern Europe.

These reforms may have made sense in economic terms. But they ran up against a basic fact: both as a matter of ideology and as a matter of real power, the party claimed control over the economy. Decentralizing or market reforms necessarily meant diminishing the party's authority. A basic tension was therefore present in any attempt to reform the economic system.

In the 1960s, the Soviet Union itself experienced a new round of discussions of economic reform, as Khrushchev sought new ways to unleash what he believed were the great potentials of state socialism. Using the modern sounding language of systems-theory and cybernetics (also popular in the West), Soviet economists presented alternatives to the cumbersome, inefficient, and often corrupt planning system in place. Underneath the fancy language of higher mathematics and computer modeling, the reformers called for decentralizing economic decision making and permitting a greater role for markets, prices, and profits.

Across Eastern Europe, party leaders responded to this new opening with plans for some form of decentralized economy. In so doing, they were not just responding to a cue from the Soviets; they were responding to problems of inefficiency, waste, and lack of innovation that had appeared in their own countries, as noted by their own economists.

The party remained, however, dominated by leaders committed to the kind of planning that they had learned about in the Soviet Union. Ulbricht looked outside of this cohort to find his new allies, in men who were both younger and less part of the party apparatus. Erich Apel and Günter Mittag, both technical experts and both under 50, rose to positions of economic authority in 1962 and 1963, and both owed their rise to Ulbricht. The two developed a new approach to the economy. Despite the opposition of some conservatives in the Politburo, Ulbricht proclaimed the New Economic System of Planning and Management (NÖSPL following its German initials) in summer 1963. The word "system" implied the height of modern, scientific economics; the word "management" stressed the central role of the leaders of individual firms, rather than central planners. The reform aimed at decentralizing economic decision making—and, even if not intended as such, decentralization meant shifting power away from party to manager.

The reformers hoped that more authority for managers would lead to a more flexible and more efficient economy. For that to happen, though, managers had to have incentives to improve their firms. Profit came back in as a factor: at issue was not whether a shoe company produced a lot of shoes, but whether anyone bought the shoes, and the more profit a company could make from selling desirable goods, the more money for reinvestment, wages, and bonuses. Profit plus decentralized management would both create an incentive to use labor and materials efficiently, and enable managers to take action toward this end. These economic levers required one further component as well: prices that reflected demand and were not set on political grounds. Otherwise, managers could avoid the incentives by lobbying planners for better prices.

Price reform puts the essential paradox of the reform in East Germany (and in the other People's Republics) into stark relief. The purpose of state socialism was to guide the economy to produce the goods necessary for society. But prices that fluctuated according to the whims of demand would have shifted that power to consumers. A free market would have implied something other than the planning of both production and consumption at the heart of the Marxist-Leninist tradition.

Shifting from production targets set centrally to production oriented toward "profits" on the basis of prices was a difficult task. Freely set prices had not existed in eastern Germany since the late 1930s. Prices that were too low could harm decent firms, while prices that were too high could help problem companies. For that reason, East Germany implemented its price reforms in stages, starting in 1964. Every change brought pain. And since the party claimed ultimate control over the economy, it was held responsible for the pain. As the irritations increased, so did the voices of those critical of reform in the party leadership. Pressure increased on the reformers. On December 3, 1965, Apel committed suicide. Many factors may have contributed to his decision, including the declining power of his reform. Just as certainly, however, rumors circulated about the "actual" cause of his death and its relationship to the reforms for years afterwards. With his demise and the rise of the conservatives around Erich Honecker, the reforms petered out.

Ulbricht had not given up, however; instead, he shifted his ideas about reform. Now he focused his attention on science and technology. Already the NÖSPL included funding for game-changing technological advances. Now that became Ulbricht's primary focus. Through investments in scientific research and development, the GDR would be able to overtake the West without actually catching up with it economically; technology would permit the properly organized state-socialist economy to leapfrog over Western economies to form an Economic System of Socialism. Socialism was no longer a brief stop on the path toward communism; it now became a separate, stable, lasting socioeconomic formation based on the predominance of science, technology, and economic planning.

A good part of the Economic System of Socialism sounded like well-worn propaganda. But Ulbricht believed in what he said. The party would now have the role, in connection with technical experts, of determining which investments would determine the structure of the economy itself—deciding where resources should flow to transform the economy. Chemicals, electronics, and data processing headed the list of potentially transformative technologies.

The number of structure-determining tasks grew rapidly, totaling some 160 by 1968, and planners allocated a disproportionate amount of investment into these areas. Other industries, such as clothing, remained neglected. Long-term planning became more and more adventurous by the end of the 1960s, supposing that the gains through technological breakthroughs could lead to increases of productivity of upwards of 10 percent a year, far higher than what the West experienced. These projections soon proved unrealistic.

Except for 1966–67, when West Germany experienced its first postwar recession, East Germany's growth rate lagged behind that of the West. Certainly the GDR saw real increases in the East German standard of living; these were, however, accompanied by images of new commodities in the West, from jeans to appliances to audio recordings, seen on television. Consumers' expectations increased. By 1969, the overall plan was acutely unbalanced—it assumed materials and products that were not actually available. The results were apparent to consumers, as items from batteries to underwear became unavailable in the stores. Even more worrisome, the planners increasingly had to rely on supplies from the West to deliver the parts and machines necessary for their own hoped-for technological breakthroughs. East Germany was not alone; the more industrialized members of the Council for Mutual Economic Assistance faced similar problems. But as a result, East Germany's bloc partners could not always deliver what East Germany needed. The West, and especially West Germany, remained a vital trading partner. But reliance on the West called into question the entire state-socialist project of breaking away from Western capitalism to create a new and different economy and society.

The economic reforms of the 1960s were thus filled with paradoxes. Nonetheless, the actual gains of the economy over the decade were substantial: The number of families with refrigerators increased from 6.1 percent to 56.4 percent (in the FRG, 65 percent of families owned refrigerators in 1965) and the quantity, quality, and variety of food rose steadily. The number of homes with televisions increased from 18.5 percent to 73.6 percent. And, in "new socialist towns" like Hoyerswerda, the regime now embraced modernist architecture and threw up its first prefabricated housing blocks, the *Plattenbau* developments for which the GDR later became famous. Each apartment was compact, well-lit, and outfitted with modern kitchens and bathrooms, though the structures themselves were ugly and often poorly built, and the apartments too small for larger families. Consumer goods were likewise overpriced, quality was often low, and supply could not keep up with swiftly rising demand. But the gains were real.

Literature between propaganda and experiment

Attempts to reform the economy revealed a basic tension. On the one hand, the party claimed to command and direct production. On the other, it sought to use the "mechanisms" of profit, price, and market to reach these goals—mechanisms that, if they were to work, were beyond party control. A similar tension appeared in the world of high culture. The GDR leadership set great store by its claim to represent the "better Germany," the Germany of anti-fascism and of creative and critical intellectuals. The quality of GDR literary production, represented by Brecht, Seghers, and Heinrich Mann, reflected on the GDR itself. But at the same time, the party claimed to be able to organize and direct the process of creating a new, socialist society. How could party control be squared with its need for the first generation of original East German intellectuals?

For Ulbricht, industrial transformation was primary: socialist culture should be part of the process of transforming production and vice versa. Joseph Stalin was wont to praise writers as the "engineers of the human soul," and Ulbricht agreed. With this in mind, he had proclaimed his Ten Commandments of Socialist Morality in 1958, which, like the *Jugendweihe*, aimed to break churches' moral and social presence by establishing a secular (or even: post-Christian) code of ethics. Cooperation, loyalty, cleanliness, decency, order, diligence, frugality, and respect for the family—Ulbricht understood these to be the values of both industrialism and socialism. One year later, the cultural leadership of the party proclaimed a new literary movement, named the Bitterfeld Way after the chemical-producing city. Their aim was a union of artistic, industrial, and agricultural production, but the initiative produced more of the same old stories of workers overcoming obstacles before becoming integrated in the grand project of socialist production: a dialectical process of conflict, challenge, overcoming, and resolution. When the new, moralizing stories became innovative and critical, intellectuals became a problem for the Socialist Unity Party. The playwright Heiner Müller, for example, brought the contradictions of socialism in real life into his work. A student of Brecht, Müller was aware of the explosive potential of irony and the dialectic. Over the late 1950s, Müller developed a drama about the forced collectivization that had created so many emigrants to the West, entitled *The Resettler, or Life in the Countryside (Die Umsiedlerin oder Das Leben auf dem Lande)*. On the surface, the story fit with socialist realism: the new farmers face the challenge of a radically different approach to production and individuals who refuse to accept change, and will eventually embrace the socialist way. But the contradictions that Müller drew were arguably too realistic for the party leadership. The freeloaders are too bold, and the disconnect between the party leadership and reality on the ground is too glaring. The contradictions, moreover, are never fully resolved, they fester. Suddenly socialist realism became a means of describing the real problems of socialism. An adventurous but ill-fated group of students at the School of Economics in Karlshorst, an institution aimed at creating party elites, sought to perform the play in September 1961, just weeks after the erection of the Berlin Wall. The students quickly found themselves under interrogation, one was jailed, and Müller's plays were not performed in East Germany again until 1969.

LOCAL SOCIALIST UNITY PARTY POLITICAL REPORT ON PERFORMING A PLAY BY HEINER MÜLLER, 1961

In this play the origins of the GDR are falsified and represented as the result of the influence of the Soviet occupation authorities—as an "export from the East," a transfer of foreign examples. In it, party and state functionaries are portrayed with disdain, the farmers as reactionary, dumb, and dull, and the alliance between workers and farmers contorted. Furthermore, the piece contains not-to-be-repeated obscenities and its depiction of women is an absolute insult. It is in essence anti-humanist, without exception all of the characters appear as caricatures (which is already clear by the names of the main figures: Cattle Driver, Heretic, Looter, Debt-Collector, and so on); there is no positive character in the entire play. The political carelessness that emerges in this case proves above all that the necessary conclusions have not been drawn from the measures taken on August 13, 1961 [i.e. the construction of the Wall] and from the new situation. . . . The comrades have not understood that even cultural activity is an important tool of political education, and that class struggle intensifies above all on ideological terrain.

Source: "Report on the Lapses at the College for Economics," October 9, 1961, from Landesarchiv Berlin C Rep. 902 Nr. IV/7/049-9, pp. 2, 9. Reprinted with the permission of the Landesarchiv Berlin

Just as in the realm of economics, however, restrictions on cultural expression began to lift in the years after the Wall was built. In 1963, the party announced that youth should enjoy more freedom to participate in political discussions and to express themselves. New works began to appear that addressed the themes of a society now twenty years beyond wartime: personal relations and everyday life in an East Germany that lived behind the Wall. The best known of these, *Divided Heaven* by Christa Wolf, combined the personal and the political: a failing romance plays out in the context of the division of Germany, and the heroine decides not to follow her ex-lover to the West. The book was received with enthusiasm in West Germany (where it was also published) but not in the East, where the heroine's attempted suicide was deemed too negative. Wolf had intended to write a book both complicated and in support of socialism. The poet and singer Wolf Biermann had a similar experience. Like Wolf, Biermann was committed to the socialist project but, unlike her, the regime already distrusted him because of his nonconformist beliefs. Nonetheless, Biermann was able to perform widely, in both East and West Germany, starting in 1963. In 1964, his first album appeared in the West. The opening track, "There's no Party without the Beer

Man," that is, Biermann, showed his wicked sense of humor, as he made fun of the "excited Stalinists who pissed on my leg." Biermann's connection to the counterculture, openness to Western music and Beat poetry, and frank sexuality went far beyond what the prudish party leadership could stand.

The moment of cultural openness came to an abrupt end at the Eleventh Plenary Session of the Central Committee in December 1965—just a few weeks after Apel's suicide. The up-and-coming Erich Honecker condemned recent literature and film in the GDR for its "nihilism" and "skepticism," and the way it called into question the grand goals of socialism and the place of the party. The criticism was not just political. Honecker and others were also offended by what they saw as "pornography" in the work of Biermann and others. Honecker's remarks sound more like those of a cultural conservative than a radical: "Our GDR is a clean state. The standards for ethics and moral, for decency and morality, are set in stone." Only one participant in the conference, Christa Wolf, then a candidate for membership in the Central Committee, dared to confront Honecker with what she called the "emptiness" of life under state socialism, the real cause, she held, of youth "immorality." Notably, though, she agreed with the characterization of sexuality and complexity as "immorality." After the conference, works by Heiner Müller, contemporary novelist Stefan Heym, and others were banned. The Central Committee itself banned performances by Wolf Biermann in the GDR—although he could continue to perform in the West.

The party's ideal socialist novel was a melodrama, focused on production, with a happy end for both party and socialism. *A Trace of Stones* by Erik Neutsch, a sprawling 1964 novel about a love triangle at a construction site, seemed to embody these qualities. The setting is a new chemicals plant, requiring thousands of workers to build. Not all of the workers are yet committed socialists: Hannes Balla, for example, leads a brigade of skilled carpenters openly scornful of the party, even anarchistic in their approach to the world. But the new party secretary, Werner Horrath, sees the need to win Balla over to his side. At the center of the story is Kati Klee, a young female engineer whom both Balla and the married Horrath love. When Klee becomes pregnant, Horrath abandons her to save his career—and thus to serve the larger social good. As the book ends, the previously scoffing Balla develops a commitment to socialism and the completion of the construction site; personal problems are set aside for the big task at hand.

Neutsch was a committed supporter of the GDR. But his book, too, came under fire at the Eleventh Plenary. At the same time, a film version of the book was being prepared, which cast the popular actor Manfred Krug as Balla. The movie was released in 1966, but only to a handful of small movie houses. Organized groups of young party members broke up the showings, and the film was withdrawn from the public, only to be shown again at the end of 1989 as the GDR itself collapsed. Once more, complexity and contradiction turned out to be too much for the cultural police. A source of particular complaint was the fate of the heroine Klee: in the film, she leaves the town to find another life elsewhere, as socialism cannot resolve her pain at being abandoned. And as Minister of Culture Klaus Gysi complained, the representative of the party—Horrath—was not a moral character, and therefore the party itself seemed merely a neutral institution, "rather than the guiding light of development."

In short, official GDR culture had a hard time accepting the potentially tragic divergence between politics and life. As official propaganda acclaimed the "scientific-technical revolution" that would resolve all pressing human issues, GDR writers took a different direction. Heiner Müller by the late 1960s entered into a deep and often violent engagement with the irresolvable conflicts of ancient Greek tragedy. Christa Wolf's *Quest for Christa T.* (1969) turned inward, investigating the role of memory, of unrealized futures, and of meaning in individual lives that reached beyond what socialist or capitalist systems could address. In 1969, Jurek Becker published his Holocaust novel, *Jacob the Liar*. Set in the Jewish ghetto of Lødz, where Becker himself had been as a child, the novel broke with the official history of the glorious liberation of the East by the Red Army. The main character, Jacob, claims to have a radio that tells about the imminent liberation of the ghetto by the Red Army. That army never arrives and Jacob is forced to confess his lie, as the people of the ghetto are deported to the death camps. Becker does not resolve the wound of the Jewish genocide but rather leaves it open in what remains one of the most moving tales of the Holocaust. Official histories of National Socialism in the GDR downplayed the specifically Jewish aspect of the killings in order to focus on a grand story of anti-fascist, especially working class, resistance. Becker's book, however, rejects that very move. It focuses on the suffering of the Jews and refuses to fold it and the Holocaust into a universal narrative of postwar political redemption.

Becker, Müller, and Wolf, like so many GDR intellectuals, were not opposed to state socialism, and indeed embraced it as a system that would resist resurgent fascism and continue to strive for a more egalitarian society. Their works were far more available in West Germany than in East Germany, however. The party leadership sought to use these writers and musicians to bolster support, even if critical, among the intellectuals of the West, while at the same time trying to protect GDR citizens from the complexities and contradictions described in the works themselves. The result was a complicated, and ultimately unsustainable balancing act between dictatorship and cultural expression.

East German Society: Normalization and change

Time and again the biggest threat to the Socialist Unity Party and its policies seemed not to be its outright enemies but people from within its own ranks. Robert Havemann, for example, was a noted chemist with an impeccable political history: a Communist in the late Weimar Republic, arrested by the Gestapo in 1943 for resistance activities and condemned to death, he was saved only because the Nazi state needed his expertise. Havemann was dedicated to the GDR, and until 1963 worked secretly for both the Soviet KGB and the Stasi, delivering reports on his fellow scientists. But starting in 1956, he began to give lectures that addressed the failure of the GDR's leadership to come to terms with Stalinism, and used his own profound knowledge of Marxism to cast doubt on the official Marxism of the party. Worst of all, he published his Marxist criticisms of the GDR in West Germany. Even when he was removed from his university position in 1964 and eventually put under house arrest, Havemann continued to publicize his dissent until his death in 1982—thanks to his FRG contacts. The party's attempt to quarantine one of their own failed.

But most of society did not consist of intellectuals. By the end of the 1960s, East German society had lived for two decades with mass organizations, the parades celebrating May 1, the international labor day, and the interminable speeches of state socialism. Younger people had adjusted to a polity that demanded the appearance of consent in return for access to higher education and social advancement. Older people adapted, or at least learned to keep their heads down. The youth of the 1960s, however, found before them a polity and a society that claimed to speak in their name, but that was ruled by men who had come of age in the 1920s and 1930s. Just as in the West, the stage was set for generational conflict. The regime was aware of this potential, and issued a communiqué in 1963 calling for more responsibility to be given to youth. The party followed up with education reforms in 1965 that opened up more opportunities for professional careers, at least for those who conformed politically.

A dictatorship that claimed not to merely represent the people but to be the people had a problem, after all: How to integrate the masses into politics? how to ensure that the people did not just become passive? One way was to improve dialogue between the state and society, which the Socialist Unity Party attempted by holding a number of controlled discussions on sensitive policy issues. In 1962, the GDR held a conference on East Germans' national status. In 1965, the Ministry of Justice circulated a new draft of the family code, encouraging public discussion. And in 1968, the party solicited feedback on its new constitution. That same constitution elevated the right to petition, previously anchored in Article 3 of the 1949 Constitution, by establishing it as one of East German citizens' most fundamental civil liberties, closely connected with the right of codetermination and participation in the affairs of state and society.

The topics for public discussion point to the importance of law in normalizing everyday life in East Germany. In 1967, the government revised the citizenship law: now GDR citizens received a passport declaring them "citizens of the GDR" rather than "German citizens." While the goal of German unification was never officially given up, in fact the GDR leadership was hoping for a uniquely East German sense of national belonging. If the new citizenship law peered optimistically into the future, many of the decade's legal reforms simply attempted to catch up with the present. They sought to develop institutions aimed at coherence and efficiency within one state, not unification.

Most important, the new legal codes were to reflect the realities of socialist society. The new family law of 1965, for example, reconfirmed the equality of the sexes as well as gender and family relations already established by decrees, court rulings, and East German women themselves. By 1962, 72.2 percent of all employable women had a job, including almost 70 percent of married women (this in comparison to 49.7 percent of working-age women in the FRG). Whether single or married, women continued to be overlooked for leadership positions and overrepresented in the service and light industries. And they still carried the burden of housework, despite the state's expansion of childcare facilities and workplace kitchens, cafeterias, and laundry. The strain placed on women and the family was reflected in the new code's stipulation that more resources go toward sex and marriage counseling centers, institutions dating back to the Weimar Republic that proved hugely popular in the GDR from the 1960s on. The clinics served the needs of both the population and the regime, with social workers gathering information about East Germans' everyday problems at the same time they sought to ease them. Of course, "help" could be highly interventionist: counselors—and, if it got so far, divorce courts—mobilized friends and family to help repair troubled marriages. Help also took the form of self-help and sex therapy manuals that East Germans consumed just as eagerly as West Germans at the time. And, in fact, the self-help literature and sex therapy that circulated within the GDR drew heavily on the work of American sexologists like Williams H. Masters and Virginia E. Johnson and feminist scholars such as Simone de Beauvoir. This expert knowledge merged with East Germans' demonstrated willingness to discuss sex openly to create something new: an image of East Germans as less uptight and prudish than their Western, capitalist counterparts. Here, too, gender equality emerged as a distinguishing feature of socialist love and marriage, and with it expectations of mutual respect and sexual satisfaction. The revised grounds for divorce reflected this: now a marriage could be dissolved if "it lost its meaning for the spouses, the children, and therefore also for society."

The new criminal code of 1968 expressly banned retroactive legislation (i.e., laws that declared actions carried out in the past criminal), a key principle of the rule of law, and stressed the principles of prevention and rehabilitation over punishment. The code reflected the actual practices of the normal police and criminal law courts. However, it also significantly widened the range of instruments legally available to the state and the Stasi in their efforts to "protect the socialist state and social order," that is, to prosecute both political crimes and social deviance. The Stasi became in fact less openly coercive over the second half of the 1960s, not cracking down on complaints as long as they involved no group action. But its potential for repression increased as it came to rely on covert surveillance and the employment of "informal operatives" (IMs) who recorded people's conversations on any and everything. Indeed, in the 1960s the number of IMs working for the Stasi increased to more than 100,000, a new high at the time but a number that would nearly double over the 1970s. There was roughly one Stasi informant for every 150 inhabitants in the 1960s, and one for every 100 by the 1980s. It is estimated that more than 600,000 IMs in total worked for the Stasi in the period between 1950 and 1984: neighbors, fellow workers and students, family members, friends at the neighborhood bar.[2]

Most important of the reforms was the new constitution approved in 1968. The new constitution sought to describe and promote citizens' participation in the republic. Over 750,000 meetings were held with citizens across the GDR to hear suggestions. Like the Soviet Constitution of 1936, the apparent model for this process, the GDR Constitution would be able to claim mass public input. The new constitution officially enshrined basic rights, including the rights of religious faith, of freedom of thought, and of freedom of the press; it also claimed to guarantee free elections with secret ballots to elect the People's Chamber and lower level officials. The People's Chamber, it proclaimed, was the "highest organ of state" in the GDR.

The People's Chamber in fact never acted as the highest legislator in the land, but rather acclaimed what the party leadership put before it; elections were not free, and secret voting did not exist. Neither were rights protected when matters of national security, politics, and access to higher education and leadership positions were at stake. But in a central matter, the constitution expressed reality clearly. Article One stated that the GDR "is the political organization of the working people in town and country under the leadership of the working class and its Marxist-Leninist party," the Socialist Unity Party. This principle stood above all the other laws of the land. Not, however, in the sense that the party decided everything—it did not—but in the sense that if the party wanted, it could step in to take extraordinary actions. The constitution thus both declared grand rights and principles and provided a way to circumvent them.

After twenty years, the population knew how to participate in party-sponsored discussions: what kinds of statements were acceptable, which were not, and how to phrase statements. Nonetheless, within the discussions about the constitution several central and controversial themes emerged: not direct challenges to party rule, but indirect hints at discontent. First, the question repeatedly came up of why the new constitution did not enshrine a right to strike in a workers' state. Whatever the answer, the question suggested that the party did not respect the working class—and implicitly raised memories of the strikes of 1953. Work stoppages did, in fact, occur in the GDR, but remained localized and disconnected from the official Free German Trade Union Federation, whose job was to integrate the workers into the state rather than to lead strikes. Second, people repeatedly raised questions about the right to travel, restricted by the constitution to the territory of the GDR. Implicitly, the constitution denied the right to leave the country; with these questions, then, people were raising the issue of the Wall. Third, women raised issues about how the right to a job fit with the reality of underdeveloped social services for women, such as childcare facilities. As Mary Fulbrook has noted, these discussions all avoided the question of the party's special place, and focused on personal issues related to quality of life instead.[3]

It was impossible, though, to cordon one's private life off from a political system that claimed to be all-embracing. From childhood to school, from higher education to employment, boys and girls, men and women had to use the right phrases, to avoid taboo topics, and to take part in empty formalities like voting for a predetermined list of candidates. Nonetheless, social life continued to exist. State control was by no means total.

That lack of total control became especially evident as new media technologies developed. As televisions became more common, for example, so did access to West German media. Only in an area of southwestern East Germany known popularly as the "valley of the clueless" could one not receive West German television shows. In the early 1960s, the Free German Youth (FDJ) tried to reorient people's television antennae to the east or remove them. The action was a complete failure. Citizens quickly learned how to create their own antennae out of metal balconies, kitchen materials, and other ready-made structures; the members of the FDJ could not police every living room. The later dissident Roland Jahn described the odd situation that children found themselves in by the late 1960s. At home, everyone watched shows from the West, but at school or at work, everyone pretended to know nothing about them.[4] Official GDR media thus never had a monopoly over news and information, not to mention entertainment. And GDR citizens grew up practising systematic lying in public places.

The normalization of life thus posed challenges to the political regime. On the one hand, the regime needed dedicated, energetic, and innovative help from the people to create the new, socialist nation. On the other, it could not exercise complete control without stifling that energy and dedication. Workers, for example, were both supposed to follow orders and to contribute creatively to reaching goals; at the same time, they were not allowed to form autonomous organizations to represent their interests. Managers, meanwhile, faced a chronic shortage of labor, and had to do everything they could to keep workers. Under these circumstances, occasional unofficial work stoppages became possible, if not legal. Furthermore, rank and file workers, with not only little possibility for social mobility but also little chance of unemployment, were not afraid to speak their minds. In early 1963, for example, workers at the Berliner Kabelswerke were asked for suggestions on how to save energy; the management reported in alarm the proposal of some that the lights be turned off at the nearby Berlin Wall. Workers certainly came to accept the social reality of the GDR, but their potential to challenge the regime remained.

Women, too, posed a problem. The economy required their participation in the workforce—large-scale immigration was not on the agenda in East Germany as it was in the West. By 1970, East German women attained the world's highest rate of employment in an industrialized economy but the party wanted more, not as a political statement but as a response to the endemic labor shortage. At the same time, the regime feared declining birthrates and thus actively encouraged women to have children. Women complained openly and loudly of the double, even triple burden of work, home, and party life. Thus women in the workforce required more social services. Party leaders like Honecker agreed with medical professionals—and younger East Germans—that abortion reform and access to contraception were also needed. As long as Ulbricht was in power, however, changes in abortion rights and "family planning" remained unofficial and controversial.

Last but not least, there was the youth. For East Germans as for West Germans, the 1960s was the age of the Beatles and the Rolling Stones, of long hair and beards for men, of androgynous clothing styles for women. The music could not be stopped: it was available over the radio and television, and increasingly through vinyl records and tape recordings. Members of the party leadership regularly condemned these new lifestyles of the young; in some cases young men with long hair were arrested and their hair forcibly cut off. But these campaigns failed, not least since so many of the members of the Free German Youth were also participating in this youth culture.

Indeed, the party was forced to give way on cultural issues. In 1963, the Sputniks formed, a rock band influenced by the Beatles and California surf music. They soon became popular across East Germany and found outlets for their songs on the youth radio station DT-64, which began broadcasting in 1964. Hundreds of other bands started as well, causing the party concern. According to Honecker, "An excess of beat rhythms stimulates young people to extremes." In the next year, facing harassment from party and state organizations, Sputnik disbanded. But the music remained popular. DT-64 would continue to broadcast youth radio to the end of the GDR—and indeed up to the present, under its current name MDR-Sputnik.

Foreign policy in the shadow of the Soviet Union

The GDR survived because of the Berlin Wall; the final clearance to build the Wall came from Moscow. East Germany remained dependent on the Soviet Union and its foreign policy reflected that dependence. New treaties with the Soviet Union (1964) as well as with members of the Warsaw Pact drew the GDR ever closer to the East Bloc states, in military as well as in economic matters.

Dependence did not mean complete Soviet control over East German foreign policy. East Germany, after all, faced problems that were different from those of its neighbors. As one of the most highly developed industrial states of Eastern Europe, it required a relationship with Western, capitalist states to ensure supplies of both raw materials and machines necessary for its economy. Furthermore, despite all of the conflict between the two Germanys, trade relations continued to exist.

Not surprisingly, then, relations with West Germany continued to dominate the GDR's foreign policy. In 1962, the Politburo released its so-called National Document, calling for a confederation of the two Germanys on the basis of "peaceful coexistence," echoing Soviet policy. Its main effect would have been to reverse West Germany's Hallstein Doctrine (discussed in Chapter 3). But the National Document had no impact on relations; West Germany did not recognize it as a sincere offer in the first place. The Hallstein Doctrine remained in effect. And in any case, East German gestures toward German unity seemed more and more like lip service after the building of the Wall. For East Germany, the aim of establishing a socialist East German nation gradually displaced the aim of reunification.

In the end, a quickly changing world of national liberation movements and decolonization did more to undermine the Hallstein Doctrine than the GDR's 1962 initiative. In early 1963, Cuba and the GDR agreed to exchange ambassadors, and in the summer Ulbricht invited Fidel Castro to East Berlin around the same time that Kennedy was to visit West Berlin. In the end, Castro was unable to come, and the decidedly uncharismatic Ulbricht reportedly harbored a distrust in any case of the charismatic revolutionary leader and his adventurous economic policies. But the GDR did agree to work closely with Cuba to develop internal security agencies, to help it circumvent the US embargo, and to build new—and highly effective—medical and education systems. Anti-imperialism offered the GDR a way out of its international isolation.

The GDR was especially active in the Middle East and Africa. It established relations with the Mozambique Liberation Movement fighting to overthrow Portuguese rule in the 1960s, for example. And in the late 1960s, it provided training for security officers in Sudan, Ghana, Zanzibar, and elsewhere—a model extended in the 1970s to Somalia, Libya, and Syria, countries where military governments had just taken power.[5] In 1965, Ulbricht was invited to visit President Nasser of Egypt after West Germany's secret delivery of weapons to Israel become public; Nasser's power as a defender of nationalism and socialism in Egypt and leader of the Non-Aligned Movement made him a significant force in world politics. In his speech on that visit, Ulbricht referred to Israel as "an imperial outpost in Arab space," denying its right to exist. Official anti-Zionism now became a tool for currying favor with the Arab states. The trip to Egypt did not culminate in official recognition—the Hallstein Doctrine formally held. But nevertheless, as the West Germans realized, the doctrine was in fact losing its value. If the Egyptians recognized the GDR, the FRG would have a hard time breaking off its own relations with Egypt and losing its place at the diplomatic table.

Soviet reservations about Nasser did not prevent them or the People's Republics (excepting Romania) from expressing their full support for Egypt and its allies in the Six-Day War with Israel in June 1967. After the war— an abject failure for the Arab side—Ulbricht again condemned the United States, West Germany, and Israel as imperialist powers. The party once more sought to draw a clear line between anti-Zionism and anti-Semitism. For a Germany only two decades removed from the Holocaust, such oversimplification and thinking in black-and-white terms was problematic, to say the least. But Ulbricht could live with the harsh criticisms of the Social Democrats and others in the West. After its support for the Arab side in 1967 (West Germany remained neutral), the GDR soon received recognition from Egypt, Iraq, South Yemen, Syria, and Sudan. The Hallstein Doctrine was collapsing.

The GDR took strong stands within the Warsaw Pact, as well, especially in response to the brewing crisis in Czechoslovakia in 1967–68. Like the GDR, Czechoslovakia had implemented economic reforms in 1963, but unlike the East Germans, the Czechs had continued the process. By 1967, an increasingly open and contentious public sphere accompanied the ongoing economic reforms. The government suspended political censorship in February 1968; by March, party leaders were even discussing whether to eliminate the constitutional clause asserting that the Communist Party was the "leading force" in the state. Such developments gained traction when the reformer, Alexander Dubček, became general secretary in January 1968. In April 1968, he announced a new political program: "socialism with a human face."

Pressure mounted for a military intervention, led by Bulgaria, Poland— and the GDR. Ulbricht feared that political reform in one country could mean the end of the party's primacy and the end of East German socialism. Leonid Brezhnev, the Soviet general secretary and a friend of Dubček, still hoped for a political settlement. But at the same time, he drew a line against the takeover of power by any group deemed hostile to Soviet Communism. This position would later become known as the Brezhnev Doctrine, enunciated in a letter of July 15, 1968. The doctrine in essence reserved the right of the Soviet Union to intervene in any of the satellite countries in order to ensure the survival of party authority and state socialism.

On August 21, 1968, around half a million soldiers from the Soviet Union, Poland, Hungary, and Bulgaria invaded Czechoslovakia, smashing the attempt at a peaceful transformation and a different vision of socialism. East German soldiers, contrary to what was believed at the time, did not participate, despite the willingness of Ulbricht's government to do so—

probably because of the still living memory of Germany's last invasion of Czechoslovakia in 1939. After the military intervention, the official newspaper of the East German Socialist Unity Party justified the intervention as a response to "counterrevolutionary elements."

Certainly many in the GDR knew that the story was much more complicated. After all, the reports from West Germany were available with the click of a dial. The Stasi was prepared for any acts of resistance within East Germany. But although there were numerous reports of graffiti and individual complaints, no major demonstrations took place. An individual like Wolf Biermann could proclaim that "the Paris Commune is in Prague," referring to the radical, socialist, insurrectionary government that briefly ruled Paris and was violently crushed in 1871. Biermann was an isolated figure. Nonetheless, the Prague Spring was a crucial experience for many intellectuals and activists in both East and West, who came to believe that state socialism could not be reformed.

If a political breakthrough occurred it did so elsewhere: Ulbricht had helped push the Warsaw Pact into action. In the same year, as noted above, Ulbricht proclaimed the Economic System of Socialism; in the context of international relations, he seemed to be saying more, that the GDR as much as the Soviet Union could be a model for international socialism. Just as another repressive leader of the East Bloc, Nicolae Ceaușescu of Romania, was starting to act independently of the Soviet Union, Ulbricht seemed to be hinting at a stronger role for the GDR in world affairs.

The new politics of détente in the West (discussed in the next chapter) paradoxically undermined Ulbricht's claims. As the West German Government set aside the Hallstein Doctrine, toothless as it had become, other states—including other People's Republics—began negotiating directly with the West. For this reason, Ulbricht's government tried to undermine détente. A visit to Erfurt on March 19, 1970, by the new Social Democratic chancellor of West Germany, Willy Brandt, led to enthusiastic applause from East Germans; was the GDR once again under threat? But the GDR's concerns went unheeded. In the end, the Soviet Union called the shots, and the policy of détente continued.

By the late 1960s, Ulbricht's power, arrogance, and openness to the ideas of experts outside of the party bureaucracy had led to increasing discontent in the top ranks of the party. But changing leaders was a problem under state socialism. The men (all men) who rose to the top across the state-socialist countries were experts at gaining and consolidating bureaucratic power. Ulbricht's chief opponent could only be someone with a similar wide party base. This was Erich Honecker, who had opposed Ulbricht's economic reforms and called for closer relations with the Soviet Union through the 1960s. On May 1, 1971, Honecker arranged to send an associate on a secret mission to Moscow, to gain Brezhnev's consent to remove Ulbricht. With this agreement in hand, he finally confronted Ulbricht, who was forced to request that he be relieved of his duties for reasons of age.

Brezhnev did not force Ulbricht out. But his approval was necessary for Honecker to succeed. Change in the GDR was predicated on Soviet agreement.

Further reading

Augustine, Doleres L. *Red Prometheus: Engineering and Dictatorship in East Germany, 1945-1990*. Cambridge: Harvard University Press, 2007.

Biermann, Wolf. *Poems and Ballads*. Translated by S. Gooch. London: Pluto Press, 1977.

Bischof, Günter, Stefan Karner, and Peter Ruggenthaler, eds. *The Prague Spring and the Warsaw Pact Invasion of Czechoslovakia in 1968*. Lanham, MA: Lexington, 2010.

Caldwell, Peter C. *Dictatorship, State Planning, and Social Theory in the German Democratic Republic*. Cambridge: Cambridge University Press, 2003.

Childs, David, and Richard Popplewell. *The Stasi: The East German Intelligence and Security Service*. New York: Springer, 2016.

Fenemore, Mark. *Sex, Thugs, and Rock and Roll: Teenage Rebels in Cold War East Germany*. New York: Berghahn, 2007.

Gray, William Glenn. *Germany's Cold War: The Global Campaign to Isolate East Germany, 1949-1969*. Chapel Hill: University of North Carolina, 2003.

Ludz, Peter. *The Changing Party Elite in East Germany*. Cambridge, MA: MIT Press, 1972.

Major, Patrick. *Behind the Berlin Wall: East Germany and the Frontiers of Power*. New York: Oxford University Press, 2010.

Müller, Heiner. *A Heiner Müller Reader: Plays, Poetry, Prose*. Edited and translated by Carl Weber. New York: PAJ, 2006.

Robinson, Ben. *The Skin of the System: On Germany's Socialist Modernity*. Palo Alto, CA: Stanford University Press, 2009.

Sheffer, Edith. *Burned Bridge: How East and West Germans Made the Iron Curtain*. New York: Oxford University Press, 2011.

Steiner, André. *The Plans that Failed: An Economic History of the GDR*. New York: Berghahn, 2010.

Trentin, Massimiliano. "Modernization as State Building: The Two Germanies in Syria, 1963-1972." *Diplomatic History* 33 (2009), 487–505.

Wolf, Christa. *The Quest for Christa T*. Translated, Christopher Middleton. New York: Farrar, Strauss and Giroux, 1979.

Wolf, Christa. *They Divided the Sky*. Translated by Luise von Flotow. Ottowa, Canada: University of Ottowa Press, 2013.

PART TWO

New beginnings, 1969–92

6

New social republics,
East and West

FIGURE 6.1 *The new Chancellery in Bonn, completed in 1976. (JOKER/Hartwig Lohmeyer)*

FIGURE 6.2 *The Palace of the Republic in East Berlin opened in April 1976.*
(ullstein bild/Messerschmidt/Getty Images)

Both East and West Germany saw important political transformations at the
end of the decade. In the FRG, the Social Democrat Willy Brandt became
chancellor with the promise to "dare more democracy" and to relax tensions
between East and West with a "neue Ostpolitik," or new policy toward
Eastern Europe. His government, a coalition of Social Democrats and Free
Democrats, also strove to reform the educational system and expand the
West German welfare state in order to empower citizens to shape their own
lives. Even before the economic crisis of 1973 and the subsequent shift in
policy, however, the project's limits were becoming apparent.

In East Germany, meanwhile, Erich Honecker took over as the leader of
the party and therefore the state, and his team immediately sought to connect
the GDR more closely to the Soviet Union. While Honecker's economic policy
returned to centralized systems of planning, his social policy went in a new
direction. Specifically, it aimed to expand the advantages of what he called
"really existing socialism," life as it was lived in the GDR at present rather than
in some distant future. While praising what had already been accomplished,

Honecker's government sought to make available more consumer goods as well as new and better housing, and expanded social rights for women.

Between 1969 and 1971, both West and East Germany experienced an important political transition. In the West, for the first time in the history of the Federal Republic the Social Democrats took over as leaders of a government coalition. With Willy Brandt as the new chancellor, two decades of Christian Democratic rule came to an end. In the East, Walter Ulbricht lost his place as party leader as the result of a carefully engineered plot organized by Erich Honecker. The break with previous administrations and spirit of progress that Brandt and Honecker both espoused drove the construction of new government buildings, buildings whose architectural style proclaimed the changed times and communicated their creators' professed values. In Bonn, a new chancellery replaced the Palais Schaumburg as West Germany's seat of government after the old building was judged too small for the offices and staff that would accompany the government's expansion of social programs. Whereas the old palace evoked a world of privilege and old social hierarchies, the new Chancellery, built in the International Style, suggested a no-nonsense administration—a government for and by the people. Helmut Schmidt, who succeeded Brandt as chancellor in 1974 and was the first to occupy the building two years later, supposedly compared its charms to a Rhineland credit union. At the same time Schmidt settled into his new quarters, the East German People's Chamber moved into the new "Palace of the Republic" on Berlin's Museum Island, where the imperial Prussian palace once stood, across from the Berlin Cathedral and next to Marx-Engels Square. The Palace of the Republic was rectilinear and featured bronze-mirrored windows and more closely resembled the modernist aesthetic of the new Chancellery than the socialist realism of Stalinallee. But whereas the new building in Bonn served exclusively government functions, its East Berlin counterpart lived up to its name by opening its doors to the citizenry for cultural and social purposes. The Palace of the Republic housed a bowling alley, a theater, numerous restaurants, a discotheque, and several art galleries in addition to two auditoriums for large assemblies.

If monumental architecture captures the self-representation and self-understanding of the new governments, the method by which both men came to power tells a lot about the nature of the countries' two political systems: in the one, change came through voting, in the other through behind-the-scenes maneuvering. In both cases, foreign policy played a big role, as well. At the same time, the parallel focus of both Brandt and Honecker on social policies—the so-called welfare state—also reveals similarities between both states. In both cases, industrial societies relied on state intervention; in both cases, social policies had political motives, either to shore up popular support for a party or for a state. As the chapter concludes, however, the differences in political and economic systems promoted two distinctly different welfare states.

Political transitions, West and East

The Social Democrats had been the number two party since the founding of the Federal Republic in 1949. During the Great Coalition of 1966–69, the party contributed to new laws resolving old questions. The 1968 Emergency Laws, for all the fears they raised, were also about regularizing West German control over internal circumstances. Similarly, the 1967 Law for the Promotion of Economic Stability and Growth gave the government the tools for economic policy already adopted by other advanced industrialized lands. The Social Democrats helped bring reform into high politics—but remained the junior partner.

That changed with the elections of 1969. The left-center Social Democrats gained 42 percent of the popular vote, which translated into 45 percent of the representatives in the Bundestag. This was far from a "win," given that the conservative Christian Democrats secured almost 49 percent. But it did mean that the Social Democrats' political strategy over the 1960s had paid off. They had adopted parts of the Christian Democratic program to increase their own popularity, and combined them with a call to overturn politics-as-usual at home and abroad. Delivered by the charismatic Willy Brandt, it was a message of change with widespread appeal that propelled the Social Democrats across the 40 percent mark and made a coalition government against the Christian Democrats possible for the first time. Neither the newly formed German Communist Party (the DKP in distinction to the banned KPD) nor the right-radical National Democratic Party were able to cross the five percent hurdle required to be represented in the Bundestag, leaving only the liberal Free Democrats, with 6 percent of the representatives, alongside the two dominant parties. But that 6 percent was just enough to present political elites with a choice: they could continue on with a Great Coalition (CDU/CSU + SPD) representing almost 90 percent of the popular vote, or form a new coalition of Social and Free Democrats in control of just 51 percent of Bundestag seats.

As noted in previous chapters, progressive and conservative impulses lived side by side in the Free Democrats, often leading to internal dissent. But just like the Social Democrats, the Free Democrats also saw a new generation of reformers rise up through its ranks, propelled to the top by the party's exclusion from government in 1966 and the soul-searching that followed. Its new leader, Walter Scheel, sought a new approach in foreign policy, and gathered behind him a socially liberal section of the party; they were willing to endorse Willy Brandt's ambitious proposals for domestic reforms and an opening of foreign relations with the East. A Social-Liberal coalition—a coalition of Social and Free Democrats—formed. And for the first time in the country's twenty-year history, the Christian Democrats did not lead the government.

Willy Brandt's inaugural declaration of October 28, 1969, equivalent to a state of the union address, gave a message of youth, renewal, and reform. He proposed to lower the voting age to eighteen, consciously embracing the politically active student movement. He called for more freedom and more responsibility, in the realm of culture as well as economy. He called for updating and reforming both marriage law and criminal law in the face of a changing population. Echoing a key demand of the intellectual and sociologist Ralf Dahrendorf and the Free Democrats, he proposed educational reforms aimed at creating "citizens able to make judgments" and a "permanent learning process." He called for better social support for the old, the sick, and the physically disabled, new laws that would allow all citizens, including workers, to accumulate property, and reforms that would offer women greater opportunities and equal rights in family, work, politics, and society. Again and again, Brandt connected the concept of democracy to active intervention by the government, and to social equality—as a precondition for genuine political and legal equality. He praised the accomplishments of the last twenty years, specifically the strong institutional foundations that had been laid, but insisted that they were just that: foundations on which to build. The goal was to ensure that all citizens had an equal chance, both in their private lives and in public discussion.

In 1969, then, the Federal Republic saw the first legal handover of power on the national level, under Brandt's slogan of "daring more democracy"— an explicit jab at the immobility of the Christian Democrats. The process in the West stood in glaring contrast to the transition of power in the GDR. In East Germany, Honecker did not replace Ulbricht by way of a public process. The change in power happened behind the scenes, as Honecker conspired with other party leaders and with top Soviet leadership to undermine Ulbricht. When Ulbricht was removed from power, there was no official announcement of the reasons for it; the media simply stated that Ulbricht was ill. The People's Chamber, nominally the leading governmental body according to the constitution, played no role in the transition, nor did the more than 2,000 party delegates at the Eighth Party Congress in June 1971. They merely confirmed what had already occurred.

With Honecker as the new first secretary of the Central Committee, Ulbricht's economic reforms disappeared. Emulating a similar shift in the Soviet Union, the Socialist Unity Party now celebrated "already existing socialism." Whereas Ulbricht unwisely suggested that East Germans might teach the world a thing or two about socialism, Honecker reasserted the Soviets' leadership of the international socialist cause, a move that linked the fate of the GDR even more tightly to that of the Soviet Union. At home, Honecker consolidated his power by taking on additional functions, including commander-in-chief of the armed forces, and placing his supporters in key positions. In short, political transition in East Germany took the form of a palace coup based on connections within the bureaucracy. And while the new leadership aimed at greater popular support, it did so by announcing projects, not by exposing itself to the people's will.

The transition in the GDR involved more than changes in policy. Honecker and his allies in the Politburo took measures to minimize Ulbricht's place in the history of the GDR, removing his picture, his name from history books, and even tearing down his house in the Majakowskiring, where the ruling elites lived. The aim was not to eliminate the cult of personality, however, but to make the uncharismatic Honecker the center of a new cult. Honecker's face was everywhere. He pushed long time party leaders aside and increasingly ruled with a few close contacts, people like the economics expert Günter Mittag and the Stasi chief Erich Mielke. He approved every decision coming to the Politburo and, like Ulbricht, controlled what information reached the Politburo. The other Politburo members grumbled, and even made use of informal contacts to complain to Moscow. But Honecker used his monopoly over official information to circumvent such complaints. In 1980, for example, when the Kremlin suggested that Mittag be removed, Honecker simply did not pass the suggestion on to his colleagues.

Both East and West Germany began the 1970s with broad plans for social reform. And in both cases, these plans ran up against hard economic restraints by the mid-1970s. All internal reforms, too, took place within the system of international relations that continued to define the two separate German states. But even here, the status quo crumbled. The attention Willy Brandt gave to improving diplomacy with the East and his success in relieving Cold War tensions demonstrated that if Germans remained defined by the international arena in which they lived, they also helped define it.

Ostpolitik

The brutal reality of the Cold War underlay Brandt's new approach to Eastern Europe. Germany was divided. Both East and West Germany belonged to well-armed and effective military alliances, whose massive arsenal included nuclear weapons. The alliances guaranteed the existing border between Eastern and Western Europe, and hence between East and West Germany, and barring a massive change in this reality, Germany would remain divided.

Brandt's aim, as he stated on October 28, 1969, was to "prevent any further alienation of the two parts of the German nation." The two Germanys, he continued, should not be foreign countries to each other. Only by accepting the current reality could conditions improve through more trade and travel. And accepting reality meant dealing with both the Soviet Union and the East German government. In short, Brandt and his main adviser on foreign policy, Egon Bahr, argued for détente (an easing of tensions) and the development of friendlier relations, or rapprochement, with the Soviet Union, Eastern Europe, and the GDR.

These aims flew in the face of West German foreign policy. The Hallstein Doctrine assumed that East Germany was an illegitimate state, which could not claim to represent the German people. Advocates for the many millions of Germans expelled from eastern Europe after the war rejected both the expulsions and the new borders created at the end of the war—meaning they denied Poland's territorial integrity. Respecting these borders, however, was the prerequisite for any diplomatic rapprochement with Poland, Czechoslovakia, or the Soviet Union.

Brandt's new *Ostpolitik* came in the context of new hopes on the part of both the United States and the Soviet Union for a relaxation of tensions in Europe. The Soviet Union faced a growing challenge from China as well as an increasing awareness of the widening economic gap between the economies of Eastern Europe and the West. Soviet leaders hoped to decrease tensions in Europe in order to focus on the Asian challenge, and to open trade paths to the West. The United States, meanwhile, was preoccupied with Vietnam, and had in fact been urging West Germany to moderate its position on East Germany in the interest of détente. Both superpowers harbored a distrust of their German allies, as well. The Soviets, after all, agreed to the removal of Ulbricht in part because he seemed less committed to Soviet predominance than Honecker. The new US President Nixon and his adviser Henry Kissinger, meanwhile, who took over in early 1969, shared British and French policy makers' concerns about the Social Democrats and their potentially nationalist German-German policies. Kissinger in particular feared that *Ostpolitik* might lead to a more independent German voice in Europe, which might contradict US interests. The Western Allies therefore demanded, and received, close consultation with West Germany about its diplomatic initiatives.

Just three weeks after coming to power, Brandt and Bahr entered into negotiations with Moscow; the new foreign minister, the Free Democrats' Walter Scheel, was not far behind. On August 12, 1970, West German and Soviet leaders signed the Treaty of Moscow, which ruled out the use of force in their foreign relations. More controversially, the treaty also recognized the existing, postwar borders—including the Oder-Neisse Line dividing East Germany from Poland. The treaty implicitly recognized the existence of the GDR as well. The West German side hedged its recognition of the GDR, however, with a separate letter on German unity to the Soviet Union, which maintained a united Germany's right to self-determination. The Soviet Union acknowledged receipt of the letter without approving the principle. That receipt allowed Brandt's government to assert its ultimate goal of unifying Germany—a goal eclipsed by that of Western integration but never abandoned by the Social Democrats—while still recognizing existing borders. A juggling act to be sure, these contradictory impulses became a major talking point in the public discussions leading up to the Bundestag's required approval of the treaty.

The Treaty of Warsaw, signed on December 7, 1970, was the logical next step: a direct treaty with a land that had suffered tremendously at the hands of the Germans. The treaty explicitly recognized the territorial integrity of Germany and Poland, a major step toward relieving Polish distrust. On the same day, Brandt laid a wreath on a monument for the heroes of the Warsaw Ghetto Uprising of 1943, and fell on his knees in an apparently unscripted moment of silent commemoration. Brandt, who as a political exile bore no personal responsibility for Nazism, expressed remorse on behalf of the German nation: a major statement, which much of the world found impressive. Matters were different at home, where a public opinion poll showed that more Germans found his gesture "excessive" than supported it. And in Poland itself, some expressed annoyance that Brandt had expressed remorse before a Jewish site rather than a site honoring all Poles. The leading party paper in East Germany, *Neues Deutschland*, did not report on the event at all.

Brandt's government hoped that the Treaties of Moscow and Warsaw would pave the way for concrete improvements in the lives of Germans in both Germanys, and especially in West Berlin. Such improvements, at least for West Berliners, were not long in coming. On September 3, 1971, the four occupying powers, the United States, Soviet Union, France, and Great Britain, signed the Quadripartite Agreement to recognize the existing

FIGURE 6.3 *Willy Brandt kneeling in front of the Warsaw Ghetto Memorial on December 7, 1970, during his official visit to Poland. (STR/AFP/Getty Images)*

borders of East and West Berlin and to ensure unhindered traffic to and from West Berlin. This Agreement reduced the heat on one burner of the Cold War.

On October 20, 1971, Willy Brandt received the Nobel Prize for Peace, in recognition of his actions to lessen tensions in Europe. His opponents viewed his actions differently. Some accused him of selling out the German nation, others of opening up the FRG to serious security threats. The Christian Democrats announced that they would oppose ratification of the Treaties of Moscow and Warsaw in the Bundestag. Some members of the Free Democrats also rejected the policies of Brandt and Scheel, as did even one Social Democrat. By April 1972, the government was in crisis, and quite possibly unable to find a majority for the treaties. Under these conditions, the Christian Democrats called for a vote of no confidence on April 25, which, if successful, would have brought the Christian Democrats back into power. By all indications, the vote was set to pass—but then failed by two votes. One Christian Democratic member admitted several years later that he had received a bribe to change his vote; evidence from 2000 suggests that another member was similarly bought off. In both cases, the money seems to have come in the end from the East German Stasi. And some leading Social Democratic Party officials seem to have been aware of the bribes.

However it happened, the Social Democrats survived by the skin of their teeth. In May 1972, the Bundestag approved the Treaties of Moscow and Warsaw, after the parties agreed to explicitly reserve the final determination of borders to the period after German unification. The Social Democratic/ Free Democratic majority remained, however, unstable, and the government was unable to pass its yearly budget. Under these conditions, the ruling coalition engineered new elections, which were to be held that November. The returns revealed increasing support for the government and perhaps more specifically, for *Ostpolitik*. With a turnout of over 91 percent, the Social Democrats received more votes than the Christian Democrats, and the Free Democrats saw their support grow as well. For the first time, the Social Democrats had more seats in the Bundestag than the Christian Democrats.

For Brandt and his government, opening up diplomatic relations with the East aimed above all to bring the GDR and FRG into direct contact. Brandt had already met with GDR prime minister Willi Stoph, on March 19, 1970, in Erfurt, where an enthusiastic crowd of East German well-wishers turned out to greet him. It was a propaganda disaster for East Germany. But the GDR pushed ahead with negotiations, starting with one firm demand: any agreement depended on West Germany's international recognition of the GDR. In other words, the Socialist Unity Party called for an official end to the Hallstein Doctrine. After many difficult negotiations, the two sides agreed on the so-called Basic Treaty of December 21, 1972. Both Germanys upheld the existing borders; each agreed not to represent the other, meaning that each state accepted that the other state represented its own population; and each established a "permanent representative" in the other's state, something less than an embassy, but more than a consulate. The way was open for cooperation on economic, humanitarian, and other matters.

With this treaty, the Hallstein Doctrine became obsolete. A flood of countries established relations with both East and West Germany. In 1973, the GDR and FRG joined the United Nations, impossible before because of the veto power of the US and the Soviet Union, respectively. Now leaders in both Germanys could express their interests directly to other powers and in the UN. East Germany in particular could claim a legitimacy previously denied it and, over the course of the 1970s, the Socialist Unity Party used this to craft a sense of a particular East German (versus all-German) nation. The Christian Democrats in West Germany eventually accepted the logic of *Ostpolitik*, as new reformers took over and revamped the party over the 1970s.

But it remained controversial. Did it open the way for better relations between East and West? Or did it not simply provide new opportunities for the GDR to find access to Western currency and prop up its failing regime? Did détente promote human rights, or offer a way for the GDR to profit from its human rights violations, by selling political prisoners to the West? These are important questions, and continue to be debated. Less clear is whether an alternative was really open, once the process of détente had begun.

The primacy of social policy, East and West

Brandt's government linked reform in foreign policy to the development of a broad array of social programs at home. Honecker, while less interested in altering the international status quo, also brought social programs into the picture as a way of stimulating production and regime loyalty (made all the more important given the changing German-German relations). Digging more deeply into the social reforms in each country and their limits reveals not only where East and West Germany converged but also where the crucial differences between the two systems lay now that both were firmly established.

East and West Germany were both industrial societies. Both faced similar social challenges, and devised similar, state-run responses. Both were in this respect welfare states. In the FRG and GDR, the average citizen's livelihood depended on their working to secure a steady income. Those who could not work faced potential poverty. Most at risk were children, mothers in later stages of pregnancy or with young children, the disabled or ill, and the elderly. Advanced industrial economies, however, require educated and capable workers. If children are neglected, the result is unhealthy and uneducated workers; if women or other members of the family have to take care of children, the economy is deprived of their skills; if there are no systems of health care and rehabilitation in place, ill or disabled workers cannot return to work.

The welfare state in both East and West responded to these needs but in different ways, reflecting the differences between the political and social systems. Most important, people in the West could vote, and older people tended to vote more than younger. Little wonder, then, that the cornerstone of the West German welfare state was a generous pensions system, where people who had worked for more than forty years could count on retiring with over 60 percent of their average take-home pay; that amount was furthermore regularly adjusted to reflect overall productivity gains, so that the elderly could count on pensions often well above the poverty level. Pensions in the East were by contrast much lower. Despite several well-publicized pension increases over the 1970s and 1980s, retired workers still received less than 45 percent of their salary through their pensions. Since many workers' salaries at the start of their working life had been quite low, then, a pension based on average earnings over the course of a lifetime could amount to 20–40 percent of a worker's final take-home pay, resulting in a dramatic decline in income. By the late 1970s around half of retirees had pensions that put them at or below poverty level. And because resources remained tight, neither family members nor other non-state institutions like private or church welfare providers were able to step in and fill the gap. Being old in East Germany usually meant continued work and the ongoing threat of poverty.

The "Unity of Social and Economic Policy" in Honecker's East Germany

Honecker was a political conservative; he sought to return to old, Soviet models of centralized planning organized around the stable leadership of the party and the power of the state. When it came to social policy, however, Honecker pushed to upend the status quo. Ulbricht had prioritized investment in production, especially in heavy industry, but over the 1960s also in advanced technologies. As he repeatedly stated, "Only what has been produced can be distributed"; in practice, the slogan meant that production was primary and consumption was deferred to the future. Honecker asserted, by contrast, that social and economic policies were intertwined: providing more consumer goods and services would help prompt workers to work better and more efficiently.

The shift to social spending reflected fear, as well. Next door in Poland, price increases led to strikes in December 1970. The Polish leadership responded with massive military violence and many deaths on December 17, but the strike wave continued and spread in early 1971. Along with demands for lower prices, the strikers called for independent trade unions, contradicting the regime's claim to represent all workers—and therefore its claim to political legitimacy. For good reason, the Polish leadership feared these developments: Solidarity, the independent trade union that formed ten years later, helped usher in the end of state socialism in Poland. The

East German leadership paid close attention to these developments and for this reason the social reforms it introduced in 1971 can also be seen as a partial response to them—an attempt by the Socialist Unity Party to prevent upheaval from spreading to the GDR.

Housing formed the first pillar of Honecker's social policy. For years, East Germans had suffered from inadequate housing, with many buildings simply never fully repaired after 1945. Unlike West Germany, where governments had developed major housing programs over the first two decades after the war, Ulbricht had focused on industrial investment instead. The new housing units for which he did finally allocate money—the modern, prefabricated buildings discussed in the last chapter—were small and not near numerous enough to meet the needs of the population at large. For this reason, large families often had to make do with a few rooms, partitioned out of what had been a larger apartment. And young families found themselves forced to live with parents for years, hoping for an eventual apartment of their own. Since the state had in practice taken over the housing market, either directly or by regulating the private housing that remained, local officials made the decisions about who would receive which housing allotment. Not surprisingly, officials, privileged groups, and intellectuals floated to the top of their lists. People blamed the state for their housing problems, and swamped officials with petitions about housing problems.

For all these reasons, Honecker announced a plan to create or renovate up to three million housing units between 1971 and 1990, and set the goal of building half a million of these already during the Five Year Plan of 1971–75. Since that planning period had already begun, the housing initiative required a sudden scramble to reallocate the necessary resources. The idea was to utilize only the most efficient production method, using prefabricated blocks to build multi-story units as part of large, organized complexes of apartments. The new units would provide adequate space for a small family, as well as toilets and showers inside the apartment—a great improvement over the old and makeshift housing units that so many postwar East Germans had lived in. The apartment complexes were to fit together in the form of planned communities, with their own parks and post offices, day care centers and discos. They were designed to spur the development of a local community but some locals experienced them as cold and alienating; one nickname for the complexes was "worker refrigerators" (*Arbeiterfrischhalteboxen*). To be sure, the new housing offered new opportunities, but it also put its residents more firmly under state control. No wonder, then, that people who moved into new communities like Marzahn, on the outskirts of Berlin, felt a fundamental ambivalence.

These huge projects were not an architectural development specific to the GDR, or even to the state-socialist regimes. From New York to Paris, from Frankfurt to Cologne, architects developed similar plans for big housing projects with integrated social centers. Many of these came under

FIGURE 6.4 *Erich Honecker visiting the Grosskopf family in their new apartment in Marzahn, one of the massive housing settlements constructed following the Eighth Party Congress, July 6, 1978. (ullstein bild/ADN-Bildarchiv/Getty Images)*

fire already in the early 1970s, as local politicians lamented the destruction of downtowns, the triumph of the automobile, and the unintended consequences of big projects that marginalized populations from the rest of cities. What distinguishes the East German case was the state's continued fixation on this kind of architectural development over other approaches, and the continued financial challenge of how to pay for them.

Little money was allocated, for example, to renovating existing units, despite the State Planning Commission's calculations that renovation might be a cheaper approach to the housing shortage. Rents, meanwhile, remained low, as part of socialism's guarantee of housing to the workers. But because rents were so low, they could not pay for the cost of upkeep and renovation, necessary in old but also in newer housing. The older parts of the cities continued to slowly crumble away, or to be torn down to make way for new housing. Newer units often remained construction sites for years, with muddy fields and abandoned materials. In short, the housing program was problematic from the very start—and very expensive, as well.

Labor formed the second pillar of Honecker's social policy. The Berlin Wall had not resolved East Germany's labor shortage. And despite full employment, the economy was not booming. The system of planning contributed to economic inefficiency. Since party leaders often changed their goals in the middle of a planning period, as the example of Honecker's decree on housing production above illustrates, firm managers sought to keep on hand as many workers as they could. That way they could respond to sudden demands from above. The result was full employment in East Germany, an achievement that the Socialist Unity Party proudly advertised in contrast to the unemployment that plagued West Germany from the 1970s on. Indeed, the GDR simply abandoned unemployment insurance in 1977. But below the surface, many workers were *under*employed or were left idle while awaiting supplies. And state socialism needed a vast number of employees just to fill party offices at the local, regional, and national level, for administration, and for the state security agencies. Together, the inefficient use of labor and ballooning bureaucracy resulted in an economy that was perpetually short of laborers.

The GDR could have done what the FRG did when faced with a similar need for workers: import foreign labor. And indeed, there were work brigades in East Germany from allied countries like Vietnam. But the regime distrusted these workers and the foreign ideas that they might bring into the country, and was furthermore concerned about negative reactions to foreigners from the native German population. If for slightly different reasons, then, foreign workers in the GDR tended to live apart from Germans much as they did in the FRG. But in the GDR, the separate housing facilities that this necessitated presented an obstacle in itself—only contributing to the existing housing shortage! The populations were furthermore heavily monitored and spied upon by the Stasi, another cost. The paranoia of the East German police state and the presumed xenophobia of its population made it impossible to use foreign labor to solve East Germany's economic problems.

Honecker's government sought to solve the labor problem, then, not with foreign workers but by creating better conditions for labor. The right to work was cemented into the revised constitutions of 1968 and 1974, and during the 1970s workers' rights gradually gained legal recognition, culminating in the Labor Code of 1978. Workers made use of these rights to demand jobs that fit their qualifications and to complain about working conditions; they did not hesitate to invoke the principles of the "socialist state of workers and farmers" to get their way. The result, however, was not a more flexible and efficient workforce, but rather a culture of complaining and intervention by local courts. The government also sought to reduce working hours in the hope that workers would respond by increasing their own productivity. This did not happen, and state, party, and companies once again turned to calls for greater enthusiasm and effort in labor.

The third pillar of Honecker's social policy involved women, and overlapped with both housing and labor policy. Women had been tapped in the 1950s as an additional source of labor. As noted in the previous chapter, 60 percent of women of working age and able to work had jobs already in 1955. By 1970, that number had surpassed 70 percent and continued to rise to nearly 80 percent in 1989 (over 90%, if women who were students or in training for a job were counted), compared to around 50 percent in

West Germany. The official ideology identified women's emancipation with employment (a position that many feminists, in East and West, shared as well) and the Socialist Unity Party continued to target women for further training and education opportunities. But the freedom to work could itself feel imprisoning when women remained the ones chiefly responsible for shopping, cooking, cleaning, and taking care of children. In this way the home—still embedded in traditional gender roles—persisted as an obstacle to women's equality, at the same time East Germany's economy of scarcity made the "double burden" of homemaking even more onerous. No wonder that so many women wanted part-time jobs. No wonder, either, that factories with a majority of women workers regularly registered more sick days, as women took time off to take care of sick children. Already in 1952, Ulbricht's government had granted a "housework day" once a month for women in full-time jobs who were either married or had children. This measure must have eased women's workdays, but it also cemented into place the double burden faced by women; the house and children were women's work.

Honecker publically noted that women still bore this unequal burden in 1971 and, over the course of the decade he adopted a number of social policies aimed at lessening the social misery of women. In the previous decade, growing numbers of women had petitioned for an abortion, complaining of being physically and psychologically exhausted; already having had several children, often in quick succession and with little time off from work, many were desperate to avoid the demands of yet another pregnancy—on already too tight living quarters and childcare arrangements as well as on their bodies and psyches. Ulbricht remained unmoved, refusing even to make contraception available. But Honecker accepted the Ministry of Health's recommendation to legalize abortion in the first trimester of pregnancy. One year later, women sixteen years and older could obtain birth control pills at no cost. For many women living in the GDR—and in the FRG, too—Honecker's decisions may have seemed revolutionary, but they were in fact fifteen years behind the social policies of the Soviet Union and even Poland. Nonetheless they gave women—and men—more freedom to plan their families according to their individual needs and desires.

Evidence suggests that Honecker hoped that the liberalization of family planning policies would promote a more positive attitude among women toward socialism, and that this in turn would lead both to women's higher productivity and a higher birthrate. By 1970, the GDR's birthrate—strong just five years earlier—had begun to decline, a development that worried government leaders and should have worked against the decade's liberal marriage and reproductive policies. Without more children, the labor shortage would just worsen. Any action that enabled more women to enter the workforce full-time thus also needed to make conditions easier for women with children.

Social policy tried to square the circle. To encourage women to have children, the 1972 the regime extended the pregnancy leave to eighteen weeks. Four years later, a new policy granted mothers twenty-six weeks of paid leave for pregnancy and birth, and in the case of a second baby a full "baby year," during which they continued to receive wages. Other regulations, such as a forty-hour workweek without reduction in salary for mothers with more than one child, aimed as well at making work and family compatible. In 1972 the government offered a special, interest-free loan to married couples under twenty-six years of age, which would be partially relieved with the birth of each child. Yet problems persisted: what, after all, should happen to small children when mothers were at work? Government and firms sought to expand the day care system.

Together, these reforms contributed to the high labor participation rate for women in the GDR, and in this respect were a success. They could also be regarded as a success in comparison to West Germany, which offered far less in the way of childcare. But each new reform created new problems. First, a reform aimed at one part of the population raised cries of unfairness from those not receiving benefits. Why should only women with more than one child receive a "baby year," for example? And what about men without a wife? In 1986, reforms extended the benefit to include these groups. In addition, day care facilities not only cost money, they required employees, precisely what the economy lacked. The government never succeeded in providing adequate day care facilities for working parents, however much it tried. The result was a continual stream of petitions demanding more and better childcare.

Social reform remained a focal point for Honecker throughout his time in power, from 1971 to 1989. As the three examples of housing, full employment, and women have shown, all cost money, which the GDR did not have. The government undertook these policies to gain popular support, in order to survive. But as Chapter 8 underscores, by doing so the government undermined its own financial health and ultimate chance of survival.

Nowhere are the limits to the GDR's social policy more apparent than with respect to those who could contribute neither work nor babies: the elderly. Old age pensions went up several times between 1971 and 1989, but the minimum pensions remained abysmally low. A supplementary pension system existed that one could pay into, but the workers at the lower end of the scale were often unable to do so. And given the persistent disparity between male and female incomes, women as a result tended to receive much lower pensions than men. By the early 1980s, some 84 percent of women pensioners lived on the minimum pensions. Given that the average pension amounted to less than half of the average wage, these pensions must have been low indeed. To be elderly, then, meant to be poor. And the elderly had no effective vote. In a society with a perpetual labor shortage, the government had little incentive to assign workers to take care of the old and the disabled, who accordingly became marginalized and isolated. Conditions in homes for the elderly and disabled were catastrophic.

At the same time, close to 10 percent of the East German population enjoyed supplemental or special pensions on top of the regular ones: pensions designed to lure workers into important economic sectors like mining, or to reward the intelligentsia, or to honor the anti-fascist resistance—those who had resisted Nazism and were also loyal to the Socialist Unity Party. Members of the Stasi and other security services had their own special pensions system, as well. The pensions system, in other words, was not equal. These special pensions were not publicized, and their full extent only became known to the public after the GDR's collapse in 1989–90.[1]

But the elderly did have one privilege that the rest of the population did not: they could emigrate to West Germany with ease. There they could receive a higher quality of care at West German expense, and relieve the East German Government of the costs of care. Of course, emigration came with a personal cost far harder to quantify: the loss of regular contact with family and friends.

"An economy that offers more freedom but demands more responsibility": Social reforms in the Brandt Era

If housing topped Honecker's list of reforms in the GDR, education lay at the heart of the Social-Liberal coalition's plans to reform the FRG. By the late 1960s, almost everyone agreed on the need to increase the educational level of the German workforce in light of technological advances. And the fact that the East Germans had already initiated the far-reaching and effective reform of their educational system put even more pressure on the West German regime to do so. For Brandt and for reformist liberal intellectuals like Ralf Dahrendorf, however, the challenge went further. In a democracy, they argued, every child, no matter his or her background, should have the equal chance at an education and access to better jobs. As Dahrendorf pointed out, however, a number of social groups were significantly underrepresented in higher education, in particular the working class, women, Catholics, and southern Germans. Democracy meant offering the potential for social advancement to all social groups, not just to those already privileged.

Indeed, evermore parents demanded that their children have access to better schools and to university. To provide more access would have meant opening up the entire school system, and breaking with the existing three-track system that essentially channeled secondary school students into their future careers. In 1969, the Social Democrats proposed a radical plan to unify the three tracks into a comprehensive school from grades five to ten, and to adopt the all-day school schedule used in the United States and elsewhere, both in order to give students more exposure to teachers and to allow both parents in a family to work full-time. These radical plans aligned with some of the ideas of the influential Free Democratic politician and trained chemist and political scientist Hildegard Hamm-Brücher, who called for a comprehensive, national educational plan. She visited the GDR and the Soviet

ON MODERNIZING AND DEMOCRATIZING EDUCATION IN GERMANY: A REPORT OF THE BRANDT ADMINISTRATION, PRESENTED TO THE BUNDESTAG ON JUNE 8, 1970

We did not decide that educational policy should be a priority merely because technological progress, economic growth, and social security depend on the the effectiveness of education and research. More than that, education and science develop the individual and cultural values that are the prerequisite for the necessary humanization of technological civilization and for the survival of a free, democratic form of society.

The German educational system developed in the 19th century, not according to democratic but according to feudal [*ständisch-obrigkeitsstaatlichen*] conceptions of order and education. . . . Despite many partial reforms, this system is no longer suitable for present-day social developments. It neither contributes to the right to education, nor does it satisfy the demand for modernization and democratization. . . .

Education should enable a person to shape his or her own life. People growing up must experience the possibility of greater mobility and freedom, so that they learn to make sensible choices for themselves. Through learning and experiencing democratic values, and through insight into social development, education should create the lasting foundation for free and democratic [*freiheitliches*] coexistence. Education should awaken joy in independent, creative work.

Source: From "Bericht zur Bildungspolitik," Drucksache VI/925, Deutscher Bundestag, 6. Wahlperiode, June 8, 1970, pp. 1–2.

Union to study the successful educational reforms implemented by those two countries, but such visits caused controversy and helped build a case against reform. Plans for reform, in fact, ran into difficulties at multiple levels. First, the Basic Law reserved to the Länder essential powers over local education, and a conservative land like Bavaria, dominated by a Catholic constituency, remained distrustful of politicians in Bonn. Second, while some parents hoped for new opportunities for their children, others feared that their gifted children would not be sufficiently educated and challenged in a comprehensive system, essentially mirroring debates over "gifted-talented" programs in the United States. Despite some local experiments, major structural changes in the system were blocked. Curricular reforms, involving both sexual education and new courses on politics and society, also drew the wrath of some parents and members of the Christian Democrats. The more radical aims of the coalition at the level of primary and secondary education were not reached.

But alongside these headline-grabbing reforms, deep changes were underway nonetheless, as the percentage of school children attending the university-oriented *Gymnasium* increased from 8.6 percent in 1950 to over 15 percent in 1970, and the percentage of students attending the lowest level *Hauptschule* dropped from around 87 percent to 71 percent. The number of *Gymnasium* students rose from just under a million students in 1965 to almost 1.9 million in 1975. This change meant that in fact more children were gaining access to higher levels of education, and furthermore that the increasing number of students would begin to put pressure on West Germany's system of higher education.[2]

Already by the early 1960s, plans were underway for new institutions of higher education, and by the late 1960s major new universities had come into existence in Bochum, Bielefeld, Bremen, Darmstadt, and elsewhere. The social sciences played a key role in many of them; Ralf Dahrendorf himself was one of the founding professors at the new "reform university" founded in Konstanz in 1966, and noted social scientists and social historians found homes in other new universities. Ever more students made more teachers, more classrooms, indeed more universities necessary: the Social-Liberal coalition developed plans to create thirty new institutions of higher education between 1970 and 1980.

Brandt's government did not just aim to provide new spots for students. It sought as well to open up universities to the voices of students and teachers who had not yet achieved the civil servant status enjoyed by professors in Germany. Such had been the aim of the radical students of the 1960s, who had wanted to influence the curriculum, something traditionally determined by professors. Professors organized in response, countering student claims in the name of their own freedom and expertise. The debate that ensued, during which each side accused the other of undermining basic freedoms of the academy, persisted for more than a decade. Eventually, the Constitutional Court stepped in to assert that tenured faculty should have the dominant say over curriculum and teaching.

Underneath the heated polemics, however, the educational system was indeed transforming. By the late 1970s, women made up an ever larger percentage of the total university population, though still underrepresented in relation to men, and the disparity between Catholic and Protestant university students had sunk dramatically. For these groups, the reform years saw a real increase at an equal opportunity in education. The number of working-class students in universities remained low.[3] But the increased number of students and a downturn in the economy after 1973 shifted the debate from diversity to time, specifically the question of how to speed up the educational process. Students attending university often found themselves facing overfilled classrooms, inaccessible teachers, and requirements that seemed more attuned to conditions decades before. A tension emerged between maintaining universities oriented toward the great humanist goals of cultivating human potential and knowledge, and creating technical elites.

That tension remains unresolved—in Germany as in other industrialized countries—up to the present day.

The concept of democratizing social reforms extended to other areas as well. Both Social Democrats and Free Democrats proclaimed their goal of expanding the system of codetermination that brought worker and owner representatives together to determine company policy, for example, and in 1972, after much debate, the Bundestag approved a new—though not significantly different—codetermination law. More important, the liberals spearheaded a major reform of German criminal law, which sought to shift away from the principle of punishment for the guilty to the principle of resocialization, of finding ways to bring criminals back into normal community life. As part of the discussion, the coalition significantly altered the law regulating political demonstrations in 1970. Now political protesters could only be prosecuted in the event of violent actions, and the burden of proof lay with the state rather than with the accused. Strongly opposed by conservatives, the new law allowed demonstrators more room to protest, protected by law.

Along with the right to an equal educational chance and the right to protest, the reformers also sought to allow individuals a broader right to shape their own lives. Of special importance in this respect were laws about marriage, which, despite Article 3 of the Basic Law, had cemented gender inequality into place in West Germany. The coalition sought to equalize the position of man and woman in marriage, and to make a divorce easier to obtain. In this context, too, the government loosened criminal laws regulating pornography, adultery, sodomy, and homosexuality. Male homosexual relations with a male under twenty-one remained illegal in 1969, although lesbian and heterosexual relations with a minor fourteen years or older were not. The language and age of consent were revised again in 1973, legalizing homosexual relations for men eighteen years and older. But Paragraph 175 remained on the books until 1994, when the Bundestag finally abolished it. The GDR followed a similar course of gradual liberalization of policies regulating sexuality. It had already ceased applying Paragraph 175 in the late 1950s, and abolished it in 1969; the law that replaced it, forbidding homosexual (but not heterosexual) relations with a minor, was suspended in 1988. East and West approved more liberal laws at about the same rate. The difference in attitude to gays and lesbians did not lie on the level of state policy, but in society. And in this respect, as Chapter 8 will discuss in more detail, East Germans were less tolerant.

Abortion proved a far more difficult topic. Unlike in East Germany, where the leadership avoided open public discussion in its legalizing of abortion, in West Germany a variety of voices—liberal and socialist, conservative and Catholic—made themselves heard on the issue. The existing law, Paragraph 218, dated from 1871, made abortion a crime unless the life and health of the pregnant woman was at risk. The newly revitalized feminist movement (discussed further in the next chapter) called for the end to the law, stating "my belly belongs to me." Opposition came quickly, especially from conservatives and from the churches, which demanded protection for the unborn. More moderate conservatives agreed to exceptions in case of medical emergency or extreme psychological strain. Examples of the failure of the law to prevent abortions and the effects of illegal abortions made their way into the debate as well. The simple solution of a dictatorship—to simply declare a right or take it away—was not available in West German democracy.

The Social-Liberal coalition sought a compromise position in 1974, with a law that allowed abortions following medical consultation. Conservatives appealed the case to the Constitutional Court, which sent it back to the Bundestag with the mandate that the life of unborn children be better protected. The ultimate result was a complicated compromise in 1976, which allowed abortions in the first trimester only in cases of medical, psychological, or "social" exigency, to be determined by a medical professional. The vagueness of the term "social" meant that different doctors could give different verdicts, leading to vast differences from hospital to hospital and region to region. Handing the ultimate decision to doctors meant taking it out of the woman's hands, as well. Paragraph 218 in its reformed version remained controversial, for both feminists who demanded a clear right and conservatives who demanded more protection for the fetus.

Last but not least, old age pensions also received a boost—and in this case, the Christian Democrats and the Social Democrats worked together. Both, after all, wanted to attract elderly voters, especially given the political turbulence surrounding Brandt's *Ostpolitik*. The government initially proposed a new, flexible retirement scheme, which would have allowed workers to retire earlier; it also proposed a minimum pension, which helped that part of the population, especially women, in low-paying, nonunionized jobs. That proposal, based on the optimistic growth forecasts of 1969, would have led to a significant surplus in the pensions fund by 1985. Over the short run, however, pensions did not increase as fast as wages and salaries. Smelling a political opportunity, the Christian Democrats proposed a dramatic increase in old age pensions—just at the time that it called for a vote of no confidence in Brandt's administration. The Social Democrats responded with its own dramatic plans, including higher pensions, paid parental leave, and other measures. The Free Democrats brought its clientele into the picture, demanding that the self-employed have the right to be part of the pensions program. Housewives were granted the right to participate as well. Soon a massive new bill was looming but the government remained confident that the pension system would operate with a budget surplus.

The Bundestag approved the measure nearly unanimously, despite growing signs of a weakening economy. All the parties sought to attract voters and very few public figures questioned the financing of the new measures. In the wake of the debate, the Social Democrats' superstar economist Karl Schiller left the party in protest, and was soon seen in the company of leading Christian Democratic politicians who favored fiscal austerity.

Liberal democracy not only gave ordinary citizens a voice. In the difficult conditions of a political crisis, it contributed to a poor policy decision. The first oil crisis of 1973 already put an end to the hopes for a dramatic extension of benefits; by 1976, as economic growth stagnated and unemployment increased, the Social Democrats, now under the leadership of Helmut Schmidt for reasons discussed in the next chapter, were forced to "delay" full implementation of the pension reform.

Democracy and dictatorship

Both East and West Germany were industrial societies, and both had a significant array of social policies in place to deal with the challenges of such a society—more than one can easily present in a short chapter. Both were concerned with how to prepare children for the needs of an increasingly advanced technological society, for example, and each offered pensions for the elderly and the disabled with significantly longer life expectancies. But there were significant differences between the two welfare states as well, which reflected the differences between dictatorship and democracy.

Dictatorship did not exclude the voices of ordinary people, who could and did frequently complain about conditions in the GDR and call for reform. The petitions for housing, abortion rights, work rules, and material goods attest to the power and persistence of the popular voice. But the dictatorship only had to respond to those it needed. It needed workers; it provided rules affording them some power in the workplace. It needed women in the workplace; it provided special policies like the "house day," so that women could balance their dual load. It did not need elderly people, and so they had no meaningful vote and could not improve their living conditions. Last but not least, the dictatorship could pass a law without extensive discussion. Apart from a timid expression of concern from Protestant and Catholic churches, public discussion about the new abortion law of 1971 simply did not take place in the GDR. Fourteen members of the CDU (a bloc party subservient to the Socialist Unity Party)—some 3 percent of the normal pliant People's Chamber Volkskammer—voted against the law. In the end, a small circle of men in the Politburo made the final decision.

In the FRG, the right of free speech, competitive elections, and opposing political parties gave citizens the ability to influence legislation, which empowered some groups, such as the elderly. The fruits of liberal democracy, however, could create problems down the road. The pensions reform of 1972, for example, made little economic sense, reflecting instead each party's effort to win over important parts of the electorate for future elections. It did not surprise Karl Schiller that from 1973 on, financial problems related to pensions repeatedly plagued the government. Public discussion about abortion, meanwhile, certainly did not lead to consensus. The result instead was a complex abortion law in West Germany that remains problematic to this day. Pandering and populism are parts of representative democracies. At the same time, though, the party dictatorship of the GDR was also dependent on popular support and capable of making decisions that would harm, indeed destroy, the national economy over the long term.

Political leaders of both East and West Germany—and in the second case, both left and right leaning—made a similar error, however, in their assumption that high growth rates would persist. Already in 1974–75, the new Social Democratic chancellor Helmut Schmidt would reverse course on social reforms, seeking to rein in public spending. Honecker took a different tack. Facing no public challenge and no opposition party, he did not have to explain the state of public finances to the People's Chamber or to voters. While West Germany entered into a period of defensive restructuring in response to the perceived economic crises, East Germany avoided structural change, with ultimately drastic consequences.

Further reading

Allinson, Mark. "More from Less: Ideological Gambling with the Unity of Social and Economic Policy in Honecker's GDR." *Central European History* 45 (2012), 102–27.

Burdumy, Alexander. "Reconsidering the Role of the Welfare State within the German Democratic Republic's Political System." *Journal of Contemporary History* 48 (2013), 872–89.

Fink, Carole, and Bernd Schaefer, eds. *Ostpolitik, 1969-1974: European and Global Responses*. New York: Cambridge University Press, 2009.

Harsch, Donna. "Society, the State, and Abortion in East Germany, 1950-1972." *American Historical Review*. 102 (1997), 53–84.

Mierzejewski, Alfred C. *A History of the German Public Pension System*. Lanham, MD: Lexington, 2016.

Offe, Claus. *Contradictions of the Welfare State*. Edited by John Keane. Cambridge, MA: MIT Press, 1984.

Rubin, Eli. *Amnesiopolis: Modernity, Space, and Memory in East Germany*. New York: Oxford University Press, 2016.

Sammartino, Annemarie. "Mass Housing, Late Modernism, and the Forging of Community in New York City and East Berlin, 1965-1989." *American Historical Review* 121 (2016), 492–521.

Sarotte, Mary Elise. *Dealing with the Devil: East Germany, Détente, and Ostpolitik, 1969-1973*. Chapel Hill: University of North Carolina Press, 2001.

Schmidt, Manfred G., and Gerhard A. Ritter. *The Rise and Fall of a Socialist Welfare State: The German Democratic Republic (1949-1990) and German Unification (1989-1994)*. Translated by David R. Antal and Ben Veghte. Berlin: Springer, 2013.

Zacher, Hans. *Social Policy in the Federal Republic of Germany: The Constitution of the Social*. Berlin: Springer, 2013.

7

Crisis and change: The Federal Republic in the 1970s

FIGURE 7.1 *View over the Rhine and town situated below the Mülheim nuclear power plant in 1979. (ullstein bild/Kucharz/Getty Images)*

Many West Germans in the 1970s sensed a looming crisis of the state. The West German economic boom and the social policies promised by the Social Democrats in power came to an abrupt end with the 1973 oil crisis. On top of that, a spy scandal forced Brandt from office, whose popular idealism was replaced by the pragmatism of Helmut Schmidt, and left-wing terrorism awakened old fears regarding democracy and the state. In a time of unemployment, the continued presence of guest workers, particularly newer migrants from Turkey, Greece, and Yugoslavia, further heightened societal tensions, tensions that challenged the established parties and benefited the far right. But in retrospect, important changes accompanied these negative developments. A left alternative milieu, born of the 1960s protest movements, pushed cultural and social boundaries as they allied with other West Germans to challenge nuclear power and technocratic rule, sexism and environmental degradation. From these new social movements and citizens groups arose the first successful challenger to the three-party system, the Alternative List/Green Party. Massive peace protests against nuclear arms divided the Social Democrats and helped solidify the Greens. Facing so many internal and external challenges, the Social Democrats were forced from power in 1982, opening the way for the return of the Christian Democrats under the leadership of Helmut Kohl.

During the 1970s the average West German felt the "good life" to be fundamentally threatened and the leaders of the FRG confronted one crisis situation after another. Though frequently mapped onto the years that Helmut Schmidt was chancellor (1974–82), the economic and political challenges that he and his coalition government struggled to address were present already under Willy Brandt. The limits to economic growth in light of limited human and material resources; rising unemployment and inflation; international and domestic terrorism (and corresponding efforts at counterterrorism); and popular unrest over urban renewal, nuclear energy, and technocratic decision making—all this took the wind out of the Social Democrats' reformist sails. Despite a second win at the polls in November 1972, Brandt proved ineffective in the face of internal government problems and intrigues, and he was forced to step down amid mounting scandal. In the chancellor's office and the homes of many West Germans, the phrase "crisis management" replaced the call to "dare more democracy."

But to remember the 1970s only as a decade of crisis and economic stagnation misses a good deal, internationally and domestically. The policy of détente led to striking improvements in German-German relations and international diplomacy more generally. At the same time, West Germany continued to draw closer to France and to help lay the political and economic framework for European integration. Just as important, if not as immediately visible, were the productive consequences of West Germans' efforts to contain their fears and to secure their future. Not only did the 1970s see a rise in political violence and state security but also an impressive mobilization of citizens eager to counter a dominating state. Citizens' initiatives formed in opposition to unwanted state intervention at the local level while new social movements pushed for greater inclusion and government accountability.

As these examples suggest, young and not-so-young West Germans continued to push against cultural, political, and social boundaries. They did so in large and diverse numbers as well as across nation-state borders. In this way the protest of the 1960s can be seen as the beginning, a push for change that culminated not in "1968" but a decade later. With the postwar consensus in tatters, however, there was now little agreement over the best way forward. Multiple voices fought for representation and found it, not only in parliament but in new media and social venues. Voices on both left and right developed criticisms of state bureaucracies and organized politics as West Germans turned to the private sphere and everyday life as places from which to organize resistance to the state, as a better site for dealing with social problems, or as the best source for cultivating one's personal potential. All of these factors played into the end of the three-party status quo with the rise of the Green Party, the only group to successfully found a new parliamentary party in the old Federal Republic.

Ostpolitik and the Guillaume affair

Social Democrats' victory at the polls in 1972 made them the largest party in parliament and delivered the clear message that West Germans were ready for change. Empowered by a comfortable parliamentary majority, the Social-Liberal coalition could finally pursue its policy of détente without fear of Christian Democratic interference. Even when rising oil prices and growing unemployment stalled other parts of the government's reform program, the FRG continued to work for better relations with the Eastern bloc countries and with the GDR in particular. Bonn continued to emphasize the unity of the German nation and the two Germanys' common history and culture, but the Hallstein Doctrine was unquestionably a thing of the past. The construction of a new highway between Berlin and Hamburg and new railway lines facilitated a travel "boom" from West Germany and West Berlin eastward and from the GDR to the West. Used by both governments to facilitate their own interests and never without tension, their rapprochement nonetheless eased the personal pain suffered by families and friends on opposite sides of the Iron Curtain and helped to establish a new norm in East-West relations.

The victory for *Ostpolitik* was ultimately bittersweet. On April 25, 1974, police arrested Günter Guillaume, a member of Brandt's staff suspected of being an East German spy. The details of his case were a gift to conservatives, demonstrating the security risks inherent in diplomacy with the East. Guillaume came to the FRG in 1956 posing as a refugee. In reality, he was a member of the Stasi and an officer in the East German army who gathered intelligence as he rose up the ranks of the Social Democrats. At the moment when his identity was uncovered, Guillaume had the job of maintaining the chancellor's diary and correspondence; he had access to state secrets. Whether the scandal required Brandt's resignation or provided an excuse for it is debated. Brandt's affairs with female journalists, revealed around the same time, hurt him at a time when he and the party could ill afford it. Brandt claimed personal responsibility for "negligence" in the Guillaume affair and stepped down on May 6, 1974. He was replaced as chancellor ten days later by Helmut Schmidt. Despite the upheaval, the Social-Liberal coalition remained firm. Free Democratic leader Walter Scheel replaced Gustav Heinemann as president and his party mate Hans-Dietrich Genscher assumed the position of foreign minister and vice chancellor.

Willy Brandt was a charismatic visionary who captured a younger generation's hopes for change. Helmut Schmidt, by contrast, was a no-nonsense pragmatist. The son of a school principal, Schmidt served in the war until captured by British forces. After his release, Schmidt studied political science and began his long career in the Social Democractic Party. As a member of the Bundestag, he established his name as a defense expert. But it was his effective handling of the 1962 Hamburg flood as that city's interior minister that first earned him a national reputation for getting things done under pressure. A reformer in his own right, Schmidt served as defense minister and as economic and finance minister under Brandt. In stark contrast to Brandt, however, he had no interest in spiritual or moral leadership. His political experience fit the suddenly uncertain times; when Schmidt took office, he confronted economic recession, terrorism, and growing doubts over the government's ability to steer the country back on track.

Schmidt spoke differently than had Brandt. While Brandt talked about hope and daring more democracy, Schmidt's speeches were filled with references to security: a militarily secure country, security in the form of reliable jobs and welfare state institutions, energy security. He sought to plug what he called "gaps" in security, revealed by the oil embargo discussed below, or by Soviet superiority in nuclear arms, or by a weakening economy. To talk constantly of security was to emphasize insecurity and fear, and to stress how the right leader could protect the population: these ideas of security and fear made up the core of Schmidt's rhetoric, including his defense of what he called "*Modell Deutschland*," the German model of social and political order. Academic discussions, which resonated widely in the media, reflected this language of security as well. Political scientists on the right, filled with dread over the student movement and its effect on the universities, raised the question of whether too much democracy could overburden the political system, rendering society itself "ungovernable," in the slogan of the time. That discussion was echoed on the left, which asked whether West Germany was facing a "crisis of legitimacy" rooted in the inability of capitalism either to pay for the welfare state or to provide a meaningful world for citizens. As much as Schmidt might have disagreed with both premises, they show how deeply his language of security and insecurity reflected the political culture of the 1970s.

The oil crisis and the limits to economic growth

In 1972, an international think tank known as the "Club of Rome" published a report on the world's economic future. The report's authors argued that the current, unrestrained pursuit of economic expansion could not continue since the earth's resources were finite. Continued growth would lead to environmental destruction, famine, and ultimately a disaster for the earth, including humans. It was a bleak picture but not quite the bombshell that is sometimes remembered to have been. Few people paid the apocalyptic report any mind until a swift downturn in the world's economy drew their attention to a particularly vital resource: oil. After a disastrous war with Israel, in late 1973, Arab countries decided to continue the fight by using their vast oil reserves against Israel and its biggest supporters. The Organization of Petroleum Exporting Countries (OPEC) raised the price of crude oil, restricted production, and declared an embargo against the United States and the Netherlands. Their decision spelled the end of cheap energy in the Western world. From $1.40 per barrel in 1970, the price of crude rose to $12 per barrel and remained high—and volatile—even after the embargo ended in March 1974, surging to $23 after the 1979 Iranian revolution and again in October 1981, to $34 a barrel. The result was a negative chain reaction in the FRG and other industrialized countries. The spike in energy and transportation costs saw a drop in both production and exports, rising unemployment, steady inflation, and growing debt.

The FRG weathered the global recession better than other Western industrialized nations but the crisis exposed the country's dependence on oil, as well as West Germans' relatively low threshold for financial pain. West Germans were primed to think of political and social stability in relation to productivity and permanent economic growth: The Weimar Republic had collapsed in the wake of the Great Depression, the Federal Republic succeeded on the basis of a strong economy. Because of this, the end of the postwar "boom" produced a general sense of societal unease. Rising unemployment (already one million in 1975) and inflation amid economic stagnation conjured up memories of Weimar and corresponding fears of political extremism and government failure. But what could be done? There were no easy answers. Unemployment alone cost the state millions in lost tax revenue, unemployment benefits, and retraining programs, so that lowering taxes or state spending was not an option—at least not for the Social Democrats. The party may have abandoned Marx but not its labor union and working-class electoral base. Free Democrats did not feel the same way. As the federal debt grew from DM47 million

CHART 7.1 *Unemployment Rate and Rate of GDP Growth in West Germany, 1950–90*
Source: Statistisches Bundesamt, "Gross Domestic Product, Gross National Income, National Income (Factor Costs)," at: https://www.destatis.de/EN/ FactsFigures/NationalEconomyEnvironment/NationalAccounts/DomesticProduct/ Tables/GrossDomesticProducSince1925_xls.html; "Arbeitsmarkt: Registrierte Arbeitslose, Arbeitslosenquote nach Gebietsstand," at: https://www.destatis.de/DE/ ZahlenFakten/Indikatoren/LangeReihen/Arbeitsmarkt/lrarb003.html

in 1970 to DM309 million by 1982, their demands to cut public spending became a major source of tension between the coalition partners. But Social Democrats refused to cut existing social programs. At the same time, though, they ceased talking about reforms already in the autumn of 1973. Though this change in course occurred under Brandt, Helmut Schmidt generally gets credit (or blame) for the end of the Social Democratic reform program. In his first address to the nation as chancellor, Schmidt summarized the new state of affairs and explained that "at a time of growing global problems, we concentrate realistically and soberly on the essentials, on that which is now necessary and put all else aside." The new government sought to combat uncertainty by essentially rebranding the FRG: it reminded West Germans that the *Modell Deutschland* was strong, resilient, and secure.

Nuclear energy, citizens' initiatives,
and the anti-nuclear movement

In response to the energy crisis, the Bundestag passed a new law empowering the federal government to restrict citizens' oil and natural gas consumption. Toward this end, Bonn declared car-free Sundays in November and December 1973, grinding West Germans to an astonishing halt, and introduced (temporary) speed limits on the country's highways. Of more lasting import, the Social-Liberal coalition reoriented the country's oil imports toward Great Britain and the Soviet Union and announced plans to build forty-two nuclear plants by 1985. This dramatic expansion of nuclear energy was understood as a win-win: West Germany could escape the turbulent oil markets, and West German citizens would not have to change their consumer habits. Nuclear energy was essential, in the opinion of both political elites and union leaders, to closing the gap in energy security, thereby regaining the FRG's economic well-being and, by extension, political and social security.

Not everyone agreed. In fact, as the decade wore on a growing number of citizens became convinced that nuclear power promised to do more harm than good. They mobilized to stop construction. Initial protest came from citizens living in areas around the proposed building sites: farmers, winegrowers, and educated middle-class residents who had the most reason to fear the reactors' negative impact on the environment, local economy, and health of those who lived nearby. The first major anti-nuclear protest took place in Wyhl, a small town in Baden-Württemberg near the French border. Its location was significant, as the entire upper Rhine region of West Germany, France, and Switzerland was slated for large-scale industrial development and French protesters were already at work. The local groups that formed in response to Wyhl's selection as a future nuclear site resembled other citizens' initiatives springing up at the time, independent of traditional institutions. Their location outside party, church, or state organizations was no accident. Whatever the specific problem or issue that citizens' initiatives sought to address, members generally connected their need to act to bureaucratic incompetency, to their government's unresponsiveness, or to both. A coal-fired power plant in West Berlin, a new airport runway in Frankfurt, and various plans for urban renewal across the country: local residents judged these, like the construction of nuclear power plants, to go against their community's interests and attempted to regain control over their lives by demanding more transparency from elected officials. In situations where those officials sat on the board of the industry directly benefiting from public investment, the residents went one step further and openly questioned whether representative democracy was working.

Government officials at local, state, and federal levels were right to see citizens' initiatives as challenging more than any single issue. The desire to register this more fundamental disquiet drew increasing numbers of West Germans (as well as French, Swiss, British, and Americans) to the anti-nuclear movement. The disposal of radioactive waste and risk of a potential meltdown loomed large in protesters' minds as did the lack of transparency involved in the decision-making process. The majority of activists were politically moderate and committed, at least initially, to working with government representatives. In Wyhl, petition drives, public forums, and a 2,000-person strong march to the proposed construction site in the summer of 1974 drew attention to local concerns and won the support of Christian and Social Democrats, Protestant pastors, university students, and farmers—but ultimately failed to sway officials at the state level. When construction began on February 17, 1975, thousands of protesters occupied the site, with people from elsewhere in West Germany and surrounding countries descending on the site by the end of the week, and an estimated 28,000 participants constructed a settlement complete with a "friendship house" and adult education center. It did not end the conflict over Wyhl's future, which raged on into the 1980s, but the protest did offer a model for future nonviolent action.

The citizens who opposed the proposed nuclear reactors could not easily be disparaged as student rebels or Communist stooges. But when they occupied construction sites, local and Land-level authorities took harsh actions against them. The events in Brokdorf, a town to the northwest of Hamburg where another nuclear reactor was planned, show how the radical response by police and political officials contributed to a radicalization of the protests. Despite a public referendum against a nuclear reactor, authorities cordoned off the proposed site and allowed the power company to begin construction in October 1976. What started as a peaceful effort to occupy the site by an estimated 30,000–45,000 people quickly turned violent when the minister-president of Schleswig-Holstein authorized wide-sweeping police action against the protesters. Demonstrators who managed to reach the construction site equipped with helmets, shovels, and rocks were met with water cannons, tear gas, and rubber truncheons, while many others got caught in the crossfire. Over 500 people were injured in the clash between police and protesters. Further occupation attempts at Brokdorf as well as at Grohnde in Lower Saxony and in Malville, France, saw similar, even deadly, violence.

Citizens' concerns went beyond what critics called a "NIMBY" ("not in my backyard") attitude. They involved a whole series of negative consequences that could follow from nuclear power. In 1977, the noted science journalist Robert Jungk published a book called *The Nuclear State* (*Der Atomstaat*), which asked about the broader implications of nuclear power for democratic societies. The phrase came to him when he was giving a speech during one of the protests at Brokdorf. Jungk argued that nuclear energy, like the nuclear bomb, posed extraordinary risks for all of humanity, exemplified by the scientific discussion of the "maximum

ON THE POLITICAL EFFECTS OF NUCLEAR POWER: THE DEBATE OVER THE "ATOM STATE"

In his internationally known book *The Nuclear State*, the physicist Robert Jungk asked not only about the environmental and military risks of nuclear energy, but also about its effect on domestic policy: "The intensification, expansion, and centralization of state surveillance," he argued, would be the result of expanding high risk nuclear power; "a perpetually endangered central source of power" would require "permanent protection"; "a nuclear industry means a permanent state of emergency justified by a permanent threat."[1]

Jungk's words linked the transnational protests against nuclear power to concerns specific to postwar West Germany. By invoking the "permanent state of emergency," he linked the politics of the nuclear state to the exceptional laws at the end of the Weimar Republic and ultimately the start of Hitler's reign; antinuclear protests started to overlap with defense of the "rule of law" and the constitutional state. Excessive police measures against critics reinforced the critique. In 1976, for example, the Ministry of Justice illegally tapped communications of Klaus Traube, a leading manager in the nuclear industry who had turned against nuclear power. In a hard-hitting editorial, the editor of *Der Spiegel*, Rudolf Augstein, asked whether the nuclear state could remain a constitutional state—opening up a crisis of state leading to the resignation of the minister of justice.[2] The left-leaning Free Democrat Ingrid Matthäus-Maier likewise invoked a series of threats from environmental to political and constitutional in a speech against the expansion of nuclear power from 1980: Jungk's critique made its way from protest groups into the center of elite protest.[3]

Jungk's words resonated on the right, as well—but negatively. In his antinuclear speeches, Jungk used rhetoric that suggested violence against property, for example, though not against things, leading the right-leaning Free Democrat Norbert Eimer to question the commitment of the left to democracy: "Violence against things," which he accused Jungk of defending, "is also violence against democratic decisions. . . . It is a mark of all totalitarian movements that they do not accept majority decisions, that they morally justify resistance against majority decisions."[4] Like his opponents on the left, Eimer implicitly reached back to scenes from the end of the Weimar Republic, when National Socialists and Communists had rejected parliamentary democracy, to describe antinuclear protests.

The debate over the environmental risks of nuclear power thus opened up a wider discussion about the deeper, historical threats facing German democracy.

credible incident," translated as "greatest acceptable accident" (GAU in the German abbreviation), a catastrophic accident whose chance experts downplayed. Some risks came directly from radioactive material, but others came from the security needs created by such high-risk technology. To protect the construction of reactors, to ensure their long life, and to guard against the misuse of radioactive waste, governments would be drawn to limit citizens' freedoms, to limit the flow of information, and to take security precautions that could upend democratic society itself. "A nuclear industry," Jungk wrote, "means a permanent state of emergency justified by a permanent threat"—a phrase that conjured up the fears of a dictatorship that haunted so much of the Federal Republic's political culture. Jungk criticized the sanitized, technocratic language about risks, which covered up the fact that fallible humans had to make decisions about reactors. His fears seemed to be borne out by the near meltdown in 1979 of the nuclear plant at Three Mile Island in Pennsylvania, when a mechanical failure nearly became a disaster because of human error. The international press reported widely on the accident. Jungk and many other intellectuals and activists contributed to a broad anti-nuclear movement by the 1970s, strengthened by growing public awareness of the potential environmental and social hazards.

Until Germany officially ended its nuclear energy program after the 2011 nuclear meltdown in Fukushima, Japan, it remained a highly contentious issue. Long before the cessation of the nuclear program, however, West German activists succeeded in dramatically reshaping their country's energy policy. Whereas the French state, facing equally stringent opposition, installed 85 percent of its proposed nuclear reactors, the FRG only built a quarter of those it originally planned. From the 1980s onward, state and private initiatives also went to alternative ("green") energy research.

Growing pains of a globalizing economy and European solutions

Not all of the country's financial woes could be blamed on the high cost of oil. By the 1970s, the coal and steel industries—the heart and soul of the 1950s economic miracle—were in dire need of overhauling, and West German manufacturers faced increasingly stiff competition on the global market. Newcomers like Japan threatened to overtake Germany in key industries like microelectronics and car production, while German textile producers faced significantly cheaper imports from developing countries. Here, too, the collapse of the international monetary system in 1971 brought home the harsh realities of a globalized economy and the wide-ranging consequences of the United States' ballooning budget deficit.

To address the economic crisis in all its facets, the Social-Liberal government pursued both national and international measures. At home, Schmidt used his strong ties to the trade unions to help legitimize a significant shift in Social Democratic economic policy. The federal government did not cut state programs designed to reawaken consumer demand by injecting money into the economy; local and regional job-creation programs as well as wage subsidies for hiring unemployed workers were part of the government's early and ongoing efforts to tackle unemployment. But the kind of deficit spending advocated by the United States and Great Britain at the time did not sit well with West German elites, unnerved by memories of the hyperinflation and political disaster of the Weimar Republic. Schmidt himself warned against the diminishing profits that accompanied such demand-oriented measures. Rather than reduce government spending he argued that the path to renewed economic growth and all that West Germans associated with it— job security, higher wages, and social progress—required greater attention to the supply side of the economic equation. "Investment" became a new guiding economic principle. Political investment meant closer cooperation between government officials and prominent business leaders and the introduction of state programs designed to encourage employers to invest instead of simply maintaining their course or, worse, downsizing. This two-pronged approach achieved momentary improvements but unemployment proved just as lasting as the new faith in supply-side economics would be.

On the international stage, the West German government spearheaded economic and security initiatives aimed at closer cooperation, especially in Europe. The European Council and the United Nations, for example, both passed international counterterrorism policy initiated by the FRG. In economic matters, Schmidt's government worked to forestall protectionism as a world response to the economic downturn, which would have hit the export-dependent FRG particularly hard. Two arenas were particularly important: the European Community (EC) and what eventually became the "Group of 7" (G7), a forum of leading industrialized nations (United States, Britain, France, FRG, Italy, Japan, and Canada). In both, the West German chancellor had a strong ally and friend in French president Valéry Giscard d'Estaing. Though they could ultimately do little to sway US policy, Schmidt and Giscard did steer the EC toward currency stability. Previous efforts were unsuccessful largely because important countries like Great Britain, Italy, and France regularly failed to fulfill the economic preconditions established for membership in the short-lived European Exchange Association. Schmidt therefore proposed to construct a new currency system that would, he assured West Germans, improve their domestic economy and give new life to European integration. Despite significant opposition from his own countrymen (who largely feared that West Germany would be left writing the check), Schmidt worked with Giscard to found the European Monetary System (EMS). The EMS, approved by the European Parliament on December 5, 1978, established fixed but adaptable exchange rates between the Western European currencies based on what was essentially a non-existing currency, the European Currency Unit (ECU). Real or not, it served as an important measuring stick. And though still a long way from the common market and currency of the twenty-first century, the ECU and EMS made both imaginable.

The world economic crisis in a way reanimated the European project, which had suffered in the 1960s under the nationally oriented politics of French president Charles de Gaulle and Brandt's focus on eastern Europe. With de Gaulle out of office, the greatest obstacle to EC expansion was removed and in 1973, Great Britain, Ireland, and Denmark became members. Greece, Spain, and Portugal were embraced as future EC-members following the collapse of their respective dictatorships. What membership in the "Europe" of the EC meant remained unclear, and already in the 1970s one could talk about a democratic or legitimacy deficit when it came to the decisions handed down from Brussels. But politically important steps included foreign policy coordination (the European Political Cooperation initiated in 1970 and strengthened in 1973) and regularly scheduled meetings of EC leaders in the European Council. Of crucial symbolic value was the first direct election of the European Parliament in 1979. The institution itself had little actual authority as yet but it implied that the project of European unification could take a more democratic and potentially more robust course. The project of the European Community moved ahead, then, as a response to political and economic challenges, not primarily because of idealistic aims. For Germany, European politics were a means to maintain competitiveness and an export economy.

From guest workers to fellow Germans?

The end of the postwar economic boom brought a different approach to the guest worker program. Already in the 1960s, government and union officials nervously observed changes in migration patterns. Guest workers were remaining in the FRG for longer periods and an increasing number sent for their families or started them in Germany, adding the needs of wives and children to the total cost of foreign labor. Officials felt their hands, however, were tied: employers demanded cheap, stable labor and family reunification was widely understood as a basic human right. Many of these same officials originally hoped that ending the guest worker program would reverse the migration trends of the past decade.

The restrictions placed on migrant labor between 1973 and 1975 aimed to reduce unemployment and to relieve pressure on state funds by shrinking the total number of foreigners working and residing in the FRG. When the federal government ended the recruitment programs, 2.6 million guest workers already lived in West Germany. As members of the EC, Italians (and later Greeks, Spaniards, and Portuguese) required no special work permits and could still come and go across borders with relative ease. Turks and Yugoslavians, in contrast, feared that they would not be allowed to return to the FRG if they left—so they stayed and sent for their families before the new policies went into effect. The result was that the Turkish and Yugoslavian populations, which had recently overtaken the Italians as the two largest migrant groups, continued to rise. By 1980, the number of noncitizens living in the FRG equaled 4.4 million. The government's plan to reduce immigration, in other words, failed. And Turks, widely considered the most "foreign" of guest workers, came to disproportionately influence West German perceptions of resident aliens and migrant labor. The original, multinational nature of the worker recruitment program was forgotten—lost to the image of the Turkish guest worker and his family.

The growing permanent population of guest workers fed into the difficult debate taking place at the same time about (white) German demographics. As had been predicted already in the 1950s, German population growth leveled off by the 1970s, after 1972, even ventured into negative territory: more Germans died than were born. An aging and shrinking population posed a major challenge for the welfare state, which relied on the young to finance the pensions of the old. Immigration appeared to help remedy the challenge of a shrinking birthrate, especially since the new immigrants had a higher fertility rate. But therein lay the deeper problem: would Germany survive by becoming more ethnically diverse, by shrinking the proportion of "ethnic" Germans?

Though only a handful of officials publically referred to the population in question as immigrants, all parties now agreed on their need for integration into West German society. But what this meant—in both theory and practice—depended on who you asked. Conservatives favored integration tempered by the preservation of national and cultural identities. The goal, as they saw it, was not to mingle the different cultures, or to encourage foreigners to become West German (whatever that was) but rather to establish the conditions needed for different and discrete cultures to exist peaceably side by side. And by encouraging migrants to retain their language and homeland traditions, conservatives left the door open to their future departure. Heiner Geissler argued, in fact, that the cost of integrating foreigners was far higher than the benefit they might bring to the German economy. Liberals, in contrast, tended to emphasize the importance of the existing legal and social order for peaceful coexistence, specifically its guarantee of basic human rights and protections. They did not demand complete assimilation to German culture and social practices but they did tie guest workers' rights to live and work freely in the FRG to their acceptance of German liberal democracy. Finally, those on the left generally held a vision of integration that involved Germans and foreigners living together. It also involved a good deal of work: Germans and non-Germans learning about the other and changing (not necessarily consciously) as a result. As the decisive voice in government, Social Democrats largely determined the framework for the new guest worker policy. But the integration of foreigners into the fabric of West German society remained controversial, with all three approaches to integration in play.

All three remained in play not least because West Germany's strong federalist system dictated that culture and education were under the control of each individual Land. That meant (and means) that how integration was pursued depended greatly on where you were, and on who controlled the local government. Most educators agreed, for instance, that bilingual education aimed to ease guest worker children's transition into the German school system and to maintain the students' home language and cultural identity. In practice, however, the tendency was to focus on one or the other of those goals, to either attempt to bring children into the German system as quickly as possible or to maintain the language and culture of the home by establishing separate national or "home language" schools. The "Berlin model" favored the former. After recognizing that they could not simply throw guest worker children into a German classroom, educators developed special intensive instruction for non-native speakers in the hopes that they would quickly catch up to their German peers and no longer need them. Supplementary instruction in the home language and culture was provided outside of school by the consulates and embassies of the workers' home countries. On the opposite end of the spectrum was the "Bavarian model," where, aside from limited instruction in German as a Second Language, children were taught in their home language until the fifth grade, when German was first used to teach regular subject matter. The basic assumption here was that a child could not learn a new language and new subject matter at the same time. Though in theory the Bavarian model also aimed to assimilate these students into the German school system, in reality it segregated them from their German peers. In an effort to find some middle ground, the Federal Ministry of Culture recommended a combined approach: minority-language children should be placed in regular German classrooms, unless the language barrier proved too great; in either case, they should receive special instruction in German as well as the home language and culture; intensive courses in German should be offered; and tutoring should also be available if needed. In short, critics noted, the ministry's "double strategy" asked guest worker children to learn the German language, the regular subject matter, and their home language and culture in the same time it took German-speaking students to master the subject matter alone. Pedagogues, parents, and politicians united in general dissatisfaction and even open skepticism over assimilation's prospects.

New social movements and the alternative milieu

The citizens' initiatives discussed above point to a more general phenomenon: a broadening of political engagement both in terms of participants and the avenues they pursued. Middle-class West Germans, many of whom did not consider themselves the type to take to the streets in protest, formed the backbone of new social movements that questioned the achievements of the postwar years. The feminist, ecological, and peace movements forced a reexamination of gender equality, the material and social costs of unrestrained capitalism, and the quality of life lived under the threat of nuclear annihilation. Similar concerns motivated others to search for alternative ways to live, not in opposition to mainstream society but alongside it—in spite of it—if possible. The result of all these varied, anti-establishment impulses was a flourishing alternative culture in which unconventional lifestyles, autonomous spaces, and the development of new consumer habits offered the possibility of change—but did not demand it.

Germans' history of environmentalism reaches back to the nineteenth century, to early efforts at conservation and critiques of modern society frequently associated with political conservatives. The ecological movement is part of this rich history but it is best understood in the more immediate context of the Club of Rome and the newfound conviction that economic growth was no longer a measure of progress but rather a fundamental threat. Like all of the new social movements born after the 1960s, the West German ecological movement evolved in conversation with similar grassroots organizations in other countries. This was perhaps more true of the ecological movement than other movements since its very subject defied nationally bounded spaces and solutions. Those active in the movement— particularly its leaders—operated on a European field as much as a West German one. At the same time, most of the movement's supporters first got involved at the local level and it was there, in their everyday life and in their backyards, that they were most active and effective. The ecological movement was thus intensely local *and* transnational. Organizationally, it was deeply wedded to grassroots forms of decision making. Members of the ecological movement placed the blame for environmental destruction not only on industrialization and the unrestrained pursuit of capitalist profit but on an understanding of human progress that pitted man against nature. They claimed that achieving a sustainable lifestyle—avoiding the earth's and humanity's destruction—required upending this existing value system and learning to think in an entirely new way.

As a guiding principle, "ecology" offered broad guidelines for organizing society and for how to live life day to day. It was also vague enough to house a large number of different projects and perspectives under one roof. In the FRG, many came to the ecological movement through local citizens' initiatives and the anti-nuclear movement. Others—traditional pacifists, Christians, feminists, and socialists among them—were drawn to it as an extension of their existing worldview. The Federal Association of Citizens' Initiatives for Environmental Protection, founded in 1972, sought to coordinate and amplify their efforts in national and international campaigns. By 1977, the association represented nearly four hundred citizens' initiatives, many though not all concentrated on fighting nuclear energy. In this, the West German ecological movement differed from similar initiatives in other countries, and its intense anti-nuclear engagement had both positive and less positive consequences. In the immediate term, it was an incredible source of energy and dynamism, and helped to centralize the movement. The downside to West Germans' more narrow focus on nuclear energy was that it made for powerful enemies, namely all three political parties and the labor unions who tied the fate of the nuclear program directly to the economic health of the FRG.

The ecological movement succeeded in raising West Germans' awareness of the risks nuclear energy posed to the environment and human health. Even the Social Democrats registered environmentalist dissent within its ranks and party leaders, as did the Christian Democrats. The result was a particularly intense and, as noted earlier, at times violent clash of opinions. The unions joined forces with the utilities companies and employers' associations to reframe the public debate as a choice between jobs and environmental protection. In the end, though, what is perhaps most striking about the movement is its success in Europe's most industrialized nation. Despite ongoing controversy over nuclear energy, West Germany's government and population proved receptive to focusing on quality of life issues rather than simply increased wealth.

This focus on quality over quantity runs like a red thread through the new social movements and alternative projects of the 1970s. The women who mobilized under the banner of feminism, for example, called for gender equality as a precondition for a more fully lived life. They, like second-wave feminists in the United States and other European countries, famously argued that the "personal was political" and understood that what happened at home or behind doors was just as important to power relations—and the formation of a more just society—as government and the workplace. Feminists drew attention to women's unpaid work maintaining the home and raising children to underscore not only women's oppression but also how West German society maintained and depended on it. Over the course of the 1960s, married women's part-time employment gained acceptance but women's work outside the home had not shaken the legitimacy of the "breadwinner/housewife" model. If anything, it helped reconcile women's duty to the family and their desire (or need) to work, and confirmed the presumed female and supplementary nature of part-time work in the FRG. Education reforms notably had not touched the average school day, which ended in time for children to go home for lunch; without public childcare facilities—never a goal of West German social policy—most women had little choice but to give up full-time positions if they had them and either stay home or seek part-time work. As a result, women continued to lag behind men in areas like education, career development, and pay. Many feminists rejected biological justifications for continuing to treat men and women differently. Famously, publicist Alice Schwarzer did not deny that the one "little difference" between men and women had "huge consequences," but she argued that gender was a cultural construct: women were nurturing and men leaders only because society defined them as such. For many feminists then, women's liberation aimed at toppling established notions of what it meant to be "male" or "female."

The women's liberation movement always understood itself to address concerns common to all women. But it was the campaign to de-criminalize abortion, touched on in the previous chapter, that first made feminism a national movement in West Germany, uniting women of diverse social and political backgrounds. Following the example of French feminists, a number of prominent West German women "outed" themselves as having had an abortion on the front page of the national news magazine, *Stern*. By demonstrating that abortion was neither rare nor limited to marginalized elements of society, feminists hoped, first, to empower other women with the knowledge that they were not alone and, second, to underscore the flawed nature of a law that not only criminalized a significant part of the population, but also risked women's lives by doing so. Reproduction rights were just the beginning: New journals like Alice Schwarzer's *Emma* and the more radical *Courage* as well as the organization of self-help and women's only groups provided different forums in which to discuss the specific needs of women and possibilities for change. West German feminists founded safe house for battered women and children in cities across the country. They also organized telephone hotlines, initiated education campaigns, and (this time copying the British) marched to "take back the night," all in an effort to break through the pervasive silence on domestic abuse and rape. Once again, success—in this instance women's liberation from physical harm—depended on the rewriting of societal norms so that violence against women, rather than talking about it, became taboo.

That conservatives opposed many of the feminists is not surprising. In the mid-to-late 1970s, the Christian Democrats undertook a political campaign against all the symptoms of modernity that they thought were undermining ethnic German reproduction: abortion rights, divorce, and new opportunities for women in the workplace. More important, however, the changes in cultural norms were reflected in Christian Democracy. The Christian Democrats could not simply return to the conservative, Catholic positions of the 1950s: society had changed, and society meant voters. Heiner Geissler, one of a group of party reformers, rephrased the problem as one of an ill-considered welfare state. Society was facing, he said, a "new social question": it was no longer working-class men who lived below the poverty line, but mothers raising children alone, families with many children, and the disabled. Along with calling for government to focus on how to pay for the care of the elderly, he also called for new social policies that would promote the family and reproduction instead of placing women before a choice of career or family. Only in this way could the declining birthrate of ethnic German families be reversed. The project would never be realized, even when the Christian Democrats came to power in 1982, because of its high costs. At the same time, it showed how a conservative party could take up matters of concern for women and indeed feminists, propose solutions, and start to imagine a welfare state that looked significantly different from that of the Social Democrats.

Feminists were not the only ones seeking to overthrow gender norms and the existing (patriarchal) order. The 1970s also marked an important chapter in gay men and women's efforts to organize against heteronormative conceptions of family and sexuality that continued to cast homosexuality as deviant. The crucial precondition, and mobilizing force, for gay liberation was the 1969 reform of Paragraph 175 (discussed in Chapter 6). In this liberalizing atmosphere it was possible to openly publish and circulate homosexual magazines, and gay action groups formed not only in the urban protest centers of West Berlin, Frankfurt, and Hamburg but in university towns like Bochum and Münster. Few of these early groups were large, and lesbians increasingly opted to organize separately, as part of or in cooperation with the feminist movement. But as the decade progressed, gay (male) activists successfully formed a national and even international network. The establishment in 1975 of two nationally distributed journals, *Emanzipation* and *Schwuchtel*, and the movement's first publishing house, Pink Triangle Press (Verlag Rosa Winkel), was both a product and engine of that success. Important, too, to the movement's self-identity was the "rediscovery" of the pink triangle, worn by homosexuals in Nazi concentration camps, with the 1972 publication of Heinz Heger's memoir *The Men of the Pink Triangle*. It immediately became a symbol of homosexuals' past and present persecution and of the gay liberation movement itself.

Some accounts of the West German gay movement nevertheless portray it as woefully behind its counterparts. One reason is certainly because, unlike in the United States and Great Britain, gay activism West Germany did not take the form of a gay *rights* movement until the 1980s. Instead, gay liberation was initially pursued from within the New Left; activists linked their particular oppression as homosexuals to the existing socio-economic order and focused their energies on transforming it. The pink triangle was worn in solidarity with (rather than in distinction to) the red triangle of socialist victims. This changed by the end of the 1970s, when— gay or straight—few leftists continued to place much hope in revolutionary projects, and gay activists in particular felt their cause negatively affected by political affiliation. Only then did West German activists adopt a language and legal framework of human rights like their counterparts elsewhere, and enter the official history of the gay rights movement.

These new social movements contributed to a broad and eclectic "alternative" culture within the FRG. Though often associated with left politics because of its roots in 1960s counterculture, those who identified with the alternative scene defy such easy labeling in part because they sought to escape the very kind of disciplined politics implied in party or left/right designations. Those West Germans who made up the alternative milieu were widely diverse in their interests and politics. Uniting them in equal measure was a rejection of mainstream society and the search for new autonomous ways of living. They did not renounce protest actions or the hope of reforming society, but those involved in the alternative scene increasingly focused on the individual as the site of change. The focus on individual change fit a general trend: therapy and self-improvement went mainstream in the 1970s, opening the doors to a new culture of self-help books, personal health and exercise regimens, alternative therapies, and New Age spiritualism seeking to address a common sense of alienation. What distinguished the alternative milieu was its insistence that individual well-being could not be achieved within the existing societal structures. "Destroy What Destroys You," a song by the West German band Ton Steine Scherben, captured this sentiment and propelled it to cult status. This deep distrust of established authorities connected the alternative scene to the new social movements and other punks and "freaks" in Western Europe.

Those attached to the alternative scene aimed to change how life was lived in the present, not by talking (a common criticism of the theory-heavy 1960s) but by doing. They not only protested *Modell Deutschland;* they also consciously carved out an alternative to it. A few sought to "drop out" or "return to nature." Some—the *Spontis*, for instance—embraced emotion and spontaneous action. Most focused on opening up spaces and lifestyles where they might eat, work, live, and play according to their own wants and needs: communally organized bookstores, journals, and art exhibitions; neighborhood cafes, organic food cooperatives, and housing co-ops; lawyers' collectives, women's houses, and squatting tenements. The cooperative aspect of these endeavors was not an accident. Rather than class or nationality, it was the deliberate cultivation of close, relaxed personal interactions and emotional warmth that drew people to this new community and that characterized its spaces and unorthodox living arrangements. Many projects failed before they got going or were short-lived, but enough survived—along with their critique of society—to sustain an alternative scene in Germany today.

Terrorism and internal security

In addition to economic recession and social unrest, the Social-Liberal government faced a third international development: terrorism. Most famous of the West German "urban guerrillas" was the RAF, formed on the coattails of the protest movement by Horst Mahler, Ulrike Meinhof, Andreas Baader, and Gudrun Ensslin. The group attacked the West German state for what it saw as its continued fascist tendencies and the FRG more generally for crimes that it attributed to Western capitalism: global imperialism, genocide in Vietnam, and the slavish dictates of consumer society. In this focus on fascism, the RAF was as uniquely German as it was international in its outlook and self-understanding. From 1970 until its dissolution, the GDR provided the group with an easy escape route as well as funding and important arms networks. The RAF's members also found at least passive support among large sections of the alternative left in West Germany who shared their distrust of the German state. That support would diminish greatly after the wave of violence of 1976–77, when many came to reject the need for and therefore the legitimacy of violent revolt in the FRG.

In May 1972, the RAF staged a major "offensive" against the FRG, the United States and NATO military forces, and the long-hated Springer Press, setting off six bombs that killed four and injured seventy-four others. By fall, its leaders were arrested and, by year's end, they were all awaiting trial in a newly constructed high security prison at Stammheim. But the time between the terrorists' incarceration in 1972, the start of their trial in 1975, and their final sentencing in 1977 proved an immense liability for the state in terms of security and public relations. Successive generations of RAF recruits joined other radical groups in actions designed to pressure the state into releasing imprisoned militants. In 1975, for example, the June 2nd Movement secured the release of several of its members after kidnapping Christian Democratic politician Peter Lorenz, a feat that the RAF tried to repeat two months later by seizing the West German embassy in Stockholm. Their failure (the militants' accidentally detonated their own bomb) and Schmidt's adoption of a policy of non-negotiation did not put an end to kidnapping attempts.

The RAF did the most damage to the FRG in prison, using their bodies as a weapon. Through hunger strikes, painful forced feedings, and their own vivid accounts of sensory deprivation, the RAF built a public case for torture. The war they waged in West Germany's prisons had both transnational and national components. It was, on the one hand, part of a larger, international movement for prisoners' rights that arose at the end of the 1960s in response to changes in prison practices and the influx of young, educated "radicals" into prisons who could shed light on these previously liminal public institutions. Ulrike Meinhof's "Letter from the Death Wing," written sometime between June 1972 and February 1973 from the Cologne-Ossendorf prison and later published by her lawyers, detailed the excruciating experience of isolation, building on imagery set in motion by IRA prisoners in England; it also referred to prison technologies pioneered in the United States, like the isolation chamber or "dead cell."

There is no ignoring the importance of the Third Reich for giving credence to the RAF's accusations of inhumane treatment or for guiding counterterrorism policies. On November 9, 1974, RAF-member Holger Meins died after nearly two months on hunger strike. The harrowing photographs of his emaciated corpse assured that Meins' name lived on and, by visually replicating the image of emaciated people liberated from the Nazi camps, it mobilized sympathy for the prisoners, if not necessarily their cause.

ULRIKE M. MEINHOF, "LETTER FROM THE DEAD WING," FROM THE PERIOD JUNE 16, 1972–FEBRUARY 9, 1973

The feeling, one's head is exploding (the feeling, the top of one's skull will actually split, peel off)—

the feeling, one's spinal column is pressing into one's brain—

the feeling, the brain gradually shrivels up like dried fruit for example—

the feeling, one is constantly, imperceptibly wired, one is remote-controlled—

the feeling, one's associations are being hacked away—

the feeling, one pisses the soul out of the body, like when one can't hold water—

the feeling, the cell is moving.

. . .

One can't tell if one trembles from fever or from cold—

One can't tell why one trembles—one freezes.

To speak at normal volume requires effort, as if one were speaking loudly, almost yelling—

. . .

the feeling, if one were to say what's wrong, if one were to let that out,

it would be like throwing boiling water at another's face, like boiling drinking water that would forever scald, disfigure—

Raging aggression, for which there is no outlet. That's the worst.

Clear awareness that one has no chance of surviving; the complete failure to communicate this....

Source: From Peter Brückner, Ulrike Marie Meinhof und die deutsche Verhältnisse *(Berlin: Wagenbach 1976), pp. 152–54. Reprinted with the permission of the Verlag Klaus Wagenbach. Translation by Karrin Hanshew.*

At the same time, the retaliatory murders undertaken by the RAF following Meins' death and the later sentencing of RAF prisoners not only threatened the justice system but conjured up memories of similarly violent acts under the Weimar Republic. The title of South African historian Jillian Becker's book, *Hitler's Children*, captures the fascist lineage that many West Germans ascribed to the RAF, asserting that a straight line ran from the terror of Nazism to the terrorism of the 1970s. And precisely because fascism loomed large in the imaginations of both international and West German publics, the RAF succeeded in mobilizing fears—and state action—disproportionate to its actual threat. The government did not reinstate the death penalty (banned in 1949) or break hostage negotiations by taking retaliatory action on imprisoned radicals as politicians Alfred Dregger (CDU) and Franz-Josef Strauss proposed. But some West Germans' open support of such measures greatly alarmed others; indeed, many Germans were terrorized as much by the responses of their fellow citizens to terrorism as they were by the actual attacks. Newspapers and politicians laid the blame for terrorism at the feet of alleged sympathizers who protested RAF members' treatment in prison as well as those, like Heinrich Böll, who turned a critical eye on the media's own terror-mongering. Accusations of terrorist sympathy even extended to the Social Democrats and members of government: the Christian Democrats issued (and then quickly revoked) a "black book" which named Willy Brandt among its known terrorist sympathizers.

Officials acted to calm public fears but ultimately added to them. Already under Brandt, in 1972, interior ministers at the Land-level approved a ban on employing so-called radicals in the public sector. Referred to as a "ban on radicals" by its supporters and as a "occupational ban" by critics, the measure opened up teachers and state employees to political persecution. Members of the Bundestag made support for violent crime (defined very loosely) a criminal offense. And to facilitate a faster trial of suspected terrorists, Social and Free Democrats revised criminal procedure so as to exclude defense attorneys found colluding with their clients and to allow suspects to be tried without a lawyer—and even in absentia. Eventually, suspected terrorists were even denied attorney-client privilege as officials moved to keep information from passing to prisoners from the outside world. While all of these measures incited criticism at home and abroad, nothing perhaps inflamed imaginations more than security experts' efforts to combat terrorism by modernizing West German police forces and expanding the power of the Federal Criminal Office. The collection and storage of information on convicted and suspected criminals, accessible to all West German police with the help of new computer databases, dovetailed with preventative efforts to identify and eliminate terrorists' possible support base. The profiling and surveillance of the population fed the public "hunt for sympathizers" and raised uncomfortable comparisons with police power under the Third Reich.

In April 1977, the West German courts sentenced Baader, Ensslin, and Jan-Carl Raspe to life imprisonment; Meinhof would have been as well had she not committed suicide the summer before. The retaliatory murders of attorney general Siegfried Buback and Dresdner bank president Jürgen Ponto followed soon thereafter. On September 5, the RAF kidnapped the industrialist Hanns-Martin Schleyer from his car after gunning down his chauffer and bodyguards. The bloody crime scene was the start of the "German Autumn," an intense five-week period in which media headlines and political soundbites enflamed public emotion, new counterterrorism legislation passed in record time, and Helmut Schmidt assumed unprecedented executive power in an undeclared state of emergency. When members of a Palestinian liberation group hijacked the Lufthansa airliner *Landshut* in solidarity with the RAF on October 13, Schmidt mobilized the GSG-

FIGURE 7.2 *A poster issued by the West German Federal Criminal Office showing wanted terrorists, circa 1980. (Keystone/Getty Images)*

9, the anti-terrorist police squad created after the 1972 Munich Olympics. In 1972, when members of the Palestinian group "Black September" took Israeli athletes hostage, no such force existed; local police handled the crisis and it ended in the death of hostages and terrorists alike. On October 18, in contrast, the GSG-9 successfully stormed the hijacked airliner when it landed to refuel in Mogadishu and rescued all eighty-six passengers. It was the first mobilization of German paramilitary force abroad since 1945, a game-changer in more ways than one. Back in Germany, the leaders of the RAF committed suicide and, two days later, Hanns-Martin Schleyer was found dead. The terrorist crisis was over but the presence of handguns and transistor radios in the prisoners' cells left the door open for continued controversy and, for those so inclined, conspiracy theories.

Heinrich Böll described the RAF's attacks as a war of six against sixty million and captured a crucial truth: left-wing terrorism did not pose a fundamental threat to the FRG. Then why the unprecedented expansion of federal police powers, infringement of civil liberties, and moral panic? When it came to counterterrorism measures, West Germany differed little from other Western democracies at the time. But far from unifying West Germans, terrorism exposed long-simmering tensions regarding the legacy of 1968, West Germans' success at "coming to terms" with the Nazi past, and the strength of German democracy itself. It also exacerbated anxieties expressed by the new social movements concerning government intervention, the dangers of technology, and the undemocratic (or unchecked) use of state power. Lastly, the new international character of terrorism in the 1970s underscored the insecurity of a globalizing age, when states could no longer safeguard their borders, the lives of their citizens, or national economies from outside threat.

Debates about "terrorism" are never just about terrorism. In this case, the debate was also about whether the Federal Republic was really a viable and legitimate democracy. The FRG's ability to weather a direct attack and to do so without reverting to a police state may seem like the minimum one can expect from a democratic state, but for many West Germans neither was a given going into the 1970s. The ability of the West German democracy to respond to terrorism and to survive as a democracy points to terrorism's larger, lasting significance. Terrorism mobilized strong emotions and undoubtedly tested the republic's democratic commitments, but it also brought clarity. And at the end of the day, the majority of West Germans concluded that the state was neither fascist nor, as conservatives traditionally feared, too weak. Many critics on the left remained skeptical of the state and parliamentary politics. But they renounced the self-destructive politics of the RAF's "death trip" and their own "violent bitterness and acid cynicism" and directed their energies to the alternative projects and new social movements discussed above as well as to the successful founding of a nationally distributed countercultural newspaper, the *Tageszeitung*, and a parliamentary party left of the Social Democrats, the Greens. Critics describe these developments as the domestication or cooptation of left radical politics for there is no doubt that they helped stabilize the existing political system. But they also changed it. If West Germany's liberal institutions and political culture had never been so secure, they had also never been as open to further pluralization.

The experience of economic stagnation, rising unemployment, and terrorism on the one hand and grassroots organization on the other, encouraged many to rethink the role of the state in their lives. So much so that by the end of the 1970s, West Germans' relationship to the state was discernibly different than it had been at the outset. The change could be seen in people's response to the new Chancellery in Bonn, commissioned by the Social-Liberal government in 1969. The winning design boasted the democratic aesthetic of modern internationalist architecture and was celebrated for capturing, in concrete, a government open and accessible to its constituency. Upon its completion in 1976, however, that same three-story building with long horizontal lines and recessed windows was read as "faceless"—representative of a bureaucratic and administrative style of government. Confidence in the welfare state's reforming and benign hand was replaced by understandings of the state as both overly interventionist and inept. A faith in modernization and progress was giving way. But to what?

Further reading

Aust, Stephan. *Baader-Meinhof: The Inside Story of the R.A.F.* New York: Oxford University Press, 2009.

Becker, Jillian. *Hitler's Children: The Story of the Baader-Meinhof Terrorist Gang.* Bloomington, IN: AuthorHouse, 2014.

Böll, Heinrich. *The Lost Honor of Katharina Blum.* Translated by Leila Vennewitz. New York: Penguin Books, 1994.

Chin, Rita. *The Guest Worker Question in Postwar Germany.* New York: Cambridge University Press, 2009.

Geyer, Martin H. "Security and Risk: How We Have Learned To Live With Dystopian, Utopian, and Technocratic Diagnoses of Security Since the 1970s." *Historia* 396 (2015), 93–134.

Göktürk, Deniz, David Gramling, and Anton Kaes, eds. *Germany in Transit: Nation and Migration, 1955-2005.* Berkeley: University of California Press, 2007.

Griffiths, Craig. "Gay Activism in Modell Deutschland." *European Review of History* 22, no. 1 (2015), 60–76.

Haeberlen, Joachim, and Jake P. Smith. "Struggling for Feelings: The Politics of Emotions in the Radical New Left in West Germany, c. 1968-1984." *Contemporary European History* 23 (2014), 615–37.

Hager, Carol. *Technological Democracy: Bureaucracy and Citizenship in the German Energy Debate.* Ann Arbor: University of Michigan Press, 1995.

Hanshew, Karrin. *Terror and Democracy in West Germany.* New York: Cambridge University Press, 2012.

Jungk, Robert. *The Nuclear State.* Translated by Eric Mosbacher. London: John Calder, 1979.

Katzenstein, Peter J. *West Germany's Internal Security Policy: State and Violence in the 1970s and 1980s.* Ithaca, NY: Cornell University Press, 1990.

Melzer, Patricia. "'Death in the Shape of a Young Girl': Feminist Responses to Media Representations of Women Terrorists During the 'German Autumn' of 1977." *International Feminist Journal of Politics* 11 (March 2009), 35–62.

Milder, Stephen. *Greening Democracy: The Anti-Nuclear Movement and Political Environmentalism in West Germany and Beyond, 1968-1983.* Cambridge: Cambridge University Press, 2017.

Passmore, Leith. *Ulrike Meinhof and the Red Army Faction: Performing Terrorism.* New York: Palgrave Macmillan, 2011.

Schwarzer, Alice. *After the Second Sex: Conversations with Simone de Beauvoir.* New York: Pantheon, 1984.

Seefried, Elke. "Towards *The Limits to Growth*? The Book and its Reception in West Germany and Britain, 1972-73." *German Historical Institute London Bulletin* 33 (2011), 1–37.

Seefried, Elke. "Rethinking Progress: On the Origin of the Modern Sustainability Discourse, 1970-2000." *Journal of Modern European History* 13 (2015), 377–400.

Smith, J., and Andre Moncourt, eds. *The Red Army Faction: A Documentary History*. Oakland, CA: PM Press, 2009.

Varon, Jeremy. *Bringing the War Home: The Weather Underground, the Red Army Faction, and Revolutionary Violence in the Sixties and Seventies*. Berkeley: University of California Press, 2004.

8

The socialist nation and the rise of dissidence: Honecker's East Germany

FIGURE 8.1 *Marzahn, on the outskirts of East Berlin, was the largest of the new housing developments built in the GDR. (Bundesarchiv, Bild 183-1987-0128-310/ Hubert Link)*

Honecker's social reforms contributed to a brief increase in production. And the construction of new apartments plus the growing number of consumer products improved material conditions and raised people's quality of life. But economic problems rooted in the state-socialist system persisted. Companies continued to hoard goods and labor, and labor remained scarce and inefficient. The costly social reforms diverted labor and resources from other necessary goods, and the GDR fell further behind in the technological changes now shaping the world economy. To counter these problems, the state increasingly relied on inventive ways of acquiring hard currency from the West. The government also sought to rally popular support by fostering a new sense of identity apart from the German nation, opening up better relations with the churches, and seeking to gain for East Germany a grander status in international affairs. By signing the Helsinki Accords, the East German government won recognition from foreign powers—but also accepted the principle of internationally binding human rights, which dissenters then used to measure government actions. New forms of dissent, from those sympathetic to socialism and those opposed to it, from church-sponsored peace activists to literary figures to punk rockers, began to challenge the regime's legitimacy.

The GDR celebrated "really existing socialism" under Honecker. The term was, first and foremost, a propaganda slogan proclaiming that the existing East German society led others on the march of progress. But it implied more than that: the phrase implied that socialism had been achieved—that it was no longer a point on the way to Communism, but its own stage of civilizational progress. Communism was, to be sure, somewhere out there in the future but a better way of life already existed, here and now in the GDR. In this way, really existing socialism encouraged citizens to take stock of the present and to support the GDR for what it provided in the here and now: a stable and comparatively egalitarian system. The term also, however, opened the way for possible criticisms of the existing state, if it did not live up to its promises.

In part, the appeal to the present over a vague, ideal future reflected Honecker's pragmatic viewpoint on the conditions under which the state could operate. As he stated in 1971, "One cannot govern against the working class." Therefore he supported the social spending and subsidies for commodities described in Chapter 6. But Honecker was equally interested in asserting—to East Germans and the world—that the GDR was a stable society able to reproduce itself. And in many ways, that is how it appeared to observers both inside and outside of the country.

But societies and cultures of any kind, including both capitalist and state-socialist ones, do not remain stable. Nor can they ultimately be reduced to the demands of the state. Just as West German society developed in unexpected ways over the 1970s, so did society in East Germany. In both cases, new movements, critical of industrial society, the Cold War, and state power developed. In the case of the East, these movements ultimately came to challenge the state itself.

Creating a DDR identity: Nationalism, localism, sports, and consumer goods

Economics preoccupied the Socialist Unity Party leadership after 1961. But so did culture. The aim was not merely to create a stable and productive economy, but also to promote individuals' sense of belonging and loyalty to East Germany. In this respect the GDR did not differ greatly from the FRG of a decade earlier, except in one key respect: by drawing an unbroken line between itself and pre-Nazi Germany, the FRG won popular legitimacy from national loyalties and emotional bonds that predated the West German state. The "crisis of legitimacy" discussed in Chapter 7 resulted, in part, from the decline in the unspoken acceptance of these loyalties and historic continuities. The GDR, by contrast, had embraced historical rupture and, at least on the surface, rejected nationalist sentiment. For two decades, the Socialist Unity Party struggled to forge emotional ties between state and citizen and between individual East Germans based on internationalism and anti-fascism, with little success; by creating the National Front to rally former National Socialists in 1949 and by attacking "American" jazz and rock 'n' roll in the name of "German culture" in the 1950s, they continued to play with German nationalist traditions. Now, under really existing socialism, Honecker announced that a "new kind of nation, the socialist nation" was developing. Beginning in 1971, government policy promoted this socialist nationalism, both through developing aspects of East German regional identity and through victories in international sports. A new constitution, more military training, and the ongoing focus on social programs actively encouraged people's loyalty to the state. And, by laying claim to a specifically German socialist community, the shift in policy fed a more general appropriation of German history and culture for the GDR.

In 1974, the People's Chamber approved several revisions to the 1968 Constitution. Most important, the new constitution dropped references to the "German nation." Indeed, outside of the obligatory reference to the German Democratic Republic, the word "German" itself only appeared four times: once as a positive reference to the "German working class," once as a negative reference to "German militarism," and twice invoking the Free German Trade Union Federation. It referred not to the German nation but to "socialist national culture."

But what was GDR nationalism? As Jan Palmowski has shown, it necessarily involved regional identities. The GDR worked to promote local identity already in the 1950s, as well as regional variations in food, culture, and dress, as a way of breaking down allegiances to an older, united Germany (whether Bismarck's or Hitler's). The task was complicated and contradictory: strong regional identities could just as easily encourage distance from the GDR, promoting regionalism rather than national patriotism. A romantic regional identity could also mean resistance to a central authority that disturbed the local environment. The early attempts to create a separate identity did not succeed in any clear cut way. Honecker's effort to reclaim broader German national traditions and historical figures for the GDR starting in 1980 was more clearly an unmitigated failure. It ended the impossible task of denying East and West Germans a common past but proved equally challenging: Martin Luther and Bismarck, previously rejected "reactionaries," were now welcomed into GDR national history as transformative eastern Germans, who helped propel both the German nation and socialism toward their culmination in the German socialist state. Even the bronze statue of Frederick the Great astride his horse returned to its place of honor on Unter den Linden in Berlin, no longer a symbol of Prussian militarism but rather a symbol of East Germany's Prussian heritage. This attempt to "re-nationalize" German history paralleled efforts by conservative historians in the FRG to bring nationalism back in the German historical conceptions in the 1980s (discussed in Chapter 9).

The GDR leadership also viewed international sporting events as a way to rally support among the population. The state funneled funds and expertise into athletics, seeking to separate out the best athletes at an early age and breed them for the Olympics. Despite having a much smaller population, they were able to field tough soccer teams consistently; in 1974, the GDR team even beat the FRG team in the first round of the World Cup. They were later eliminated, and the West Germans won the tournament, but the team had proven its power. The East German sports industry was a world leader in the use of performance-enhancing drugs such as anabolic steroids as well as blood transfusions. While this wrecked the bodies of many, it also resulted in the resounding success of GDR athletes at the Olympic Games. Suspicions of other countries were confirmed in 1977, when shot put champion Ilona Slupianek tested positive for steroids. The trainers reacted to the embarrassment, not by ending the program, but by more carefully timed doping and comprehensive testing to avoid their athletes' failing the test. The East German team came in second in the world, in both the summer and winter games, in 1976, 1980 (when the United States and other Western countries boycotted the games over the Soviet invasion of Afghanistan), and 1988.

Preparation for possible combat with West German imperialists and fascists made up another part of the GDR's program. Since the building of the Berlin Wall, East German men were required to serve in the military. In 1978–79, as part of an attempt to bring the need to "defend the GDR" to the people, the government required "defense education," including paramilitary training, as a school subject starting with the ninth grade. Despite protests from parents and church leaders, defense education remained obligatory until 1990, when the only democratically elected People's Chamber removed the requirement.

As Chapter 6 already described, the Socialist Unity Party hoped that increased social security would lead to greater worker initiative at the

FIGURE 8.2 *At the 25th anniversary of the building of the wall, children in the Thälmann Pioneers' group cheer on members of the "Combat Group of the Working Class" as they march down the street in East Berlin. August 13, 1986. (ullstein bild/Stiebing/Getty Images)*

workplace. In addition, the 1974 constitution added new labor rights, which were codified in a revised book of labor law in 1977. The new rights combined with the endemic shortage of labor resulted in job security. It was very difficult for a worker to be fired. As a result, it continued to be in managers' interests to hoard workers: quantity over quality. Subsidized materials added to the disincentives in the system to become more efficient and productive. Not only were workers' jobs secure, but anyone could see that some workers got by doing little while others did a lot. Despite all this, a work ethos did develop in the firms. Workers were critical of those who did not work, referring to them as "asocials," a term made all the more problematic for having been used by the Nazis. Social pressure was thus exerted against those who did not measure up to the average. Workers themselves aimed, however, at the average. Official propaganda reflected the underlying tension of the workplace. On the one hand, it proclaimed loudly the stability and security of really existing socialism, and proclaimed ever new triumphs in production. On the other hand, the propaganda repeatedly demanded new, heroic efforts from the population, and state authorities repeatedly called for more efficiency and less waste. If the system was so successful, then the pleas for efficiency would not have been necessary.

In all advanced industrial societies—and such were both East and West Germany—labor and commodity production play a central role, and workers are paid at unequal rates. Some jobs, especially more skilled jobs populated mostly by men, paid higher wages in both East and West, for example, while service jobs carried out mostly by women paid less. In other respects, however, the societies looked far different. In the West, work tended to be separate from shopping, health care, and other non-work social functions. In the East, by contrast, larger firms had their own stores and sometimes even clinics, making the place of employment an important center of social life. Wages in the East were adequate for basic needs. Rents were subsidized and extremely low, as were basic commodities like meat and bread. Fresh vegetables, however, cost much more. And consumer goods like televisions and autos cost proportionately much more in the GDR than in the FRG. Special shops—Delikat and Exquisit—sold these more upscale goods. The Intershops, meanwhile, originally intended to attract foreign visitors from the West able to pay in Western currency, were opened up to East Germans in 1974—so long as they could pay with the West German Mark. Few were so lucky, but those who were obtained Western currency either from visiting relatives or through black market currency exchanges with visiting foreigners. The Intershops offered merchandise otherwise not available in the East—and priced accordingly. The higher prices allowed the state to mop up the "overhang" of demand in the GDR, represented by the growing savings accounts of citizens with little to spend the money on.

The Trabant or "Trabi," the East German two stroke automobile, provides a good example for how the state absorbed consumers' money. A small but relatively cheap car produced from 1958 on, it was marketed as a car for the people, a symbol of their modernity and mobility made out of the most modern of materials—plastic. East Germans themselves had a love-hate relationship with the car. Its weak engine and cramped interior was already outdated by the end of the 1960s, its cheap materials and poor construction the subject of countless complaints, and its replacement parts scarce. But for most it was the only car on offer, and relatively affordable. People signed up for a Trabant years in advance, often as soon as they turned eighteen; the waiting list stretched to well more than a decade. And since the state did not offer credit for automobile purchases, that period was spent saving money for the car—thereby removing that potentially inflationary currency from the economy.

State planners did take the people's demand for new kinds of consumer goods seriously. A new Institute for Market Research in Leipzig began investigating the people's needs already in the 1960s. From jeans to vinyl record albums, from women's fashion to colorful plastics for home furnishings that could have challenged the aesthetic claims of the worst dayglo orange tables on offer in the West in the 1970s, the State Planning Commission responded to consumers' demands. As Jonathan Zatlin has pointed out, however, those who worked for the Commission did not necessarily do so without grumbling over the consumerism of citizens of a socialist nation.

The party leadership and the party ideology asserted that the kinds of economic crises facing the West could not happen in the East. But they did. A gap between production and consumption arose, resulting in a growing deficit—especially to West Germany and other Western countries. Again and again, the leadership of the State Planning Commission pointed this fact out. Again and again, Honecker returned to his position that governance against the workers was impossible. The leadership placed its bet on the imminent collapse of the capitalist economy and on some breakthrough in technology that would suddenly put the GDR and the socialist world in the saddle of the world economy. Starting in 1977, for example, the planners threw massive resources at microelectronics, hoping to jump ahead of the major firms in the West investing in semiconductors and thereby gain valuable foreign markets. The huge investments led to a breakthrough in 1988, a one megabyte chip. It cost far more than its counterpart in the West, was less reliable, and was soon left in the dust.

The world economy kept getting in the way of the leadership's visions. The oil crisis of 1973 did not immediately affect the GDR thanks to the Soviet Union, which sold oil to its Eastern European allies far below international market value. By 1970, the Soviets already satisfied 80 percent of GDR crude oil needs, and faced increasing shortages at home; by 1972–73, the Soviets were forced to purchase oil on the world market, from Iraq, in order to satisfy its client states' need for oil. What the Soviets got from this deal was continued political stability and East German goods, though often of a lower quality than desired. Meanwhile, the GDR got much more than oil. By processing Soviet oil at massive plants and then selling the petroleum products to the West, it secured a new stream of Western currency. Economically, the Soviet Union could not afford to go on this way. Their own dependence on goods from the West, whose prices had increased due to the price of oil, finally led them to increase the price for oil to the GDR in 1974. Continued wrangling over oil muddied relations between East Germany and the Soviet Union for the next fifteen years. It ultimately encouraged the GDR to increase economic relations with the West, leading to further strains, and to a growing distance between Brezhnev and Honecker.

The destabilization of world oil prices, then, ended up affecting the GDR after all. In response, East Germany cut its use of oil in order to reserve these resources for trade with the West, and increased its use of the inefficient brown coal (lignite) available especially around Cottbus, in an area predominantly populated by the minority Sorb population. The result was environmental degradation, the destruction of many Sorb villages, and heavy reliance on one of the more inefficient and polluting forms of fossil fuel available. Anyone who spent time in the GDR after 1970 knows the smell of brown coal, which people used for their furnaces, and which seemed to seep into every corner of a building and every article of clothing.

Under Ulbricht's leadership, the Socialist Unity Party succeeded in establishing a stable political system. Honecker now used the policies of consumer socialism and socialist nationalism to establish a specifically East German culture and identity. It was an attempt to shape society from above not at all unique to state socialism or to Germany. But several things worked against the creation of patriotic East Germans. First, the heyday of nation-building, when all Western states (including the United States) rushed to industrialize their economies and invent a national culture using food, language, and newly found traditions, had occurred a full century earlier. However, it was not just the lateness of Honecker's undertaking but what had happened in the meantime to discredit nationalism: two world wars, Nazism, genocide. Precisely because of this dark past, socialism—with its open rejection of nationalism—continued to attract postwar Germans in both Germanys. Honecker's efforts to win popular support by reneging on this and other ideological commitments (including equality, as will be discussed below) cost the regime its lingering supporters. Or, more precisely, it sapped the energy from a small but critical cadre of social workers, lawyers, judges, and the like who enforced or facilitated the very policies designed to create the conditions for socialism. From the mid-1970s on, the Socialist Unity Party itself began to suffer from a lack of political conviction. The one thing that most clearly distinguished East from West Germany and argued for two separate states—the socialist project—began to matter less at exactly the moment when the regime hoped it would matter most.

This loss of faith was not specific to East Germany. Over the 1970s, ever more Marxists developed criticisms of state socialism. Like their predecessors, the "revisionists" of the 1940s and 1950s, they found in Marx's own work ammunition to aim at a state bureaucracy claiming to act in the name of the proletariat and a system of centralized planning that ever more emulated the big corporations of capitalism. The economic functionary Rudolf Bahro stands out in the East German context.

Despite a commitment to state socialism, Bahro had grown increasingly critical of official government policy over the 1960s, as Ulbricht's New Economic System gave way to renewed emphasis on centralized planning. Over the first half of the 1970s, Bahro penned a monograph highly critical of the Soviet model of economic development. Fearing that the Stasi were on to his project, he managed to get his book, *The Alternative in Eastern Europe*, smuggled out of the country in 1977. Parts of it appeared in the West German news magazine *Der Spiegel*. Bahro called for a second revolution against the new class society of state socialism. In many ways, the book remained within the mindset of the state-socialist tradition— but used its very categories to take apart those states' claim to legitimacy. Bahro was immediately arrested and jailed for two years on charges of espionage. Pressured by international protests, the regime released him and, in 1979, deported him to the FRG. There Bahro became an active member of the new Green Party, breaking with Marx and turning instead

to Christian liberation theology and environmentalism. His trajectory from
Lenin to radical environmentalism epitomizes Eastern intellectuals' gradual
disenchantment with the state-socialist project. It also reflects a wider turn
of critical intellectuals, in both East and West, against the "high modernism"
that celebrated grand, planned projects aimed at transforming society.

Even more than this loss of faith in the socialist project, the existence
of West Germany undermined the development of a unique sense of East
Germanness. There was always an alternative to the GDR. The Socialist
Unity Party could try to deepen citizens' commitment to the state through
international success in sports and other areas. New rights proclaimed in the
constitution could seek to increase people's sense of having a stake in the
system. Compulsory military service could seek to inculcate a proper militant
attitude toward West Germany and the capitalist world. Social programs
could aim to make people more grateful and hence more productive. But
West Germany remained just over the border, offering automatic citizenship,
basic rights, and a higher standard of living.

East German society: Within the state and beyond the state

It is among people—in families, extended families, friendship networks,
and workplace communities—that notions of civilized behavior or of work
expectations arise. States can foster these norms, but they cannot dictate them.
In this sense, East German society could never be fully reduced to the state.
It followed its own course, in ways that official ideology neither predicted
nor condoned. For all of its slogans about equality, society splintered into
many different groups, organized according to status and opportunity, and,
just like in capitalist countries, higher status mapped onto greater wealth.
Those who learned to speak the language of Marxism-Leninism and to
read and follow the overall party line had much greater opportunities in
secondary and higher education, as well as in the world of work. One could
become a leading technical expert without complete mastery of the official
language, but political docility remained a prerequisite. And intellectuals
and artists, so long as they remained loyal to the state despite occasional
transgressions, also enjoyed a higher status. In addition to nicer apartments
and other material benefits, they might be granted the right to travel to the
West—though travel often also required filing a report with the Stasi upon
their return.

These advantages added up to a sort of privileged middle class, not unlike
that in the West. More access to money, including Western currency, combined
with some travel freedoms, meant greater access to consumer goods. But just
like elsewhere, social inequality went deeper. Parents with education and
good jobs could teach their children how to act and pull strings to help them

in life: privileged classes tend to reproduce themselves. Leaders no doubt had good intentions. They did not oppose better conditions and opportunities for all, better quality schools and homes, better neighborhoods and social services. But reality diverged from the ideal, and ordinary people knew it.

Life differed greatly, moreover, depending on where one lived. East Berlin received more state investment than other parts of East Germany because of its position as a showplace for the West. But beyond that, much of the country remained relatively rural. Even in 1989, almost a quarter of its inhabitants lived in communities of 2,000 people or fewer. Collectivization had eliminated private farms, and the Socialist Unity Party ran politics and local government, but these communities retained their own characteristics. Catholic villages continued to celebrate their holidays, for example. Villages of the Sorbs, a Slavic minority in the eastern part of the country, also retained their language, customs, and sense of community, even as open-face coal mining destroyed the land around their towns and the government pressed for German as the official language.

Despite the demands placed on average East Germans to participate in mass organizations like the Free German Youth or in military exercises after work, they still found time to spend with family and friends and for holidays, book reading, and hobbies. Though this had always been the case, under Honecker one's private life took on more importance—for both East Germans and the state. Leisure time expanded with the introduction of shorter workdays and the Socialist Unity Party increasingly acknowledged that the state's social contract with its citizens included a comfortable domestic life. The 1970s were, according to Paul Betts, the "high period of Socialist Biedermeier." Gardening, family camping trips, and quiet evenings at home compensated for the disenchantment with socialist ideals, alienation at work, and lack of control over one's public life. Nude bathing, part of a longer tradition in German history, became ever more widely practised; the party at first criticized the movement, but eventually decided to claim it as its own, proof of socialism's more natural relationship to the human body. Not that East Germans confined themselves to the kinds of middle-class, familial pleasures that the Socialist Unity Party—now just as much as Christian Democrats in the FRG—extolled. The amount of time dedicated to watching television, for example, only increased with the growing numbers of televisions in people's homes. And that meant a lot of time was spent soaking up sounds and images from the West. And some of these East Germans, particularly youth, adopted and adapted these as their own. Jana Hensel, born in 1976, remembers the pride with which she and her friends sported homemade knock-offs of Adidas and Puma, and the social status granted a classmate wearing western blue jeans. Rebellious East German youth similarly adopted the music and style of British punk bands brought to them over West German airwaves. Punk's revolutionary and even anti-capitalist ethos did not cancel out its anti-establishment, anarchist politics and the Socialist Unity Party quickly condemned it. Punks, whose numbers the government estimated at 1,000 with some 10,000 "sympathizers," were chased underground and kept under the close eye of the Stasi.

The GDR also experienced its own sexual revolution, as Josie McLellan has documented. The gradual provision of better housing, the availability of contraception, the turn from Ulbricht's overbearing moralizing rhetoric to Honecker's more pragmatic approach to society, as well as the change in generations from one marked by the scarcity and violence of war to a postwar generation living in (relative) abundance: all of these factors contributed to a new approach to sexuality. No doubt West German television had an impact as well, but the Communist tradition itself had radical roots in its pre-Stalinist youth culture and critique of bourgeois morality. There remained a gap between the more prudish leadership and a society that seemed to increasingly accept sexuality, including outside of marriage. The sexuality accepted in the GDR by both state and society was furthermore private and heterosexual. Both official rhetoric and personal opinions considered homosexuality to be abnormal. Whereas in the West a public and increasingly political gay scene developed over the 1970s, its parallel in the East remained less visible.

People did indeed seek to live in their social niches, in the phrase made famous by the television talk show host Günter Gaus, who was appointed West Germany's "permanent representative" in 1974. But the image of a "niche society," suggesting East Germans' retreat from public life, has its limits. Families or friendship circles required protection, which meant outward conformity. Parents could opt out of state-socialist rituals at home, but only if they maintained those rituals at their jobs. The Socialist Unity Party furthermore cared a great deal about East Germans' private lives, especially insofar as they influenced job performance and the birthrate. And East Germans were not simply objects of state paternalism or silenced by repression. Most people figured out ways to navigate their social environment, conforming where necessary and taking advantage of what Socialist Unity Party institutions offered from sports to crafts to parties. They also used the state's own language, particularly its promises of equality and prosperity for all, and politicized the domestic sphere to meet their own demands for things such as childcare and reproductive rights. In this way East Germans protected their private lives from public scrutiny and control as best they could.

If the Socialist Unity Party promoted the private sphere as a place of really existing socialism, it also never fully trusted what people did in the privacy of their homes or weekend gardens. For this reason, the Stasi blossomed in both size and importance in what was otherwise a period of détente and relative liberalization. By 1977, the Stasi grew to over 70,000 official employees; in 1989, an estimated 91,000 people worked for the Stasi, making it the GDR's largest employer. In its last two decades the Stasi exchanged brute force and imprisonment (although these measures remained always available) for more subtle methods of preventing and subverting dissident behavior. New recording devices, secret video equipment, and automated letter-opening machines helped the Stasi keep tabs on religious leaders and dissident Christians, on conscientious objectors, on those who applied to leave the country, on nonconformist youth, and even on party officials and its own agents. With the information it collected, the agency also sought to break up dissident groups by playing on internal rivalries and disagreements, and to discredit individuals by sending incriminating photographs (sometimes doctored) or anonymous letters to spouses and friends. In these instances, surveillance was sometimes deliberately unsubtle, in order to unnerve and intimidate the person or group being watched.

Perhaps even more impressive than the professional Stasi apparatus was the ballooning of informal operatives who reported as needed on friends, family, colleagues, and acquaintances. Many saw it as their duty to report to the Stasi if asked; others no doubt did it for the thrill or sense of importance it inspired; while some were coerced into cooperating. Whether one worked officially or informally for the Stasi, there was no question that it paid, in favors, privileges, and status. The Stasi's power lay not in its surveillance technology but in its ability to give or withhold goods and jobs. By 1989, roughly one in thirty GDR citizens had assisted the Stasi at one time or another. The state security system and East Germans' participation in it produced a culture of self-censorship and secrecy, and, after 1990, a myth of the Stasi as omnipresent.

Culture does not remain stable over time, and the same held in East Germany. As in the West, an immediate postwar generation, concerned with jobs, security, and adequate consumer goods, gave way to a society more interested in individual self-expression and a broader range of consumer goods to fit the personality. Honecker's policies accelerated this process, promoting a turn to individualism and a parallel turn away from public life.

The Helsinki Accords

All of these changes took place within the foreign policy framework opened up by *Ostpolitik*. But *Ostpolitik* posed challenges for the GDR. Détente and peaceful cooperation between East and West opened the way for Soviet cooperation with West Germany. Soviet support for East Germany, however, tended to rise and fall in relation to the level of tension between East and West. Détente made the GDR more vulnerable, not less. After he came to power, Honecker made a point of stressing the GDR's connection to the Soviet Union for this reason, even asserting an "eternal bond" between the two in the 1974 Constitution. The 1975 Treaty of Friendship, Cooperation, and Mutual Assistance between the two powers underlined their connection.

At the same time, Honecker, like Ulbricht, sought new possibilities for independent action in foreign policy. Already by 1973–74, for example, secret meetings began to take place between Honecker and his closest collaborators and leaders of the Federal Republic, to discuss transportation and trade relations between the two states; even the Soviet Union was not informed about some of these discussions until they were near completion.[1] But it was ultimately the Helsinki Accords that offered Honecker a way to make his international role public. The GDR had a place at the table in the Conference on Security and Cooperation in Europe (CSCE), which started meeting in 1973 to help ease tensions in Europe. After two years of negotiations, the group agreed on the Helsinki Accords of August 1, 1975. For Honecker, the Accords were a great victory. All the states of Europe as well as the United States agreed to recognize existing borders and existing states; the signatories renounced the right to intervene in other states' internal affairs. Now Honecker stood and talked as an equal with Helmut Schmidt, and even had the chance to meet with President Gerald Ford of the United States.

Voices in the West, and not only on the right, condemned the Helsinki Accords for granting legitimacy to dictatorships, and this criticism continues to the present day. Certainly, Honecker viewed the GDR's enhanced legitimacy as the main result of the conference. More important over the long run, however, were the sections declaring human and civil rights, including the right to free travel, the right to the free flow of information, and the right to cultural exchange. The GDR had affirmed its respect for individual rights in its constitution and, now, in a major international treaty.

The leadership of the Eastern European countries did not consider these affirmations of human rights significant. To be fair, neither did US or Soviet leaders. But the populations of Eastern Europe and Russia did. In Czechoslovakia, for example, leading intellectuals signed the Charter 77 in 1977. It called upon the state to recognize the rights of citizens—and led to harsh retaliation from the authorities. Attentive East Germans read the Accords as well, reprinted in full in *Neues Deutschland*. In response, applications to emigrate increased by over 50 percent in 1976. Granting that right, of course, would have meant in essence tearing down the Berlin Wall. When the state refused to grant the petitions, one petitioner, the doctor Karl-Heinz Nitschke, took action. Since 1964, he had been trying to emigrate, and had landed in jail for his attempts. Nitschke was not especially political: he wanted to start a practice in the countryside, and did not want to do so under East German conditions. By 1975, after being arrested in Romania and coming under intense surveillance and harassment from the Stasi, he had had enough. He began to contact the press and human rights institutes in the West. And now his fellow citizens of the town of Riesa joined him in a collective petition with dozens of signatures. The result was a huge media spectacle, and the GDR responded with force, arresting many of the signatories. On August 26, 1977, after the FRG had agreed to pay for his release, GDR authorities deposited Nitschke in West Germany.

Payments from the West to release either jailed citizens of the FRG or troublesome GDR citizens like Nitschke had the virtue of bringing additional Western currency to the GDR. But they illustrated as well the continued desire of many easterners to leave the GDR. The Stasi reported to the government extensively on this problem, and on a deeper issue related to the approval of the Helsinki Accords: Amnesty International and other "hostile organizations" could now "misuse" the Accords for ideological reasons, for espionage, and to promote emigration. And indeed, dissent became an ever bigger problem for the GDR, which both relied on its security agency to keep the population in order and was increasingly dependent for economic reasons on a West Germany sensitive to human rights violations.

The Nitschke episode involved ordinary East Germans. The Biermann episode brought in the country's intellectuals. The state barred singer-songwriter Wolf Biermann from performing in East Germany already in 1965, as Chapter 5 described. But he continued to live in East Germany, inviting other regime critics to his house and producing records that were marketed in the West. In November 1976, Biermann received permission to travel to the FRG on the invitation of the I. G. Metall trade union. He gave a performance in Cologne on November 13, broadcast across West Germany, in which he both declared his dedication to the socialist experiment in the GDR and criticized political conditions there. After hearing of the matter, Honecker ordered the Stasi to strip Biermann of his citizenship and to not permit him to return home. Biermann had no choice but to take up permanent residence in West Germany.

The intellectuals who were permitted to earn their living as writers or performers in the GDR had made a deal with the state. They could work, they could even on occasion cross a political line into critique, so long as they remained dedicated to the state. Biermann was a particularly tough case: he did not hesitate to criticize the GDR as a bureaucratic state but he was a loyal socialist. Twelve leading figures, including Stephan Hermlin, Stefan Heym, Christa Wolf, Heiner Müller, and Jurek Becker, publicly asked the government to reconsider its decision. The GDR could, they stated, put up with such trouble; Biermann had never called into question his ultimate allegiance. They were soon joined by more than a hundred other public figures.

The Socialist Unity Party leadership was not prepared for such a response. They left the most important intellectuals alone. Others received a reprimand from the party, or were removed from the party. And some they forcibly expelled from the GDR. They made clear: to be an intellectual, with the special privileges that this entailed, public figures had to be loyal to the state—to a far greater degree than the intellectuals had anticipated.

The Biermann affair represents a major break in the history of GDR intellectuals. They had entered into a bargain with the state that required a kind of loyalty test and excluded explicit opponents of the state. Now the freedoms that they had gradually carved out seemed less secure. They voted with their feet, in ways that ordinary GDR citizens could not. In the aftermath of the Biermann affair, Jurek Becker, for example, moved to West Berlin, after being thrown out of the party; so did Manfred Krug, a famous actor now deprived of the right to act. He would become a beloved detective on the West German television show *Tatort*. Others, like Christian Kunert, were expelled. All of these cases called into question East Germany's adherence to the Helsinki Accords.

East German dissenters

Dissidence that went beyond the small group of relatively protected, state-supported intellectuals grew at the end of the 1970s, and began to take on a more openly critical tone. Dissent, however, can mean different things. At its most general, dissent includes those who explicitly rejected their society, but not necessarily on political grounds. The punk movement in East Germany, for example, initially formed around music, dress, and hair, rejected the norms of East German society—and in East Germany as in other parts of the world, much of society rejected the punks. The difference, of course, lay in the relationship between punk rock and the state: in East Germany, the Stasi became involved. In the early 1980s, they sought to dissolve the entire movement. By the mid to late 1980s, the Stasi had learned to make distinctions: they carefully removed the more politically active punks, and in October 1987 tolerated an attack by right-wing skinheads (also coming from the punk scene) on other punks at a concert organized by the Zion Church in East Berlin.

Open political dissent was a different matter. Those who organized in opposition to the state remained outsiders in the GDR. Indeed, across Eastern Europe dissenters represented a small minority, except for Poland, where a combination of Catholicism and the powerful independent trade union, Solidarity, made for a different kind of challenge (and one that concerned the GDR leadership). The collapse of the GDR in 1989–90 indicates how weak the state's legitimacy was before that point; it does not, however, indicate an active desire for change on the part of the general population.

Dissent nonetheless increased across Eastern Europe and the Soviet Union in the 1970s. Intellectuals, even some of the most privileged, now lent their voices to pacifism, environmentalism, and human rights—themes of dissent that were simultaneously mobilizing citizens in Western Europe. In the GDR, dissent developed in particular around the Protestant Church. The Catholic churches were small, were not centrally located, and kept to themselves; the Protestant churches, by contrast, were in the major cities, in particular East Berlin, and their religious leaders stayed in contact with the official Protestant Church in the West. Relations with the Socialist Unity Party leadership were never easy. In the 1970s, however, the Protestant

FIGURE 8.3 *Punks hanging out on the fringes of a concert in East Berlin.*
(ullstein bild/Volker Döring/Getty Images)

leadership adjusted its course in order to gain concessions from the regime. First, it broke off its official relationship to the Protestant Church in West Germany (though not West Berlin). Second, it completed its theological shift to a conception of the church as an ethical entity that existed for others, including for those not in the church. Third, the Protestant leadership declared in 1971 that theirs was a "church, not next to, not against, but in socialism." After decades of conflict over the *Jugendweihe*, over the right to remain part of the West German Church, and over persecution of church members who refused military service, they now accepted the state—not coincidentally at the same time as the government began trying to connect Martin Luther's Reformation to an East German identity. Some church leaders did so willingly, looking for the opportunity to reform the society within which they were located. Others did not easily accept the truce with a state that, on principle, denied the church's right to an autonomous existence.

In 1978, Honecker reached a decision with the church leadership that granted churches the right to control their own spaces. The aim was not social autonomy for the church, but for the state to gain a tool that would ensure church cooperation monitoring potential dissidents. And indeed many church officials entered into the bargain, submitting reports to the Stasi. The 1978 decision, however, also opened up a semi-public space for dissent and free discussion, protected from party structures. Here critics *not* enjoying the privileged status of the state-supported intellectuals could find their voice, from human rights advocates, environmentalists, and members of the peace movement to punks and gays and lesbians.

The big issues confronting citizens and governments in the West—nuclear war, environmental degradation, civil rights—had an official and unofficial place in the East as well. The official peace movement, for example, condemned the proposed stationing of missiles on West German soil: West Germany was the aggressor and imperialist. Their slogan was "oppose NATO weapons, create peace" (*Gegen NATO-Waffen Frieden schaffen!*).The Protestant Church took a somewhat different view. In the early 1970s, it adopted the Biblical phrase "from swords to ploughshares" to call for a reversal of the arms race and, in response to the introduction of paramilitary training in 1978, it spoke of "education to peace." The church offered space for pacifists to meet and to discuss Bible verses on war. Out

---

"BERLIN APPEAL" AGAINST NUCLEAR WEAPONS, 1982

Make Peace without Weapons

1. If there is war in Europe, this war can only be a nuclear war. It will transform Europe into a desert. The weapons of all kinds piled up in East and West will not protect us, but will kill us. That's their only purpose. The soldiers in the tanks and rocket bases and the general and politicians in the bunkers will be the last ones to die. . . .

2. If we want to prevent war, because we want to live, we must destroy the weapons of war. We therefore demand as a first step: get rid of atomic weapons. All of Europe must become a nuclear weapon free zone. We suggest negotiations between the governments of both German states concerning the removal of all nuclear weapons from Germany.

. . .

5. Make peace without weapons: that means not only creating security for our own survival. It also means the end of the senseless waste of labor power and the wealth of our people for the production of tools of war and the arming of huge armies of young men, who are thereby removed from productive labor. Shouldn't we help those with hunger across the world, rather than continuing to prepare our own death?

Source: Rainer Eppelmann and Robert Havemann, "Berlin Appeal," January 25, 1982, Robert-Havemann-Gesellschaft/RH 022/2 Bd. 080. Reprinted with the permission of the Robert-Havemann-Gesellschaft

of these groups developed pacifist positions that also criticized the Soviet Union and the GDR. At first, the state was hesitant: perhaps the "swords to ploughshares" contributed to socialism. Then, in 1981 the state declared that the movement muddied the political waters by not specifying that the West was the enemy. In response, in early 1982 the East Berlin pastor Reiner Eppelmann issued his "Berlin Appeal." Formulated with the help of the Marxist dissident Robert Havemann, it called for the removal of atomic weapons from both Eastern and Western Europe. From this point on, the East German peace movement grew slowly, persecuted by the state but growing within the Protestant Church and publicly supported by Western peace movement activists.

The peace movement also found support from Christa Wolf, a member of the Socialist Unity Party and one of the most important and valued intellectuals of the GDR. In 1983, she published the novel *Cassandra*, a feminist and pacifist retelling of the Greek story of the battle of Troy. The main character, Cassandra, has been granted the power to tell the future and the curse that nobody will believe her. As a woman, an outsider, an object of men's desires, she sees through the arguments for war. Like the pacifist movement, she foretells violence and destruction, carried out by men who cannot see the truth, who claim to fight for beauty (Helen) but instead fight to fight. It is no wonder that her book was censored in East Germany, where state leaders insisted on paramilitary training for school children and only allowed a peace movement that criticized the other side.

The environment was another important issue. East Germany was an industrial state, and like West Germany it suffered from environmental degradation. Also like West Germany, state and economic elites acted in collusion to avoid regulations that might slow the economy. The effect of strip mining for brown coal on Sorb communities in the Lausitz has already been mentioned: despite the official endorsement of regional identities, the economic plan demanded the destruction of the Sorb region. Basic criticism, indeed basic reporting, on environmental degradation could count as anti-state activity.

On April 26, 1986, a string of events led to the meltdown of one of the reactors at the Chernobyl nuclear power plant in Ukraine, then part of the Soviet Union. The resulting explosion produced a radioactive plume that drifted across northern Europe. The disaster was catastrophic, and was made even worse by the Soviets' response. Local villages were not evacuated for twenty-four hours, after many people had already fallen sick from radiation poisoning, and no official announcement of the disaster was made until April 28. Even thereafter, Soviet officials acted to limit the spread of information.

Criticism of the Soviet Union was taboo in the GDR. Environmental activists thus lacked information, about Chernobyl and about local environmental issues like the status of East German reactors, of groundwater, or of air quality. Information about the environmental conditions in East

Germany could serve as a tool for organizing, as they realized in the aftermath of Chernobyl. In 1986, the Zion Church in East Berlin granted environmental activists space in the church basement to start an unofficial library. The aim was an egalitarian, open space to read and discuss the relationship between environment and industrial society. The library also produced an underground newsletter, which would become one of the chief organizing tools of GDR dissent. The Stasi thoroughly infiltrated Berlin's Environmental Library, and cracked down on its leaders in 1987. But the West German press reported extensively on the event, and in the end the East German state released the dissidents. In 1988–89, churches in other East German cities founded their own environmental libraries.

The environmental movement also found its author in Monika Maron. Her stepfather, Karl Maron, was a leading GDR official who served for a time as minister of the interior; she was thus able to study theater and become a writer. In 1981, she published *Flight of Ashes* with a West German publishing house. Based on her experiences as a journalist around the heavily polluted city of Bitterfeld, the novel describes the machinations of the party as it defends a brown coal power plant, poisoning the land and the people. Even more than Wolf's novel, which set the story in ancient Greece, Maron's novel takes aim at the hypocrisy of the party and passivity of the population. Maron remained part of the political elite. Not permitted to publish in East Germany, however, she emigrated to West Germany in 1988.

Both pacifism and environmentalism raised questions about basic rights to information, to speech, and to peaceful protest. Unsurprisingly then, civil rights formed a third major theme around which dissent groups coalesced. The grassroots dissidents who gathered under the wings of the church in

---

MONIKA MARON DESCRIBES BITTERFELD

These smoke stacks like cannon barrels aimed at the sky shooting their charges of filth at the town day in day out and night after night: not with a roar, no, but quietly, like snow that falls slowly and gently, that stops up drainpipes, covers roofs where the wind blows without waves. In summer it swirls through the air, dry black dust that flies into your eyes. . . . Only strangers stand still and rub the soot from their eyes.

And the way people clean their windows. Every week, better still every day. Everywhere clean windows in this god—awful filth. They wear white shirts, the children, white stockings. You have to imagine it: going through the black, greasy rainwater with white stockings.

Source: Monika Maron, Flight of Ashes, *trans. David Newton Marinelli (New York: Readers International, 1986), 8. Reprinted with permission of Readers International.*

the late 1980s were different from the intellectual dissenters of the 1970s. Reunification and capitalism were not on the agenda for either group; both aimed to reform or to transform the existing state rather than to bring about its end. But as a group, the new dissenters lacked the sense of commitment to the GDR as a state-socialist project. For them, the system was dictatorial, hypocritical, and stifling. And they were no longer willing to tolerate its suffocating policies.

One of their leaders, Bärbel Bohley, made a name for herself in dissident circles over the 1980s, as an organizer and as an open protester of the military draft in 1983. In 1988, she and dozens of other dissidents connected with the so-called Church From Below and the Berlin Environmental Library and tried to participate in the commemoration of Rosa Luxemburg's murder during the German Revolution of 1918–19. Luxemburg was a hero of the GDR; she was also a harsh critic of Lenin's dictatorial tendencies. Many of the members of the group were arrested before the march: the Stasi was, as always, well informed. Those who succeeded in making the march carried a banner emblazoned with Luxemburg's famous quotations: "Freedom is always the freedom of those who think differently" and "The only way to rebirth: the broadest democracy." They were quickly arrested by the Stasi and eventually charged with treason, with the choice of long jail terms or expulsion to the West. The Socialist Unity Party's only response to the correct citation of one of its saints, in other words, was brute force. Though a small part of the demonstration, the incident received heavy coverage on West German television and was therefore viewed by many or most East Germans. The dissidents had succeeded in putting the regime's hypocrisy in full view. They remained peripheral to society at large. But over the next year and a half, their disruptive events spread, contributing to the GDR's gradual loss of legitimacy.

Further reading

Augustine, Dolores L. *Red Prometheus: Engineering and Dictatorship in East Germany, 1945-1990*. Cambridge, MA: MIT Press, 2007.

Bahro, Rudolf. *The Alternative in Eastern Europe*. London: Verso, 1978.

Barck, Simone, Martina Langermann, and Siegfried Lokatis. "The German Democratic Republic as a 'Reading Nation': Utopia, Planning, Reality, and Ideology." In *The Power of Intellectuals in Contemporary Germany*. Edited by Michael Geyer, 88–112. Chicago: University of Chicago Press, 2001.

Bathrick, David. *The Powers of Speech: The Politics of Culture in the GDR*. Lincoln: University of Nebraska Press, 1995.

Dale, Gareth. *Popular Protest in East Germany, 1945-1989*. New York: Routledge, 2005.

Dennis, Mike. *The Stasi: Myth and Reality*. New York: Routledge, 2003.

Fulbrook, Mary. *The People's State: East German Society from Hitler to Honecker*. New Haven: Yale University Press, 2008.

Gieseke, Jens. *The History of the Stasi: East Germany's Secret Police, 1945-1990*. New York: Berghahn, 2015.

Madarász, Jeannette Z. *Working in East Germany: Normality in a Socialist Dictatorship, 1961-79*. New York: Palgrave Macmillan, 2006.

Markovits, Inga. *Justice in Lüritz: Experiencing Socialist Law in East Germany*. Princeton, NJ: Princeton University Press, 2010.

McLellan, Josie. *Love in the Time of Communism*. New York: Cambridge University Press, 2011.

Pence, Katherine, and Paul Betts, eds. *Socialist Modern: East German Everyday Culture and Politics*. Ann Arbor, MI: University of Michigan Press, 2008.

Richardson-Little, Ned. "Between Dictatorship and Dissent: Ideology, Legitimacy, and Human Rights in East Germany, 1945-1990." *Bulletin of the German Historical Institute* 56 (2010), 69–82.

Rubin, Eli. "The Trabant: Consumption, Eigen-Sinn and Movement." *History Workshop Journal* 68 (2009), 27–44.

Tyndale, Wendy R. *Protestants in Communist East Germany: In the Storm of the World*. Burlington, VT: Ashgate, 2010.

Zatlin, Jonathan. *The Currency of Socialism: Money and Political Culture in East Germany*. New York: Cambridge University Press, 2008.

9

The paradox of West German conservatism

FIGURE 9.1 *Döner Kebab Imbiss, 1984. (ullstein bild/Harry Hampel/Getty Images)*

Helmut Kohl's Christian Democrats returned to power in 1982, leading a government focused on financial retrenchment and nationalist identity politics. At the same time, the peace movement achieved broad public support as nuclear disarmament found favor among environmental activists, members of the alternative scene, left-leaning Social Democrats, and even some Christian Democrats. In response to the growing body of scholarship that linked particular German traditions to National Socialism and the Holocaust, a new cohort of conservatives attempted to fashion a more nationalistic, or patriotic, approach to West German history. The result was a heated debate on how to come to terms with the past. Could Germans ever escape their history? The fact that millions of guest workers had by now become permanent residents of West Germany played into the debate, as Turks and Kurds, Serbs, Croats, and Kosovars, and many others brought their own pasts to bear on the present—and future—of the FRG. In the end, a return to tradition and the nation could not resolve the challenges of identity faced in West Germany.

The 1980s has a reputation as a conservative decade. In the United States, Great Britain, and the FRG, conservative parties regained power after a decade or so of labor or left-center governments. Their resurgence reflected the waning confidence in liberal solutions—like the welfare state and Keynesian economics—to solve the world's problems, in particular the energy crisis, inflation, and unemployment that continued to plague the West. The shift rightward also reflected broader unease and feelings of dislocation following the social and cultural tumult of the previous two decades.

In West Germany, the Social Democrats were under fire from all sides: from its coalition partner, the Free Democrats; from conservatives; and from its own party base. Meanwhile, the Christian Democrats, under the leadership of Helmut Kohl, underwent significant internal reform; they eagerly reclaimed the reins of government in 1982, when confidence in Schmidt collapsed and the Free Democrats threw their weight behind the CDU. As chancellor, Kohl promised a new era of economic liberalism and "spiritual-moral" rejuvenation. The so-called conservative turn entailed cuts to public spending, efforts at restructuring labor and industry, and a renewed German patriotism. But for all of the conservatives' language of radical new beginnings, there was considerable continuity between Schmidt and Kohl. In fact, the decline of the Social Democrats can be blamed at least partially on the fact that West German conservatives championed many of the positions held by conservative Social Democrats regarding the counterculture, immigration, and political stability. This is certainly how millions of peace protesters viewed the situation, and it is one of the reasons a new parliamentary party, the Greens, entered the political stage at this time, demonstrably to the left of the Social Democrats.

The image of 1980s West Germany as one of overwhelming conservatism is not wrong but it leaves out a great deal. Not only did West German conservatives travel a parallel but different path from their Anglo-American counterparts, but the FRG also saw considerable activity and organization on the political left and, perhaps more significantly, outside the traditional left-right political spectrum altogether. While the 1980s was a decade of conservatism, it also witnessed the largest mass demonstrations in FRG history. The Green Party brought environmentalists, feminists, and former student rebels into parliament and Land-governments. And thirty years after its founding, West Germany was a far more pluralist, multicultural, and multiethnic society than it had been even a decade before. What connected many the seemingly divergent trends, conservative and progressive, was a strong emphasis on the individual: needs, solutions, and rights.

Helmut Schmidt and the peace movement

Previous chapters have traced the long history of the peace movement in West Germany. In the 1950s, it opposed rearmament and the atomic bomb. In the late 1960s and early 1970s, it came to be dominated by the student left, and characterized by opposition to the Vietnam War. In the late 1970s, it returned to its roots as a movement—although the distrust of the United States that had deepened during the Vietnam War certainly did not go away.

In the late 1970s, the United States and the Soviet Union were in talks about nuclear disarmament. Chancellor Helmut Schmidt defended the strategic arms limitation treaty as essential to military and political stability and to East-West détente generally. But he did so while pointing out the presence of new, medium-range Soviet SS20 missiles in Eastern Europe and the absence of similarly modern missiles in Western Europe. NATO slept, he argued, while the Soviets modernized, and no other nation would be more negatively affected by a Soviet stockpiling of weapons than West Germany—the United States' principal NATO ally. It was not just the threat of physical annihilation that worried Schmidt; the SS20s gave the Soviets a weapon with which they could politically blackmail the country. In the assessment of Schmidt and many others, military parity was thus essential: the sides should be balanced to ensure that one side did not have a greater incentive to start a war than the other. For this reason, Schmidt advocated stationing medium-range nuclear missiles in West Germany unless the Soviets removed theirs. This was essentially the tactic NATO adopted in what became known as the dual-track decision.

At the same time, the Cold War intensified after a decade of détente. In 1979, revolution brought a left, socialist-leaning government to power in Nicaragua, replacing a sordid, American-supported dictatorship. The same year, the Iranian Revolution left both the United States and the Soviet Union unsure about the future of the Middle East. The US response under President Jimmy Carter appeared halting and indecisive. Last but not least, the Soviet Union invaded Afghanistan. Ronald Reagan was elected president in 1980 largely in response to the sense that the United States was adrift, weakened by the Vietnam War, the Nixon Watergate scandal, and continued economic recession, and now growing international unrest. Reagan and his military advisers called for modernizing US and NATO forces. And they started to fund, arm, and train internal opponents of the regimes in Nicaragua and Soviet-controlled Afghanistan, who undertook armed attacks on the existing states. Defended as "freedom fighters" by their supporters, their opponents termed them "terrorists." Among the people supported by the United States in Afghanistan was the later anti-American terrorist Osama bin Laden, showing just how changeable the labels could be.

President Reagan himself was not prone to moderation. Soon after taking office, he made public jokes about shooting off nuclear missiles and referred to the Soviet Union as an "evil empire." Members of his administration speculated about whether the United States could win a nuclear war. In this context, plans to station medium-range missiles in Western Europe resurrected German fears of nuclear death and enflamed anti-American sentiments among German antiwar activists. The foreign and defense ministers of NATO together agreed to the dual-track decision to simultaneously pursue arms negotiations and deploy 108 midrange Pershing II missiles and 464 cruise missiles in Western Europe. The long-range but slow cruise missiles were to be placed in West Germany, Sicily, Great Britain, the Netherlands, and Belgium but the Pershing II missiles were to be stationed in the FRG alone, within range of Moscow. And though stationed in the FRG, the United States held the launch button for the Pershings, which could fly so fast as to make a response impossible before they hit. What might be a purely tactical decision in Washington, D.C. could mean the obliteration of Germany, East and West, in the kind of midrange engagement for which the missiles were designed.

A flood of citizens' initiatives greeted the proposals for Pershing missiles. Protests swelled into the hundreds of thousands, and even millions, uniting not only Germans but Europeans (as well as Americans), Mohawk-sporting punks and clergy in common cause. The Krefeld Appeal, calling for a nuclear-free Europe, attracted some four million signatures in West Germany alone. Its success was unexpected and reached, again, across society. Underlying the protests in the West was a basic theme, echoed in the dissident peace movement of the East: the protesters trusted neither nuclear superpower.

The "missile crisis" culminated in 1983, the year the United States deployed the missiles. It was also the peace movement's high-water mark. American commentators anxiously noted that, while 72 percent of West Germans said that the FRG should remain in NATO, only 46 percent would do so if given the choice between rejecting the missiles and leaving NATO versus accepting the missiles and staying in.[1] Why were Americans so concerned? NATO commanders claimed that without West Germany, the military alliance lost its ability to deter or defend. And though they ultimately ignored the peace movement, relying on the passive and active support of the millions who did not protest the missiles deployment, the statesmen and women who backed the double-track decision—on both sides of the Atlantic—understood its reach. Rumors circulated about Communists having infiltrated the movement, but they failed to discredit the millions of protesters. In fact, their message and their fears seeped into popular culture and bridged language barriers. In Europe, Japan, and the United States, "Neunundneunzig Luftballons" by the German singer-songwriter Nena (aka Gabriele Susanne Kerner) topped the charts in 1984. The song's lyrics painted a not unbelievable, if unlikely, scenario in which ninety-nine red balloons trigger a nuclear war with the help of trigger-happy pilots, power-hungry war ministers, and panicked nations. The conflict ends with no winners; surrounded by ruins, the singer releases a lone red balloon.

Challenges to the Social Democrats: Environment, peace, citizens' movements, and the founding of the Greens

In the 1970s, the Social Democrats did not expect a parliamentary challenge from the left. They had already won a political battle against the Communists in the 1950s, when the KPD faded away to insignificance before being banned. A new version, the DKP, was founded in 1968; it was closely aligned with and indeed funded by the Socialist Unity Party in East Germany. It, too, never had any significant support among the population at large, although it attracted support from a number of left intellectuals and activists.

But now the Social Democrats' basic positions were under attack, also from within the party. Disagreement over the government's build-up of police and surveillance powers as well as its willingness to suspend some civil liberties in the fight against terrorism split the Social Democrats into left and right wings. Those two positions mapped roughly onto party members' different relationship to extra-parliamentary movements, whether they saw them as correctives to established politics or as unwelcome interlopers. Social Democrats who joined the anti-nuclear and environmental movements discussed in Chapter 7 and the peace movement discussed above, found themselves increasingly divided between their party and their politics. The Social Democratic future involved industrial growth; the environmental movement questioned its presuppositions. The Social Democrats under Brandt and Schmidt had favored détente, yes, but also accepted the premise that West Germany would be aligned with the West and with the United States. The peace movement questioned that alignment, and many proposed a neutral central Europe. And no matter their cause, the citizens' initiatives challenged the mostly parliamentary orientation of the Social Democrats. Schmidt won international praise for his level-headed solutions to the financial and security crises besetting the industrial world, but at home and within his own party opinions were extremely mixed.

Schmidt nonetheless won the elections of 1980. His opposing candidate was Franz Josef Strauss, whose redbaiting rhetoric and staunch conservatism (he once admitted a hankering for monarchism) did nothing to help the Christian Democrats, and quite a lot to help Schmidt. Also, Schmidt's own record and personality, particularly his air of pragmatic decision making and sober realism, drew centrist voters, regardless of their party affiliation. Conservatives looking to remake their Cold War warrior image paid heed to exit polls that noted the average voters' preference for competence and a "man of the people." Strauss remained a political fixture as the head of the Bavarian government until his death in 1988, but the brand of conservatism that he represented moved to the margins with his 1980 defeat.

There was, however, a new party in the elections: the Greens. Whatever one thought of parliamentary politics—and many Greens supporters thought very little of it—the appearance of a new party on the federal level was evidence of the FRG's growing pluralism. Since the Social Democrats renounced Marxism and set its sights on becoming a center-left party in 1959, left activists and intellectuals had dreamed of a parliamentary alternative. But the potential engines—the DKP, the German Peace Union, the Democratic Union—each failed. The Greens' initial base was broader; it formed out of the complex milieu of the citizens' initiatives and the anti-nuclear movement, movements with single-issue goals that reached across traditional party lines. Their members included members of tiny communist splinter parties; Social Democrats disappointed in Schmidt; Christian Democrats and Christian Socials infuriated by the heavy-handed tactics of their local party leaders; and long-standing ecological clubs, some far to the right of Christian Democracy. Minority groups and Third World/anti-imperialist organizations also joined the "alternative list" initiative as did concerned Christians like Christa Nickels and artists like Joseph Beuys, in pursuit of a third way. It was a truly colorful group, which, from 1977 on, contested local elections, usually not reaching 5 percent of the vote. They had different names: Green, Alternative, Democratic List. In 1979, a group of them met in Frankfurt to bundle their voting potential in preparation for elections for the European Parliament. Their leaders included Herbert Gruhl, a former Christian Democrat, whose book *The Planet Is Being Plundered* was a bestseller among ecological groups, and Petra Kelly, a leader of the citizens' initiative movement more generally.

Born in the American Zone of Occupation in 1947, Petra Lehmann became Petra Kelly when her mother married a US Army officer. Her dual nationality parents opened the way for her to experience American culture and politics. She moved to the United States in 1959, where she participated in the civil rights movement and even campaigned for Robert

Kennedy before returning to West Germany in 1970. She was a political science major, and worked for the European Commission, at the same time becoming more involved in environmental and alternative politics. She quit the Social Democrats in 1979 and quickly became one of the leaders of the new Green movement. Intense and charismatic, she proved to be a hero for others, including for Major General Gert Bastian. Bastian was an officer in the Second World War, later chosen to build a democratic army in the postwar Federal Republic, and a member of Strauss's Christian Social Union. Firmly anti-Soviet, he nonetheless believed that Soviet foreign policy was primarily defensive, not offensive. He also feared that the new generation of missiles made nuclear war more, not less, likely. Because of this fear, Bastian finally resigned his commission in 1980 to join with Kelly and the Greens. Side by side in politics and in life, Kelly and Bastian captured the broad coalition that had, by the 1980s, coalesced around issues of peace and environmentalism.

The Greens were not just another party, but a kind of anti-party, whose very existence stood as a critique of the existing West Germany political system. A soccer metaphor helped describe the intended relationship of the party to its base: the Greens were to have one leg firmly planted in grassroots movements and one "kicking leg" in parliament. Instead of the "one-dimensional productionist politics" of Bonn, the Greens promised a more holistic and future-looking approach, a politics that was ecological, social-minded, grassroots, feminist, and nonviolent. The party's work derived from these core principles.

The Greens formed under chaotic circumstances in 1980. They faced all kinds of questions: Should they allow members of the dogmatic, communist splinter groups to join, given their different conception of a party and rejection of pacifism? Should members be allowed to belong to multiple parties? And what should be on the platform? The platform of 1980 called for shutting down the nuclear power plants, unilateral disarmament, the end of NATO and the Warsaw Pact, as well as the full legalization of abortions, incontrovertibly establishing themselves as part of the environmental, peace, and feminist movements. Campaign slogans like "Alternatives for Everyone," "Neither Capitalism nor Communism—We Need a New Path," and "Courage for a Political Spring" (in reference to the Prague Spring) similarly spoke to members of the alternative milieu and to the politics of 1968. Because of the new party's connection to radicalism and advocacy of abortion rights, many conservative elements, including Herbert Gruhl, abandoned the party-movement. In the 1980 elections, the Greens received 1.5 percent of the votes, and were thus denied representation. But only a couple of months later they crossed the 5 percent hurdle in Baden-Württemberg. And in 1983, with 5.6 percent of the vote, twenty-eight Greens entered the Bundestag for the first time, breaking the three-party structure that had dominated since the 1950s. The new delegates appeared in jeans, carrying potted plants to their seats.

PETRA KELLY ON GREEN POLITICS

We have little reason to place our hope in governments or established political parties, for their primary interest is always in extending their own power. But we can find hope in the strength and imagination of people working at the grassroots to create positive change. We Greens work within the political system solely for the benefit and empowerment of those at the grassroots. Our efforts within the halls of government are not to replace work at the grassroots. Our commitments are, first and foremost, to those who elected us. We must work with them, nonviolently, for life-affirming solutions to the problems of our day.

Green politics is based on direct democracy—our effort is to redefine and reorganize power so that it flows from the bottom up. We seek to decentralize power and maximize the freedom and self-determination of individuals, communities, and societies. This means moving power out of the hands of centralized bureaucracies—above all, the military-industrial complex—and empowering people on the local level. It also means reaching across national borders and ideologies to build alliances with others also working for peace and ecology. It means moving government power away from the state towards smaller and smaller units of organization. In economics, grassroots democracy means a production system that maximizes workers' self-management and minimizes corporate or government control. It means units of production scaled to a comprehensible human dimension and that are locally responsive and globally responsible. The day may come when the Greens find a truly democratic and ecological partner among the established political parties, but until then we must work in government as an anti-party party, an experiment in radical parliamentary opposition unwilling to compromise fundamental values for the sake of expediency.

Source: Petra Kelly, "Thinking Green!" *From Thinking Green! Essays on Environmentalism, Feminism, and Nonviolence (Berkeley: Parallax, 1994), 42–43. Reprinted with permission of Parallax Press, Berkeley, California, www.parallax.org.*

Origins of the *Wende*: Helmut Kohl and the Christian Democrats

The Greens were a challenge to the Social Democrats, but also to the Christian Democrats, insofar as the Greens took over some of the focus on conservative and regional values. The new party even caused the Free

Democrats some concern. Who was more in favor of individual rights, the Greens or the Free Democrats?

But the Social Democrats had other problems. Under Schmidt the economy continued to see high unemployment and in 1981, German economic growth was negative. The deficit increased dramatically. And by the end of 1981, the Social-Liberal coalition was at a crossroads. If the Social Democrats continued to follow its own policies, maintaining social expenditures and providing subsidies to help workers who were losing jobs in basic industries, the Free Democrats feared that the economy could veer out of control, into high inflation without growth. On the other hand, if the Social Democrats cut social benefits, they hurt their base of support, the industrial working class.

On September 9, 1982, the Free Democratic minister of economics, Otto Graf Lambsdorf, released a paper that read like a radical turn to economic liberalism: he demanded that the government dramatically cut social spending, lower the deficit, liberalize rents and reform labor law, and cut taxes for business. Many of these ideas existed within the Social Democrats' conservative wing, associated with Helmut Schmidt. But winning over the party and its base to the uncompromising economic plan laid out by the Free Democrats was hard. Making labor more "flexible," for example, meant cutting the rights of labor—a position antithetical to the party's history and, many argued, its core ideological commitments. When Schmidt ultimately refused to accept the demands of the Free Democrats, they abandoned his cabinet in a move that left them free to ally with the Christian Democrats.

In the political seesaw that characterized Free Democratic politics, economic commitments now trumped social agendas. This was true even for Hans-Dietrich Genscher, who originally spearheaded the Free Democrats' reformist agenda but now actively strategized with Kohl to topple the existing government. On October 1, 1982, Helmut Kohl called for a vote of no confidence. It succeeded, the only time that it has in the history of the Federal Republic up to this day. Some Free Democrats were upset, especially those committed to liberal reforms. But with the exception of a few representatives who joined the Social Democrats in protest, they fell in line behind the leadership of Lambsdorff and Genscher. Soon, Germany had a new, conservative face—and a new, Christian Democratic-Free Democratic coalition government.

It was new because the Christian Democrats were no longer the party of Adenauer, though it continued to pay homage to him. For nearly a decade, Helmut Kohl had been working if not to reinvent the party then to thoroughly spruce it up. The Christian Democrats' core constituency, aside from being Catholic, was aging, and détente and the peace movement greatly weakened the party's go-to strategy of anti-Communism. In short, it was past time for change. With the assistance of other younger members of the party, Kohl repositioned it to appeal to the center, particularly to northern Protestants and to younger voters and women—swing voters who were increasingly decisive to elections. Updating the Christian Democrats' image required a new party platform and actively demonstrating that conservatives, too, had good ideas.

When Kohl became chairman of the Christian Democrats in 1973 he called for the reinvigoration of a conservative "community of values and ideas." He and his fellow reformers blamed older leaders for neglecting the party's soul—its beliefs and cultural dimensions—and assuming that past economic successes would continue to get it reelected. Christian Democrats complained and offered doom-and-gloom predictions but offered West Germans no constructive alternatives; the party knew what it opposed, but what did it stand for? Under the leadership of Richard von Weizsäcker, the future president of the new conservative government, a special commission spent two years crafting a new party program that answered this question. Completed in 1976, it took another two years of intense party debate before the Christian Democrats officially accepted a new program in 1978. It declared the Christian Democrats' commitment to "freedom, solidarity, justice" and to the defense of the existing order. Here, "defense" included strong support for NATO and nuclear armament but also a "spiritual-moral" turn aimed at restoring pride and personal investment in the institutions of the FRG. The new message was particularly welcomed by West Germans who were tired of social unrest and what they experienced as a young generation's destructive—not to mention ungrateful—disparagement of all they had accomplished after the war.

While Kohl was regenerating the Christian Democrats, the main party of the CDU, the Bavarian Christian Socials took a different course. Between 1966 and 2008, the CSU had gained the absolute majority of votes in Bavarian elections. This achievement rested on the Christian Socials' ability to represent the special interests of Bavaria while avoiding the shrill tones of other Bavarian federalist parties: only the Christian Socials managed to build up a modern election machine, to open the party to the minority Protestants in parts of Bavaria, and to be represented in important ministries at the federal level. The party maintained support as well by means of a conservative populism closely identified with the strong personality of Franz Josef Strauss. The party at times adopted anti-foreigner slogans and professed to reject the principles of *Ostpolitik* (the emphasis on professed—it did not in reality do so). Popular support also rested on success: the Christian Socials put in place economic policies that gradually transformed Bavaria from a relatively backward, agricultural land to a leader in technological innovation. The Christian Socials became the party furthest to the right on the party spectrum, a position it held until the rise of the short-lived Republicans in the 1980s and the Alternative for Germany after 2010 (discussed in Chapter 13). As such, it often opposed its close partner, the Christian Democrats.

Christian Democratic leaders meanwhile offered new initiatives in social policy. Heiner Geissler, as noted in Chapter 7, called to embrace groups that had been marginalized, including women. A few years later, he was joined by Rita Süssmuth, a professor of education and one of the relatively few women professors in the FRG at the time. Süssmuth joined the Christian Democrats in 1981 and quickly rose through its ranks as an advocate for working mothers, a dramatic move for a party that just a few decades before had insisted that a woman's place was in the home. The Christian Democrats had become a home for reformers.

As a leader, Kohl was no less important to Christian Democracy's reform, breaking as he did with the authoritarian style of Adenauer and Strauss. Kohl drew on a language of pragmatism and unruffled realism to craft an image of strength not unlike that of his rival, Helmut Schmidt. In addition, he delegated power in a reorganization of the Christian Democrats that helped invigorate the party's base. For twenty years, the party had essentially been run out of the chancellor's office. Now, local and regional party offices gained full-time staff and greater responsibility. Kohl also recruited young campaign strategists to revolutionize the party's electioneering and

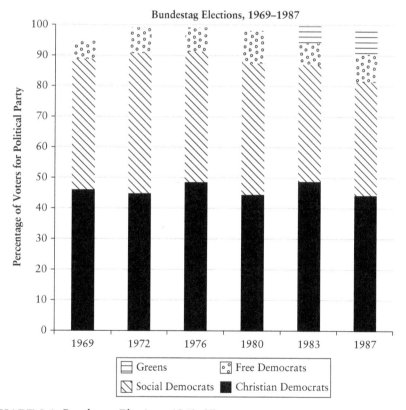

CHART 9.1 *Bundestag Elections, 1969–87*
Note: *Where figures add up to less than 100%, the remaining votes went to parties that failed to fulfill the conditions (in particular the 5% hurdle) required to enter parliament.*

communication techniques. And in the end, his efforts paid off. In the 1983 federal elections, the Christian Democrats succeeded in taking nearly 49 percent of the vote—results that clearly affirmed the Union's new path and nearly secured it a majority of the vote. Kohl would end up chancellor for a total of sixteen years, longer than Adenauer. When he left office, he was the furthest thing from a reformer—but both he and the Christian Democrats owed their long reign to the reformist energies he once championed.

Neoconservatives in power

Economic policy

For all their brave words about enacting an abrupt change in economic policy, the Kohl-Genscher government ended up looking quite moderate compared with those of Margaret Thatcher in Britain and Reagan in the United States. In both of these countries, the neoconservative governments came to power calling for a dramatic break with the policies of the postwar period. They called for a renunciation of Keynesian measures to stabilize and guide the economy, for a reversal of social spending, for the privatization of services provided by government such as post offices and schools, and for replacing social security systems with fixed contributions to private investment accounts for retirement. Many of these projects failed in the real world of US and British politics, but even so their rhetoric was much more radical than that of the German conservative coalition. The "German model" tempered Anglo-American neoliberalism with traditional German corporatism and a social market economy that emphasized the social obligations of the state, and thus swam against the tide by maintaining a level of cooperation between government, unions, and corporations.

First, the government called for cleaning up finances and reversing the deficit. In practice, that did not mean major cutting of social spending, but it did mean declaring a halt to new social spending. Schmidt had de facto already moved in this direction. In practice, several increases were delayed and several marginal programs cut slightly. In addition, the government began moving toward privatizing some state-held firms, including Volkswagen, but also Lufthansa and the federal train system. These were one-off sales that brought a one-time influx of cash. But at a cost. Privatized transportation and hospital services meant under-provisioning certain groups, such as the elderly and rural populations. Until German unification, West Germany did not see any major new expenditures, which was one way the government managed to get the deficit under control.

Second, the government called for the "flexibilization" of labor. In practice, making labor more flexible meant reducing the work week and increasing the number of part-time and temporary jobs. The effect was to open up a new field of low-paid work for the less skilled—those who tended, in any event, not to be in unions—and to move men into a sector of the economy previously associated with women's work. Employers favored the reforms, while the left harshly criticized them. In the FRG, such reforms remained relatively limited in any case because the government continued to treat the unions as a key partner in policy making.

Third, the government, in conjunction with unions, tried to help ease people out of the industries in decline, especially as cheaper steel from other lands undermined the West German steel industry. It did not respond as Thatcher had in Britain, by allowing massive plant closings. As a result, the FRG avoided the extremely painful labor strikes and mass layoffs of miners, steelworkers, and other blue-collar workers that wracked 1980s England. But these policies, including short term job-creation schemes, had little effect on the country's overall economic health. And neither they nor efforts to make labor "flexible" solved the problem of unemployment. The number of West Germans without work hit an all-time high of 2.2 million in Kohl's first years in office and remained high through the 1980s.

In all of these areas, Kohl's minister of labor, Norbert Blüm, played a role. From the trade union movement, he helped to integrate Catholic workers into the party. More important, he became known as the protector of pensions—and as a guarantor of future Christian Democratic success. With Blüm's energy, a new long-term care component was added to the social security system. Blüm was the first minister of labor who had to confront a looming crisis of the pensions insurance system: the graying of the West German population. A declining number of workers would be paying for an increasing number of retired people. Demographers made dire predictions over the 1980s about how contributions to social security could double or more over the coming decades, eventually reaching one-third or more of workers' salaries. Blüm promised that pensions were secure in the electoral campaign of 1986. To ensure that the system remained solvent, however, he was forced to introduce mechanisms gradually raising the retirement age.

Kohl's Foreign Policy: Continuity of Ostpolitik, Expansion of Europe

Kohl saw himself in the tradition of Adenauer: a fervent advocate of Western Europe. But when he became chancellor, the entire EC, including West Germany, faced high deficits, high inflation, and high unemployment. The states also faced the dramatic pressures of new competitors, especially Japan, with its high-tech products, but also China, enjoying a jump in production with its turn toward state capitalism. Kohl and his French counterparts both knew that the West German economy had already become the hegemonic economic power in Europe. The newly elected French president Francois Mitterrand, leader of France's Socialist Party and president nearly as long as Kohl was chancellor, at first tried nationalizing key firms and traditional

Keynesian measures to restart the French economy. After just two years, his government reversed course. In addition to adopting austerity policies, Mitterand turned to his adviser Jacques Delors, who had become president of the European Commission in 1985. Delors proposed a European rather than a single state (French or West German) solution: bring the European economies closer together in order to reduce costs and increase pressures for efficiency. Kohl was receptive. Despite significant political differences, he and Mitterand worked well together, improving Franco-German relations and helping to reinvigorate the European project. In 1986, the European Community voted to revise the Treaty of Rome, in a decision known as the Single European Act. Its aim was to create a single market by ending border controls and tariffs by 1992. The two men eventually authored the Maastricht Treaty, responsible for creating the Eurozone and the formal structures of the European Union (discussed further in Chapter 11).

Otherwise, Kohl continued Schmidt's *Ostpolitik*. His government was very concerned to stand beside its US allies. But they were also concerned to keep East Germany stable, fearing what might happen to existing borders. Honecker was equally concerned to protect German-German relations from Cold War tensions and, later, the unpredictable climate ushered in by Mikhail Gorbachev in the Soviet Union. While the two superpowers' relations fluctuated wildly, then, German leaders on both sides of the Cold War divide doggedly maintained—and even deepened—contact. Behind the scenes, the FRG continued to buy the freedom of East German political dissidents, eventually spending almost 3.5 billion Deutschmarks, and, none other than Franz Josef Strauss, the fervent anti-Communist and fierce critic of Social Democrats' *Ostpolitik*, put together a $397 million private bank loan in June 1983. Publicly, the two governments arranged for 10,000 GDR citizens to visit the FRG in 1984. And in 1987, Kohl extended an official state invitation to Honecker and accorded the East German head of state full diplomatic honors. The GDR thus reached the pinnacle of its international prestige just as glasnost and perestroika were shaking up the People's Republics of Eastern Europe. When Honecker visited Bonn after speaking of future unity in his hometown of Wiebelskirchen (in the Saarland), Kohl spoke in favor of the German nation—but said explicitly that "unification is not on the agenda of history" at the time.

What do we make of this foreign policy? It was characterized by a good deal of continuity, and very much oriented toward the status quo. Kohl's government—not unlike Honecker's—did not think much of Gorbachev's reform policies, and would be surprised by the dramatic changes of 1989.

The 1980s: The return of the past

Having survived the challenges of terrorism and, before that, mass student protest, few doubted the FRG's political stability from the late 1970s on.

Perhaps it was no accident that it was then that the past returned to the center of West German consciousness. The groundwork for this change of consciousness had been laid over the 1970s, as young teachers, many of whom came of age in the 1960s, began bringing the history of the Holocaust into the classroom, encouraging students to do research on the fate of Jews in their own communities—often against the wishes of parents and local leaders. Discussion intensified after the airing of the American television miniseries *Holocaust*. Experts had panned the miniseries as sentimental and fluffy, and so it was not aired on the main national channels but rather on the so-called third channels administered by the Länder. The show electrified West German viewers when it aired in 1979. Twenty million West Germans—half of the adult population—tuned in each night to watch history unfold from the perspective of a German-Jewish family and a rising SS-officer (who ends up as a cold-blooded killer). Of course, not all of them liked what they saw and a special historians' "hot line" set up after each episode was overwhelmed by questions and by angry callers. Regardless of how West Germans responded to it, the miniseries brought the discussion of the Holocaust into the mainstream.

It also reflected the work of a new generation of historians. Trained in the late 1960s and committed to writing history from the ground up, they joined scholars in France and the Netherlands to ask who did what during the war years. And, in the spirit of the citizens' initiatives of the 1970s, they involved ordinary people in their research. Local histories, often carried out by high school students, received official sanction in 1980–81, when President Karl Carstens, himself a former member of the Nazi Party, declared that the annual German president's History Competition for Young People would focus on "everyday life under National Socialism." Thousands of German schoolchildren carried out local historical research. The project was a huge success, and the best results published in several volumes. It was also highly controversial. The 1990 film *The Nasty Girl*, based on a true story, tells how a schoolgirl from the conservative Catholic town of Passau in Bavaria wins the competition and then faces personal attacks at home for having "dirtied the nest" by investigating what local people had done during the dictatorship. By not restricting their inquiry to great men, known Nazis, or even Germans, the new generation of German historians (and their students) upended old narratives of ignorance, innocence, and resistance. A history that had been fairly black and white was now a sea of complicated moral grays.

Helmut Kohl also wanted to muddy the historical waters. He bemoaned young Germans' lack of attachment to their homeland, even locating the roots of the youth revolt and terrorism in Germans' inability to feel proud as Germans. From his first day as chancellor, Kohl aimed to right this imbalance and to create a "spiritual home" for the younger generation by stressing the positive side of German history. He gave speeches emphasizing Germany's many cultural, scientific, and entrepreneurial contributions.

And he commissioned a new West German history museum celebrating the country's many achievements. Kohl did not ignore the Nazi past in his promotion of a national identity, but he did his best to draw a line between it and present-day Germans. On a trip to Israel in 1984, for example, Kohl, who was born in 1930, referred to the "grace of a late birth," a comment interpreted to mean that he and the majority of Germans alive bore no direct responsibility for Nazism. By following a visit to the Bergen-Belsen concentration camp with a commemoration service at the Bitburg military cemetery, Kohl—with President Reagan's help—blurred the distinction between Germany's victims and its war dead, the questionably innocent Wehrmacht soldiers and members of the Waffen-SS buried there. All were mourned as part of the general catastrophe that was the Second World War. Germans' Nazi past did not, however, pass away into history as conservatives wished. Their statements mobilized politicians and intellectuals on the left, sparking a prolonged national debate over what lessons should be taken from Germany's Nazi past.

The most famous of these was the so-called Historians' Quarrel (*Historikerstreit*), a debate between left-wing and right-wing intellectuals over the nature of Nazi crimes that lasted nearly three years. The quarrel began in May 1986 with the *Frankfurter Allgemeine Zeitung*'s publication of historian Ernst Nolte's essay, "The Past That Won't Go Away." Nolte asserted that Auschwitz was a defensive response to the Stalinist gulags, that Germans had copied rather than originated the camp system, and that these copies paled in comparison to the horror of the gulag. It was not the first time Nolte had argued as much, but this time Jürgen Habermas publicly refuted his claims in the newspaper, *Die Zeit*. Habermas accused Nolte of using Stalinist crimes to reduce or even cancel out the crimes of Nazism. He criticized Nolte as well as historians Michael Stürmer and Andreas Hillgruber for trying to whitewash the German past—Stürmer by citing the Germans' need for a positive history (his influence as Kohl's main speechwriter was unmistakable), and Nolte and Hillgruber by comparing Nazi crimes with those perpetrated by the Soviets or suffered by German expellees. Carried out almost entirely through the two newspapers, the debate, which involved some twenty historians, lacked nothing in heat and vitriol. It provoked lasting public discussion of the uniqueness of Nazi crimes and, relatedly, the Jewish genocide; Germany's peculiar or not so peculiar historical trajectory; whether comparative history, in this case the comparison of Nazism and Stalinism, necessarily lead to moral relativism; and last but not least whether all Germans, regardless of age and distance to the Third Reich, bore the guilt of Nazi crimes.

The debate was by no means reducible to the politics of left and right. It was Federal President Richard von Weizsäcker of the CDU who made one of the most important contributions to the debate in an address to the Bundestag commemorating the fortieth anniversary of the end of the Second World War. Von Weizsäcker himself was from a conservative noble family in the south of Germany, and had been involved with the conservative resistance to Hitler—

although he served in the German army until the end of the war. May 8, 1945, he noted, was "not a day for Germans to celebrate" because of their personal experiences of bombing and invasion, of death and of the disappearance of men into prisoner-of-war camps. But at the same time, he proclaimed, May 8, 1945, was "the end of an aberration in German history, an end bearing seeds of hope for a better future"; it was in fact a "day of liberation" from dictatorship—though not from the guilt for the atrocities and genocide carried out in the name of Germany. He called for Germans "to face up as well as we can to the truth" of the German past. And part of coming to terms with that past meant repudiating the hatred of foreigners both abroad and at home, "to learn to live together, not in opposition to each other."

Integration and multiculturalism

Conservative attempts to reassert a German national identity came at a time when West Germans were just beginning to grapple with the fact that theirs was a multicultural, multiethnic society. In 1900, 8 percent of the German population, or 4.5 million residents, did not have German as their mother tongue; during the Third Reich, this number dramatically increased as Germany brought millions of foreigners into the country as forced laborers. After the postwar settlements, however, things looked quite different. In 1950, Germany was as homogenous as it had ever been—or would ever be again. Of the 68.5 million people who lived in the FRG and GDR, fewer than 100,000 were foreign residents. There were, of course, migrants, as every fifth German was an expellee. But there were so few "foreigners" in either Germany that the notion of an all-German Germany—not as racist fantasy but as lived norm—took hold. That notion has proved the most enduring of the postwar founding myths.

In the 1970s, the leaders of the Christian Democrats, Free Democrats, and Social Democrats all declared that the FRG was "not a country of immigration." Some West Germans pointed to the guest workers and asylum seekers in their midst and rejected such statements as absurd: like it or not, the FRG had become a country of immigration. Still, West German citizenship remained a blood right—granted to children born of German parents regardless of where they lived. This meant that guest workers who had lived in the FRG for decades could not become citizens. And that their children and grandchildren, the so-called second- and third-generation immigrants, also had no access to citizenship even if they had been born in West Germany. This situation contrasted sharply with the situation facing new arrivals from Eastern Europe: as the Eastern Bloc began opening up in the mid-1980s, people with German heritage could claim the right to immigrate to West Germany. With often limited German language skills and decades of experience in societies with significant anti-German sentiment, they were also immigrants—but immigrants whom the Basic Law automatically granted citizenship. Though complaints, particularly regarding their insufficiently "German" state, were widespread, this did not fundamentally change the fact that the majority of West Germans shared 1950 as a reference point and assumed Germany to be a historically homogenous nation. Integration and West German multiculturalism therefore also worked from this basic premise.

The Social Democrats pursued integration for guest workers and resident aliens already living in the FRG at the federal and local levels starting in the late 1970s. Schmidt's government passed new legislation allowing foreigners to obtain unrestricted resident permits and, in 1978, created a new Federal Commissioner for the Promotion of Integration among Foreign Workers and Their Families (the commissioner of foreigner affairs for short). Its name alone acknowledged the change in demographics: gone were the days of predominately male guest workers living in dormitories. The population in question now included spouses, children, and parents. By 1982, 48 percent had been in the FRG for ten years or more.[2] Despite this, guest workers and their families remained isolated. They could not vote and decisions that affected their lives were made by faceless administrators, often whimsically or arbitrarily (or so it seemed to them). The high drop-out and failure rates among second-generation immigrants in German schools did not offer much hope for their future social and economic advancement: 50–60 percent of students from guest worker families did not complete their education to the ninth grade. The reasons for the high drop-out and failure rates among second-generation immigrants were many, ranging from familial expectations and cultural constraints to official policies and school practices, but the end result—little chance for social and economic advancement—was the same. Heinz Kühn, the first commissioner of foreigner affairs, declared an urgent need to offer these immigrants, young and old, "unconditional and permanent integration" into West German society.

As the former minister-president of North Rhine-Westphalia, home to the largest guest worker population, Kühn grasped better than most the potentially devastating consequences of denying labor migrants and their children access to education, employment, and political rights in the FRG. But he was not alone. Trade and religious charity unions joined forces with local citizens' initiatives dedicated to "helping foreigners help themselves." Together they offered German language and adult education courses, legal aid, translation services, and neighborhood support groups. Technical colleges, too, began training teachers and social workers attuned to the specific challenges of migrant populations and second language acquisition. None of this came to an end in 1982 with the change in government. Rather it was in the 1980s that the integrationist policies pursued by Social Democrats, still prominent on the local and state levels, came into their own, provoking more change—and criticism, too.

Supporters of integration generally assumed that success rested on a mutual appreciation of difference; peaceful relations and intercultural communication would follow. Literature written by non-native German speakers, especially guest workers, offered one potential way into another's culture. Minority writers had begun publishing in German and even organizing their own writing and publishing collectives within the alternative milieu, but this "migrant" or "guest worker" literature only gained a commercial audience in the 1980s. Most popular were works that traced migrants' experiences before and after they came to the FRG, granting native readers access to unfamiliar lives and customs as well as an opportunity to see West German society from an outsider's perspective. Authors and essayists such as Aras Ören, Franco Biondi, and Zafer Şenocak each won the Chamisso Prize, created in 1985 to honor the literary achievements of non-native German writers, at least in part for their ability to help mainstream readers understand the "foreigners" in their midst. But the authors wrote for other migrants as much as they did for native Germans. In accepting the Chamisso Prize, Ören explained his desire to bridge the Turkish and German communities, to connect "fantasy with fantasy, idea with idea, language with language, individual with individual."[3] His acclaimed Berlin trilogy used the hustle and bustle of a city street to suggest what a unified, multicultural society might look like. Set in West Berlin's working-class district of Kreuzberg, the three novels trace how Germans and Turks of different backgrounds came to live side by side and how they coexisted, if not always peaceably, then with some hope that they one day might.

That works such as these were prized for their portrayal of migrants' difference and thus tended to encourage exotic stereotypes rather than debunk them was not lost on the authors. Many rebelled against cultural tokenism and their being pigeon-holed as writers of migrant literature. Emine Sevgi Özdamar, the first non-native German speaker to win the prestigious Ingeborg Bachmann Prize for literature, simultaneously delighted and appalled cultural elites with her whimsical use of the German language to relate not only her experiences as a guest worker and aspiring actress in 1960s West Berlin but also to expose persistent cultural assumptions about Turks and guest workers, German culture, and national belonging. Others, like Şenocak, wrote soberly about the challenges of multiculturalism, just as critical of those who glorified the foreign as he was of those who demonized it. If the latter insisted on full assimilation, the "disappearance of Anatolian faces behind German masks," he argued that the former safeguarded German culture by promoting a society in which different peoples existed side by side but did not touch one another. Şenocak insisted that, at a minimum, Germans of Turkish origin should have rights of citizenship (denied them until 2000) but also that the mere acceptance of difference was not enough. A multicultural society demanded an end to cultural ghettos, a "comprehensive change of consciousness" that would leave neither German nor Turkish culture untouched. The tension that he perceived to exist between the two identities would not be resolved. Instead, it would be the impetus for a third, new culture.

First- and second-generation migrants were not the only "outsiders" to find their voice and to challenge ethnic definitions of German national identity in the 1980s. African American writer, feminist, and civil rights activist Audre Lorde spent several weeks as a visiting professor in West Berlin in 1984 and then returned annually, intensely interested in how the African American experience both diverged and converged with that of Afro-Germans, a term she in fact helped coin to underscore the transatlantic ties of the black diaspora. Convinced that the greatest difference between the situation of black people in the United States and in Germany was the isolation experienced by Afro-Germans, Lorde touched the lives of many black German women in her efforts to relieve some of that isolation. In addition to raising Germans' awareness of their place in a transnational, diasporic network, she helped a number of female artists and writers like Ika Hügel-Marshall, May (Opitz) Ayim, and Helga Emde find their voice and community in the FRG as Afro-German women. Ayim and Emde contributed to the 1986 book *Farbe Bekennen* (translated in English as *Showing Our Colors: Afro-German Women Speak Out*), which, through its collection of personal histories, poems, group testimonials, and key secondary texts, provided a groundbreaking examination of the Afro-German experience generally and a forum for Afro-German women specifically. It was also in *Farbe Bekennen* that the term Afro-German was first published and defended.

Once mobilized, the Afro-German movement grew quickly. Political and cultural organizations like the *Initiative Schwarze Deutsche* and ADEFRA (an acronym for Afro-Deutsche Frauen, or Afro-German Women) formed in cities across the FRG with the goal of fighting racism and bringing black Germans together at the local and national levels. And the publication of new magazines like *Afro-Look* and *Afrekete* (geared toward women) gave

ON BEING AFRO-GERMAN

66 Afro-German" seemed appropriate to us since many of us have an African father and a German mother. . . Our essential commonality is that we are Black and have experienced a major part of our socialization and life in confrontation with West German society—a society that is not ninety-nine percent white but has always behaved as though it were, or should be. By the term "Afro-German" we mean all those who wish to refer to themselves as such, regardless if they have one or two Black parents. . . We want to propose "Afro-German" in opposition to more commonly used names like "half-breed," "mulatto," or "colored," as an attempt to define ourselves instead of being defined by others.

Source: Katharina Oguntoye, May Opitz, and Dagmar Schultz, eds. Farbe bekennen. Afro-deutsche Frauen auf den Spuren ihrer Geschichte *(Berlin: Orlanda Frauenverlag, 1986), xxii–xxiii. Reprinted with permission of Orlanda Frauenverlag.*

further shape and visibility to nonwhite Germans. Though the editors of *Farbe Bekennen* argued for inclusivity—and tended to use "black German" and Afro-German interchangeably—the movement's identification with the African diasporic community clearly limited its appeal and its ability to represent other minority groups. For this reason, black German (and, today, "black people in Germany") came to replace Afro-German as the term used to unite Germans of Asian, African, and other non-European descent.

International travel and exposure to new cuisines also contributed to a more consciously multicultural West Germany. In fact, when viewed alongside the popularity of migrant literature, it seems that postwar Germans' expanding leisure time did as much for intercultural exchange as government policies. Many West Germans embraced foreign travel as a means of experiencing new cultures, though more probably traveled abroad in search of warmer weather. Whatever the reason, the end of the postwar boom did not adversely affect West Germans' travel; in fact it reached a record high in 1975, despite that year's negative economic growth. By the mid-1970s, a yearly vacation of at least five days was part of most West Germans' normal lives, an assumed lifestyle more than a conscious choice, and the number of West Germans who took that vacation abroad exceeded the number who stayed in the FRG. Innovations in air travel brought affordable airfare, matched in the 1980s by a booming trade in vacation "package deals"; German "colonies" sprouted up on the coasts of Spain, Italy, southern France, and other Mediterranean locales.[4] Back home in the FRG, West Germans could relive their travels or demonstrate their knowledge of other cultures in the growing number of ethnic restaurants that graced even rural areas of the FRG by the 1980s. There had long been eating establishments owned and visited by migrants. Now former guest workers and, more commonly, newly arrived entrepreneurs opened restaurants for a West German clientele, students with little money and those interested in getting to experience another culture through their stomachs. "Authentic" and often regionally specific cuisine began to replace that of generic, culturally blind "Asian" and even "Italian" restaurants.[5]

The attention to authentic cuisine dovetailed with broader concerns regarding authenticity expressed in the alternative and punk (and now post-punk) scenes as well as in the attention given to food, water, and air purity—something that went from fringe to mainstream following Chernobyl. The desire to expose the artificial, to live an "authentic" life, to learn about and from other cultures, and to embrace difference contributed to a more pluralist West German society. It was pluralism based just as much on the pursuit of individual taste and needs as it was on acknowledged cultures, ethnicities, and special interests. Whereas previously one could speak of a common public sphere, from the 1980s on there was a growing multiplicity of publics—newspapers, television channels, magazines, and the like that catered to a particular subset of the West German population rather than the population as a whole. One might judge the development as isolating;

increasingly, different parts of the population could live in their own social and political bubbles. But it also contributed to a vibrant society, a diversification of identities tangible in the multiculturalism discussed above as well as in West Germany's thriving gay and lesbian community, and in the larger-than-life music personalities like Nina Hagen.

Hagen first rose to stardom in the GDR before emigrating to the FRG in 1976 on the coattails of her stepfather, Wolf Biermann. Before settling down in West Berlin she spent time in London, mixing with the Sex Pistols and earning a reputation as the "Godmother of punk." In the 1980s, Hagen's style attracted an international audience. From start to finish, it was unconventional: outrageous outfits, music drawn from punk, heavy metal, and German new wave, and—harkening back to an early career in theater— high theatrics. In 1982 she produced her first English-language album and added reggae, funk, and opera to the mix. Hagen's politics matched her music, impassioned and sometimes bordering on the bizarre (she increasingly referenced alien sightings). In November 1985, German *Vogue* made Nina

FIGURE 9.2 *Nina Hagen on tour in Canada, July 26, 1987. (Toronto Star/Rick Eglinton/Getty Images)*

Hagen their cover girl: she was undoubtedly, perhaps even uncontrollably, one of West Germany's new faces.

The last West German Bundestag elections of 1987

The Social Democrats by the late 1980s remained a divided party. On the left, the firebrand Oskar Lafontaine was on the rise. He joined the Greens in rejecting military blocs and calling for the FRG to leave NATO, a return to early postwar neutralism in response to a similarly "hot" phase of the Cold War. But while the Greens busily contacted dissidents in Eastern Europe, Lafontaine focused on West Germany: he was one of a new generation that was simply not that interested in the project of German unity. Under his influence, the Social Democrats downplayed civil rights issues in the GDR, saying that peace came before human rights. It was a position that they would shortly regret, when, in the aftermath of Germany's unanticipated unification, the party faced a former East German constituency. Others within the Social Democrats continued to underestimate the Greens' ability to attract support away from Social Democrats. The Social Democrats before unification, then, stood before a dilemma. It was under attack economically and politically. The party's conservative members could not stomach what they understood to be Lafontaine's anti-Americanism; its leftist members wanted a more radical stance on European neutrality and less compromise on social and economic policy at home.

At the same time, the Christian Democrats seemed to have run out of steam. Kohl's government lacked concrete proposals for change and suffered from a general sense of malaise. Rainer Barzel, Kohl's predecessor as chairman of the Christian Democrats and Bundestag president as of March 1983, was forced to resign his position in 1984 along with the minister of economics, Lambsdorff, amid mounting scandal. Both men were accused of accepting bribes from CEO Friedrich Karl Flick in exchange for helping the Flick company evade taxes. Barzel was eventually exonerated but not before a parliamentary committee determined that politicians from every party except the Greens had received "donations" from Flick to the tune of 25 million marks. Kohl tried and failed to amnesty the offenders, a move that only seemed to confirm government and party corruption. Then, three years later, on the eve of the 1987 Bundestag elections, another scandal erupted, this time around the minister-president of Schleswig-Holstein and Christian Democratic candidate Uwe Barschel, involving smear tactics and his use of government resources for the surveillance of his Social Democratic rival. Barschel resigned and then turned up dead, adding to the tale already being spun by mainstream media: a man's lust for power leading him to pursue criminal acts and the abuse of justice. Kohl's administration did its best to ride out the scandal and to avoid any direct responsibility. The absence of any real reform, once again, suggested to many West Germans that the existing political system lacked either the desire or the ability to prohibit such activities.

Further reading

Bahro, Rudolf. *From Red to Green*. London: Verso, 1984.

Cooper, Alice H. *Paradoxes of Peace: West German Peace Movements since 1945*. Ann Arbor: University of Michigan Press, 1996.

Dirke, Sabine von. *All Power to the Imagination! The West German Counterculture from the Student Movement to the Greens*. Lincoln, NE: University of Nebraska Press, 1997.

Heyl, Matthias. "Holocaust Education in (West) Germany—Now and Then." In *Never Again! The Holocaust's Challenge for Educators*. Edited by Helmut Schreier and Matthias Heyl, 165–79. Hamburg: Krämer Verlag, 1997.

Hügel-Marshall, Ika. *Invisible Woman: Growing up Black in Germany*. Translated by Elizabeth Gaffney. New York: Continuum, 2001.

Knowlton, James, and Truett Cates trans. *Forever in the Shadow of Hitler? Original Documents of the Historikerstreit, the Controversy Concerning the Singularity of the Holocaust*. Atlantic Highlands, NJ: Humanities Press, 1993.

Maier, Charles S. *The Unmasterable Past: History, Holocaust, and German National Identity*. Cambridge, MA: Harvard University Press, 1988.

Mende, Silke. "'Enemies at the Gate': The West German Greens and Their Arrival at the Bundestag. Between Old Ideals and New Challenges." *German Politics and Society* 33 (2015), 66–79.

Michaels, Jennifer. "The Impact of Audre Lorde's Politics and Poetics on Afro-German Women Writers." *German Studies Review* 29 (Feb. 2006), 21–40.

Milder, Stephen. "Between Grassroots Protest and Green Politics: The Democratic Potential of the 1970s Antinuclear Activism." *German Politics and Society* 34 (2016), 25–39.

Oguntoye, Katharina, May Opitz, and Dagmar Schultz, eds. *Showing Our Colors: Afro-German Women Speak Out*. Translated by Anne V. Adams. Amherst: University of Massachusetts Press, 1992.

Ören, Aras. *Please, No Police*. Translated by Teoman Sipahigil. Austin, TX: Center for Middle Eastern Studies, University of Texas, 1992.

Özdamar, Emine Sevgi. *Life is a Caravanserai: Has Two Doors, I Came in One, I Went Out the Other*. Translated by Luise von Flotow. London: Middlesex University Press, 2000.

Shahan, Cyrus. *Punk Rock and German Crisis: Adaptation and Resistance since 1977*. New York: Palgrave Macmillan, 2013.

Sollors, Werner. "Good-bye, Germany!" *Transit* 1, no. 1 (2004), 1–14.

10

Collapse, revolution, unification: 1989–90

FIGURE 10.1 *On October 9, 1989, seventy-thousand Leipzig residents claimed the city's main thoroughfare in the Monday night demonstration. (ullstein bild/ Christian Günther/Getty Images)*

The Berlin Wall opened on the night of November 9, 1989, signaling the collapse of the East German experiment with state socialism. An apparent error of a spokesman for the East German leadership was the immediate cause of the fall of the Wall, but three other deeper changes had already undermined the GDR. First, by 1988–89, East Germany was facing a major financial crisis as its debts to the capitalist world ballooned. The state-socialist dream of decoupling from capitalism was at an end. Second, the other state-socialist countries in Eastern Europe were starting to dismantle their economic and political borders with the West, and the Soviet Union under Gorbachev refused to intervene. Once Hungary opened its borders to Austria, the outflow of East German citizens to the West began and the Wall started to lose its key function. When Solidarity, the trade union in Poland led by Lech Wałęsa, became powerful enough to force Poland's Communist Party to implement democratic reforms, East Germany increasingly stood alone as a defender of the old line. Third, leaders of East Germany themselves began to hesitate and express self-doubt—allowing dissidents new openings for protest. The stage was set for the dramatic protests of 1989, the removal of Honecker from power, and, eventually, German Unification on October 3, 1990.

Three different stories are told of Germany in 1989–90. The first narrates the collapse of the regime in the face of political and economic crises. The second story turns from political and economic structures to the individuals who attacked the regime: the epic story of revolution against dictatorship. The third story is one of reunification and the end of Germany's division. These three narratives have different implications.

The story of regime collapse raises questions about how stable modern nation-states are. From 1961 until the late 1970s, East Germany was stable, and in many ways appeared normal and legitimate to most of the population. Over the course of the 1980s, however, it rapidly lost legitimacy, largely because it could not deliver the economic goods. The state's inability to deal with environmental problems, with crumbling cities and infrastructure, and with consumers' demand for up-to-date products finally caught up with the claims of the party dictatorship. Modern states seek to promote economic growth and to provide social benefits in part to ensure their own legitimacy, as Chapter 6 discussed. East Germany could provide neither. Its collapse shows how dependent modern states are on the functioning of industrial society.

The story of revolution focuses on the dictatorship and the individuals who broke with it. For a variety of reasons, a small set of people, often unconnected to one another, began to demand that the rights granted to citizens on paper be respected in practice, and to draw attention publicly to the effects of dictatorship. The crumbling infrastructure and ever more obvious failure of the state to ensure a functional economy led an increasing number of people to sympathize with the revolutionaries. When the regime revealed its own hesitancy and weakness, the people took to the streets— in East Germany as well as in Poland, Hungary, Czechoslovakia, Bulgaria, and Romania. East Germans toppled their country's dictatorship and, so doing, placed themselves in the grand tradition of revolt against despotism dating from the great American and French Revolutions of the eighteenth century. It took active revolutionaries to take advantage of the economic and political challenges of the first narrative.

The third narrative of national reunification appears because the revolutionaries failed. They did not establish a new democracy, impose a new constitution, or present a new face of the people to the world. Instead, the newly elected People's Chamber of the GDR voted itself out of existence, opting to unify with the Federal Republic. The sense of national belonging trumped revolution—and left many of the original dissidents feeling surprised or betrayed. Here the story becomes complicated. On the one hand, nationalism and the drive for national unity had a long tradition in Germany. On the other hand, the National Socialist regime, discredited by both East and West Germany, had used nationalism for genocidal and imperialist aims. But with the sudden disintegration of legitimacy, the purpose of the East German state became less clear. Unlike any other state in Eastern Europe, the GDR was linked—linguistically, culturally, even economically—to a rich neighbor state. The Basic Law granted East Germans West German citizenship, and the FRG was both economically stable and a democracy founded on basic rights. In this narrative, nationalism is the obvious endpoint of the revolution in retrospect.

All three narratives are necessary to understand what happened in 1989–90, and this chapter will make use of all three. The overlapping narratives, however, also show what was and remains controversial about the moment. Collapse, revolution, or reunification: the choice of term implies what the narrator thinks is the main story.

Financial and economic crisis

The GDR leadership faced a dilemma in its economic policy, as Chapter 8 discussed. In order to ensure the loyalty, quiescence, and productivity of the working population, it felt compelled to provide social programs and to ensure that consumer goods were available. But the economy could not produce enough to pay for these goods and services. The economy entered a vicious cycle, borrowing more from the West, putting off reinvestment at home, and throwing resources at prestige projects like microelectronics, in the hope for a technological solution to the dilemma. Economic leaders in the State Planning Commission and the State Bank repeatedly noted that planned expenditures did not equal real production, and repeatedly expressed their concerns about the growing debt to the capitalist West. The Socialist Unity Party leadership, increasingly reduced to Honecker and his chief economic helper Günter Mittag, brushed aside such complaints. But neither governments nor businesses in the capitalist lands wanted the East German mark in return for their goods. They wanted money that they could use across the world without restrictions: they wanted hard, Western currency.

The GDR's leadership thus had to scramble to find hard currency. They permitted Westerners to travel into East Germany starting in 1971, but required that visitors purchase East German marks at a 1:1 ratio and pay 25 marks for every day they stayed. The exchange rate was set at a fixed, high rate in order to generate revenue for the state, a rate they raised several times along with the required daily amount. All Western visitors thus subsidized the GDR. Many of these visitors had friends or relatives in the East, and brought them hard currency as a gift. Knowing this, the GDR opened up the Intershops, discussed in Chapter 8, selling quality goods from the West at a markup price. In addition, the GDR negotiated billions of dollars in credits from the FRG, from both Social Democratic and Christian Democratic administrations, all interested in maintaining stability in the interest of East German citizens. As mentioned in Chapter 9, in the context of Kohl's continued *Ostpolitik*, the SED government traded in political prisoners and negotiated for Western loans—leaving itself open to being pressed for concessions. And last but not least, Alexander Schalck-Golodkowski developed a shadowy office in the Ministry for Foreign Trade that arranged sales of valuables from East Germany and negotiated directly with West German politicians, including, as we saw, the CSU's Franz Josef Strauss. His work may have averted a financial collapse of the GDR already in 1983.

Such financial crisis management came at great cost. The GDR was increasingly in debt to the country that it referred to as an enemy. And a chronic shortage of resources had an effect on the country itself. With rents amounting to about five percent of income, money flowing into housing stock could not cover necessary repairs, and the state could not allocate additional subsidies. Officials therefore deferred repairs. By the late 1980s, the facades of older buildings were crumbling. Environmental challenges, from drinking water to polluted air to the dying trees around coal plants, remained unaddressed. Industrial equipment in sectors not deemed innovative and vital, such as textiles, remained in use long after more productive equipment was available; increasing repairs took ever more of a bite out of production. Living conditions for the elderly, dependent on pensions, remained terrible. Over the long run, the GDR's economy was devouring itself and impoverishing East Germans' daily lives.

Foreign policy growing tensions with the Soviet Union

The GDR's economic dilemma had effects on all other aspects of governance, including its foreign policy. Indebtedness to the West increasingly limited what the GDR's leaders could do in their own country. West German politicians understood that the GDR was a dictatorship and proved willing to work with the regime. But gross human rights violations could have led the FRG to cut off its credits to the GDR. As dissent grew, then, the ability of the GDR to respond to that dissent in a repressive manner declined.

International pressure—and the financial crisis management pursued by the Socialist Unity Party—even forced the party to suspend the order to shoot those trying to cross over to the West in April 1989.

Tensions with the Soviet Union grew as well, first and foremost over economic issues. The Soviet Union faced the same kind of problems of economic decline as the GDR. But the Soviet Union was a superpower and an empire, and was furthermore deeply involved in Afghanistan since 1979. In the wake of the oil crisis of the 1970s, the Soviet leadership had built up a lucrative trade in energy with the West, and the FRG was one of its leading partners. In 1981, faced with economic challenges and new opportunities to sell oil in the West, Brezhnev let Honecker know that the Soviet Union would start to deliver less oil to the GDR. Honecker responded that less oil would destabilize the GDR. But the Soviets held firm. Tensions grew in the years that followed, as the Soviets complained of low quality goods from East Germany; in 1984, the Soviets threatened a further reduction in deliveries.

Losing subsidies from the East meant even more economic reliance on the West. In order to avoid endangering his special credit line to West Germany, Honecker planned to attend a summit in 1984 with Helmut Kohl. The new Soviet general secretary Chernenko, aiming at a more confrontational course with the United States, summoned Honecker to Moscow to forbid the meeting. The GDR relied on Western credits for its economy, but on Soviet tanks for its existence. Honecker therefore gave in, and canceled the meeting.

The tensions at first seemed to ease after Mikhail Gorbachev assumed the position of general secretary in 1985. Gorbachev began to restructure the Soviet relationship with Eastern Europe, on the basis of a renewed détente with the West. Not only did the shift permit a closer relationship to West Germany; Gorbachev also apparently considered the East German economy to be efficient and a potential modernizer for the entire East Bloc. The honeymoon quickly came to an end, however, as once again the Soviets cut deliveries of oil and other raw materials—and Honecker and the Socialist Unity Party proved unreceptive to Gorbachev's political reforms.

In January 1987, Gorbachev called for the introduction of the secret ballot and the fundamental democratization of society and polity, stating, "We need democracy just like we need air to breathe." The Socialist Unity Party politburo member and chief ideologue, Kurt Hager, responded in an interview with the West German magazine *Stern*, "If your neighbor repapered the walls, would you feel obliged to do the same?" The two governments' differences only grew. In 1988, Gorbachev announced Glasnost, or a policy of openness. Already under his rule the realm of free speech had broadened; now he used a term associated with Soviet dissidents to demand greater attention to rights and the rule of law, and a wider range of opinions on hot-button issues like government policy and Stalinism.

The SED leadership feared that Glasnost would spread like bacteria to East German society. It increased its attempts at censorship in 1988, even interfering with internal newspapers of the Protestant Church. In the same year, the GDR banned the Soviet journal *Sputnik*. The result was not a consolidation of the party's authority, but intense criticism of the action from within the Socialist Unity Party itself as well as from the population as a whole. Honecker had come to power, after all, asserting that the Soviets were a model for the GDR: why not now? The crude censorship also indicated to Gorbachev Honecker's unwillingness to change.

Honecker indeed had grounds for concern about the Soviet Union under Gorbachev. The GDR, as had been clear from the very start, depended on the Soviet Union for its own existence. Gorbachev, however, began to paint a very different picture of what the Soviets expected from their client states. He allowed them more "freedom of choice" in the way they developed socialism, breaking with the Brezhnev Doctrine, which had justified Soviet intervention in Eastern European states. The East German leadership greeted this change: it offered them more flexibility in their own policy making. They did not immediately grasp, however, that such a policy might also imply that the Soviet Union would not prop up the GDR, militarily or economically—a new reality slowly dawning on all the Eastern European state-socialist regimes. What became known in late October 1989 as the "Sinatra Doctrine"—alluding to the American crooner's popular song "My Way"—was a double-edged sword for a state whose existence depended on the Soviet Union. Comments by Soviet officials or intellectuals about the possibility of a united, neutral Germany added to Honecker's distrust.

In short, the GDR's economic predicament was bound up with a foreign policy predicament. It relied on the Soviet Union to survive politically, but the Soviet Union was cutting supplies; it relied on the Federal Republic for financial help, but too much reliance would mean moving away from the Soviet Union, again threatening the existence of the GDR. The multiple foreign policy crises contributed to the general crisis of 1989.

1989

Gorbachev made the rule of law a centerpiece of his reforms. However, there could only be rule of law if the state followed its own laws, as dissidents throughout Eastern Europe braved to point out. Over the 1980s, East German activists spread across dozens of groups began to come together in umbrella organizations, often connected with the church: the "Action Group Law of Citizenship" of 1987, for example, or the "Initiative for Peace and Human Rights" that carried banners with slogans from Rosa Luxemburg into the official parade honoring her memory on January 17, 1988, already discussed in Chapter 8. Indeed, the role of the Protestant Church cannot be underestimated in the story of 1989. The special status of the churches offered the opportunity for critics—environmentalists and civil rights activists—to carve out a space relatively protected from state interference, in which they could discuss, collect information, and organize.

There were not many active dissidents: the Stasi estimated their total number at about 2,500 in summer 1989, which was a tiny percentage of the overall population. The state's strategy was to provoke disagreement and internal disputes with well-placed Stasi provocateurs, and to deport those who remained a problem. In spring 1988, for example, they expelled fifty-three people, including leaders like Bohley, Vera Wollenberger, Stephan Krawczyk, and Wolfgang and Regina Templin, in the wake of the Rosa Luxemburg demonstration. For such a small group of dissenters, the loss of these leaders should have been devastating.

But citizens beyond the dissidents took up the language of rights. The number of petitions in general increased during the last years of the GDR. By 1989, East Germans were writing over a million letters a year to state authorities, letters that took up hot-button issues. Starting in 1984, for instance, the number of requests to leave the GDR—usually to go to the West—increased to 40–50,000 per year. This right, as Chapter 8 discussed, was guaranteed by the Helsinki Accords of 1975, but in practice petitioners were subjected to harassment; more and more people were now willing to take that risk—and cited freedom of movement as their socialist as much as human right. Even some within the Socialist Unity Party, eying Gorbachev, began to propose legal reforms in the name of a modern socialism; their proposals show how far the dissident language of rights had seeped into the consciousness of GDR society. The language of rights accompanied every step of the East German Revolution of 1989.

Voting with their feet: Emigration through Hungary

A new emigration law came into effect at the start of 1989, an attempt by the GDR to both appear to honor its obligations to the Helsinki Accords in the eyes of the international community and simultaneously to regulate and slow any movement out of the country. Thousands of people nonetheless applied to leave the country. Honecker fanned the flames by declaring that the Berlin Wall would continue to exist in hundred years.

At the same time, momentous changes were underway in neighboring Hungary. At the beginning of the year, the Hungarian Socialist Workers' Party (i.e., the official Communist Party) gave up its monopoly over politics; over the next two months, the country shifted to a multiparty democracy, and began to break down the divide between East and West, on cultural, political, and economic levels. On May 2, the Hungarians began dismantling the barriers dividing their country from Austria. Mikhail Gorbachev, meanwhile, made official his break with the Brezhnev Doctrine in early July. From this point on, the Hungarians, seeking greater political and economic contact with the West, were increasingly less likely to follow East German commands. East Germans now began to travel to Hungary, seeking to cross its border into Austria and from there into West Germany. The successful flight on August 9 of several hundred East Germans in Hungary to Austria increased the pressure on all sides. The Hungarians continued to honor an agreement they had made with the GDR, however, and returned the would-be emigrants with a stamp in their passport that would have made them susceptible to criminal charges at home. A direct intervention by Chancellor Kohl with his Hungarian counterpart Miklos Németh, however, led to the release of around 8,000 East Germans at the West German embassy in Budapest to travel to the West on September 10; the GDR government furiously accused the FRG of inciting illegal emigration and the occupation of diplomatic spaces—both violations of existing treaties and GDR national sovereignty. The Czechoslovak leadership, like Honecker opposed to reforms, agreed to close their borders to East Germans to keep them from exiting through Hungary.

Recognizing an opportunity, some East Germans began to gather in the West German embassies in Prague and Warsaw in late September, seeking asylum; thousands scaled the walls to reach the embassy grounds in Prague, without being stopped by Czechoslovak police. Under considerable pressure, the countries' foreign ministers reached a compromise: the GDR permitted the squatters' emigration on the condition that they be formally deprived of their GDR citizenship. More specifically, they had to travel back over East Germany in closed trains so that they could then be legally "expelled" to the West. It was, to say the least, a desperate play by Honecker's government to re-exert state authority that only encouraged panic at home. As the trains from Prague moved through on October 1, other East Germans tried to jump on. Two days later, the GDR suspended free travel to Czechoslovakia, to try to fend off a route of escape to an embassy or to Hungary. On the next day, a second transport of expellees from Prague led to mass protests in Dresden; some 10,000 East Germans blockaded the tracks, and fights broke out with the police.

Strikingly "flat footed" is how one scholar sums up the regime's response to events. The SED leadership was unquestionably out of touch: The East German government issued an official declaration condemning the emigrants for trampling on the basic values of socialism. Honecker, battling cancer at the time and so not immediately involved in matters, apparently managed to add another sentence for good measure: "One should therefore shed no tears for them." Such sentiments did not quell unrest but rather inspired outrage among ever more East Germans. The GDR government faced a potential mass exodus of its population greater even than before the Berlin Wall. What started as a tense diplomatic-political situation was, by the fall of 1989, a full domestic crisis.

Rights, elections, and free speech: From Dresden to Plauen to Leipzig

At the same time as some East Germans sought to leave, others increased the internal pressure on the regime. Peace protesters in Leipzig chanted, "We are staying here!" a declaration that was both a challenge to the state, which could not count on dissidents' leaving the country, and a promise of further political opposition. In either case, rights were at issue. The political aims of the dissidents began to coincide with the aims of the people in general. Gradually the demand for rights became a demand that the people, not the party, be sovereign.

The pressure over rights increased over the course of 1989. On May 7, local elections took place across the GDR. The elections followed the old model: one unity list of candidates, giving the voter the chance to vote either yes or no. East Germany still refused to reform voting laws, despite examples from the Soviet Union, Poland, and Hungary. Dissidents called for a boycott of the elections. They then declared their intention to monitor the elections, a right accorded them in the 1974 constitution.

Official news media declared that nearly 99 percent of the eligible population had voted, and that almost 99 percent of them voted yes; 1.15 percent of the voters voted no, the largest such vote reported (and one that required courage on the part of a voter, since these were not secret ballots). Local monitors, however, recorded significantly more no votes (even though the total number remained quite small). They could prove that the state had falsified the election, and they transmitted this evidence to the Western media, which reported the news back to GDR citizens.

A gap remained between dissidents and the population as a whole. Weekly prayer meetings for peace in the St. Nicolas Church in Leipzig saw, to be sure, a gradual increase in numbers starting at the end of 1988. But repeated Stasi actions against dissidents and protesters kept the numbers low. Nonetheless, Leipzig residents were aware that these nonviolent meetings, carrying an implicit criticism of East German military policy, enjoyed the protection of the Lutheran Church. With the emigration crisis, the significance of the meetings began to change. On September 4, others joined the dissidents to demand their right to leave the country. When Stasi operatives intervened, the protesters moved against them, shouting "Stasi out!" They dared to stand up to the feared secret police.

Soon thereafter, the dissidents dared another big step by applying for official recognition of their autonomous organizations following the laws regulating their formation. The group New Forum filed the first application on September 9. Officials predictably denied it, citing a security risk, but the organization formed anyway. Next, Democracy Now filed an application on September 12, followed by Democratic Awakening on October 2. Most provocatively, the Social Democratic Party applied on October 7, rejecting the 1946 forced merger of the Communist Party and the Social Democrats. By the last part of September, the Stasi had determined that it could no longer effectively destroy the movements by means of subversion or force.

Later commentators have criticized the dissidents for acting within the law, as though the existing system could be reformed. But they had solid reasons for pursuing change as they did, beyond the practical desire to avoid imprisonment and their still small movement's violent suppression. The Communist tradition laid claim to the model of social change through revolution, and national Communist parties set themselves up as the revolutionary avant garde, who knew what the revolution should bring. The dissidents rejected that model, inherited from the radical phase of the French Revolution of 1789 and the Russian Revolution of 1917. They wanted instead, as the names of their organizations suggested, to open up a new realm for political discussion, a way for engaged citizens to express their opinions: they did not want any single group, including themselves, to claim the right to shape and guide society. They were, like the Greens, critical of the party system in West Germany; their aim was not to implement rule by the right party, but to move beyond rule by parties per se.

The Monday protests in Leipzig, meanwhile, were increasing in number. On October 2, they took on a new quality, as some 20,000 people marched in open opposition to the Stasi and the Socialist Unity Party. Five days later, on October 7, between 10,000 and 20,000 people protested in the Saxon town of Plauen and refused to disperse, despite arrests and brutal attacks by the Stasi and police. On that same day, the Socialist Unity Party celebrated the Fortieth Anniversary of the GDR in Berlin. Gorbachev visited

THE NEW FORUM REJECTS UNIFICATION

D ear Friends of New Forum!
      We are involved with New Forum because we are concerned about the GDR—we want to stay here and work here. We ask that those who have made a different decision not misuse our endeavors in order to emigrate more quickly.

For us "reunification" is out of the question. We presuppose that Germany will be divided into two states and will not strive for a capitalist social system. We want changes here in the GDR. . . .

We do not want to, and cannot, define in advance what reform means for our land; we want to develop a comprehensive discussion process instead. We need this solidaristic conversation that seeks consensus, without sweeping different opinions under the table. . . .

Our goal is to create a legal political platform that can put urgently necessary social dialogue into motion. Nobody should be excluded because he or she belongs to the Socialist Unity Party or to any other organization.

Source: Pamphlet of New Forum, October 1, 1989, available at https://ia802705.us.archive.org/26/items/DieErstenTexteDesNeuenForum/89_NeuesForum_Die-ersten-Texte-des-NEUEN-FORUM.pdf   (collective commons).

the triumphant celebration, and East Germans greeted him, and the content of his speech, enthusiastically. Gorbachev delivered a clear message to the party leaders standing beside him—and in other People's Republics—who rejected reform. He made clear that the survival of the GDR was at stake, and warned his comrades not to miss the opportunity to change. On the night of October 7–8, the Stasi and police intervened with force against a handful of protesters, beating them and arresting over five hundred. Their aim was to stop the coming Monday demonstration in Leipzig.

But the Leipzig demonstration on October 9 took place nonetheless. The organizers, fearing violence from police and Stasi, stressed nonviolence. Their fears were well warranted: four months earlier, the Chinese government had savagely crushed prodemocracy protesters in Tiananmen Square and all signs indicated that Honecker was prepared to do the same. The government sent thousands of police and Stasi members to Leipzig, and even called up the National People's Army. Nonetheless, some 70,000 protesters marched that night, chanting not only "Gorbi!" and "We are staying here!" but also "We are the people!" In other words, they rejected the Socialist Unity Party's claim to represent the people. Dissidence had become revolution.

The state did not mobilize its forces against the marchers. Argument has ensued about who made the decision on the part of the Socialist Unity Party to avoid violence. Honecker certainly seemed to think that violence would be justified, and he remained powerful, although ill and away from his office at this time. Other party leaders, however, knew that they lacked military support from the Soviets in the event of a crackdown. Egon Krenz, a leading member of the politburo eager to oust Honecker, had been in touch with the Soviet ambassador on precisely this issue. He and others in the party leadership knew that they were no longer dealing with 2,500 dissidents, but with hundreds of thousands of protesters. There was no turning back the clock. In this sense, the decision not to intervene in Leipzig made October 9, 1989, into the turning point of the revolution.

Party and masses: Berlin, October 1989

By now the legitimacy of the party was in free fall. The Stasi reported on the growing number of party members who were voluntarily leaving the party. Egon Krenz chose this moment to challenge Honecker's hold on power. The conspiracy successfully ousted Honecker on October 17. To the end, the party had no normal means for removing old, recalcitrant leaders from power.[1]

Krenz spoke the language of reconciliation and perestroika; he promised a new law regulating travel. But he remained a representative of the old regime. After all, as East Germans remembered, just a few months before he had visited China to congratulate the party leadership there on its violent repression of the Tiananmen Square protests. On October 24, for the first time ever, the People's Chamber did not vote unanimously to approve Krenz as the head of the party. The following weeks saw more protests, more challenges, and the gradual crumbling of party power. Internally, the party leadership finally confronted the huge debts to the West, which had been accumulated over the previous two decades. The only alternative, the head of the State Planning Commission stated, was an austerity regime. But the party leadership had, since 1953, made an implicit deal with the workers: no austerity in exchange for the acceptance of Socialist Unity Party rule. They were faced with a contradiction that they could not solve.

On November 4, a number of prominent intellectuals called for a rally on East Berlin's Alexanderplatz in support of the GDR, if not as it was, then for what it could be. Some half million people showed up, in this most privileged of East German cities, to hear intellectuals associated with East German socialism but critical of it, like Stefan Heym and Christa Wolf, as well as dissident activists like Marianne Birthler. Party leaders approved such an event because they hoped to co-opt the dissidents. But talking with autonomous social organizations meant giving up the Socialist Unity Party's claim to represent society alone. Discussion itself called into question the premise of the party.

In the meantime, the border with Czechoslovakia had been reopened, and thousands of East Germans were on their way to West Germany: they voted with their feet. Nearly a week before the fall of the Berlin Wall, East Germany had lost its border with the West.

The fall of the Wall and the opening up of the East German polity

Mary Elise Sarotte has told the gripping story of the many errors that went into opening the Berlin Wall on the evening of November 9. Underlying the errors, however, is a deeper theme. The Socialist Unity Party had lost its compass, its sense of how to maintain power and the purpose of doing so. More concretely, its leadership could not develop a new travel law, since it still sought to reconcile two, contradictory aims: to keep the working people at home and to give them the right to leave. When it did develop a half-hearted reform of the travel law, aimed again at appeasing the people and slowing travel across the border, its poor implementation ended up speeding the process of dissolution.

Gorbachev had warned that the existence of the GDR was at stake. The party leadership hesitated, provided half measures, and then apparently avoided even careful reading of its own draft travel laws. When Günter Schabowski, as press spokesperson, introduced the new travel regulation on the evening of November 9, he seemed barely informed of the details. The room erupted in response to the statement that the politburo had decided to "implement a regulation that allows every citizen of the German Democratic

Republic (um) to (um) leave the GDR through any border crossing," surprising Schabowski and sending him in search of his glasses and the official announcement, which he promptly read out loud: "Applications for travel abroad by private individuals can now be made without the previously existing requirements. . . . The responsible departments of passport and registration control in the People's Police district offices in the GDR are instructed to issue visas for permanent exit without delays and without presentation of the existing requirements of permanent exit." Asked when the law would go into effect, he paused, again consulted his papers. "Immediately, without delay." That is also how quickly reporters from the West German media broadcast the news, making East German citizens aware of their government's apparent change in policy.

Citizens assembled at the checkpoints in Berlin, and local border guards could not figure out what the new rules were. In retrospect, it is clear that no plans had been made for the opening of the border, which would at the very least have required the notification of the Soviets and of NATO. But as the crowds grew, guards at checkpoints along the Berlin Wall ultimately decided to not risk violence or their own necks: they raised the traffic barriers and let East Germans cross. Television cameras captured these first border crossers and the flood that followed them. The fall of the Wall was an instant media event, broadcast live to the world as a heartfelt reunion, a spontaneous street party, a joyous rock festival. It happened because of the incompetence, but even more because of the insecurities of the party: proof positive that its time, too, had come.

But the crisis of the GDR did not mean the victory of the dissidents. They had been a minority before. Now the broad masses of the people joined them in the streets. But the dissidents called for a new forum, a new democracy; the masses called for unification with West Germany. The slogan "We are the people" was replaced by "We are one people." For many dissidents, this shift came as a rude surprise. They had aimed for a new kind of democracy based on the direct participation of society, with social as well as ecological and pacifist goals at its heart. Unification implied simply adopting the model of West Germany, with its industrial capitalism, its commitment to NATO, and its existing political parties.

The dissidents have been criticized for their elitism in rejecting what the people wanted. This criticism operates on a moral level, but both dissidents and East Germans calling for unification need to be understood on a different, historical level. The dissidents, unlike many of the latecomers to open protest, had developed their understanding of the regime and change in a different period, and not surprisingly had a different point of view from those who had chosen personal security over open confrontation. To be a dissident before 1989 meant precisely to go against the flow; they were hardly likely to give up their critical perspective just because the masses were behind them. With a few exceptions, meanwhile, the citizens who came out into the streets only in the last months of the regime used the language of nationalism. The East German economy was, by November, in free fall. But unlike other states in Eastern Europe, the GDR bordered on a wealthy, capitalist state that spoke the same language and whose constitution guaranteed citizenship rights to GDR citizens. German nationalism meant in the context of the Revolution of 1989 the ability to dump a failed state and economy and join with a wealthy neighbor. To many, unification seemed an easy, even natural way forward. For the dissidents, it meant giving up the grand goals of constructing a new society based on post-consumerist, participatory values, for consumer goods and comfort.

The diplomacy of unification and the Round Table

German unification was not just a German affair. It operated within a wider international context, involving the Allies of the Second World War and the alliance systems of the Cold War. Between November 1989 and early summer of 1990, the fate of East Germany was decided in two very different realms: international diplomacy and internal, revolutionary transformation.

The division of Germany into East and West had taken place between 1946 and 1949 not as the result of a final peace treaty ending the Second World War, but in place of one. The Allies never reached a formal resolution of the war and remained involved, legally, militarily, and politically, with the divided Germany. The GDR and FRG had been integrated into two different international systems and their reunification now posed a challenge to both. It also posed a challenge to the Warsaw Pact and NATO, as well as to the individual states of Europe. Forty-five years before, a horrendous war started by Nazi Germany had come to an end: should Germany be allowed to reunite? It was an emotional as well as political question for Europeans and their governments.

The East German crisis was thus potentially an international crisis. The Soviet Union had made the decision not to intervene to protect Honecker's regime; that was very different, however, from agreeing that East Germany should leave the Warsaw Pact. Similarly, the Western Allies had to view any discussion of German unification with trepidation: would unification take place at the cost of German commitment to NATO? A neutral German federation or confederation would bring costs to both sides—and while the tensions of the Cold War were abating, it and the division of Europe had certainly not come to an end.

The West German government watched with concern over the summer and fall, fearing violence and instability. Kohl's government worked to ensure the safe passage of East Germans to the West, and Kohl himself declared in August that German unity remained a West German goal. On November 8, when the fall of the Berlin Wall still seemed a distant dream, he took a dramatic next step. In a speech to the Bundestag, he reaffirmed the goal of a united Germany, and demanded free elections, pluralism, political democratization, and the end of the state-socialist economy. He also asserted that European unification, that is, stronger ties among the members of the European Economic Community, should occur at the same time as German unification. Kohl's statements reached East Germans and guaranteed that the West German chancellor was now associated with the demands for German unification.

Kohl's speech was also aimed at all those outside of Germany, who feared a united Germany. Britain's Margaret Thatcher had a visceral reaction to a strong, united German nation, rooted perhaps in her memories of the Second World War; France's François Mitterrand reacted negatively as well. So long as the West Germans still refused to recognize the Oder-Neisse Line as the German border to the East, that line that had removed large parts of territory from Germany, the neighboring Poles remained skeptical to say the least. Americans and Soviets, too, expressed unease, doubtful about the possibility of a strong, neutral, united Germany. The specter of German militarism loomed large.

After the fall of the Wall, the discussion broke out in full force. Within Germany, despite the protests of some dissidents in the East and some critics of Kohl in the West, the question quickly became, not whether to unify, but how. On November 28, Kohl surprised the Bundestag with a speech that laid out a path to stabilization, confederation, and finally federation, in other words a roadmap to unification. Most Germans, no matter where they lived, supported the goal of unification, as did all major parties in West Germany. Those predominately younger West Germans who did not found their position represented by the Greens, who were linked to the dissident movements in East Germany and rejected German nationalism. Internationally, however, Thatcher and Mitterrand were furious, Gorbachev rejected unification, the United States rejected any change that would take Germany out of NATO, and Israeli prime minister Yitzhak Shamir expressed his fears that a united Germany would pose a mortal threat to Jews. Kohl notably said nothing about the East German border with Poland, the Oder-Neisse Line. Indeed, he refused to address that issue. Some members of his party began speaking of the German borders before 1937. This did not help calm fears of German nationalism.

At the same time, the GDR still existed and was moving quickly toward a fundamental change of the regime. On December 1, the People's Chamber eliminated Article One of the constitution, which had guaranteed the guiding place of the Socialist Unity Party in politics. Two days later, the entire SED leadership resigned. And on December 7, following the example set by Poland not long before, a Round Table of the leading dissident groups plus the Socialist Unity Party formed, with the aim of working out a new constitution and new laws for democracy. They had no official standing. But then again, the People's Chamber was hardly a democratically elected body. In a sense, the unelected Round Table was more representative, since it included leaders of social groups independent of state and party. The Round Table saw its role as a transitional rather than a governing body, laying the foundations of greater freedom and representation of all social groups.

But this lofty aim confronted a bitter fact. Somehow the existing economy had to be stabilized. Hans Modrow, a member of the Socialist Unity Party but a committed reformist and now prime minister of the People's Chamber, approached Helmut Kohl on December 19, asking for a 15 billion mark credit. Kohl refused until free elections took place and the constitution reformed. Although the two sides reached other decisions about free movement and a more realistic exchange rate of 1 West to 3 East German marks, Kohl's decision doomed the East German economy.

In the face of an impending collapse of the GDR, the Round Table agreed in late January 1990 to move elections ahead to March 18, 1990. The next few months saw a flurry of activity: the Socialist Unity Party renamed itself the Party of Democratic Socialism (PDS), the Christian Democrats and Liberal Democrats broke from their bloc party status to form independent parties, the dissidents formed their own electoral groups. While the government, such as it was, engaged in extensive damage control, and all the while East Germans continued to flow over the border to the West.

Debating unification, East and West, and the elections of March 18

Unification was not only a matter for discussion in the East. West German political parties contributed time and money to the East German election, campaigning hard for their desired outcome. But in the West, reunification, which implied the end of the old Federal Republic, was controversial as well. According to public opinion polls, starting in the 1970s an increasing number of younger people in the FRG viewed the GDR as a foreign country. They identified furthermore with Western Europe, not with Eastern Europe, reflecting four decades of Western European economic, social, and cultural integration. In addition, the ongoing, heated discussions about a united Germany's actions in the Second World War left many feeling ambivalent about the prospect of unification. The Greens, representing younger people and following their anti-nationalist principles, rejected unification as a goal. Older intellectuals on the left like Jürgen Habermas and Günter Grass questioned the German nationalistic tendencies behind the campaign for unification, and younger politicians like Oskar Lafontaine of the Social Democrats questioned whether the nation-state was still on the agenda at the end of the twentieth century. Lafontaine received hearty applause for his position in Young Socialist circles in West Germany. But others within the West Social Democrats criticized Lafontaine: Willy Brandt campaigned for the Social Democrats in the East, symbolizing by his very presence his belief in German unity.

On March 18, 1990, the East German people spoke in their first free elections since 1932. Against expectations of a Social Democratic victory, the conservative Alliance for Germany, connected to the Christian Democrats, swept the elections, with nearly 50 percent of the vote; the Christian Democrats alone received over 40 percent of the votes. The Social Democrats received only 21 percent, to their surprise. The Party of Democratic Socialism (the reformed Socialist Unity Party) gained 16.4 percent of the vote. The parties representing the dissidents, the Greens and Alliance 90, received less than 5 percent of the vote: they were the big losers.

The diplomacy of unification continues

On December 11, 1989, the Four Powers met in the same Allied Control Council building in Berlin that the Soviets had left in anger in 1948. Three of the four, all but the United States, opposed unification. The question was whether they really could guide the developments.

The US position would, over the next half year, win out. President Bush and Secretary of State James Baker made it a point to avoid polemics and enthusiasm: the point was not to humiliate the Soviet Union, if a peaceful resolution of the crisis was to be reached. Bush and Baker laid out four principles to guide the coming process. First, any decision on the future should be based on the principle of German self-determination. Second, the process should be deliberate and carried out in steps, not abrupt. Third, existing borders in Europe were to be respected. Fourth, a unified Germany would belong to both NATO and the EC.

It would have been hard for any of the four to reject the notion of German self-determination: what else was Gorbachev standing for, after all? Similarly, calling for a steady and deliberate process was hardly controversial. Recognizing borders meant setting a condition for Helmut Kohl: his government would have to recognize the Oder-Neisse Line. Again, despite Kohl's stubbornness on the point, it was hardly a position that one could reject. The controversial demand was that Germany remain bound to NATO.

Gorbachev tentatively agreed to unification in principle by the end of January 1990—but only if Germany remained neutral, which meant leaving NATO. The question of NATO membership would remain the sticking point for the next months. The Soviet government was divided between those willing to make concessions and those viewing East Germany as an essential part of Soviet defenses. Given the fact that East Germany was in free fall, and after the elections that amounted to a referendum for unification, the Soviet position seems in retrospect chaotic and contradictory: their bargaining chip was in the process of dissolving. As for Great Britain, Prime

Minister Thatcher, against other parts of her government, simply opposed unification. But hers was hardly a forward-looking policy that could provide an acceptable alternative strategy. President Mitterand of France, by contrast, developed a clear notion of the way forward, insisting that a united Germany must bind itself more closely with Europe. All of the Allies came together in what became known as the Two plus Four process: putting the representatives of the Germanys at the same table as the Allies to stress that any resolution to the crisis would not be simply a decision of the victors of the Second World War, so many years after the war, but would include representatives of East and West Germany at the table.

The breakthrough with Gorbachev came at the end of May, when he accepted the condition of Germany's membership in NATO. On the surface, he was accepting the principle that a nation-state had the right to choose its own alliance system, which under the leadership of Kohl meant NATO. What really changed his mind was a growing internal crisis within the Soviet Union, which faced not only the inability to provide basic goods to Soviet citizens but also the beginnings of its own collapse, as the Baltic states declared their independence from the Soviet Union. Under pressure from all sides, Gorbachev gave in; US and German diplomats grabbed the opportunity and ran with it—fast, since even Gorbachev and his foreign minister Eduard Shevardnadze expressed fears of a possible coup attempt. In the end, the Soviet agreement was not cheap. The West German government agreed to massive subsidies of about 12.5 billion West German marks to build housing and facilitate the removal of the hundreds of thousands of Soviet soldiers who would have to return to the Soviet Union.

That left one key decision unmade: recognizing the Oder-Neisse Line as the border between Poland and Germany. Kohl resisted for a long time, whether for nationalist or more likely political reasons: the lobby representing those Germans expelled from eastern Europe after the Second World War remained strong in Bonn. His government also resisted its recognition, since with that would come the question of reparations owed to Polish forced laborers in the Second World War. Other European countries responded to Kohl's resistance with harsh criticism. In response, Kohl changed course. The Bundestag and the People's Chamber released a joint resolution of June 21–22, 1990, recognizing all existing borders, and soon after unification Germany and Poland signed a treaty to that effect.

On September 12, 1990, state leaders of both Germanys, the United States, the Soviet Union, Great Britain, and France, signed the Two Plus Four Treaty, formally bringing an end to the Allied occupation of Germany and opening the way to German unification. With German unification, the division of Europe following the Second World War finally came to an end—although, as we will see later, tensions between East and West would certainly remain.

It is hard to see what a realistic alternative would have been. But one always has a clear vision in retrospect. In fact, the structures of the Cold War, including missiles and alliance systems, were still in place throughout the negotiations; in fact, while it may be hard to envisage another peaceful and stable outcome, unstable and less than peaceful outcomes are imaginable. As the political scientist John Ikenberry has argued, the US approach toward the German problem succeeded because it aimed also at a sustainable, long-term peace, at incorporating a united Germany into a stable alliance system that could restrain it, and at opening up both NATO and the Conference on Security and Cooperation in Europe to make them less of a militant anti-Soviet force.

The currency of unification

Meanwhile, the two German states were moving rapidly toward currency unification. A common currency was becoming necessary as the border disappeared; the East German currency, still propped up by official exchange rates, was declining precipitously, and the West German currency was, in any case, spreading across the East. But official transactions remained in East German marks, from the capital of individual firms to the savings accounts of individuals.

Between the fall of the Berlin Wall and the end of 1989, some 300,000 East Germans had migrated westward. The Social Democrat finance expert Ingrid Matthäus-Meier noted already on January 19 that the East Germans needed a "signal to stay" at home, if the East German economy was not going to collapse; she and others began to talk about a currency union—just as her party mate Oskar Lafontaine started calling to slow the process down, possibly by offering East Germans fewer rights to social benefits as a way of dissuading them from abandoning ship. Economists, meanwhile, argued against a quick currency union, which they predicted would undermine the East German economy, with its subsidized wages and labor hoarding, while overburdening the West German economy with debt.

The debate on monetary unification was long and hard, and, as the economists had feared, focused on politics—minimizing hardship—rather than economic performance. Advocates for the East Germans called for a 1:1 exchange rate in the interest of fairness, to avoid wiping out individuals' savings; those concerned with West German financial stability and the very different levels of productivity in East and West suggested a far lower rate, of 1:3 or less, also to ensure the competitiveness of East German firms. The final result saw a 1:1 exchange rate for a certain amount of savings, and a 1:2 rate for other amounts, and left businesses with their existing debt—as a signal to East Germans to stay, and as a gift to East German voters for the upcoming election. The GDR and the FRG agreed to a detailed treaty on currency, economic, and social unity on May 18, 1990, which took effect on July 1, three months before political unification. On that day, Western banks opened their doors in the east, as did many Western chain stores selling coffee, groceries, and insurance.

When the currency union officially took place on July 1, 1990, it had the result of putting some extra hard currency in citizens' pockets, but also of making huge numbers of East German firms insolvent from one day to the next: they were forced to pay wages at Western rates and now owed debts in the West German currency, while the productivity rates of East German workers, especially given the state of the industrial plant, remained far below that of the West. And since East German firms were now selling their goods for hard currency, many of their former customers to the east were unable to pay. By the end of 1990, the unemployment rate in Eastern Germany had surpassed 10 percent. Many economists had hoped that the sudden shock of the currency unification would lead to a rapid recovery. In fact, the unemployment rate continued to increase, eventually rising to nearly 20 percent by the end of the 1990s.

It is unclear, however, what the alternative might have looked like. The East German economy was going to come under intense pressure no matter what, and political unification was rushing ahead. A unified state with two economic zones would not only have created massive administrative headaches, the western part would still have been forced to provide subsidies for eastern firms. And to maintain those firms, it would have had to find ways to stem migration, amounting to some kind of new wall, even if just in the form of different rights. Not only would that have left lasting political resentments, it also would have been unconstitutional. Finally, the exchange rate agreed to, while already generous to East Germans given the state of their economy, was still low enough to create wide resentment. There were no good choices, and the two German governments came up under these circumstances with a compromise that was at least less bad than alternatives.

The constitutional politics of unification

At the same time as the diplomats worked out the international conditions for German unification and the economic experts and political parties wrangled over how to integrate the two, very different economies, a public debate developed over the question of how the two countries should unify. On the East German side, the questions were not so difficult: after the March elections, it was clear that the GDR was about to be dissolved. On the West German side, however, the questions were less straightforward.

According to Article 146 of the Basic Law, on the day that a "constitution freely adopted by the German people" was approved, the Basic Law itself would cease to exist. Article 146 thus suggested that German unification would require a period of constitution-making. Even though a substantial majority would stand behind the principles of the Basic Law, the process could still have led to important changes. Article 23, by contrast, stated that when new Länder joined the Federal Republic, the Basic Law would apply to them. Article 23 required no revision of the Basic Law.

Political expediency won the day. Leading public figures like Jürgen Habermas on the political left and Dieter Grimm, a justice on the Constitutional Court, argued that the citizens of a new republic had a right to affirm their own constitution, and furthermore deserved the political respect that would be accorded them by opening up such a process. But the ruling coalition in the Bundestag opted not to open what they saw as a can of worms. The People's Chamber made the political decision to join the Federal Republic, which took the legal form of a decision by the five Länder of the GDR, formally reconstructed in 1990, to join the FRG.

Instead of a debate on basic constitutional principles, German unification took the legal form of a massive thousand page Treaty on Unification, approved on August 31, 1990, which deferred further discussion on basic constitutional questions to future sessions of the Bundestag. Political unification was set for October 3. The vast majority of People's Chamber and Bundestag delegates voted for unification—the PDS and the Bündnis 90, representing the ex-Communist Party and the dissidents, respectively, voted against in the East, while the Greens and a handful of delegates from the Christian Democrats voted no in the West. October 3 was then declared a national holiday, the Day of German Unity. November 9, the date of the opening of the Berlin Wall, might have seemed a more logical choice, but November 9 was also the date of Hitler's attempt to take over Germany during the Beer Hall Putsch in 1923 and the date of the "Night of Broken Glass," when National Socialists burnt synagogues across Germany and radicalized their attacks on the Jewish population in 1938. Even longer memories knew it as the date of Germany's 1918 revolution, whose success or failure, depending on how one looked at it, set the stage for the other two events. No doubt about it: the German past continued to haunt the German present at the moment of unification.

The treaty amended the Basic Law in minimal, but important, ways. Article 23 was revised to state that no more Länder were to join the Federal Republic, underlying the principle of respecting existing state borders. Key issues were left unresolved: the different rights of women in the east, where they had access to free and legal abortions, for example, and the west, where abortions were restricted, childcare was less available, and less provision was made for mothers who worked. No account was taken either of the dissidents' demands for greater public participation in decision making, for new social rights, and for constitutional principles affirming the state's commitment to the environment. Some of these became incorporated in the constitutions of the Länder; the Basic Law remained, with a few exceptions, the same. In 1991, following a heated debate, Berlin became the capital of Germany once more. The old West German parties were divided over the matter. Some politicians, on both left and right, stressed that Bonn had been the capital of Germany's first successful democracy.

Others, also from both sides of the spectrum, argued that a reunified Berlin should become the country's capital as a gesture to those who strove for freedom and democracy in the East. Religious tensions underlay the debate as well. Bonn was an old Catholic city, and Catholicism had helped to shape West Germany; Berlin was a majority Protestant city (with a good number of people outside of any church by the end of the twentieth century), and a majority of the population of united Germany would have a Protestant background. In short, the decision to make Berlin the capital symbolized many things: German unity, the democratic revolution of the East Germans, but also an end to confessional parity and a return to the capital of Prussian militarism.

Collapse, revolution, and unification

The story of 1989 in Germany can be read as a brutal comedy of collapse, a tragic story of doomed heroism, or a happy ending to an unnatural separation. Dirk Philipsen's extraordinary collection of interviews with East Germans shortly before unification poignantly illustrates how people had different experiences of the revolution and even contrary understandings of what it was about, depending on their politics and their place in society.

The SED regime had watched for two decades as the contradictions in economy, society, and polity grew worse and worse. Under Honecker, it resolutely avoided the contradictions; it received bad news from the Stasi, but found no way forward. The story of its collapse is almost like a comedy: huge amounts of information paralyzing an indecisive leadership, the transformation of the great party into a group of men unsure how even to challenge their incompetent leader, all the way down to the incoherent laws and public statements that finally led to the opening of the Berlin Wall. At any moment, of course, the comedy could have turned bloody: Honecker's party was not above employing the "Tiananmen Solution."

The dissidents had played a marginal role in the GDR, and probably would have played even less a role had the government not felt exposed to the West German media and therefore compelled to exercise some restraint. To be a dissident, however, was to make harsh compromises in life, to be excluded from most higher education and better jobs, and to be exposed to constant monitoring by the Stasi, possible violence, and expulsion. The dissidents were small in number. Their actions gradually ate away at the legitimacy of the state, just as the Stasi had feared. But then, as legitimacy collapsed and the population rose up, the dissidents found themselves marginalized yet again. Some would resurface in leadership positions in the newly united Germany; others retreated as the various parties and grassroots organizations that sprang to life that autumn dissolved or joined their West German counterparts.

VOICES FROM THE 1989 REVOLUTION

Doris C., Berlin worker: "So more and more people went to the church, not because they liked church, but because they were seeking protection in the church. Women my age all of a sudden ran to church on every 7th of the month, lighting candles and all, simply because we no longer knew what to do with our bottled-up anger. All of those double standards, all of this arbitrariness came to our attention after a while, even though we used to say to ourselves 'there is nothing you can do anyway.'"

Ludwig Melhourn, founding member of Democracy Now: "Not even as late as November 9 were we able to provide leadership for the people. Things were happening on the streets, but not in any organized fashion. It really was spontaneous mass enthusiasm, and also an enormous willingness to take immense risks, particularly when you look at the 70,000 or 80,000 who demonstrated in Leipzig [on October 9] when things were still extremely dangerous. . . ."

Cornelia Matzke, founding member of the Independent Women's Alliance: "You see, the nice thing about this country called the "GDR" before the Wende was that we all had something in common with each other, something about which we all agreed, which was complaining about the leadership. But the reasons why people disliked the system were very different. . . ."

Maria C., Berlin worker: "All we wanted was to be able to travel . . . We wanted to be able to go wherever we felt like, and for as long as we wanted. . . But this kind of open Wall, well, let me tell you, that is not what I wanted. And I also did not want to get rid of socialism. . . You have to realize, we looked wide-eyed at Gorbachev, what he was trying to do in the Soviet Union. That came right out of our own hearts; that's what we wanted to happen here. . . ."

Peter R., Berlin worker: ". . . And then this valve opened, and we had so much hope that we could perhaps still save the whole thing. And then we got Egon Krenz, who had been fed the same shit, who was, in fact the same old shit. Nothing, absolutely nothing, was possible with him. . . ."

Source: Dirk Philipsen, ed., We Were the People: Voices from East Germany's Revolutionary Autumn of 1989 *(Durham, NC: Duke University Press, 1992), 125, 215, 249, 281, 285.*

National unification was not on the agenda until fall 1989. As the party collapsed and as dissidents raised demands for comprehensive and complex political renewal, workers and others in society saw a collapsing economy, a power vacuum, and a neighbor that had inscribed national unity on its

264 GERMANY SINCE 1945

banner. National unity is a comforting term, one that implies solidarity and belonging. In fall 1990, as a united Germany prepared for its first national election, Kohl's Christian Democrats ran a political advertisement featuring an elderly couple separated by the Wall, but finally able to reunite in old age—a wonderfully romantic story.

Further reading

Bösch, Frank. "Energy Diplomacy: West Germany, the Soviet Union and the Oil Crises of the 1970s." *Historical Social Research* 39 (2014), 165–84.

"Günter Schabowski's Press Conference in the GDR International Press Center, 9 November 1989, 6:53–7:01 pm." Cold War International History Bulletin 12/13 (1990), 157–58.

Horster, Maximilian. "The Trade in Political Prisoners between the Two German States, 1962-89." *Journal of Contemporary History* 39 (2004), 403–24.

Ikenberry, John. *After Victory: Institutions, Strategic Restraint, and the Rebuilding of Order after Major Wars.* Princeton: Princeton University Press, 2000.

Jarausch, Konrad. *The Rush to German Unity.* New York: Oxford University Press, 1994.

Jarausch, Konrad, and Volker Fransow, eds. *Uniting Germany: Documents and Debates, 1944-1993.* Providence: Berghahn, 1994.

Müller, Jan-Werner. *Another Country: German Intellectuals, Unification, and National Identity.* New Haven: Yale University Press, 2000.

Pfaff, Steven. *Exit-Voice Dynamics and the Collapse of East Germany: The Crisis of Leninism.* Durham: Duke University Press, 2006.

Preuss, Ulrich. *Constitutional Revolution: The Link between Constitutionalism and Progress.* Translated by Deborah Lucas Schneider. Atlantic Highlands, NJ: Humanities Press, 1995.

Sarotte, Mary Elise. *The Collapse: The Accidental Opening of the Berlin Wall.* New York: Basic Books, 2014.

PART THREE

The Berlin Republic, 1990–2017

11

Tensions of unification

FIGURE 11.1 *Outside the unemployment office in Leipzig, July 9, 1991.*
(ullstein bild/Eckel/Getty Images)

German unification brought economic, political, and social challenges.
Economically, the sudden union of the East and West left a tremendous
gap between the two economies, which led to a collapse of eastern industry
and skyrocketing unemployment in the new Länder. As the new holding
company for former East German assets, the Treuhandanstalt, began to sell

those companies off at rock-bottom prices and put more people out of work,
discontent rose in the east. Politically, ever more easterners came to support the
new Party of Democratic Socialism, the heir of the old Socialist Unity Party.
Their frustrations took the form of harsh criticisms of western "annexation"
of the east, and were echoed by increasing anti-easterner views among
westerners, who experienced higher taxation to fund reconstruction in the east.
And socially, resurgent nationalism in the former GDR dovetailed with anti-
foreigner sentiments voiced by Germans throughout the newly united country.
Initially shunted off as an "Ossi," or eastern, problem, specifically as evidence
of East Germans' democratic deficiencies, right radicalism and deadly attacks
on foreigners proved to be a nationwide phenomenon, raising international and
domestic fears about a united Germany. Added to this were the harsh debates
among easterners in both law and literature, about how to come to terms with
their dictatorial past.

Between fall 1989 and fall 1990, a regime collapsed, a revolution took shape
and then disappeared, currencies were unified, and the division of Germany
brought to an end. When the West German soccer team won the World Cup
in the summer of 1990, the players also sang the *Deutschlandlied*, including
the important word "unity and justice and freedom," and streets of Germany
filled with flag-waving fans. Over the next decade and beyond, however,
the more difficult problems of unification appeared. Unsurprisingly, forty
years made a difference, economically, politically, and culturally, as did the
process of unification itself. Once the rush to unification subsided, Germans
confronted the consequences of separation.

The year 1989 signaled the defeat of state socialism. The end of state
socialism was more than the end of a stagnant economy run by an aging
collective, however. It meant the end of an entire way of life, for everyone
from workers and farmers to professionals and students to party leaders
and even dissidents. Customs, codes of behavior, as well as the rules of how
to get by socially and financially changed for East Germans in a way that
simply was not true for West Germans, whose everyday habits, values, and
institutions remained essentially untouched. Individuals reacted to these new
circumstances in a wide variety of ways but, as Dirk Philipsen's interviews
of former East Germans reveals, nearly all of them experienced 1989 as
fundamentally dislocating. Young East Germans, who had not yet come of age
when the Wall fell, adapted most readily as did those whose skills transferred
relatively easily to the new job market. Those who struggled most included
older East Germans, forced into early retirement, and recent graduates or
students in their final years of apprenticeship. Rather than stepping into
promising careers and the lives for which they had been preparing, these
young adults found their degrees declared illegitimate (presumed products of
a corrupt ideology), their training deemed inferior, and their jobs gone. And
then there were those East Germans who, at least initially, did not want to
adapt because West/unified Germany was not the democratic society they had

imagined or desired. For the thousands of protesters who took to the streets, part of what made 1989 disorienting was not only the swiftness with which the regime collapsed but also the swiftness with which their newfound voices were silenced. As an East German bishop noted with evident frustration, "It is constantly suggested that we [former East Germans] are not capable of anything, and that everything we have done was wrong... all of our experiences belong on the trash heap of history. Apparently it is not worth listening when we are saying anything. But we can no longer take this permanent know-it-all manner and our degrading treatment as disenfranchised failures."[1]

After 1989, all of the former People's Republics faced similar challenges: Their models of political organization collapsed; competitive markets replaced planning and coordination from above; and old trading connections were broken from one day to the next. In the German case, unification exposed eastern firms to direct competition from western ones, which operated more efficiently and often produced higher quality goods. The transition from state socialism to capitalism across central and eastern Europe proved far more difficult than imagined by most economists, and eastern Germany was especially hard-hit. Production declined, and workers faced the possibility of unemployment and exposure to a competitive labor market often for the first time.

Political unification trailed economic unification by three months, and by October 3, 1990, the official day of German unity, the immediate consequences of the transition were becoming clear. In eastern Germany, as in other former state-socialist lands, the Socialist Unity Party reorganized itself in defense of the "losers" of unification: this new Party of Democratic Socialism would, as this chapter discusses, reshape the party landscape, claiming both to outflank the Social Democrats to the left and to represent easterners. In addition to disrupting the politics of the old Federal Republic, unification had an effect on German nationalism. At first, the peaceful process of unification symbolized a new, mature German people; but soon after unification, violent attitudes toward foreigners, with roots in the pre-1990 period in both East and West, became manifest, and in the hands of skinheads and neo-Nazis took the form of murderous attacks on refugees.

Finally, the unification of Germany transformed the European project. Throughout the 1990s, the German government faced the difficult question of what its new role should be internationally: too much initiative raised fears of a resurgent Germany, too little raised fears of a German nation avoiding responsibility.

Managing industrial collapse in Eastern Germany: The Treuhandanstalt

The currency union of July 1, 1990, thrust eastern German firms into the cold water of Western capitalism. In his television address of that day,

Helmut Kohl promised "blossoming landscapes" across the former East Germany within a short time. Economists knew that the transition would be difficult, but they, too, predicted a rapid adjustment to the new economic environment. They assumed that with the social market economy in place, eastern Germany would experience the same "economic miracle" that West Germany had in the 1950s. Instead, eastern Germany experienced a dramatic economic collapse. After united Germany created a new Treuhandanstalt, or "trustee corporation," to administer the failing public firms, former East Germans came to view it as the western-dominated destroyer of the GDR economy. Of course, the Treuhandanstalt did not create the problems of economic transition. But it nonetheless served as a focal point for a new source of division between the east and west.

Already in early 1990, the East German Communist Party, renamed the PDS-Socialist Unity Party in December 1989, engaged in extensive discussion about how to reform the state-socialist economy. Up to that point, the State Planning Commission had set planning targets for the thousands of "people's firms." But on March 1, the PDS-SED leader Hans Modrow suggested replacing the planning agency with a new trustee organization. The party never got the chance. Eighteen days later, East Germans voted overwhelmingly against the PDS-SED and for a conservative government; its leader, the Christian Democrat Lothar de Maizière, took up the proposal, but altered it significantly. The first democratically elected government in the GDR reconceptualized the Treuhandanstalt as a kind of massive holdings company whose aim was to take over around 8,500 state-owned firms in the GDR and their four million employees, try to keep them viable and protect jobs, and, most important, to privatize them. The suggestion came from the new East German government, and West Germany agreed to the plan as part of the 1990 contract creating an economic and social union.

The new Treuhandanstalt faced a crisis from its very first days in summer 1990. The currency union had suddenly exposed the less productive and often inefficient eastern firms to western competition, while requiring former trading partners from Eastern Europe to pay in hard, western currency as they faced their own economic crises. The new agency inherited the job of the former State Planning Commission of the old GDR, just as the entire old economic system was falling apart. Detlev Rohwedder, a West German executive famous for reviving the faltering metals and alloys corporation Hoesch in the 1980s, took over as director of the Treuhandanstalt in July 1990. He hoped that selling off the individual firms would bring in some six hundred billion German marks. Like many economists and business professionals, he believed that the GDR's economy was stronger than it was in reality.

His great dream quickly turned into a nightmare. Firms remained burdened with the debts carried over from the old system; in addition, many of them sat on environmentally contaminated areas, an additional cost for potential purchasers. To the overall inefficiency of so much East German

MAP 11.1 *Unified Germany.*

production was added their often outdated and inefficient equipment. Many also suffered from the loss of their best workers to firms in the west. In addition to these problems of low productivity and high clean-up costs, firms predating 1945 were open to claims by former owners, which could tie a sale up in courts for years. These factors made selling firms difficult to say the least. To entice would-be buyers, the Treuhandanstalt offered subsidies—and opened the door to potential corruption.

A deeper problem plagued the privatization of previously state-owned firms. These firms often produced items like textiles, steel, and coal, and other products of the first industrial revolution. But it was precisely this older industrial economy that had been in a process of decline for more than twenty years in West Germany. The long transition to a service and high-tech economy had begun there in the late 1950s, when basic industries like coal and steel first came under pressure, and reached its painful conclusion in the early 1980s. The eastern German industrial economy had virtually no time to make this same transition. Even if the industrial plants had been more productive, even if the economy had not been hemorrhaging skilled workers, it is questionable whether these industries could have competed in the global economy. Further, the presence of cheaper labor in the transitional economies further east, such as Poland, Slovakia, Hungary, and the Czech Republic, made the survival of eastern German companies even more tenuous. The Treuhandanstalt went from managing a transition to managing the end of an economy. Certainly, the leaders of the Treuhandanstalt aimed at ending the state-socialist system; their intent was not to put millions of people out of work.

On October 2, 1990, the day before political unification, the Treuhandanstalt began to shut down the Pentacon camera factory in Dresden, which was unable to produce cameras at a competitive price; in the end, over 5,000 employees lost their jobs. A few months later, the entire auto industry in the former GDR came under fire. Car manufacturers in western Germany either had enough production lines or wanted to build new plants rather than inherit old ones. The East German Trabant, or Trabi (also affectionately known as the "little stinker" in reference to both its size and exhaust fumes), was about to become an endangered species. As symbols of the GDR industrial culture fell to the transition, popular anger rose.

Not only Rohwedder but almost all of the top-level managers of the Treuhandanstalt were West German. In contrast, the majority of the Treuhandanstalt employees were East German. Not surprisingly, easterners' anger turned against the Treuhandanstalt as a tool of and for western Germany. West German unions, meanwhile, inherited the job of representing employees in the new Länder. They added their voice to the growing wave of protests in early 1991. The PDS also came out in force against what one of their leaders, the former GDR economist Harry Nick, called "an unparalleled destruction and squandering of economic assets"; he and others called for the state to take over the firms and reinvigorate them instead of trying to privatize them. The protests were aimed at Rohwedder in particular, as a representative capitalist manager from western Germany.

On April 1, 1991, an unknown assassin murdered Rohwedder. The RAF, which had continued its fight against NATO and heads of capitalism even as many, older members retired in anonymity to the GDR, took responsibility for the killing. At that point the protests died down, and the Treuhandanstalt began to promise a new approach to reinvigorating and selling the factories. But protests flared up again in the summer of 1991, after revelations of corruption and sweetheart deals between some members of the Treuhandanstalt and individual companies like the French oil company Elf Aquitaine. The protests reached their high point in 1993, when major East German enterprises like the steel-producing Eisenhütten Kombinat Ost and the potash mine at Bischofferode came on the chopping block: existing big producers did not want such expensive plants when they could acquire cheap raw materials from other global sources. A hunger strike at Bischofferode brought worldwide attention to the crisis of industry in eastern Germany. The German government responded with a major—and expensive—plan to phase jobs out slowly and provide social support for the unemployed.

For ordinary workers, the Treuhandanstalt was a catastrophe. The workplace in the GDR had been a primary site of social interaction. Firms connected people with housing, with friendship circles, with goods, and even with medical care through clinics located in the factories. With the loss of their workplace, former East Germans lost the feeling of security and of community. Even former supervisors and experienced managers lost their jobs, replaced by administrators who had training and experience in the Federal Republic. Unemployment reached beyond those firms affected by the Treuhandanstalt. Thousands of academics lost their positions in the first years after unification. In some cases, fields were simply incompatible. East German law now ceased to exist, and as a result lawyers from western Germany poured into the new lands, taking over as attorneys as well as judges. Many scholars and professors had produced little in the ideologically charged environment of the GDR or what they had produced was now deemed tainted or outdated, and some had been directly involved with the Stasi; thousands found themselves out of not just a job but a career. The high unemployment of the first years continued for more than a decade and a half, at times reaching nearly 20 percent in all of the former GDR, and significantly higher in areas like Sachsen-Anhalt.

While both women and men in the east suffered from unemployment, women were especially hard-hit. Nearly twice as many women as men were registered as unemployed between 1991 and 1995. This was at least partially because women were concentrated in those sectors most exposed to competition from western German companies and from abroad: textiles, light industry, and food production. Just as important, with the end of the GDR came the end of the childcare facilities and generous maternity leaves

CHART 11.1 *Unemployment Rate in Unified Germany, 1991–2015*
Source: Statistisches Bundesamt, "Arbeitsmarkt: Registrierte Arbeitslose,
Arbeitslosenquote nach Gebietsstand," available at: https://www.destatis.de/DE/
ZahlenFakten/Indikatoren/LangeReihen/Arbeitsmarkt/lrarb003.html

that helped women juggle both children and a job. The GDR had, in part because of these accommodations, experienced both a higher birthrate and a higher rate of single parenting than the FRG; more women in East Germany opted not only to work but also to remain unmarried. Now the social supports that made this possible were gone, replaced by the West German system. It provided unemployment benefits, pensions for early retirement, and aid for mothers, but still functioned with the traditional nuclear family and male breadwinner in mind. Coupled with high unemployment, importing the western system of social services meant a sense of deep social insecurity for many of the women and men in the new federal lands.

Abortion rights represented another point of controversy for women. As Chapter 6 discussed, women in East Germany had the right to an abortion during the first trimester of a pregnancy, while women in West Germany could only have an abortion after a third party professional determined that physical, mental, or social exigencies justified such an action—otherwise, abortion was a criminal act. Negotiators were unable to resolve these differences in abortion law before unification. The new Bundestag eventually approved a law in 1992 that legalized abortions in the first trimester following counseling and a three-day waiting period. It did not take long, however, before suits brought both by individuals and the state of Bavaria forced the law's review by the Constitutional Court. After considerable deliberation, the Court issued a tortured and contradictory ruling: abortions in the first trimester were illegal, but the Bundestag had the right to fashion a law that did not punish women who had an abortion. The new abortion law, passed in 1995, thus curiously both criminalized abortion and made it a right for women in the first trimester, following counseling and a waiting period. It was a mishmash of East and West if ever there was one, with real and symbolic significance for all Germans.

The PDS and growing numbers of disillusioned easterners referred to the entire endeavor as a West German takeover, even colonization, of the new Länder. Certainly, that's how it appeared to many who saw western German managers coming into factories and firing workers. In the end, about two-thirds of the firms were privatized or taken over by municipalities; some 30 percent were closed down. The total number of employees fell from about four million to around one and a half million in 1995. Instead of gaining six hundred billion German marks from selling the industry off, the Treuhandanstalt lost over 250 billion marks in concessions, clean-up costs, and other incentive offers. In addition, the state spent huge amounts on social benefits: unemployment, pensions, and retraining.[2] All of these factors sent the entire German economy into a two-year recession starting in 1992.

Was the Treuhandanstalt, with its goals of privatizing East German industry, a failure? The East German economy had entered into free fall before the Treuhandanstalt began its work. Its collapse was not merely the result of the currency union with West Germany, but also the general crisis associated with the collapse of state socialism across Eastern Europe. Under these conditions, and given the inefficiencies and widespread hoarding of labor in the East German economy, an alternative policy that sought to subsidize the weaker state-socialist firms would have only added to the German debt and the overall German recession. Certain firms, of course, might have been supported and saved, and perhaps the Treuhandanstalt should have been more discerning. But its options were in fact limited—especially in view of the structural changes already underway in the advanced industrial economies.

The Treuhandanstalt's solution, as awful as it was for those who lost their jobs and the communities that went with them, at least slowed down the process—especially after its change of course starting in 1991. It also perversely gave unions, government, and populace a scapegoat for a process of transition, as Wolfgang Seibel has argued, and a way to avoid confronting the reality that unification simply cost a lot of money—it was a financial burden for all Germans.

The new political landscape

The first elections in united Germany took place on December 2, 1990, just as the full scale of eastern Germany's economic collapse was becoming evident. The Constitutional Court required a special set of rules for this election, which would ensure that the new Länder would have the chance to put forward their own political parties. Most important, the Court suspended the rule that a party had to receive at least 5 percent of the entire vote to be represented as a party in the Bundestag; for this election, and only this one, a party only had to receive 5 percent in the eastern or in the western Länder, a ruling that opened the way for the PDS.

In a contest with five serious parties, the overwhelming plurality of the voters endorsed Helmut Kohl and his team. The Christian Democrats won over 40 percent of the vote in both eastern and western Germany. Its ally, the Free Democrats, also received more than 10 percent of the vote in both east and west. The election could thus be read as affirmation for the end of the GDR, for Germany's remaining firmly part of NATO and the Western alliance, and for immediate economic transition—despite the costs that were already becoming apparent.

The West German left lost badly. The Social Democratic candidate for chancellor, Oskar Lafontaine, swam against the tide with his call to slow down unification, warning of its costs, and to rethink the country's relationship to NATO. Not that Lafontaine was wrong in his assessment of the costs of unification: Kohl had stated that unification could take place without sacrifices on the part of western German voters, and Lafontaine correctly understood this to be false. Later he would say that he had underestimated the irrational euphoria around unification. But more decisively, he failed to offer a positive, forward-looking message. To be negative about a major project like unification was not the way to win voters. The Social Democrats failed to attract support in the east and lost it in the west. The party saw its worst results since 1957.

The Greens, meanwhile, had supported the East German dissidents more than any other West German party, and had wanted to see the GDR revolution go further. They gave their eastern counterparts, the Bündnis 90 (or Alliance 1990), free rein, and did not create a single, overarching party platform; the Greens and Bündnis 90 did not unite, in other words. The original Greens themselves, after all, criticized political parties as forces of stagnation and therefore did not want to extend party rule to the former East. They were the only western political party that was in this sense aligned with the party-critical dissidents of the east. This meant, however, that they essentially did not compete to represent the majority of former East Germans, and in the former FRG, the Greens failed to reach 5 percent. Suddenly the very existence of the Greens was in question. The Bündnis 90, meanwhile, squeaked by. Their message of environmental reform, political renewal through grassroots roundtables, and new social rights did not resonate with the majority of the population; the dissidents remained marginalized in the new Germany. After 1990, the Bündnis 90/Greens struggled to reform and to work as one. Existing disagreements came to a head in a harsh clash between the "Fundis" or fundamentalists, who wanted their party to represent a radical, environmental alternative to capitalism and representative democracy, and the "Realos" or realists, who wanted the Greens to further a reform-oriented agenda from within the existing system—which meant winning elections. The "Realos" won the power struggle but not without lasting bitterness and notable disaffection.

In the former East, the PDS captured over 11 percent of the votes. The party relied, first and foremost, on those voters who still identified with the old Socialist Unity Party regime, though many were also attracted by its leader, the charismatic Gregor Gysi, a young, fast-talking lawyer, a chain smoker, and an East Berliner of Jewish ancestry. Gysi's father Klaus had been one of the leading party officials of East Germany, active as a diplomat and in cultural affairs; Gregor made his name in the GDR defending critical intellectuals in the 1970s and 1980s. After unification, his quick retorts, energy, and ethnicity made him stand out from all other parliamentary leaders. He tapped into both East and West Berliners' portrayal of themselves as hard hitters with a scathing sense of humor. And, in fact, Gysi's presence at the head of the party helped to explain a lot of its staying power. But a good part of its members consisted of older people, connected with the regime, and displaced socially but also morally by the new, anti-GDR discourse surrounding them. By the end of 1991, the party would also become a collecting point for a colorful mixture of activists, ranging from an open "Communist Platform" to anarchists to anti-fascists and pacifists. Protest against western German control, as embodied in the Treuhandanstalt, united the disparate group.

Many assumed that the PDS would gradually disappear as the years went by. But it didn't. As the social and economic shock of unification spread across the eastern states, support for the PDS increased. In the federal elections of 1994, the PDS received nearly 20 percent of the vote in the new Länder but only about 1 percent in the west; as a result, they did not cross the 5 percent hurdle into parliament, which only reinforced eastern voters' sense of unequal treatment and disenfranchisement in the new Germany. The party soon became a fixture of eastern German politics. During the first decade of unified Germany, the PDS gathered between 13 percent and 25 percent of the votes in eastern Land elections. Many of their supporters had been part of the Socialist Unity Party apparatus; these men and women, with strong personal connections and experience in administration and communication, gradually built up local support. At the top level, the party defended socialism in vague terms, and criticized NATO; at the local level, the PDS engaged in projects like building playgrounds and improving quality of life. But what kept it alive was former East Germans' sense of grievance. The fact that the other parties, which western Germans dominated, refused to work with the PDS, only increased its luster with alienated East Germans. By 1998, the PDS had become the clearly identifiable party of the east, a visible protest against the western domination of the new Germany. In the election of that year, it received over 21 percent of the vote in the new Länder, and crossed the 5 percent threshold for the Bundestag.

FIGURE 11.2 *In the run up to the 1994 elections, Christian Democrats launched a "red sock" campaign against their left political opponents. This poster reads: "Forward into the future, but not in red socks!" The green clothes pins allude to the possible alliance between the Greens and the "red" PDS. (Konrad Adenauer Stiftung/Welzel & Hardt/Wikimedia Commons)*

As a protest party, the PDS could live with the many contradictory positions in its ranks. After all, its members represented eastern Germans, and Gysi's charisma and biting humor kept the party present in national politics. But over the long run, the PDS faced dwindling numbers of members, as its voter base aged. Furthermore, by the mid-to-late 1990s, the PDS had become popular enough that the other parties had to cooperate with it: the Social Democratic government in Saxony-Anhalt relied on the PDS's support starting in 1994, and in both Mecklenburg-Vorpommern in 1998 and in Berlin in 2002, the PDS formed a coalition with the Social Democrats. Nothing hurts an oppositional party like being in power and having to make decisions that alienate some of its voter base. In the Bundestag elections of 2002, the PDS saw its voter numbers shrink, and commentators once again predicted the party's dissolution. Despite the importance of the East-West, or rather Ossi-Wessi (easterner-westerner), divide, discussed below, former East Germans were scarcely united behind the PDS.

"Ossis," "Wessis," and the Divided East

Unification created tension between easterners and westerners over the course of the 1990s, as well as within the former East Germany itself. These tensions took many forms, from cultural conflicts to denunciations of neighbors to harsh political polemics and radical politics. They also drove popular stereotypes of easterners and westerners—of so-called Ossis and Wessis. A Wessi was an overbearing and arrogant know-it-all ("Besserwessi"), who drove a Mercedes; an Ossi was a whiny provincial with a little Trabi. Wessis were materialistic and individualistic, Ossis more interested in community and family.

One can easily exaggerate the importance of these stereotypes. As much as they were discussed starting in the 1990s, they were not connected with outbreaks of violence, as were the stereotypes against asylum seekers discussed below. They did, however, express resentments felt by many in both the east and the west. It was all too apparent to people in the east, for example, that not only the leadership of the Treuhandanstalt but also their new judges, city administrators, upper level managers, and professors were disproportionately former West Germans. The political house-cleaning that followed the GDR's collapse was thorough: public-sector employees who had been members of the Socialist Unity Party or had collaborated with the Stasi (a significant portion of the population, don't forget) were dismissed, as were those like teachers, who were judged unfit to educate new, democratic citizens. Western judges presided over the trials of former Socialist Unity Party leaders for the murder of GDR citizens at the Wall. Critical and aggrieved observers noted how differently justice played out now than it had when former Nazis—and the Third Reich— were on the stand in FRG. Now the state seemed all too willing to go after every injustice, whereas after 1945, many in West Germany had sought to sweep the past under the rug. At the same time, the decision to incorporate the five eastern Länder into the FRG rather than draft a new constitution, which theoretically might have wed the positives of one system with that of the other, lent further credence to the colonization thesis. Somewhat ironically, there were East Germans who felt themselves disenfranchised at the very moment they became part of a working democracy.

Former West Germans, meanwhile, who had not supported unification felt increasingly vindicated by expressions of eastern German disgruntlement. Western Germans found themselves saddled with higher taxes, a so-called solidarity supplement (*Solidaritätszuschlag*) on top of western Germans' already high tax rates. Put in place in 1991, it persisted twenty-five years later and captures the heart of the matter: German unity cost 1.5–2 trillion Euros between 1990 and 2014, a huge amount. Hundreds of billions went to repair and replace crumbling infrastructure, to clean up environmental disaster areas, to help new businesses in the east, and to provide social help for the many unemployed or underemployed. West Germany itself suffered from unemployment and deficits before unification, and some westerners from the decaying rust belts of the Ruhr Valley understood themselves to be passed over in favor of recipients in the east. Others simply could not fathom how eastern Germans could complain or feel themselves the victims of unification in the face of such huge financial bailouts.

Like all stereotypes, the Ossi-Wessi distinction simplified or ignored the complexities of post-unification German society. At the same time, polling information did indicate differences between the populations of the old and new Länder—differences that, of course, varied greatly from person to person, and that were also no doubt skewed by the massive migration of so many people from east to west. Nonetheless, polls taken at the tenth, fifteenth, and twentieth anniversaries of German unification suggested that those who came of age in the FRG and GDR differed in their professed values and priorities. Even as late as 2015, eastern Germans still demonstrated fewer social stigmas against unwed parents and a greater propensity for gender equality. Not surprisingly, however, these differences existed far less among the generation that came of age after 1990. They adapted quickly to the new social customs and cultural codes of the West, even if not always painlessly. As Jana Hensel described it in her international bestseller, *After the Wall: Confessions from an East German Childhood and the Life that Came Next*, "the first West Germans from eastern Germany" were not unlike first-generation immigrants, operating as important intermediaries for older parents and family members who felt themselves foreigners in a strange land.

However real, it is fair to say that the Ossi/Wessi distinction also served to conceal the deep tensions that existed in the east, between former East Germans. They were divided, for example, about how to evaluate their recent past. The Bundestag commissioned a critical commission for the "Coming to Terms with the History and Consequences of the Socialist Unity Party Dictatorship in Germany." The result was a massive report spread

"OSSIS AND WESSIS" IN PUBLIC
OPINION POLLS

Public opinion polls taken around twenty-five years after German Unification show that the divisions between "Ossis" and "Wessis" have persisted.

From the Magdeburg *Volksstimme*, for example: two-thirds of easterners viewed westerners as "arrogant" and "religious," while over half saw them as too oriented toward money and egotistical. More than half of westerners, meanwhile, saw easterners as "frugal," "reserved," and possessing a "sense of community."[3]

The GfK Verein, meanwhile, reported that more than half of all Germans, and more than 70 percent of easterners, still saw important differences between easterners and westerners: in other words, a sense of difference had become a solid part of eastern identity. In addition, easterners viewed themselves as having a greater sense of family, and reported a far lower level of religiosity in their families than westerners did in theirs. (Interestingly, both saw their own group as especially industrious [*fleissig*], suggesting the perseverance of older national conceptions of hard-working Germans.[4])

across many volumes detailing the economic, social, military, cultural, and political aspects of the GDR. It was a report on a dictatorship, the result of intense work by scholars trained in the East and the West, and not surprisingly critical. Some members of the PDS, including the legal scholar Uwe-Jens Heuer, complained that the report only described the GDR as a state based on illegality (*Unrechtsstaat*). And, indeed, one interpretation of the GDR positioned it as the successor to the Third Reich, echoing the arguments about totalitarianism of the 1950s. This interpretation equated the Communist and National Socialist dictatorships, effectively condemning the GDR and all aspects of its society and politics, while reconfirming the FRG and its approach to democracy as the only legitimate option. Pushing back against this interpretation, Heuer and others contributed a counter-report that stressed the aspects of the GDR that followed the rule of law, that defended anti-fascism, and that provided a social safety net. They condemned the Bundestag's report as an example of victors writing the history of the defeated. In short, an important debate about dictatorship and German history was underway, but one that was skewed by attempts by some to highlight only the positive parts of the GDR and its political project, and by others to hold up the Federal Republic as the only legitimate inheritor of the German democratic tradition.

The divisions reached also into the realm of culture. Even the critical intellectuals with the sharpest eyes for the contradictions of state socialism, for example, had been part of that state. Christa Wolf, for example, had like few others developed a fundamental critique of the violent, patriarchal militarism of both East and West Germany in her novel *Cassandra* (1983), discussed in Chapter 8. In November 1989, she welcomed the revolution proclaiming that "every revolutionary movement also liberates language." "Revolutions," she continued, "start from the bottom," reversing values, and in the case of the GDR put "the head back on its feet" by making the people the basis of socialism. Her speech famously concluded: "Imagine there was socialism and nobody ran away!" Wolf's relief at the opening up of the GDR in 1989 reflected her personal experiences: in a widely discussed novella entitled *What Remains*, written in 1979 but first published in 1990, she described the feeling of being watched by the Stasi, of the claustrophobia of the GDR, the disappearance of authentic language and communication, and the retreat into inner monologues. And yet: Wolf was an intellectual in the service of the state, who, like so many East Germans, also briefly worked as an unofficial informant. And while she herself was monitored, she was also permitted to travel abroad, to write and publish controversial novels abroad, and to teach students at places like the University of Texas.

Thomas Brussig, by comparison, had no such privileges in the GDR; born in 1964, by the late 1980s he was working a series of odd jobs with little hope for escaping a life he saw as boring and unhappy. Then came the revolution, and he was directly involved in the demonstrations. His 1995 novel, *Heroes Like Us*, describes the revolution from below—and puts a leading intellectual like Wolf in a very different light. Uhltzscht, the main character with an unpronounceable last name, is a low-level Stasi officer, following in the footsteps of his dull, pedantic father, weighed down by the moralizing pronouncements of his mother, and obsessed with his own penis. On November 4, 1989, he takes the risk of attending the demonstration at East Berlin's Alexanderplatz, and arrives in time to hear, but not to see, Christa Wolf's speech. He makes the crucial error of thinking that the speaker is really Jutta Müller, a figure-skating coach and object of his sexual fantasies, and associates "Jutta" with "Mutter." In other words, he hears the voice of a mother-like, moralizing surrogate, who refers to the revolution as a moment "when demands are becoming rights, in other words, obligations." Uhltzscht rejects Müller/Mutter/Wolf's "demands-into-rights-i.e.-obligations nonsense." Brussig implied that underlying Wolf's call for a hopeful and free socialism was just more of the same narrow-minded moralizing that characterized GDR society.

The dispute went deeper. In *What Remains*, Wolf had described the experience of peeking out of her window to see a car, presumably filled with Stasi officers, observing her building; Brussig described the Stasi officers in the car as bored and ineffectual, the Stasi itself as a holding place for careerists. Where Wolf's narrative retained the somber tones of introspection and self-examination, Brussig's story was brash, satirical, and grotesque, more in the tradition of Günter Grass than of Wolf: the "hero" of his story finds his way to the porn scene in West Berlin, where his oversized penis opens the way to a new career. Brussig's story devolves near the end into an ad hominem attack on Wolf for her portentousness, her use of ambiguity to avoid taking clear political positions, and her status as the moral soul of socialism in the GDR. And indeed, Wolf was not a dissident; other intellectuals, especially from the west, pointed out that she had not published *What Remains* in 1979, when it might have made a difference. Indeed, by waiting until 1990 to publish the piece, she appeared to some to be casting herself, not as a privileged part of the Socialist Unity Party system but as its victim. Brussig's novel was just one part of this complex debate—albeit one that engaged in especially personal attacks.

The contrast between Wolf and Brussig illustrates the vast divides in eastern German society that continued to persist twenty-five years later. The dissident intellectuals, with dreams of a renewed, grassroots democracy, found themselves scorned, or worse: simply ignored. Many older people, especially those in Berlin who had had important positions before 1990, were dismayed by the GDR's collapse. And many younger people, especially professionals able to find good jobs, broke with the old regime entirely. The vast majority might be said to share all and none of these positions. Having never been part of the East German elite, they generally regarded the GDR's collapse as a good thing. But those over thirty years old and trained (and even retrained) in a job or profession for which there was no need, struggled to not feel obsolete.

The Federal Commissioner for the Stasi Records

Across postwar Europe, new democracies had faced the question of how to come to terms with a dictatorial past. East and West Germany, as we have seen, had different approaches: both denouncing the past, both eventually pursuing major criminals, but especially in West Germany not looking with much care into the actions of West German leaders under National Socialism. After 1990, a united Germany took a far more active role in assessing the Socialist Unity Party regime. Historians discussed the significance of the GDR, and huge numbers of documents became available for examination, not least through the Bundestag inquiries mentioned above. Official inquiries and academic writings are one thing, however, and personal encounters with the past something else. After a period of intense discussion, the Bundestag decided to open up the documents of the Stasi to public review, albeit under strict guidelines.

The Stasi files had been secured only through direct protest during the revolution. The GDR's People's Chamber, in one of its last acts, appointed Joachim Gauck, a Lutheran pastor, dissident, and co-founder of the New Forum, so instrumental to the 1989 revolution, to administer the Stasi records; following unification, the Kohl government named him the Federal Commissioner for the Stasi Records. His office's initial functions were to investigate cases that would require legal rehabilitation and compensation for illegal persecution by the Stasi, to review representatives and civil servants and remove those from office who had been Stasi employees, and to investigate and prosecute criminal acts by the Stasi. At the end of 1991, the Bundestag approved a complex law regulating the use of the Stasi archives; Gauck remained head of the office until 2000. The Federal Commissioner gained the additional task of providing access to those investigated by the Stasi. Demand for information grew steadily over the 1990s. By the mid-1990s, the office employed over 3,000 people to help evaluate requests for information, often from ordinary citizens.

The East German revolution had called for the new office, the government of unified Germany approved it, and yet the office of the Federal Commissioner for the Stasi Records quickly became controversial in the east. Gauck's investigations led to the downfall of a good number of eastern German leaders. Heinrich Fink, for example, also a Protestant theologian and a leading member of the Evangelical Church, had taken over as rector of the Humboldt University in eastern Berlin in 1990, where he worked to reform the university and also to save the positions of East German academics within it. Fink was also a member of the PDS. Although the Stasi had destroyed many parts of Fink's file at the end of 1989, enough remained for Gauck to accuse Fink on November 25, 1991, of having worked with the Stasi from 1968 to 1989. The material led the city government to remove Fink from his post. Students, faculty, and intellectuals in Berlin demonstrated in solidarity with Fink; the novelist Stefan Heym compared Gauck's role to that of the Spanish Inquisition. But Gauck stuck to his guns, and as Fink and others were removed from their offices, western professors often stepped in to fill the vacated posts.

What became known, especially to its opponents, as the "Gauck office," targeted a host of former East German leaders—indeed, those few who had succeeded in politics despite the transition. The leading East German Christian Democrat Lothar de Maizière, for example, and Günther Krause, one of three eastern Germans whom Kohl appointed to his cabinet, lost their positions amid rumors of Stasi collaboration. The Gauck office also accused many leaders of the PDS of having worked for the Stasi, not least Gregor Gysi himself. And indeed, the Stasi files indicated that Gysi had provided information to them under several code names. It did not, however, explain how, and in some cases the Stasi gave code names to sources who were not aware that they were being monitored. Gysi maintained that he had never given such permission, and the Gauck office was never able to make its accusations stick. The theologian Manfred Stolpe, to cite another example, joined the Social Democrats and became the popular minister-president of Brandenburg in 1990. As a leading theologian in the Protestant Church during the GDR, he regularly met with representatives of the Stasi as part of his official duties, a fact that he never denied, and that did not make him a Stasi agent. The Stasi listed him, however, as an IM—an informal collaborator. Gauck's office therefore accused him of being a Stasi informant. Like Gysi, Stolpe claimed that he did not knowingly pass on information that could harm anyone, and furthermore argued that he had no alternative given his position in the church but to meet with the Stasi. Stolpe kept his position of minister-president from 1990 to 2002, and thereafter served as a minister at the federal level.

But Gauck's investigations were only half of the equation: victims of the Stasi could request to see their files and in this way, it was hoped, work through their troubled past. Revelations of who had spied on whom did not necessarily bring relief, however. They also broke up close personal relations. The wide network of Stasi spies reached into homes, workplaces, and clubs; husbands reported on wives, parents on children, friends on friends. The alternative literary scene in East Berlin's bohemian Prenzlauer Berg district, it turned out, was riddled with Stasi informants. Wolf Biermann accused the edgy poet, author, and underground rock musician Sascha Anderson of spying in 1991, for example, and the documentation later revealed that Anderson had indeed informed on many of his closest associates in the scene even after he emigrated to West Berlin in 1986. Christa Wolf herself was shocked to find, among the many thousands of pages that documented the Stasi's monitoring of her activities, evidence that she had served as an informal collaborator between 1959 and 1961, at the start of her career. Wolf, unlike Anderson, made the records public and began an intense self-examination of an episode in her life that she had herself forgotten. In both cases—and many more could be cited, not just from the intellectuals—opening up the Stasi files served truth, but also destroyed friendships, communities, and individuals' sense of their own selves.

Under the leadership of dissidents Marianne Birthler between 2000 and 2011, and Roland Jahn since 2011, the office of the Federal Commissioner continued to provide access to the Stasi records. The office continued to review civil servants and to offer private individuals a look into their lives in the GDR. More and more, however, it compiled histories of everyday life in a surveillance state and of the role of the Stasi itself in the history of the GDR.

Anti-foreigner sentiment and right radicalism in West and East

Unification was about pulling together the German nation. For some, this meant a reinvigoration of ethnic politics. Anti-foreigner sentiment was nothing new to West Germany. The National Democrats (NPD) traded in racist and anti-immigrant fears since its founding in the 1960s. And in the 1980s, when the FRG first started to come to grips with long-term unemployment, established conservative leaders in the Christian Democrats began to take a hard line against foreigners. They concentrated on those seeking asylum. The sensationalist media reported on those lying about their circumstances in order to come to rich Germany; right-wing politicians talked about the abuse of the system; and ordinary West Germans, especially those more exposed to the big economic changes of the times, condemned people they saw as lazy, as endangering their social benefits, and even as endangering their jobs.

The Christian Democratic federal government had no clear policy on immigration. Kohl emphatically insisted that Germany was not an "immigration land." And yet, the German economy depended on cheap migrant labor and immigrants who would do the jobs that German citizens did not want to do. This was no less true in the 1990s than it had been in the 1950s and 1960s, when Adenauer's government established the guest worker program and actually brought foreigners to Germany. And for this same reason the Christian Democrats had more recently worked with businesses to extend these workers' visas and bring their families, essentially creating permanent residents. To reject Germany's status as a country of immigration was thus not so much to deny immigrants but rather to deny immigrants citizenship—formal recognition of their belonging.

Anti-immigration parties formed as well, some seeking an official party to the right of the Christian Democrats. Others rejected the democratic system per se. The most successful right-radical party of the late 1980s and early 1990s was the Republicans, led after 1984 by the former member of the Waffen-SS Franz Schönhuber, who left the Bavarian Christian Social Party to form a party to its right in 1983. Schönhuber asserted that "the boat is full" and criticized an allegedly widespread "misuse of the asylum right" that he said allowed economic migrants to enter and stay, often illegally, in Germany. The Republicans received more than five percent of the vote in some local elections as well as European elections, giving the far right a face in politics. They strove to stay inside the broad framework of the constitutional order and thereby avoid being legally banned, but to provide an opening for a xenophobic, nationalist voice in politics. In this, the Republicans roughly approximated right nationalist parties elsewhere in western Europe like the National Front in France and the British National Party.

The Republicans aimed at electoral success, which required the party to try to appear respectable. Other West German groups, however, often with neo-Nazi affiliations, were less interested in respectability and more with direct action against foreigners. Racially motivated attacks against Turks increased over the 1980s. The perpetrators were harder to monitor: often violent and on the margins of society, self-organized around new cultural forms like right-wing punk rock, they rejected compromise with democracy. Neo-Nazi groups maintained contacts with each other, and often with extremists outside of the country. US neo-Nazis, enjoying the protection of the First Amendment, published and helped smuggle into Germany old and new Nazi propaganda, thereby circumventing German laws against extremist literature. These groups helped organize the far right in eastern Germany after the end of the GDR.

Not that right-radical groups required outside help or the GDR's collapse to form. The former East German neo-Nazi Ingo Hasselbach has described the development of a right-radical milieu in the GDR, composed of outsiders who used the swastika and Nazi language to express their hatred of the state. The GDR, as we have seen, did not have a huge guest worker program, and the guest workers who did come, especially from Vietnam and Mozambique, were small in number and segregated from the ethnic German population. But as Jonathan Zatlin has argued, a country whose economy is characterized by both scarcity and autarkic tendencies, meaning it seeks to produce all the goods it needs for itself, tends to view foreigners who purchase scarce goods as an enemy. The East German government, meanwhile, simply asserted that racism was antithetical to socialism—that it was a product of capitalism and did not exist in a socialist society—and therefore did not undertake any special measures to teach about racism in its schools. Even in the face of incontrovertible evidence, the Socialist Unity Party refused to take right radicalism seriously. The state denied that it was a problem until October 1987, when an attack by right-wing skinheads on an oppositional gathering led to a crackdown.

With the collapse of Marxism-Leninism went the collapse of its ideology and an opening of political discussion about German nationalism. In this context, the turn to the nationalist rhetoric of unification in fall 1989 opened the way to radical nationalism as well. The right-radical skinhead scene was embraced by right radicals from the West, who brought with them their international contacts, the detailed and convoluted works of "historical revisionism" denying the death camps and Auschwitz, and their more focused anti-Semitism and racism. The collapse of state socialism led to a pluralist democracy and to rights, which also entailed greater freedoms for violent, right-wing youth who embraced what might be called "anti-antifascism," rejecting the ideological justification of the GDR by defending, not democracy, but fascism itself. The newly radicalized right-wing youth came to these positions in the context of the highly charged debates about asylum in the West and amid the staggering unemployment of post-unification economic collapse. When viewed altogether, conditions were ripe for right radicalism's revival in eastern Germany.

The asylum crisis and anti-foreigner violence

As Chapter 12 will discuss in more detail, the end of the Cold War reopened old conflicts in eastern Europe that the different Communist regimes had been able to suppress. This is what happened in Yugoslavia. Serbian nationalist Slobodan Milošević deliberately stirred up previously checked ethnic tensions, which developed into outright civil war in 1991. The series of ethnic conflicts fought on and over former Yugoslavian territory did not end until 2001. West Germany had long-standing economic ties with

Communist Yugoslavia, which, under the leadership of Josip Tito, pursued its own form of state-socialist economics and a path of "non-alignment" with either the United States or the Soviet Union. Starting in 1968, hundreds of thousands of Yugoslav guest workers moved to West Germany, many of them settling permanently. When the Yugoslav wars began, Yugoslavs in Germany quickly changed identity, distancing themselves from the Communist state as well as many of their fellow citizens. Neighborhood restaurants no longer served Yugoslavian cuisine but rather Serbian, Croat, or Bosnian dishes. And Yugoslav immigrants sought to bring their relatives to Germany, out of harm's way. More specifically, many wanted political asylum—for family members and themselves—from the massacres and ethnic cleansing that increasingly characterized Serb and Croat military actions.

The drafters of the 1949 Basic Law adopted a generous constitutional guarantee of asylum out of recognition for all those who fled, or sought to flee Nazi persecution. In the four decades that followed, the number of refugees seeking asylum in the FRG grew, as opportunities for communication and transportation across the globe increased. By 1988, those seeking asylum surpassed 100,000 for the first time. Over the next two years, unification preoccupied the government. But with the Yugoslav wars, hundreds of thousands of new asylum seekers were on their way. In 1992, over 400,000 refugees sought asylum in Germany, over 25 percent of them from the Balkans. Joining the asylum seekers were the ethnic German "resettlers" (*Aussiedler*) from eastern Europe discussed in Chapter 9. And somewhere between these two groups, Soviet Jews were likewise granted refuge and eventual citizenship amid reports of rising anti-Semitism in the crumbling Soviet Union. To put the challenge confronting Germans into perspective, nearly two million people immigrated to West Germany between 1950 and 1989. Between 1990 and 2000, more than two million came, 1.7 million from the Soviet Union or the states that formed after the Soviet Union's dissolution in 1991.[5]

The large numbers of immigrants and asylum seekers coming to Germany in the early 1990s fed already existing fears about national security. Conservative pundits and politicians voiced what many feared, namely that asylum seekers would seek Germany's social benefits and overwhelm a system already weakened by unification. They also accused asylum seekers of not working (in fact asylum seekers' right to work were subject to limitations) and of bringing radical ideologies with them. Here one can see how anti-foreigner rhetoric teamed up with general anxieties about Germany's future. Conservatives began to call for abolishing the right to asylum or revising it to limit the number of applications in Germany.

Over the first half of 1991, the new Länder saw a rise in the number of attacks against "*Asylanten*" and "*Ausländer*"; both terms were ambiguous, since the main object of attack were people with darker skin, whether or not they were seeking asylum or were noncitizens of Germany or, for that matter, were citizens that did not "look" German. Every week brought new attacks, often by drunken young people in the desolate industrial landscapes of the former East. These reached their climax in the small town of Hoyerswerda on September 17, 1991, when neo-Nazis attacked a dormitory for foreigners in which asylum seekers and former East German guest workers lived. The number of protesters increased on the second night; emboldened, they threw stones and Molotov cocktails at the building. In the end, the dormitory residents had to be relocated by bus for their own protection: the police had lost control of the streets. The protests simply shifted to another building housing refugees the next night, with the same result.

The events in Hoyerswerda inspired nearly two dozen similar attacks over the next months. These attacks took place more often in eastern than in western Germany, but some of the worst occurred in the old FRG Länder: children burned, adults thrown out of windows or beaten into unconsciousness. The wave of violence reached new levels on November 23, 1992, when neo-Nazis, yelling "Sieg Heil," set fire to two houses where Turkish families lived in the northwestern town of Mölln. The perpetrators were from the west not the east, and three of their victims, a woman and two girls, died. On May 29, 1993, another group of neo-Nazis murdered five Turks in the western industrial city of Solingen. The total number of murders in the wave of violence reached nearly fifty.

In the face of these events, hundreds of thousands of Germans from across the country joined in peaceful demonstrations to denounce the violence against foreigners. The majority in unified Germany did not approve of such actions. By demonstrating they sought to deny not only the radical right's racism but also its claim to represent and protect the German people— even if many were also critical of loose asylum regulations. Under pressure from the population and rising violence, the Christian Democrats and the Social Democrats came together to reform the right of asylum in the Basic Law. Regardless of the compromises each side made, they both implicitly accepted the argument—and racist logic—that "foreigners" were gaming the system and had to be stopped. According to the new law, anyone applying for asylum had to come directly from a country that did not follow the principles of the Geneva Convention on Refugees. Because all of Germany's neighbors adhered to the convention, it essentially excluded anyone coming by land from having the right to apply.

Until the late 1990s, the NPD and the German People's Union (DVU), both right-radical parties with roots in West Germany, failed to translate racial violence into electoral victories; their occasional victories, such as when the German People's Union gained nearly 13 percent of the vote in Saxony-Anhalt in 1998, were protest votes with little lasting effect. But the organizers did succeed in creating a small but violent right-radical milieu. For years following, one could not visit a train station in eastern Germany without confronting beer-swilling, right-wing skinheads. More insidiously, across united Germany an underground network of neo-Nazis formed, linked by a common anti-foreigner sentiment as well as a growing subculture of right-wing punk clubs, and capable of committing violence.

At least one group made the transition to terrorism. The National Socialist Underground, with roots in the right-radical scene around Jena, carried out a series of brutal murders and bombings between 1999 and 2007, directed especially against people of Turkish heritage. Alongside them grew a new group of far right intellectuals, clustered around the journal *Junge Freiheit* (Young Freedom). Founded in 1986 in southwest Germany, the journal moved its headquarters to Berlin in the mid-1990s. One of their writers was Horst Mahler, the radical '60s lawyer and founding member of the left-wing RAF. By the late 1990s he had become a far right defender of the German *Volk*, against foreigners, against the European Union, and against NATO and the Atlantic partnership.

Germany in Europe

In 1990, the French president Francois Mitterrand worried about whether a united Germany would remain committed to the project of European unity. But with Helmut Kohl as the first chancellor of the new Germany, he could rest assured. As part of the negotiations on unifying Germany and officially ending the Second World War, Mitterand convinced an already amenable Kohl to agree to measures that would bind a united Germany closer to (Western) Europe.

These discussions, widened to involve the rest of the members of the EC, culminated in the Treaty of Maastricht, signed in 1992. That treaty aimed to transform the European Economic Community into an integrated community by developing a common foreign policy, new judicial organs, and a common currency—the Euro. Not all states were interested. The European Union, or EU, first formed as a subgroup of the EEC with the voluntary exclusion of, most notably, Great Britain.

The judicial reforms posed some big problems, especially after the members of the European Union formulated a new set of rights. Would a European court really be able to trump the German Constitutional Court? Other aspects of the European Union bothered people at a local level—for example, the drive to develop common administrative rules across all EU states, which notoriously led to detailed rulings on how to produce cheese and what could be labeled a cucumber.

But most controversial were in fact the economic rules. Maastricht set down firm guidelines for membership. Annual government debt, for example, should not exceed 3 percent of the GDP; total debt should not exceed 60 percent of GDP. And by the late 1990s, the European Union fixed exchange rates among the EU nations. These rules made it much harder for individual states to enact inflationary policies, and laid the foundation for a unified European currency. In 2002, after years of preparation, the Euro became the common currency in seventeen European nations, and the de facto currency in others. It was—and is—the second largest currency zone in the world. Since 1998, as well, there has been a European Central Bank (ECB)—essentially modeled on the German Bundesbank, with a similar structure, operating independently of the states and narrowly focused on fighting inflation and deflation.

These developments, dry as they may seem, were revolutionary. They suggested a far more unified Europe, one that limited individual state sovereignty in a way that the original European Economic Community did not. The German government pushed hard for these rules: they did not want the powerful German economy to be sucked into paying for the inflationary policies of less responsible members of the European Union. A strange thing happened on the way to the bank, though. Germany's unification cost more than expected. Germany fell out of compliance with the 3 percent rule in the early 2000s. At the same time, united Germany had become a powerhouse of the European economy. The rules would be bent to protect Germany (and also France), but German social policy would also have to change to accommodate European rules, as the next chapter will discuss.

Further reading

Beattie, Andrew. *Playing Politics with History: The Bundestag Inquiries into East Germany*. New York: Berghahn, 2008.

Behrend, Hanna, ed. *German Unification: Destruction of an Economy*. London: Pluto Press, 1995.

Braunthal, Gerard. *Right Wing Extremism in Contemporary Germany*. New York: Palgrave Macmillan, 2009.

Brockmann, Stephen. *Literature and German Reunification*. New York: Cambridge University Press, 1999.

Brussig, Thomas. *Heroes Like Us*. Translated by John Brownjohn. New York: Farrar-Straus-Giroux, 1997.

Frölich, Margaret. "Thomas Brussig's Satire of Contemporary History." *GDR Bulletin* 25 (1998), 21–30.

Hasselbach, Ingo, and Tom Reiss. *Führer-Ex: Memoirs of a Former Neo-Nazi*. New York: Random House, 1996.

Jarausch, Konrad, ed. *Uniting Germany: Debating Processes and Prospects*. New York: Berghahn, 2013.

Müller, Jens-Werner. *Another Country: German Intellectuals, Unification, and National Identity*. New Haven, CT: Yale University Press, 2000.

Nick, Harry. "An Unparalleled Destruction and Squandering of Economic Assets." In *German Unification: Destruction of an Economy*. Edited by Hannah Behrend, 80–118. London: Pluto Press, 1995.

Patton, David F. *Out of the Past: From PDS to Left Party in Unified Germany*. Albany: State University of New York Press, 2011.

Philipsen, Dirk. *We Were the People: Voices from East Germany's Revolutionary Autumn of 1989*. Durham: Duke University Press, 1992.

Quint, Peter. "German Unification and the Federal Constitutional Court: A
    Retrospective View after Twenty Years." In *German Unification: Expectations
    and Outcomes*. Edited by Peter C. Caldwell and Robert R. Shandley, 153–71.
    New York: Palgrave Macmillan, 2011.
Wolf, Christa. *What Remains and Other Stories*. Translated by Heike
    Schwarzbauer. Chicago: University of Chicago Press, 1995.
Wolf, Christa. *Parting with Phantoms. Selected Writings, 1990-1994*. Translated by
    Jan van Heurk. Chicago: University of Chicago Press, 1998.
Zatlin, Jonathan. "Scarcity and Resentment. Economic Sources of Xenophobia in
    the GDR, 1971-1989." *Central European History* 40 (2007), 1–38.

12

The Berlin Republic, the Red-Green coalition, and the identity of the new Germany

FIGURE 12.1 *The Reichstag building in Berlin, following restorations and the installation of a new glass dome. After some debate, Germany's parliament convened there for the first time on April 19, 1999. (Photothek/Raphael Huenerfauth/Getty Images)*

Unification raised critical questions about Germany's place in Europe and the international order. It also called into question three fundamental ideas of the old Federal Republic. First, that German foreign policy, because of the Second World War, had to be restrained and defensive. Second, that a broad and deep social welfare state ensured social peace and fostered higher production. And finally, that Germany was not an immigration nation. It was not until Chancellor Kohl left the political stage and a new government formed, consisting of newcomers from the Social Democrats and the Greens, that the new Germany came into focus for the first time. In 1999, the capital shifted from Bonn to Berlin, a move that lent political weight to the claim that united Germany was not simply a geographically enlarged FRG. While continuities abounded between the old Federal Republic and the new "Berlin Republic," the differences became increasingly clear—and important. The Berlin Republic developed a more independent approach to foreign policy commensurate with its power in the European Union; broke with core parts of the West German welfare state; and announced a dramatic shift in energy policy aimed at replacing carbon-based fuels with renewable energy sources. These were more than just policy changes: they reflected a new sense of German identity in Europe.

The Red-Green coalition

Gerhard Schröder became the Social Democrats' candidate for chancellor in 1998. He was fifty-four. The candidate for the Greens, Joschka Fischer, was likewise from a younger generation, specifically a generation that had not experienced the Second World War directly. Schröder never knew his father, a soldier killed in action at the end of the war. Schröder himself entered the working world at fifteen years old, in retail and as an unskilled construction worker. He took night classes to complete high school, and eventually went on to receive a law degree. As a Young Socialist, or *Juso*, he was, like most Social Democrats under the age of thirty-five, decidedly to the left of the party leadership. But Schröder was also quite serious about rising through the ranks. Indeed, he seemed as driven in his political career as he had been to finish school and university in the 1970s. As the story goes, one evening Schröder, now the leader of the *Jusos*, stopped outside of the Chancellery, grabbed the gates, and yelled "I want in!" Strong willed and keen to advance his own agenda and career, he turned toward a different model of social democratic politics, no longer focused on the old working class.

Joschka Fischer was also a product of the postwar era. His family was expelled from Hungary in 1946, and he grew up in a small, scenic town in Baden-Württemberg, the son of a butcher. Fischer dropped out of school in 1965. Two years later, he joined up with the student movement in Frankfurt am Main, where he participated in heated discussions about Marx, Mao, and communist revolution; sought to organize autoworkers in the nearby Opel factory; and became embroiled in street fights with the police. The *Spontis* and the alternative left milieu were his political and social home, and it was as a member of this scene that Fischer—amid the terrorist crisis of 1976/77—came to declare political violence a dead end street. He, along with other former student activists like Daniel Cohn-Bendit and Antje Vollmer, joined the Greens and quickly became one of the party's leading members. By the 1990s, he had weathered the storm of unification (which he initially opposed) to become the charismatic standard bearer of the Greens.

The Greens offered a platform with a clear and focused program of reforms. Their party had gone through a period of intense soul-searching since the debacle of 1990. In 1993, they officially unified with Alliance 90, the civil rights activists of the East German revolution. And the "Realos" gradually emerged as the leaders of a less radical, more pragmatic party. The Greens still fought for environmental regulation and still defended citizens' initiatives but now, for instance, they abandoned their own self-imposed term limits. Enacted to narrow the gap between representatives and their base—and to prevent professional politicians altogether—the limits also unfortunately prevented members from gaining seniority and influence in the Bundestag. In keeping with this adjustment to the status quo, the party ceased their attacks on the parliamentary system as well. Their leaders included committed advocates of human rights like the Bavarian Claudia Roth, old guard pacifists like Hans-Christian Ströbele with his home base in Berlin's proudly "alternative" neighborhood of Kreuzberg, and Cem Özdemir from Baden-Württemberg, the son of a Turkish guest worker and the first person of Turkish origin elected to the Bundestag. Through the 1990s, the Greens became partners with the Social Democrats in five Länder (all in the former FRG; they remained underrepresented in the east). The leaders of both parties sought a similar red-green alliance on the national level.

Differences remained between the two parties, however—some of them sharp and all of them indicative of their members' and organizations' very different histories. The Social Democrats still claimed to be the party of the industrial working class—the "old" left, closely tied to the labor movement and rightly aware of its history as such. The Green Party rose in conscious opposition to traditional left politics. Its members focused on social and cultural politics, and called for reforms not necessarily to the liking of the Social Democrats; their supporters tended to be educated professionals rather than workers. They rejected atomic power, and made the phasing out of nuclear power a condition of their joining the coalition; the Social Democrats, by contrast, had up through Helmut Schmidt firmly defended nuclear power. The Greens were in many ways the champions of "1968," calling not only for a dramatic shift toward renewable energy but also for a reform of citizenship law to reflect the ethnic diversity of Germany, gay marriage, and policies that better accommodated women's career paths.[1] None of these policies were completely accepted within the SPD, many of whose members continued to conceive of class as the major obstacle to social and political inclusion and the German worker as male, blue-collar, and full-time.

But the timing proved right for a Red-Green government—in large part because it was so bad for the Christian Democrats. In 1995, news first

broke of an undeclared contribution to the Christian Democrats from
arms industry lobbyist Karlheinz Schreiber. A parliamentary investigation
soon revealed that it was not a one-time incident but that the CDU had
a well-organized system for accepting secret campaign donations. Between
1993 and 1998, Kohl alone received around two million deutschmarks. In
exchange for what? That was the question. Kohl denied that the money had
influenced government decisions; he essentially pleaded guilty to violating
party funding laws but not to political corruption. More digging uncovered
more money: it was discovered that the privatization and sale of the East
German Leuna oil refinery to Elf, for example, came with DM50 million in
bribes. The money and Kohl's public support of the sale was not enough to
make corruption charges in this or any other instance stick. The scandal did,
however, cost more than one politician their job, including Helmut Kohl's
as chairman of the party in 2000. But even before that, it cost the party
the election and Kohl his government. In the Bundestag elections of 1998,
the Christian Democrats received only 35.1 percent of the vote, suffering
particularly poor returns in the eastern states, where economic realities
had dimmed Kohl's bright picture of flourishing landscapes. The Social
Democrats and the Greens won 40.9 percent and 6.7 percent, respectively.
With that vote, Red-Green held nearly 52 percent of the representatives
in the Bundestag and took up the reins of government. For the first time
in the history of the Federal Republic, a coalition came to power because
of electoral results, rather than because a swing party (i.e., the FDP) had
shifted its allegiance.

The end of Kohl's sixteen-year chancellorship was reminiscent of the
end of Adenauer's long reign, and many approached it with an optimism
similar to that which accompanied Brandt's rise to power in 1969. But
the first year of the Red-Green government was troubled. Schröder was
authoritarian and media-oriented. And similar to his American and British
counterparts Bill Clinton and Tony Blair, his instinct was to continue
many of his predecessors' moderate to conservative economic policies. The
Social Democrats, too, remained internally divided, split between older
conservatives and younger progressives on the one hand and between labor
loyalists and neoliberal reformers on the other. Of the voices contradicting
Schröder's, the most important belonged to Oskar Lafontaine, the SPD's
candidate for chancellor in 1990, its chairman since 1995, and finance
minister in the new Schröder government. Also a child of the postwar
era, Lafontaine came from the Saarland, an old steel and mining region,
and he worked for the traditional, unionized working-class base that
Schröder's policies most hurt. The Social Democrats' coalition partners
only exacerbated these internal frictions. Members of the Greens demanded
major changes in Germany's very sense of itself as a nation, starting with
a different approach to immigration, integration, and citizenship. Neither
partner, given Kohl's long period in power, had had much experience in
actually governing at the national level.

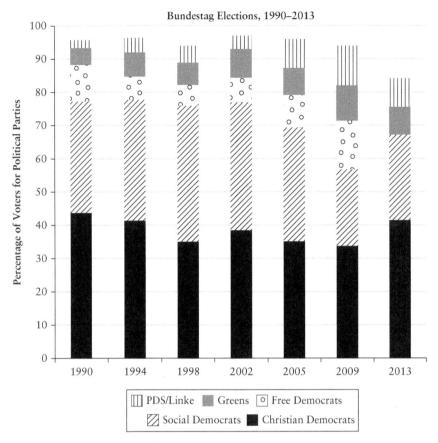

CHART 12.1 *Bundestag Election, 1990–2013*
Note: Where figures add up to less than 100%, the remaining votes went to parties that failed to fulfill the conditions (in particular the 5% hurdle) required to enter parliament.

The challenge of foreign policy

During German unification, the states with the strongest militaries and foreign policies in Europe—the Soviet Union first and foremost, but France and Britain as well—had all expressed an acute concern about having a strong, unified Germany in the middle of Europe. These concerns dovetailed with the Germans' own reluctance to engage in military activity; the disastrous and genocidal wars of the Third Reich had made many Germans pacifists or, at the very least, aware that the past spoke against using German force. Germany avoided playing a major role in the First Gulf War, then, both for internal reasons and to avoid giving the impression of a newly united Germany bent on military action. As the decade progressed, however, other

European and NATO states increasingly looked to Germany to develop a foreign policy in line with its economic and political clout, one that included possible military intervention abroad.

The First Gulf War (1990–91): German abstention

On August 2, 1990, the Iraqi dictator Saddam Hussein ordered his troops to occupy Kuwait. Heavily in debt after his recent war with Iran, he had his eye on Kuwait's rich oil fields. The invasion incited international condemnation and a coalition of thirty-four countries soon formed against Saddam with the explicit support of the Soviet Union. The United States led the massive military assault on Iraq and Iraqi forces in Kuwait in early 1991, having already established troops in Saudi Arabia as part of a "defensive mission" to protect it (and its oil). Hundreds of thousands of Germans took to the streets to protest the war, agreeing with the Brandenburg bishop Gottfried Fork who described the Gulf War as meeting one injustice with an even greater injustice. But after Saddam fired rockets on Israel, the tenor of the conflict changed. First, antiwar protesters expended considerable energy condemning German companies, which not only provided Iraq with its weapons but, with financial guarantees from Kohl's government, had helped improve the very Soviet-made Scud rockets now being used against Israel. More controversially, right radicals now joined in the antiwar protest, invoking comparisons between the UN bombing of Baghdad and the Allied bombing of Dresden; graffiti for peace covered walls alongside graffiti calling to "burn Zion." In the newspapers, a major debate erupted among left-wing intellectuals about the nature of anti-Americanism in this protest: to what extent did the antiwar movement reflect nationalist or even anti-Semitic values?

Kohl's government was preoccupied with the immediate challenges of unification, still not complete. Article 87 of the Basic Law permitted the use of German armed forces only in cases of self-defense, an article that Kohl vowed to amend but ultimately used to avoid committing troops. Instead, Germany contributed money ($9 billion by January 1991) and logistical support to the anti-Iraq coalition. Leading politicians in the United States and elsewhere criticized the government's legalistic avoidance of military action. Viewed alongside the expressed fears of Germany's possible military resurgence, it is safe to say that the international community was unsure of Germany's new place in the world—as were the Germans.

The end of the Cold War led to crises elsewhere as well, as old systems of legitimacy collapsed and US-Soviet animosity no longer kept individual states in check. Around the periphery of the Soviet Union, which ceased to exist at the end of 1991, civil wars broke out to determine new state borders. Ethnic conflicts rose up where the ideology of state socialism had suppressed them for decades. These conflicts, so close to home, forced Germany to develop a more active foreign policy. Communism's collapse had done more than open the door to old conflicts; it also reopened unsettled questions regarding the international community's commitment to human rights and humanitarian intervention. Germans, in particular, had to decide which of the post-1945, post-Nazism lessons they would follow. Would they cling to anti-militarism or to a moral duty to prevent future atrocity, including but not limited to genocide?

The Balkan Wars and the threat of genocide in Kosovo: German intervention

After the Second World War, Croats, Serbs, Slovenes, Kosovars, Albanians, and Macedonians were united in the new socialist republic of Yugoslavia under the charismatic leadership of the anti-fascist hero Josep Broz Tito. After Tito's death in 1980, tensions among the different groups resurfaced— or were imagined anew with the help of local nationalists. As Yugoslavia's economy entered into the same kind of structural economic crises seen in other state-socialist countries, ethnicity became a mobilizing force for separatist aspirations, especially those of Serb nationalist leader Slobodan Milošević. But Milošević called not only for the restoration of (largely mythical) greater Serbia; he envisioned Serbia as Europe's last Christian stronghold against Islam.

In June 1991, the northernmost regions of Yugoslavia, Slovenia, and Croatia announced their secession following months of increasing military confrontation. The German government took the lead in recognizing the new states. Other leaders accused the Kohl government of backing secession and thereby limiting the possibility of a negotiated settlement, although the dissolution of Yugoslavia was already well underway. Both Serbs and Croats engaged in what was termed "ethnic cleansing": the forced removal of the other ethnic group from their lands to create a more ethnically homogenous population. The conflict spread as other parts of Yugoslavia proclaimed secession and finally erupted in civil war within Bosnia-Herzegovina. Sides were drawn between Serbs and Croats, but also between Muslims and Christians. The violence culminated in the takeover of Srebrenica by the Bosnian Serbs in 1995, and the murder of some 8,000 male Muslims in addition to organized mass rape and the indiscriminate execution and pillaging of the local population. The German state, after having taken the lead in recognizing the breakup of Yugoslavia, provided little protection for the victims. Mass expulsions and executions of civilians and a brutal racialist and nationalist justification for violence brought back memories of the Second World War, when the Germans had played a pernicious role in facilitating the development of a fascist Croat state, concentration camps, and mass murder. Now Germany seemed simply to stand by and watch it happen again.

The Constitutional Court determined in a 1994 ruling that the German army could under certain conditions participate in "out of area" operations if they were part of the military alliance (NATO) to which it belonged; the

Basic Law could no longer, then, serve as a way to avoid questions about military action. German participation in the Yugoslav civil war remained minimal. Even with the new ruling, the government could not risk dramatic intervention: fifty years was not enough to erase memories of German atrocities in the area. Then, too, Europeans as a whole appeared paralyzed in the face of the Balkan conflict, reflecting their own different relationships with ethnic groups in eastern Europe as well as their continued ambivalence on coordinated European action. The United States finally took the lead, organizing a NATO bombing campaign in 1995 against Serbian forces in Bosnia. The 1995 Dayton Accords, signed in Paris by the presidents of Serbia, Croatia, and Bosnia-Herzegovina in front of Clinton and the leaders of France, Great Britain, Germany, and Russia, officially ended the war and brought international recognition for five new states where Yugoslavia once stood.

The peace agreement, however, failed to bring stability to the region. The predominantly Muslim province of Kosovo stood under Serbian control. In 1997, irregular Kosovar units began attacking Serbian police. The Serbs responded with massive retaliations, which targeted civilians. Hundreds of thousands of refugees left the country. The United Nations did not intervene because China and Russia, both members of the Security Council, declared that they would veto any action. With journalists and international aid organizations reporting on Serbian war crimes and, increasingly, what many feared to be genocidal actions, NATO and the United States prepared a response despite the lack of a UN mandate. Schröder and Fischer as foreign minister had to make a decision: to be unreliable allies or to directly participate. The government agreed to participate, and in early 1999 collaborated in a massive bombing operation against Serbia.

So, for the first time since the Second World War, German soldiers engaged in warfare. More precisely, they attacked a country that had not first attacked Germany, and without a mandate from the United Nations. Fischer justified this decision by declaring: "Never again war, never again Auschwitz; never again genocide, never again fascism." To the pacifist slogan "no war," in other words, he added the imperative "no genocide": that Germany not permit the atrocities of the past. His slogan implied a comparison between the Serbian attack on Kosovo with genocide, fascism, and even Auschwitz. Chancellor Schröder notably provided a very different justification: that Germany, as a normal party to the NATO alliance, should also participate in a NATO action. Both positions echoed the left's confrontation with terrorism in the 1970. Schröder ultimately proved himself Helmut Schmidt's heir. German politics were dictated by the normal needs of a nation and the Social Democrats would demonstrate its willingness to govern. For Fischer and many of his fellow Greens, the path to nonviolence had been bumpy, not abstract but deeply personal. To renounce it now was no small thing, whether one was a former radical or lifelong pacifist, and the decision for military intervention led to a harsh and bitter fight within the Greens. On May 13, 1999, one outraged member of the Greens threw a paint bomb at Fischer, sending him

GERMAN MILITARY INTERVENTION IN KOSVO

The Bundestag debate in response to accusations raised in German news media over whether the Red-Green government manipulated the facts to gain parliamentary support for war.

GREGOR GYSI OF THE PARTY OF DEMOCRATIC SOCIALISM

"This war, this attack on Yugoslavia, was, as you know, highly controversial, legally as well as morally and politically. . . . The foreign minister [Joschka Fischer] spoke of a concentration camp—and he did not choose this word by accident—in the Pristina stadium. On that point, I would like to say the following: we should try to avoid attributing conditions to another country as they existed in Germany between 1933 and 1945. . . . There is no second Hitler in the world. The foreign minister went still further and even compared the conditions [in Pristina] with Auschwitz, which is intolerable." [Gysi followed with several examples of unclear evidence to support accusations of massacres.] "We have the right not to be lied to and betrayed."

ANGELIKA BEER OF THE GREENS

"The accusation of the film 'It Began with a Lie' is unconvincing since it, in my view, negligently ignores the entire prehistory [of the war]. . . . The decision to intervene militarily in Kosovo was made in, what was then, a clear political context. . . . It had two levels: first, the humanitarian situation in Kosovo, years of at times grave human rights violations in Kosovo on the side of the Serbs, and, second, the development throughout the entire region of the threat of growing political destabilization in the region. . . . We cannot forget that [Serbian president] Milosevic is responsible for four wars in the Balkans! . . . We knew that there is no such thing as a 'clean war.' We knew that in war there are no winners or losers that instead it brings victims to all sides."

[Interjection of Ilja Seifert of the pds: "Only Losers!"]

"We have not given up the goal of non-violence. [laughter from the PDS] Our policies are intended to progressively restrain the use of violence over time."

Source: Protocol of the Bundestag plenary session of February 12, 2001, pp. 15037, 15040–41.

to the hospital. Even as some cursed Fischer, however, he remained true to the student movement's anti-fascist principles. For him, German politics were dictated by the special responsibility of Germany in light of its past.

The Red-Green government decided to act militarily, without UN mandate, to stop potentially worse things from happening and to support allies. In this way, the Kosovo War of 1999 marked a decisive break in German foreign policy. Not all accepted it. Left-wing Social Democrats and the pacifist core of the Greens complained bitterly. But a precedent was set.

Terrorism and the Second Iraq War: Breaking with the West?

Two years later, the Red-Green government found itself confronted by a different kind of problem. On September 11, 2001, terrorists connected to the radical Islamic group Al-Qaeda carried out a deadly, multipronged attack on the World Trade Center and the Pentagon in the United States. It quickly became apparent that several of the leaders had connections to a terror cell in Hamburg, Germany. The day after the attack, Schröder announced Germany's "full solidarity" with the United States. On September 14, over a million people assembled at the Brandenburg Gate to express their sympathy and solidarity.

German support went beyond words. Schröder agreed to back a NATO military mission in Afghanistan. Recognizing the opposition to militarism within the ranks of his own coalition, he called for a vote of confidence by the Bundestag. It was a calculated risk that instead of toppling his government, seemingly gave Schröder the mandate to press ahead. With the Red-Green coalition still intact, Schröder began a military exercise that would last more than a decade. It aimed ultimately to eliminate both the terrorist bases connected with the Taliban and Al-Qaeda and to build a new, hopefully stable and democratic state.

The US president George W. Bush wanted to use the terrorist attacks of September 11, 2001, as an opportunity to remake the entire Middle East. Already in late September, he was consulting with advisers about an invasion of Iraq. The United States justified the war either by claiming that Iraq was involved with the terrorist attacks or by a claim that Iraq was developing weapons of mass destruction that posed an imminent threat. There was, however, no clear connection between Saddam Hussein and the terrorist attacks in the United States. And the United Nations was in any case already monitoring Iraq's weapons programs and setting limits to Saddam's military power. The two main reasons for going to war with Iraq therefore seemed questionable to the German leadership. The Bush administration had furthermore alienated many Germans by pursuing unilateral policies in a variety of areas. It repudiated the Kyoto Protocol on climate change, denying that the problem existed, for example, and broke with a series of conventions limiting the use of biological and nuclear weapons. Both cases directly contradicted the views held by most Germans and suggested that the United States did not feel bound by international law or diplomatic agreements. The United States, (West) Germany's closest postwar ally, suddenly appeared unreliable.

German support for a war against Iraq would have been difficult to obtain under normal circumstances. It would have meant a break with the Federal Republic's entire tradition of foreign policy since 1949, which explicitly rejected participation in aggressive wars, a term that is taken in international law to include wars to prevent potential future aggression. The Bush administration bore the burden of proving that the war it planned against Iraq was not "preventive," then, but rather "preemptive," in the sense that it responded to a clear and present threat.

On top of the challenge the Bush administration's plans presented to German foreign policy doctrine, Schröder also faced a major problem at home. New elections were coming up in fall 2002, and the polls looked bad, especially because of his government's cuts in social programs (discussed further below). Schröder knew that he was losing the support of his coalition partner. Both principle and opportunism pushed Schröder to break with the United States in its call for a second war in Iraq.

On August 5, 2002, Chancellor Schröder announced that Germany would not support the United States on pragmatic grounds: "They should not only know how they're going to go in but also how they're going to get out," he remarked. The announcement helped save the Red-Green coalition, which barely squeaked by in the elections of September 22, 2002. But it also resulted in a dramatic break with the United States and President Bush, who felt personally betrayed by Schröder.

Relations between the United States and Germany worsened over fall 2002, as the Bush administration offered a series of justifications for invading Iraq, foremost the claim that Iraq possessed a secret store of weapons of mass destruction. These arguments seemed ever more like excuses. Germany teamed up with France and Russia to counter US ambitions. At one point in early February 2003, Joschka Fischer publicly rejected every argument for war presented by US defense secretary Donald Rumsfeld, including his claim about weapons of mass destruction, telling him in English, "You have to make your case. Sorry, you haven't convinced me." The United States responded by distinguishing what it called "new Europe," made up of Poland and the other NATO newcomers in eastern Europe, from France and Germany, which Rumsfeld disparaged as "Old Europe"; he also vilified Germany by listing Germany along with Libya and Cuba as states that would not attack Iraq. German support for the US war and, indeed, respect for the United States in general, plummeted.

Washington's war against Iraq was, in retrospect, a disaster, and the criticisms raised in Germany, France, and Russia seem prescient. At the time, however, the critical question arose of whether the harsh dispute signaled something deeper. Certainly Germany had already crossed the line with respect to military involvement. Was it now declaring its independence from the transatlantic partnership that had shaped the Federal Republic from its inception?

This is certainly what scholars like Stephen Szabo argued. Schröder, according to this interpretation, was shifting his focus from NATO and the European Union, and the embeddedness in transnational institutions and multilateralism that had defined West German foreign policy since 1949, to a more pragmatic, self-oriented foreign policy. It painted Schröder as an opportunist who viewed Germany as a "normal" nation, no longer beholden to the moral imperatives arising from the Holocaust. And it expressed the fear that Germany's future foreign policy would focus narrowly on its own interests.

Hanns Maull and others countered such fears with the argument that Germany's foreign policy, even as it broke with the United States over Iraq, showed remarkable continuity. Germany acted like a "civilian power" rather than primarily a military power, concerned first and foremost with cooperation and recognizing mutual vulnerabilities of states; it was therefore oriented toward peace keeping. First, at issue in the Iraq war was whether war itself was "just," a major issue that shaped German foreign policy, in both East and West, after 1945. The US case did not seem fully compelling to the Germans at the time, and in retrospect has found ever fewer defenders. Second, West German foreign policy stressed multilateralism, which implied consultation among allies. The Bush administration threw that tradition aside, defending unilateralism and a "coalition of the willing" rather than consultation with long-standing allies. Then, too, the European Union as a possible political counterweight to the United States emerged for the first time, despite American efforts to relegate its core members France and Germany to the dustbin of history. Whether Schröder was opportunistic or not, Germany's decision not to participate in the Second Iraq War fit with its longer standing diplomatic traditions.

Reforming the German welfare state

A second defining component of the old Federal Republic was an extensive welfare state, which connected social security and disability to work, and provided broad health care and social benefits. Ever since the Federal Republic was founded, critics on the right had declared that the welfare state was going to bankrupt the state, destroy the initiative of individual workers, and undermine the economy. In fact, the expansion of health care, pensions, and unemployment insurance had contributed to the stability of the state, and had accompanied unprecedented levels of prosperity and domestic peace.

The structural adjustments to the economy since the 1970s slowly but surely changed this relationship. Higher unemployment, for example, meant that the employed had to pay higher contributions to the unemployment insurance funds, as somebody had to help pay unemployment benefits. The greater the social insurance taxes, however, the higher the cost of labor and the greater the need for the employer to reduce those costs, often by rationalizing production or outsourcing labor to cheaper areas. A vicious circle of increasing costs and stagnant or declining employment ensued.

A second set of issues revolved around pensions (or what we call social security). As people lived longer, the birthrate declined, and people put off having children until later in life, the demographic structure of the society changed. In 1991, some 15 percent of the population was over 65; twenty years later it rose to 21 percent and the number was only predicted to increase. One solution was to simply cover the pensions by increasing the amount individuals contributed to the pension fund. But the obvious result of that policy was to increase the cost of labor.

The West German economy assumed high wages and high contributions. But with the internationalization of the economy, both of these came under fire. Unless productivity remained far higher than that of other countries, then German wages would start to become uncompetitive. People working in industries with lower productivity were threatened with unemployment. If they did not have specialized education and training, they would have difficulty finding a new job.

The German labor market, then, was a problem, and that problem was connected to social benefits. Clearly, more jobs had to become available; just as clearly, the existing system inhibited job creation because of the price of labor. And the comfortable, neo-corporatist system of the old Federal Republic, where labor unions and employers together played a role in implementing social policy, limited the ability of any government to alter conditions of labor. At the same time, the elderly, disabled, and unemployed voted. And precisely because they feared alienating these voters, Kohl's government had identified the problem but avoided actually confronting it.

Reforming pensions in a global age: Conflicts in the first Red-Green coalition

Schröder came into power with clear notions of how to reform the labor markets. His own party, however, was divided on the issue. His minister of finance Oskar Lafontaine called for expanding the existing welfare state as a way of injecting money into the economy. Those who agreed with Lafontaine recognized the important changes in the economy, but they feared that giving way on social programs would mean the gradual dismantlement of worker protections and greater income inequality—in short, an end to the achievements of German Social Democracy.

Schröder went his own way. In 1999, he released a paper coauthored with British prime minister Tony Blair entitled "Europe: The Third Way/Neue Mitte." The manifesto called for a defense of core social democratic values, such as solidarity and justice, but also for more individual responsibility, for lowering the costs of labor, for investing in human capital and dynamic new industries and services rather than propping up old industries. The state and the social security system should open up new opportunities, but society and individuals should act on their own initiative to find the greatest opportunities.

Even while Schröder and Blair sought to draw a clear distinction between their positions and those of neoliberalism, in the end, they had a similar critique of the old welfare state and of old, union-oriented labor policies. It was not surprising, then, that Schröder and Lafontaine came into conflict. Lafontaine resigned his ministerial position, and then left the Social Democrats altogether in early 1999.

The social security system established in 1889 and reorganized on new principles in 1957, as discussed in Chapter 2, had worked well in the context of an expanding population and an expanding economy. The Red-Green reforms of 2001 and 2004 now altered the system in three ways. First, the reforms aimed to reduce pensions in the short term from 70 percent to 67 percent of workers' previous wage or salary levels, and to win even deeper cuts over time. Second, lower level worker's pensions would be subsidized by the state, so that workers at a lower salary would receive pensions closer to those at a higher salary. Third, another kind of voluntary pension was added (the so-called Riester Pension): between 1 and 4 percent of a worker's income would be invested in a private account, which would allow workers themselves to decide where and how much to invest, would add to the capital available to companies, and would lower the amount that the state needed to pay out. All of the reforms would lower the overall cost of labor for employers, in theory giving them an incentive to create more jobs.

In order to force his party to fall in line behind him and to pass the reforms, Schröder called for a vote of confidence, essentially threatening to resign. Most Social Democratic and Green representatives voted to keep Schröder. The passage of the pensions reform brought forth extreme comments from all sides. The unions complained about abandoning the principle of solidarity. Neoliberal economists, seeking to build on what looked like a growing loss of faith in public solutions to social problems, demanded the complete end of public pensions and the "freedom" for markets to provide, despite the fact that market turbulence following the 2000 recession called into question pensioners' ability to rely on the stock market. Most relevant, though, privatizing retirement income did not, in the end, provide a solution to the problem of an aging population. The same problem remained of how a smaller number of workers could support a larger number of non-workers.

The Hartz reforms and the decline
of the Social Democrats

Schröder's hard line against the Second Gulf War combined with his successful management of a major flood in eastern Germany in August 2002 saved his government in that year's national elections by a thread. Continuing unemployment and the deficit soon dominated the second Red-Green government and led Schröder to seek more radical reforms. He named Peter Hartz, chief human relations officer for Volkswagen, to head a committee to reformulate labor-related social policy. Hartz had solved massive problems at VW in the 1990s. Now he was to manage the problem of unemployment and save Germany, suffering from lower growth rates and an unbalanced budget, from its fate as the apparent sick man of Europe.

The first three sets of proposals from the Hartz Commission involved reforming the process of linking up unemployed workers with jobs, providing additional training for unemployed workers, and creating new categories of part-time and flexible jobs (so-called mini-jobs). These first reforms occasioned some grumbling, but they remained within the realm of Social Democratic politics. The so-called Hartz IV reform, however, went further. The new proposal gave employers a greater ability to hire workers for short periods and to fire workers. It also lowered unemployment benefits in the name of making the German economy more competitive in a demanding global environment. Schröder described the reforms as "change, so that the welfare state can be retained under new conditions."

Schröder criticized long-term unemployment but also seemed to criticize the long-term unemployed. In a speech of March 14, 2003, defending the reforms, he said, "Whoever is able to work but refuses an appropriate job should have his support cut. There is no right to laziness in our society." The controversial Hartz IV reforms accordingly reduced the time a worker under fifty-five could spend on unemployment insurance to twelve months, and reduced payments after that period to the minimum level of guaranteed social assistance.

The Hartz reforms had some impact on the economy, though they cannot alone explain Germany's recovery after 2005. "Mini-jobs" grew, part-time jobs without additional social security payments, and with them job insecurity. Unemployment decreased, then, but employment itself was less secure. And wages remained flat. The weakened German trade unions provide only a partial explanation for the flat wages. More important was the expansion of the European Union to the Czech Republic, Poland, Hungary, and Slovakia in 2004, which gave German firms the opportunity to outsource production to low wage lands; German labor may have gotten cheaper but there was still cheaper to be had, and this, in turn, worked to keep wages in Germany at a standstill. German exports became relatively cheaper, and after 2005, Germany developed even stronger export markets from China and Russia to the United States. In short, the Hartz reforms were not the only reason for Germany's economic recovery, but they did contribute to it.

The reforms cost the Social Democratic leadership its party base. In 2004, union members and Social Democrats took part in massive protests against the Hartz IV reforms. The party began to lose elections at the Land level, while the Red-Green coalition lost its support in the Bundesrat. Schröder came to the conclusion that only another grand coalition of Social and Christian Democrats could continue his policies. He therefore engineered a vote of no confidence to bring about new elections in 2005. The SPD lost by a hairsbreadth to the CDU, both parties doing so poorly that neither could secure a majority in parliament without the other. In short, Schröder got his Grand Coalition but not quite as he had imagined it: Angela Merkel, who became the Christian Democrats' first female party leader in 2000, now became Germany's first female chancellor, while Schröder entered into early political retirement (and several lucrative business positions). In the next national election, in 2009, the Social Democratic Party lost its place in government as its numbers continued to fall.

With the dramatic decline of the Social Democrats came the dramatic return of Lafontaine as the defender of old Social Democratic values. In the summer of 2005, he joined a new group called the "Voting Alternative—Labor and Social Justice" (WASG, following the first letters of its German name), consisting of leftists, trade unionists, and Social Democrats who, like Lafontaine, left the party in distress over the direction Schröder had taken it. The WASG took aim at what it saw as a neoliberal ideology that favored business over workers. It pointed to the fact that since 1990, real wages in western Germany had stagnated and even declined, and inequality had increased. And many who joined the group were critical of Germany's foreign policy.

Many of the political positions of the WASG corresponded to those of the PDS, a party that was itself in flux as eastern German disgruntlement faded or evolved beyond it. In 2007, Lafontaine helped unify these groups in a new party, the Linke, or "the Left." The Linke succeeded by rallying protest votes against cuts in social spending under the Social Democrats and Greens. In both 2009 and 2013, the party received over 5 percent of the votes nationwide, meaning that now five parties fought to win Germans' favor, not only in the east (where the PDS had competed) but in the western Länder as well. With the Social Democrats joining the Christian Democrats in yet another Grand Coalition in 2013 (Chapter 13), the Linke lived up to its name as the representative of the traditional left.

The Renewable Energy Sources Act: A revolution in energy policy?

One might wonder what the Greens got out of a coalition with the Social Democrats, knowing how unpopular Schröder's foreign and economic policies were with many of that party's supporters. The environment was one key area of reform that the Greens in government were able to pursue, specifically the replacement of carbon-based and nuclear energy with energy derived from renewable sources. The Red-Green coalition approved a bundle of programs with this aim in mind, fueling the development of a new "green" economy as well as environmental protections.

First, the coalition approved new taxation policies that took account of the environmental costs of energy production. Carbon-based fuels, for example, were taxed higher than wind or solar power to reflect the costs of climate change. The Renewable Energy Sources Act of 2000 guaranteed renewable energy producers a fixed price for the energy they produced for a twenty-year period. Now small-scale producers, including individual households, received an incentive to produce their own energy. Second, the coalition provided low-interest loans for individuals and companies willing to install solar panels. Additional incentives and tax rebates were provided for investments in wind energy. Together, these initiatives resulted in a rapid transformation of the German landscape after 2000, with the proliferation of wind parks and solar panels. Third, the government invested heavily in research and development, especially in photovoltaic cells. Finally, the government promoted increased energy efficiency, through regulatory and tax policies as well as through education. Even when the Red-Green coalition collapsed in 2005, the environmental policies they forged remained largely intact.

They remained intact because, by then, social and political consensus was on their side. Up to 2004, the conservative parties opposed the policies, but back in power they came to support them, too. In an important 2007 statement, the CDU officially recognized the pressing need to respond to global warming by subsidizing renewable energy sources, not least because so many conservative homeowners had installed solar panels. Only a handful of politicians, mostly pro-business Free Democrats, denied climate change, but even they recognized Germany's need to find domestic energy sources in order to reduce the country's dependence on Russia and other foreign suppliers.

Merkel's government continued the commitment to renewable energy even after 2009, when the Christian Democrats formed a new ruling coalition with the Free Democrats. True, the conservative coalition initially reversed course and favored maintaining nuclear energy as one component in a future energy mix, partly because the Free Democrats represented the interests of big utility companies, and partly because Merkel herself, as a trained physicist with a PhD in quantum chemistry, endorsed the peaceful use of nuclear power. But on March 12, 2011, a massive tsunami damaged a nuclear power plant at Fukushima in Japan, leading to nuclear meltdown and the ongoing release of radiation. Merkel was one of the few international leaders with the scientific training necessary to grasp the event. Several months later, during a debate on nuclear power in Germany, she stated that the accident had changed her mind. That year, her government approved a broad array of further energy initiatives, linked together under the term *Energiewende*, or energy revolution (the word "Wende" is the same used to describe 1989 in the GDR). But the *Energiewende* would take place without nuclear power, as the government agreed to phase out all nuclear reactors on German soil by 2022.

When the 2013 elections brought the Social Democrats back into government alongside the Christian Democrats, the tendency to conceive of environmental and labor interests as fundamentally opposed returned, too, and slowed down the *Energiewende*. The Social Democrats, trade unions, and big utilities once again combined forces to defend the coal industry, for example, and the continued "exemptions" from the government's alternative energy surcharges that it received. It was a fight with both symbolic and material stakes. The big companies fought to protect their profits, while the Social Democrats fought to protect "the worker" whose job would be lost if those profits took a dip or "dirty" utilities like coal were phased out altogether. Nonetheless, the effects of Germany's changed environmental policies remained huge. When Red-Green came to power, renewable energy accounted for 3.4 percent of Germany's electricity. By 2015, that amount had jumped to 32.6 percent, about 12.5 percent of its total energy use (counting nonelectric energy sources such as natural gas).[2]

Imagining the Berlin Republic: Migration and citizenship, historical memory, identity

This chapter has focused heavily on shifts in political parties and policies, shifts that helped define a "Berlin Republic" different from the "Bonn Republic" for the first time. It is difficult to discuss these and at the same time describe what was occurring at the cultural and social level, but none of what was outlined above came about in a void. Politics, society, and culture hang together, and the changes in high politics reflected changes Germans experienced in the fabric of their daily lives and even in what it meant to be German. During the Cold War, Berlin not only served as a magnifying glass for superpower rivalry but also social and cultural transformation. This was no less true after 1990. By 2000, the new capital of united Germany had become a very different city, with its significant foreign populations; its Russian, Turkish, and Arabic language newspapers; its visible Jewish community; and its unabated reputation as a haven for drifters and social misfits.

Culturally, socially, and politically, the definition of "German-ness" presented a significant challenge. The still widely held perception of Germany as a land with a clear and common ethnicity and set of values did not match the reality of mixtures and migrants that it had become.

The present book has stressed that postwar Germany was, in some sense, from the start such a land. A quick look at religious affiliations shows that Catholics and Protestants were hardly on the same page over the course of German history. And since 1945, because of the upheavals of war and ethnic cleansing in the eastern European lands, their communities had been forcibly mixed, but also exposed to international influences, increasingly open borders, and the decline of religiosity. German Jews' presence had never been fully removed from Germany, despite Hitler's efforts, and in fact Jewish communities grew rapidly after 1991 as the result of an earlier treaty with the Soviet Union. More than 200,000 Russian Jews and their relatives immigrated to Germany during the first two decades after unification.[3] Islam was, of course, represented by the several million Turks in the land. And to these one must also add the huge number of atheists or agnostics, especially those from former East Germany. The refugee crises of the 1990s and again of 2015 (see Chapter 13) added hundreds of thousands more people to the diverse mix. Germans, in sum, were not only struggling to understand their new place in the world but the place of the world in Germany.

Immigration reforms, 2000–2005

The Greens made issues of migration central to their platform in 1998, but also more generally issues of multiculturalism and respect for different kinds of people. As the platform stated: "Of the more than 7,000,000 non-Germans in our land, more than half have lived here for more than ten years, a quarter for more than twenty. The majority of their children have been born here. We do not want our domestic laws regarding foreigners to continue to deny them the most important rights and to treat them as 'foreign' and 'guests'." Many ethnic Germans from eastern Europe, by contrast, had never spent a day in Germany and could not speak German, but nevertheless received automatic German citizenship. The Greens called for the complete revision of the 1913 Citizenship Law, which had established citizenship on the basis of bloodlines as a means of refusing the children of Polish and Jewish guest workers citizenship. Nearly ninety years later, these laws continued to block guest workers' and their children's entrance into the German nation. The reform of immigration and citizenship law was, alongside the environment, the most substantial reason for their joining Schröder's government and the party's most lasting contribution.

The Greens originally proposed a new immigration law in 1998–99 that would have permitted dual citizenship. German popular opinion strongly opposed it, however, and they settled instead for a revised citizenship law, approved in 2000. That law broke with the 1913 law by automatically granting citizenship to children born of parents with a valid residency permit or who had lived in Germany for eight years. At age 23, the child had to decide whether to retain German citizenship, which required giving up any other citizenship: dual passports were not permitted. (That law was amended in 2014 to allow dual citizenship in some cases.) The law also created a route to citizenship for adults not from the European Union, which required a clean criminal record, knowledge of German, commitment to the free democratic principles enshrined in the Basic Law, and ability to support him- or herself. By denying dual citizenship, the 2000 law most likely reduced the actual number of applications for naturalization, forcing, as it did, Turkish and other long-term immigrants to formally cut ties with their homeland. Far from just a legal tie, it was an emotional tie that many proved unwilling to sever.

Chancellor Schröder also sought to open the way for more immigration of skilled foreign labor into Germany, through a green card program like that of the United States. The program became quite controversial, as trade unions complained about bringing more competition into German labor markets during a period of high unemployment. One Christian Democrat called for an alternative approach that would promote childbirth among ethnic Germans rather than immigration, summed up in the phrase "Children not Indians" (*Kinder statt Inder*), revealing some conservatives' continued ambivalence about immigration—not to mention the unreflective use of racial slurs. While the Red-Green government began to consider a broader set of policies to help with migration, the Christian Democrats called in 2000 to officially respect the "dominant culture" (*Leitkultur*) in Germany. That said, the Christian Democrats, like the Social Democrats, were not unified on the issue. Christian Democratic reformers like Rita Süssmuth as well as realists like Wolfgang Schäuble recognized the need for a serious approach to immigration, integration, and also citizenship. At issue for both center-left and center-right was how to integrate migrants into Germany. The September 11, 2001, attack on the World Trade Center, however, added another, no less emotionally fraught ingredient to the debate on immigration. Some of the attack's leaders, as noted above, had been part of radicalized immigrant communities in Germany.

The development of the new Migration Law of 2005 thus took place against a background of increasing concerns about security. The law was a compromise. It promoted immigration of skilled workers of different sorts, kept immigration of others difficult, and made it easier to deport foreign nationals involved with terrorism, including those who had received asylum. Most important, it contributed to the integration of foreigners into Germany by allotting money for things such as language and civics courses.

Multicultural Germany and *Buntes Berlin* (colorful Berlin)

The policy debate about migration and citizenship was part of a wider debate about German culture in general. Germany was the home to a broad set of cultural groups, of groups with different values, different social norms, different ways of living. When the Christian Democrats called to recognize a German dominant culture, it ran into the problem that so many different values and norms coexisted.

The fact that Germany was home to multiple cultures, whose forms of expression actually bled across ethnic and religious lines, reappeared throughout post-1945 Germany: in Günter Grass's Danzig Trilogy, for example, German "ethnicity" was always intermingled with a variety of other ethnicities, Slavic or otherwise. Rainer Werner Fassbinder's 1974 film *Fear Eats the Soul,* with its portrayal of an affair between an older cleaning woman and a Moroccan guest worker, brought West German prejudices against both the elderly and guest workers to the surface. The Afro-German movement of the 1980s, associated with the poet May Ayim, among others, called for the self-recognition of black Germans in a society that often denied their very existence. A Turkish-German hip-hop culture developed at the end of the 1990s and one of Germany's most internationally acclaimed film directors at present is Fatih Akin, born in Hamburg to Turkish parents. Unifying Germany was no longer about unifying a single German ethnicity or culture.

Self-declared "new Germans" represented a departure from the 1980s and 1990s, however, by rejecting the goal of assimilation. They spoke fluent German, and they embraced the basic principles underpinning German democratic society. But, as Khuě Pham, Özlem Topçu, and Alice Bota, editors of the weekly newspaper *Die Zeit*, explained, it was simply no longer possible for them to ignore their Vietnamese, Turkish, and Polish heritage.[4] Difference, in this instance, was not antithetical to their understanding of German-ness but essential to it. If Şenocak saw his two identities (Turkish and German) in tension, this younger generation embraced multi-racialness as part of their individual and social identity.

Though not without opposition: the anti-foreigner violence following unification showed that even if the term "race" (*Rasse*) had disappeared from public discourse, racism lived on. And despite calls for inclusivity, German identity remained—and remains—bounded by race. After the neo-Nazi band White Aryan Rebels released the song, "This Bullet Is for You, Mo Asumang," Asumang, an actress and director as well as Germany's first Afro-German television personality, turned her attention to the themes of racism and integration. Her 2007 documentary *Roots Germania* is a defense of her Ghanaian-German identity—and a direct challenge to neo-Nazi claims on her German homeland. Dressed as Brunhilde, the warrior queen of Germanic lore, Asumang suggests that Brunhilde could have, in fact, been black, having first provided her viewers with a history of Africans in Germany going back "not decades but centuries." Driving a Harley-Davidson and dressed all in black, she seeks out her neo-Nazi tormentor at a Berlin motorcycle club; his failure to show is read as a victory over fear and racist intimidation. The film ends with Asumang and an Asian and Caucasian woman posed as classical matrons on the steps of the new Reichstag building—offering a new vision of Germania while an "Africanized" national anthem plays in the background. The Berlin-based DJ Erci Ergün likewise tapped into German culture in an exploration of Turkish-German identity from 2013, "Deutschland Sensin" or "Germany, It's You." He pronounces, "I am nearly 40, baby/I was born here, Berliner Erci/That can't still be an issue/A guest worker?—nobody believes that," making the words rhyme by using Berlin's own dialect. In his appeal to Germans to look at themselves and give up their hate, Ergün evokes the 1844 poem "Night Thoughts," written by Heinrich Heine, a German of Jewish descent living in French exile: "Germany, I think of you at night," laying claim to the critical nationalism of an ethnic and political outsider.

Society's diversity was apparent across Germany but perhaps nowhere as much as in "colorful Berlin" (*Buntes Berlin*). Before 1990, West Berlin had been the outpost of Turkish guest workers and asylum seekers, of young men avoiding the draft, of international bohemians like David Bowie and Iggy Pop, of radical Marxists and of the nihilistic punk counterculture. In summer 1989, West Berlin hosted the first Love Parade, which became a national and even international celebration of peace and sexuality to the sounds of technopop. In 1990, the Christopher Street Day Parade in Berlin, celebrating gay liberation since 1979, topped 10,000 participants. During the 1990s, the city remained poor as its citizens addressed all the complicated issues of how to pull its two different halves together. But at the same time, it became more and more a tourist destination, especially for younger people. The crumbling old buildings of Prenzlauer Berg in former East Berlin, before 1989 a center of the GDR counterculture, gradually transformed into a bohemian hot spot filled with young people from across the world and bars and restaurants open until late in the night. Further east, in the Friedrichshain neighborhood, clubs like the now famous Berghain popped up in abandoned factories and condemned commercial buildings, establishing Berlin's reputation as Europe's best clubbing city and the "world techno capital."

The gritty, postindustrial aesthetic and hedonistic experimentation of Berlin's nightlife was undoubtedly related to the city's particular experience of unification and the sense, if fleeting, of unlimited freedom in the wake of the Wall. "Wessi" youth looking for excitement and greater authenticity than they believed was on offer in the old FRG were drawn to the city, and Americans and Australians were particularly well represented among the international set. If they visited Berlin for its novelty and nightlife, many of them stayed for its low cost of living (a fraction of the other major European cities') and the opportunities—to make money, start a new career, open a business—that arose as soon as it was decided that Berlin would replace Bonn as the seat of government.

In 1991, the Bundestag voted to move the capital of united Germany to Berlin, and to use the old building of the Reichstag for parliamentary meetings. That building had been heavily damaged in the war, and during the Cold War sat isolated at the edge of the British zone, directly across from the Berlin Wall. At most, it had served as a backdrop for concerts, not all as famous as Bowie's that kicked off a protest in East Berlin. The Reichstag now had to be restored, renovated, and redesigned before it could again become a functioning home for the Bundestag. The entire process took nearly a decade. In 1995, as the planning was still underway, the artist Christo and his wife Jeanne-Claude transfigured the heavy, gray, pockmarked building by wrapping it with a silvery cloth. Skepticism changed into enthusiasm that summer, as millions of people came to Berlin to view what now seemed a shimmering, almost weightless entity. Four years later, the Reichstag building was completed, and in 1999 the Bundestag moved in. The old dome, destroyed in the Reichstag fire of 1933, was replaced with a new, transparent dome through which visitors can see the parliament in action, a symbol of the principles of transparency and democracy.

In 2001, the Social Democratic politician Klaus Wowereit ran for election to become mayor of Berlin. The Berlin tabloids, he found out, were ready to reveal that he was gay. He beat them to the punch, stating, "I'm gay, and that's a good thing." With this statement, he knocked the issue from the table and ushered in thirteen years during which Berlin resumed its position as one of the leading cultural centers of Europe. Wowereit's Berlin contained not only the old residents of East and West Berlin, including the many Turks and other guest workers of the old Federal Republic, it also contained a growing and ever more vibrant Jewish community. The reconstruction of the New Synagogue in the Oranienburgerstrasse of former East Berlin, which took place over the 1990s, coincided with its reinvigoration as site of worship for an active religious community. The revival coincided with the construction of a new Jewish Museum. The building itself, designed by the architect Daniel Libeskind, expressed in its fragmented and zigzag form the difficulty of representing Jews in Germany, while the content stressed not only the Holocaust but also how German Jews were interwoven with German history, both before and after National Socialism.

A handful of blocks north and west of the Jewish Museum, the Topography of Terror museum laid out the history of the SS in detail. Not far away from it, in the no-man's-land that used to be the death strip of the Berlin Wall, the Memorial for the Murdered Jews of Europe opened in 2005. Across Berlin, other historical monuments and museums appeared as well, commemorating atrocities carried out against Sinti and Roma, homosexuals, and others; the Berlin Wall and the East German dictatorship; the workers' movement; and women in German history. Berlin seemed to become a huge outdoor museum to the travails of the twentieth century.

FIGURE 12.2 *The Jewish Museum in Berlin. (ullstein bild/Schöning/Getty Images)*

Identity politics in Germany: Normalization, *Ostalgie*, and critique

The public exploration of postwar German history was not limited to Berlin. A traveling exhibition documenting atrocities carried out by the German army against Jews, partisans, prisoners of war, and civilians during the Second World War elicited major controversy starting in 1995. The exhibition directly contradicted the distinction made by defenders of the army during the Historians' Quarrel between the bad aims of National Socialism and the patriotic aims of the army defending the homeland. It was not purely an academic distinction, however, but an emotional one as well. More Germans than not wanted to remember the average German soldier as honorable. They did not want to think about fathers, sons, husbands, brothers having been involved in the atrocities of the eastern front. The exhibition's goal, though, was to deprive them of such convenient "truths"— and for this reason it provoked outrage and even acts of physical violence.

The notion of a homeland in need of defense returned to an early image of German victimhood at the hands of the Allies that resonated through the postwar years—an image which even icons of the literary left echoed. Günter Grass's 2002 novel *Crabwalk* returned readers to Danzig in 1945 to tell the tale of the *Wilhelm Gustoff* passenger liner and the nearly 10,000 Germans who, in seeking to flee the advancing Red Army, died in the icy waters of the Baltic when the ship was torpedoed by a Soviet submarine. Though

Grass rejects all straightforward narratives of German victimization, the book questions whether Germans could ever overcome their past if they ignored their own suffering; it seemed there was plenty of wreckage still to be scoured for therapeutic purposes. Responses a year later to a book on the Western Allies' bombing of Germany suggested that this was indeed the case. Written by the respected historian Jörg Friedrich, he used terms like "crematoria" to describe the brutal effects of the firebombing of Dresden on civilians. Some on the far right took the book as a way to justify their own stories of Germany as victim of the Allies. More important, however, was the mainstream discussion of the dual role ordinary Germans played in the war, both as part of a murderous state and as victims of the war itself.

The debate about the Dresden firebombing took place in the political context of the Red-Green government, the first generation of leaders whose personal memories came decisively after 1945. The author Martin Walser (born in 1927, so actually from an earlier generation) had already in 1998 raised the issue of whether German national history could finally be "normalized" after Auschwitz, in an impassioned and controversial speech about the Berlin Holocaust Memorial. Walser's comments were echoed by Chancellor Schröder, who asserted that a normal Germany should be able to promote its own interests. His own foreign minister, Joschka Fischer, notably insisted on putting German responsibility for the Holocaust in the fore. The postwar generation was not in agreement. And their own children were even less so as the perpetrators—their grandparents—entered their twilight years and passed away.

Underneath, however, a bigger change had taken place. Almost unremarked, Auschwitz had become a symbol relevant not only to Germany but to the entire Western world and beyond. In the schools, the Holocaust was still a required part of children's general education but now it needed to be historically contextualized for a new generation of students unfamiliar with the history of the Weimar Republic and Nazi Germany. Children from immigrant families required even more background, and a narrative of the Holocaust that stressed its universal relevance: it could no longer just be taught as part of German history. German kids may have had more education about the Holocaust, but as several recent pedagogical studies have shown, very similar kinds of Holocaust education were taking place in the public schools and Holocaust museums of, for example, the United States.

Similar questions arose in eastern Germany about how to remember the GDR. Millions of people had grown up there, going to school, making a career, forming families, enjoying picnics—living, in other words, everyday lives within the parameters set by the party dictatorship. In 1989, their political world disappeared. In the decade that followed, united Germany had poured money into rebuilding and restoring the towns and cities of eastern Germany. The result was an urban and rural landscape that was no longer the one people had grown up with. Already in the 1990s, movements arose to save aspects of GDR everyday life that seemed innocent of high politics.

In 1995, for example, a movement arose to save the *Ampelmännchen*, the illuminated pedestrian walk/don't walk sign in the former GDR. Unification had brought with it the standardization of such signals, but eastern Germans (as well as some westerners and many tourists) loved the jaunty hat and squat profile of the cute *Ampelmännchen*. Similar discussions took place around East German icons like the Trabi. Other products, from T-shirts to reruns of the old GDR crime show "Polizeiruf 110," revealed a big market for a kind of ironic remembrance of the recent past.

In Eisenhüttenstadt ("Iron Foundry City," named "Stalin City" before 1956), this eastern nostalgia, or *Ostalgie*, took the form of an entire museum dedicated to everyday life in the GDR, housed in a former kindergarten building. Rooms were filled with pictures of children in Young Pioneer outfits, with original training toilets from childcare centers, with all the objects that made up everyday life in the GDR. Founded in 1993, the museum was resolutely unpolitical, unlike the dozens of museums that have opened across the former GDR that focus on the Stasi. Unpolitical—but not necessarily harboring a yearning for dictatorship. As Jana Hensel described in her memoirs, there was a need to remember, not just the big history of high politics and Stasi, but also one's own life.

Sometimes this form of nostalgic commemoration ran the risk of forgetting what the dictatorship meant. The 2003 movie *Goodbye Lenin*, for example, made the GDR little more than a funny, inconsequential state, whose fake news and self-representation is preserved in fake news broadcasts and fake Spreewald pickles used to keep the protagonist's mother, a committed SED member, unaware that the Wall fell while she was in a coma. Concern about the negative effect of *Ostalgie*—or the possible disaffection it might register—was exaggerated and itself a characteristic of the new Germany. *Goodbye Lenin* was written and directed by former West Germans, and from that perspective can be read as patronizing, the nostalgia for universal childhood innocence. And for every piece of GDR nostalgia, there was also a museum like the Stasi museum in Berlin, a critical film about the Stasi like *The Lives of Others* (2006), or a critical article about the East German past in the newspapers to keep the debate vibrant.

Further reading

Asumang, Mo. *Roots Germania*. MA Motion, 2007.

Clarke, David, and Ute Wölfel. *Remembering the German Democratic Republic: Divided Memory in a United Germany*. New York: Palgrave Macmillan, 2011.

Friedrich, Jörg. *The Fire: The Bombing of Germany, 1940-1945*. Translated by Allison Brown. New York: Columbia University Press, 2006.

Hagen, Cornelia, and Axel Kleinlein. "Ten Years of the Riester Reform: No Reason to Celebrate." DIW Berlin-Deutsches Institut für Wirtschaftsforschung 2:2 (Feb. 2012). Available at: https://www.diw.de/documents/publikationen/73/diw_01.c.392354.de/diw_econ_bull_2012-02-1.pdf.

Hensel, Jana. *After the Wall: Confessions from an East German Childhood and the Life that Came Next*. Translated by Jefferson Chase. New York: Public Affairs, 2008.

Hockenos, Paul. "Die Energiewende—The Result of a Powerful Mass Movement from Below." May 23, 2013. The German Energiewende (blog). Access at: http://energytransition.de/2013/05/energiewende-powerful-mass-movement/?pk_campaign=nl4

Hockenos, Paul. *Joschka Fischer and the Making of the Berlin Republic*. New York: Oxford University Press, 2007.

Klusmeyer, Douglas B., and Demetrios G. Papademetriou. *Immigration Policy in the Federal Republic of Germany: Negotiating Membership and Remaking the Nation*. New York: Berghahn, 2009.

Lauber, Volkmar, and Staffan Jacobsson. "Lessons from Germany's Energiewende." In *The Triple Challenge for Europe: Economic Development, Climate Change, and Governance*. Edited by Jan Fagerburg, Staffan Laestadius, and Ben R. Martin, 173–203. New York: Oxford University Press, 2015.

Libeskind, Daniel. *Jewish Museum Berlin*. Berlin: Verlag der Kunst, 1999.

Maull, Hanns W., ed. *Germany's Uncertain Power: Foreign Policy of the Berlin Republic*. New York: Palgrave Macmillan, 2006.

Mazon, Patrica, and Reinhild Steingröver, *Not so Plain as Black and White: Afro-German Culture and History 1890-2000*. Rochester, NY: University of Rochester Press, 2005.

Meseth, Wolfgang. "Education after Auschwitz in a United Germany: A Comparative Analysis of the Teaching of the History of National Socialism in East and West Germany." *European Education* 44 (2012), 13–38.

Opitz, May, and Katherina Oguntoye, eds. *Showing Our Colors: Afro-German Women Speak Out*. Amherst, MA: University of Massachusetts Press, 1991.

Pearce, Caroline. *Contemporary Germany and the Nazi Legacy: Remembrance, Politics, and the Dialectic of Normality*. New York: Palgrave Macmillan, 2008.

Röhrkasten, Sybille, and Kirsten Westphal. "Energy Security and the Transatlantic Dimension: A View from Germany." *Journal of Transatlantic Studies* 10 (2012), 328–42.

Saunders, Anna, and Debbie Pinfold. *Remembering and Rethinking the GDR: Multiple Perspectives and Plural Authenticities*. New York: Palgrave Macmillan, 2013.

Szabo, Stephen F. *Parting Ways: The Crisis in German-American Relations*. Washington, DC: Brookings Institution, 2004.

13

Economics, politics, and diplomacy of a civilian state, 2007–17

FIGURE 13.1 *Children watch the construction of a container village for refugees in Köpenick, in southeast Berlin, December 4, 2014. (Getty Images/Sean Gallup)*

As this book has shown, foreign policy affected all aspects of post-1945 German history, from politics to economics, from society to culture. The same held true after German unification: now Germany was a medium-sized state with a powerful economy, whose economic vitality presupposed extensive, peaceful trade relations within a broader European economy. But the years after unification, and in particular those following the Great

Recession of 2008, proved difficult. Germany went from being the country necessarily restrained by the European Union to the country at the center of the European Union, and as such had to deal with three simultaneous and potentially existential crises. First, the Great Recession exposed weaknesses within the European Union, especially, if not exclusively, in the southern states, and the crisis in Greece in particular exposed sharp disagreements among members about economic policy. Second, the expansionist and interventionist policies of Vladimir Putin's Russia brought conflict to the European Union's borders. Third, upheavals and civil wars in the Middle East and Africa brought millions of refugees to Europe. In each case, Germany, under Chancellor Angela Merkel's leadership, found itself the de facto leader of the European Union. And in each case, Germany's decisions on how to best contain the crisis proved controversial. Across Europe, and also in Germany, new populist groups arose to challenge German and EU policies—and, in some instances, the existence of the Union itself.

By the end of the first decade of the new millennium, Germany was the most powerful country in Europe, economically, politically, and diplomatically. As a result, Germany found itself—to the surprise of many Germans—playing the role of leader, or even hegemon, in a Europe facing a multiplicity of crises.

The German economy boomed just as the rest of Europe experienced the shock of the Great Recession. The high educational level of German workers, management's focus on efficiency and productivity, and a tradition of engineering excellence gave German exporters a special niche in the world economy. The new EU lands to the east, meanwhile, offered German firms and German capital new opportunities for investment. And Schröder's reforms lowered the cost of labor.

The political system, meanwhile, proved stable and oriented toward the center. Germany remained committed to the European Union, perhaps the most committed of the large countries. Its European focus reflected, certainly, a rejection of the kind of nationalism that had led to two world wars; Europe, too, offered an alternative to the burden of being German, which may have lessened with time and each new generation but had not disappeared (and some have argued should never disappear). The European Union also offered clear advantages for a strong exporting nation with immense capital reserves: a huge, cheap internal market for goods, a range of investment opportunities with low transaction costs, and a source of skilled workers from a total population of over half a billion people.

Last but not least, Germany's role as a civilian power, discussed in the last chapter, made it a useful mediator in diplomatic and military crises. German politicians became the leading point of communication for the United States as well as for Russia during these years. Chancellor Angela Merkel developed a strong relationship with US president Barack Obama, just as she became the key contact for prime minister and then president

Vladimir Putin in Russia. Now, as some said, people knew who to call when they wanted to talk with Europe.

Germany's rise was not sudden, but three interrelated crises made it appear sudden. First, a major financial crisis began in 2007, which ten years later was still the source of political and economic problems, especially on the periphery of the Eurozone. Second, the crisis created by Russia's conflicts with Georgia and Ukraine put Germany's civilian power under pressure: could it really negotiate a path forward? Last but not least, the refugee crisis of 2015 led to a strong challenge to political centrism within Germany. All three emergencies had implications for both foreign policy and domestic politics—and signaled the potential limits to Germany's power as much as its expansion.

All three crises cast doubt on German assumptions that their interests aligned with those of the European Union. By 2015–16, it seemed possible that the entire European project might fall apart, as Greeks considered exiting the European Union and the British left the EC. All three crises converged within Germany as well, as a significant segment of the population turned against the European Union and against immigration. Thus at the same time that Germans continued to throw up "container villages" to house the influx of refugees, Germany's commitment to the European project—a matter of consensus in the western half of the country since the 1950s—was called into question.

Chancellor Merkel: Pragmatism and change

In the first years following 2000, Germany seemed the economic "sick man" of Europe. It fared quite well, by contrast, as other parts of the world suffered during the financial crisis of 2007–08 and the international recession that followed. Following a slight upward tick at the start of the crisis, the German unemployment rate continued to sink slowly, declining below 5 percent in 2015, its lowest point since the 1970s. Debt remained manageable, as Germany remained the third largest exporter in the world. With the largest economy in the European Union, Germany was also one of the most stable. But despite its wealth, wages for workers stagnated; prosperity, unlike in the FRG of the 1950s, was not distributed across society as a whole.

Wage stagnation and growing economic inequality helps to explain the paradox that just as Germany emerged as the healthiest major economy in Europe, its political system became more fragmented and contentious. The two main parties, the Social Democrats and Christian Democrats, saw a decline of support in general elections after 2002, with the Social Democrats no longer the party of labor and working-class interests and the Christian Democrats still reeling from the corruption scandal and the failed promise of economic prosperity in the new federal Länder. New parties arose but perhaps even more significantly, fewer Germans bothered to vote for any party at all. In 2009 and 2013, nearly 30 percent of those old enough to vote in the national elections did not, significantly lower than the postwar norm.[1] Already in the 1970s, the major parties were aware of a new kind of voter—what in the United States might be called a swing voter: someone not aligned or loyal to one particular party, who often votes on one or two specific issues rather than a candidate's platform. But by the late 1980s, younger Germans in particular appeared disaffected. Many still took to the streets to advocate for a cause or against government policy but now they increasingly did so instead of, rather than in conjunction with, the established procedures of parliamentary politics.

Chancellor Angela Merkel dominated German politics starting in 2005, when she took over as chancellor of the second Grand Coalition in the Federal Republic's history. Her rise to head of the Christian Democrats and then of Germany itself marked, even more than Schröder's rise, a generational transition. Merkel was the daughter of a postwar refugee from Danzig/Gdańsk and a Lutheran minister who voluntarily moved his family from West to East Germany the year Angela was born to take over a parish for the Evangelical Church. To counterbalance her Lutheran confirmation, an easy way to smash career prospects in the GDR, Angela Merkel joined the Communist youth organization, the Free German Youth. She went on to receive a degree in chemistry from the University of Leipzig and worked as a research scientist in East Berlin—an indication of the greater opportunities afforded women in the GDR. Merkel became active in the pro-CDU Democratic Awakening at the end of 1989, and was elected to the Bundestag in the first elections of December 2, 1990. Helmut Kohl chose her in 1991 to become his minister for women and youth, a ministry not very important for his politics; it had, as a rule, become the position for token female ministers since it was held by Franz-Josef Wuermeling and his immediate successor Bruno Heck. Merkel, however, was important for Kohl: a woman from East Germany with an unblemished political past and ties to the Protestant Church, she could increase the Christian Democrats' hold on eastern voters and help balance the still Catholic-dominated party. In 1994, Merkel became head of the Ministry for the Protection of the Environment and Nature and Reactor Security. After the devastating Christian Democratic loss in 1998, she became the party's general secretary.

Merkel rose quickly as an efficient and effective organizer. It took the 1999 scandal over illegal donations for her to become the head of the Christian Democrats, as she thrust Kohl aside and profited from the involvement of his heir apparent, Wolfgang Schäuble, in the affair. Suddenly a divorced woman scientist turned career politician from the former GDR was head of a party associated with cultural conservatism and traditional gender roles.

Merkel gave the appearance of a taciturn but friendly politician, someone willing to talk out issues rather than take strong stands. But she was also capable of acting quickly to exploit an opportunity. She proved her ability to act when the Red-Green coalition fell apart in 2005. Merkel became the first woman chancellor in German history and would remain chancellor for over a decade, first in a Christian Democratic government allied with the Social Democrats, then in an alliance with Free Democrats until 2013. When the FDP failed to cross the five percent hurdle that year—and found themselves excluded from parliament for the first time in the history of the Federal Republic—Merkel once again partnered up with Social Democrats in a Grand Coalition.

Merkel faced strong personalities and a changing political environment, and possessed a different leadership style than Gerhard Schröder's. Whereas Schröder had been charismatic and overbearing, she adopted a pragmatic style, allowing for diverse opinions and often only offering her opinion at the end of a coalition discussion. For some critics, her style smacked of indecision and opportunism: her decisions, they felt, were driven by opinion polls rather than by substance. For others, she remained open to argument and made decisions that took account of many different positions. However she reached her decisions, a quick review of her chancellorship demonstrates that they have left a mark on Germany.

As noted in the previous chapter, in 2011 she waded into the controversy over nuclear energy in Germany, reversing her own position as well as her government's so as to end the country's nuclear program in eleven years' time. Merkel's government also opened the way for more women in cabinet positions, and a willingness as well to consider issues related to women and family not on the table during Kohl's long chancellorship. She appointed Ursula von der Leyen, for example, a woman with a higher degree in medicine and seven children, to lead the important Ministry of Labor and Social Affairs in 2009, where she expanded preschools and introduced a controversial monetary payment for parents of small children. Even more trailblazing, starting in 2013, von der Leyen served as the first female minister of defense.

Germany and the expansion of Europe

German unification accelerated the pace of European unification and, by doing so, raised the uncomfortable question of what the European Union actually was, a decentralized confederation or an ever more centralized federation. In accord with the Maastricht Treaty, in 2002 physical Euro coins and bills replaced the national currencies of the states that had joined the Eurozone. By 2015, nineteen countries were part of the Eurozone. The Euro became the second most widely held reserve currency in the world, after the US dollar. Not all EU member states were part of the Eurozone. Great Britain, for example, refused to join and Denmark opted out as well.

MAJOR MOMENTS IN THE DEVELOPMENT OF THE EUROPEAN UNION SINCE THE 1980S

1985: *Schengen Agreement*, supplemented by the 1990 Schengen Area, which came into force in 1995. Abolished most border checks among signatories to the agreement, which now number 26 European countries, including several outside of the European Union (Switzerland, Norway, and Iceland).

1992: *Maastricht Treaty* (in force in 1993). Established the European Union, introduced direct European citizenship, and set limits to member states' debts and deficits as well as a formal exchange rate mechanism to make way for a unified currency.

1997: *Treaty of Amsterdam*. Devolved some powers from member nation states to the European Union and provided for more coordination on immigration and criminal justice.

1998: *European Central Bank* established, situated in Frankfurt am Main, Germany; fixed currency rates among the Eurozone countries.

1999: *The Euro* is introduced. Established a single currency and with it a single monetary policy for all of the Eurozone. The physical Euro currency was introduced in 2002.

2004: *failed* Treaty to Establish a Constitution for Europe. Attempted to create a constitution above the level of the member states, which failed after being rejected by French and Dutch voters in 2005.

2009: *Treaty of Lisbon*. Increased the power of the directly elected European Parliament, created a second chamber alongside the Council of Ministers, and declared the EU Charter of Fundamental Rights legally binding.

A single currency meant a single central bank. The ECB formed in 1998, becoming the Eurozone's lender of last resort. It was housed in Frankfurt and for the first decades its president was not a German so as to stress the European nature of the institution. Nonetheless, there was considerable continuity between the ECB and the West German Bundesbank. Like the Bundesbank, its primary aim was to ensure price stability. But price stability assumes a stable currency, which necessarily limits how much individual states can control their own finances. To ensure price stability, states joining the Eurozone had to sign the Stability and Growth Pact of 1998–99. That pact required states to keep their deficits under 3 percent and their overall debt under 60 percent of GDP. Many states that had suffered from inflation and deficits over the 1970s and 1980s, including Italy and Greece, helped to structure that pact and willingly signed it, in order to break away from their unstable fiscal past. The workability of the pact came into question in 2002, as both France and Germany, the central powers of the Eurozone, violated the provisions. Since that time, it was treated more pragmatically, although the goals of limiting deficits and debts remained important.

The economic rules of the Eurozone barred individual states from engaging in inflationary spending to respond to an economic downturn. Their banks were directly linked to the ECB, which unlike the Federal Reserve Bank in the United States, only aimed at price stability, not at unemployment or other aims. At the same time, individual states retained the ability to set rules for their own banking institutions, setting how much or how little capital should be on hand to cover loans, for example. The economic provisions of the Eurozone do not render individual states impotent.

In addition to the common currency, the Maastricht Treaty also aimed to strengthen the political authority of the European Union. It aimed for a Common Foreign and Security Policy, to be articulated by summits of the individual heads of state. After the movement to establish a European constitution with a collective foreign ministry collapsed in 2004–05, this system of summits took the form of an official European Council established by the Treaty of Lisbon in 2009. The Council of the European Union, by contrast, was chosen by the democratically elected representatives in the European Parliament, and in this way empowered to decide a whole series

EUROPEAN COUNCIL OR COUNCIL OF THE EUROPEAN UNION?

The government of the European Union is confusing in itself, but sometimes the names of its most important institutions lend to that confusion.

The *European Council* consists of the heads of state or of government of all the member states of the European Union, together with the president of the European Council and the president of the European Commission. Established informally in 1975 as a way to coordinate the policies of the different European states, it became an official institution of the European Union in 2007 in recognition of its centrality for policy making, in particular in the realm of foreign policy.

The *Council of the European Union*, by contrast, is one of the two major legislative assemblies in the European Union. Formally named in 1993, with the Maastricht Treaty, it had existed in some form since the 1950s, mainly as a council of ministers from different member states with responsibility for a specific area, such as agriculture. With the increased powers of the elected European Parliament, the Council of the European Union's legislative power has decreased. (A third institution, the *Council of Europe*, is not actually part of the European Union, consists of a far broader membership including many former Soviet republics in Central Asia, and is primarily interested in coordinating policies on human rights and the rule of law.)

of regulatory and judicial issues. The Council of the European Union, then, acts as if Europe is a single, democratically elected entity, while the European Council assumes a kind of confederacy of sovereign, democratic countries. The coexistence of two institutions with very similar names was evidence of the tension within the European project as a whole: was it a confederation of sovereign states or a federation of states with a combined democratic basis? The existence of these two competing notions of the European Union played into the crisis years of 2008–15.

To add to the complexity, in practice, the leading states (Great Britain, France, and Germany) conducted their own foreign policies alongside the foreign policy of the European Council. The European Union did not in fact have a single position on either the First or the Second Gulf War, and as we saw in Chapter 12, it let NATO and the United States take the lead during the Kosovo Crisis of 1999. The European Union likewise did not play a leadership role as the Arab world descended into civil war after 2011.

On a judicial level, the European Court of Justice had existed since the 1950s to deal with disputes across borders. The Treaty of Maastricht declared the Court one of the pillars of the European Union, and the 2009 Treaty of Lisbon expanded the Court's jurisdiction by adding a bill of rights for the European Union. Here, too, tensions were bound to emerge, and did. The German Constitutional Court, for example, so central to the moral, political, and cultural identity of the FRG, had developed a set of values and principles for democracy out of the Basic Law. Now the question arose: did the Basic Law remain Germany's fundamental law or was it overridden by European law? And could European law ever claim a deep emotional and symbolic hold on Germans?

The quarter century following German unification saw a tremendous increase of powers claimed by the European Union, embodied in the offices noted above. At the same time, individual national electorates rejected or qualified attempts at closer union. Voters' ambivalence to the European project was clear. The 2004 treaty establishing a constitution for all of Europe, for example, was rejected by both Dutch and French voters in 2005, two of the nations most in favor of a unified Europe. Furthermore, as difficult decisions became necessary, the European institutions themselves came under fire, as the next three sections show. Notably, though, European institutions weathered the storm, and even increased their authority during crises that seemed to challenge their existence. In the middle of a crisis, they offered tools for remedying the crisis; in other words, European institutions seemed useful, even if not necessarily beloved.[2]

The Great Recession in Europe

Over the first decades of the new millennium, US banks engaged in risky lending practices, offering mortgages with hard to understand terms to people with poor credit ratings and little collateral. The mortgage companies then bundled the mortgages in complex packages and resold them to other lenders and investors. They were able to spread these risks because of changes in US law that deregulated capital markets and left less room for governmental oversight. Globalization and deregulation meant the spread of risky loans across the world.

The US bubble began to burst in 2007, with international ramifications. One of the first foreign banks to come under pressure was the German IKB Deutsche Industriebank, which had invested in risky US loans. The banking industry in Germany is closely connected to politics, and German leaders judged a default of IKB to be risky, economically and politically; the bank was bailed out by the Kreditanstalt für Wiederaufbau, a government-owned development bank, together with other German banks in fall 2007. In so doing, they prevented the bank from defaulting, which would have led to its creditors' losing money.

Over the next year, the "subprime" crisis, so named because of the mortgages made to lower-than-prime borrowers, threatened the entire US financial system. One of the leading US banks, Lehman Brothers, collapsed in fall 2008. Its collapse endangered a series of other financial institutions. The result was the biggest threat to the US financial system since 1929. The complex world of packaged and repackaged debt implicated insurers, reinsurers, hedge funds, and other institutions.

Risky mortgages in the United States were only a part of the crisis, however. Underlying the crisis was a long-term decline of profits and productivity growth on a global scale, especially in the more industrially developed countries, a process that began already in the 1970s. Investors in search of higher profits had made riskier investments, in both the United States and Europe. The result was a flurry of new investment activity based on a dramatic expansion of private debt, including a building boom in Spain and Ireland that went far beyond what the market would bear. In Europe, as in the United States, the result was a lending bubble.

Germany was well positioned to respond to the crisis on the national level. The Merkel government increased spending to spur economic growth, and Chinese demand for German goods—made cheaper by an increasingly weak Euro—kept German factories humming. Conditions were not so good in the less developed and more indebted countries in southern Europe, which could neither increase debt nor print money, because of the rules governing the Eurozone, nor could they rely on a strong export market.

The Greek crisis and the European crisis

Although its economy was relatively small—about 2 percent of the Eurozone as a whole—Greece was at the center of the crisis. In late 2009, its government announced that the country had for years concealed its real public debt in order to remain in the Eurozone. Greek bonds and other investments were now held by banks across the European Union. As payments came due, it became clear that Greece could not meet its obligations. Costs of borrowing skyrocketed for the country. Greece faced possible default on its loans. European leaders were spooked. Especially after the Lehman Brothers disaster of 2008, they feared "contagion" in the form of a financial panic. They resisted a default, which would have meant that creditors would have had to bear some of the cost for the risky investments, fearing the psychological effects of such an action on the business world. Only slowly did the EU leadership act to shore up Greek banks. The slow reaction meant increasing nervousness on bond markets, which by 2010 meant a spread of the panic to countries with more solid public finances, but with large amounts of private debt, like Spain, Ireland, and Italy. Interest rates increased for the exposed countries, leaving them ever less able to borrow money. The countries responded by cutting their own budgets in order to decrease debt; in response, workers, pensioners, and the young began staging strikes and public protests, some of them violent, over the course of 2010. The Great Recession began to have political consequences.

All of the countries within the Eurozone had agreed to its rules, and they participated in choosing the leaders of both the ECB and the European Union itself. The leader of the ECB was notably not German but Dutch. In other words, the Central Bank was ultimately responsible to European voters, and not under the control of the Germans. Its actions, however, came increasingly to be identified with a Eurozone bureaucracy and the Germans, not least because Merkel and her finance minister Schäuble were playing such central roles in the discussion. Both of them affirmed the principles of the Eurozone limiting public debt and the manipulation of money. Led by the Germans, EU leaders teamed up with the Central Bank and the IMF in 2010–11 to bail out Greek banks with loans to be paid back by Greece. This "troika," as it was called, did not just extend loans to Greece but set extraordinary conditions for them, going so far as to specify which austerity programs Greece had to impose on its population.

Herein lay the political crisis. The Troika, with strong German leadership, dictated Greece's domestic policies; they demanded, for example, that Greek pensions be reduced further, despite the previous, painful cuts. One can argue that the European Union was, ultimately, elected by the people of the Eurozone and that the Central Bank leadership was appointed by democratically elected politicians; one can also argue that structural reforms in these countries were necessary, given the ongoing weakness of the banks, massive debt, and systematic tax evasion especially by the very wealthy. For Greeks, however, the actions of the Troika appeared to be the undemocratic decisions of an external power, with horrible consequences for ordinary people's lives. National politicians in Greece, Spain, Italy, and Britain, of course, had every reason to blame someone else for the mess (and to take the credit for any positive developments).

On a broader level, the policy of austerity meant less spending in the middle of an economic downturn. It pulled money out of the economy just as the economy was already in collapse. The result was a deeper recession. By mid-2012, the unemployment rate in Greece had passed 24 percent, where it would remain until 2016; youth unemployment surpassed 50 percent. The Spanish government, which had voluntarily initiated austerity measures to avoid a Troika ultimatum, experienced a similar shock to employment. As jobs disappeared, pensions declined. And in both these countries, even strong firms suddenly found that they could not find banks willing to grant loans. In sum, EU policy reinforced the economic downturn and made matters worse in the south.

The most stable European states in the north, however, most important Germany, experienced no crisis. Instead, they were awash in credit. The European Union had intervened to protect creditors, which meant to protect those wealthy enough to make loans—including the Germans. German politicians were in fact elected by Germans, not by Greeks; they had to answer to people holding Greek bonds in the form of a pension fund, for example, if Greece defaulted. While German citizens themselves complained about stagnant wages and worse living conditions, their fellow Europeans in the south saw a stable, indeed wealthy country sitting atop a pile of credit owed to it by the poorer countries. Germans preferred, it seemed, to stand on questionable principle rather than use that credit to alleviate their pain or to spur investment.

The brief discussion here only hints at the complexity of the Eurozone economic crisis of 2009–15. Economic experts continue to debate what was done and what should have been done. Some argued that Germany should have done more to relieve the pressure by allowing defaults that would have wiped out some of the creditors' wealth. Others, including the Leibniz Institute for Economic Renewal in Halle, lent weight to this argument with data indicating that the German government saved more than 100 billion Euros between 2010 and 2015 as a result of the European crisis. What was bad for Greece was good for Germany, in other words, and Germany's financial health was not, as Angela Merkel insisted throughout the crisis, solely the result of austerity measures imposed by her government. German finance minister Wolfgang Schäuble, who was central to the entire process, dismissed such arguments, noting, for example, that low interest rates alone would not necessarily bring investor confidence back. Demand alone would not suffice; structural reforms, including loosening labor markets and reducing debt burdens—essentially what Germany had done between 2002 and 2005—would make the Eurozone competitive again and give businesses the incentive to invest. The economic debate was hardly specific to Germany or the German ordoliberal tradition: in the United States as well, economists debated whether a response should focus on supply or demand, business confidence or consumer buying power. But the crisis had deeper political ramifications for a system like the European Union that sought to combine national sovereignty and an international federation.

Morality plays of the Great Recession

As governments bailed out banks and proved more interested in cutting public spending than in regulating the kind of shady investment practices responsible for the Great Recession, a popular backlash was not unexpected. Perhaps less expected was the successful mobilization of protest across national borders and a critique of the status quo that quickly went beyond international financial institutions. The Occupy Movement, inspired by the Arab Spring and the 2009 wave of anti-austerity protest movements, first grabbed headlines in fall 2011. With the famous slogan, "We are the 99%," Occupy attacked the growing concentration of income and wealth in the hands of a tiny minority—the 1 percent. The problem, as they saw it, was not only that large corporations controlled the market in a way that disproportionately benefited a relatively small group of investment bankers, hedge-fund managers, and corporate lawyers, but that such gross economic inequality undermined democracy and state stability. Participants occupied sites of power in over eighty countries on October 15, 2011, in solidarity with Occupy Wall Street launched one month earlier. In Germany, protesters gathered in some thirty-three towns and cities, with the largest demonstrations outside the Reichstag in Berlin and the ECB in Frankfurt. Some vented their anger at corporate greed and government cutbacks, others hoped to ignite an international movement for social justice.

The Occupy Movement was by definition extra-parliamentary and in many ways floundered on its own commitment to direct democracy. Others far beyond Occupy also attacked rule by finance, even the former Christian Democratic labor minister Norbert Blüm, who denounced what he called "Finance capitalism's" attack on "honest work" in a provocative book from 2011. Across southern Europe, however, popular protest was joined by new populist parties on the left and right. In the specific context of the European crisis, they rose to challenge the traditional parties for kowtowing to the European Union and Germany. In Greece, a neo-Nazi, anti-European party appeared on the right, Golden Dawn, which received 6–7 percnt in the national polls between 2012 and 2015, and almost 10 percent in elections to the European Parliament in 2015. On the far left, Syriza, or the Radical Coalition of the Left, rose in protest against the old center-left parties, gaining over 1/3 of the popular vote in the elections of January 2015 on a platform opposed to the terms of the bailout but not against the European Union. Syriza was able to assume the leadership with the support of a right-wing party skeptical of the European Union. Syriza's popular leader, Alexis

FIGURE 13.2 *Protesters, including one holding a sign in Greek that reads:*
"Defend democracy and a socially-oriented state, here and in Europe!"
demonstrate in solidarity with the economically stricken nations of southern
Europe during a "national day of action" on November 14, 2012. (Getty Images/
Sean Gallup)

Tsipras, struggled for better terms from the European Union in order to
reverse the austerity policies Greece had been forced to follow. They did
so by invoking national history. Germany, Syriza leaders argued, had left a
trail of destruction in Greece during the Second World War, and therefore it
should pay war reparations. Discussions reached their low point in 2015, as
anti-German sentiment on the Greek side was met with stereotypes about
Greeks as a lazy and corrupt people in the German popular press.

Great morality plays, as Martin Sandbu has called them, began to replace
the complex problems of the Great Recession in Europe. For some Greeks,
Germans became once again the Nazi occupiers of the Second World War,
complacent creditors profiting from their debtors and demanding austerity
and hardship—a story that allowed them to shift focus away from the
deep problems of poor regulation, corruption, and client politics that had
hobbled the Greek economy. Inside Germany, and also in other countries,
the real problems faced by Greece turned into a fable about a corrupt
Greek nation that spent above its means and needed to grow up: the only
alternative was strict parental disciplining. Underlying both of these tales
was a conception of nations and national character at odds with the entire
logic of the European Union, which assumed combined decision making of
sovereign states based on mutual respect.

Protest movements grew elsewhere as well. In Spain, a new left-wing party critical of the European Union and austerity, Podemos, helped paralyze the party system. In Italy, the Five Star Movement, an anti-elitist party with an ill-defined ideology but a skeptical approach to the European Union, became the second most popular party in the general elections of 2013. In France, the National Front, with its roots in racist, anti-immigrant, and authoritarian politics, gained strength in national polls and elections as the French leadership itself appeared ineffective and indecisive. In Britain, a populist movement that cut across left and right politics put its Euro-skepticism into action, in the form of a successful national referendum in 2016 to leave the European Union (Britain, as noted, did not belong to the Eurozone). And in Germany, the Alternative for Germany (AfD) formed in 2013 after a number of German ordoliberals rejected the Eurozone's bailout of Greece and successfully gathered financial and political support from some businesses as well as from disgruntled citizens. It did not take long before the group's anti-EU platform was overshadowed by anti-Islamic and anti-immigrant positions.

The financial crisis of 2007–08 thus led to a political crisis of the European Union by 2015. At the center of that crisis was Germany, as the leading creditor state but also as the state whose politicians were most directly and publicly involved in trying to deal with the crisis.

The Russian crisis: Germany and EU foreign policy

The tension between sovereign state and supranational union was nowhere more evident than in foreign policy. France and Britain, the two EU powers with the strongest militaries, clung to their former great power status. As a civilian power, German pursued its own interests as well, through economic diplomacy; it also stressed the importance of international institutions like the European Union and the United Nations. German policy makers hoped that economic interest and participation in international institutions would reinforce each other.

Over the two decades following unification, both NATO and the European Union had expanded into eastern Europe. For centuries, most of the states in eastern Europe had been within the orbit of Russian and then Soviet control. Their decision to reorient themselves politically and economically toward the West was as much anti-Russian as it was a bid for economic prosperity. And the rise of Vladimir Putin, an increasingly authoritarian leader with roots in the Soviet secret police (KGB), was in part a reaction to NATO and EU expansion. In 2014, tension with Ukraine erupted into open conflict, as Russia annexed the Crimean Peninsula and promoted civil war in the eastern provinces of Ukraine.

The roots of the crisis lay in the diplomatic agreements enabling German unification in 1989–90. At that time, the Soviet Union and the United States initially disagreed about whether the former GDR should become part of NATO. For the Russians, the problem was that NATO, an anti-Russian alliance, would expand eastward. For the Germans, the transatlantic alliance was at stake, an alliance that was central both to West Germany's foreign policy and national identity. In the end, Gorbachev acquiesced.

Diplomats in 1990 gave no clear answer to the question of whether the newly independent states of eastern Europe might be able to join NATO. After Russian and then Soviet domination, however, it was no surprise that these nations sought security against Russia. As the issue arose, Russian leaders began to argue that in fact the West had agreed not to enlarge NATO, and that it was now breaking its promise. The leading scholar of the Cold War in the United States, Mark Kramer, has asserted that no such agreement was ever made. It nonetheless continues to be part of the public debate.

The NATO bombing campaign against Serbia in 1999 brought US and NATO forces into eastern Europe, without UN authorization; Russia protested, to no avail. The Second Gulf War deepened the level of distrust. Between 1999 and 2004, meanwhile, NATO expanded to include ten states in eastern Europe, including the newly independent Baltic states and six other former Soviet satellites.

MAP 13.1 *European Union Expansion, 1993–2016.*

After 2004, President Bush and other Western leaders began to talk of a further NATO enlargement to include Georgia and Ukraine, both of which directly bordered Russia. Both of those countries had experienced protests in 2004, which had led to the removal of pro-Russian presidents. Despite President Bush's strong support for expansion, French and German diplomats argued that further expansion would undermine relations with Russia. The NATO summit held in Bucharest in April 2008 deferred the decision until December. But NATO clearly put the issue on the table.

Between April and August, violent confrontations began to take place in two contested regions of Georgia, both areas that the Russians claimed. In a well-planned move, the Russian government invaded in August, claiming that it was undertaking a humanitarian intervention and bombing Tiblis, the capital of Georgia—imitating, in other words, the arguments made by NATO when it had attacked Serbia in 1999.

In this context, Chancellor Merkel, herself not a strong supporter of NATO enlargement, acted. She visited Tiblis, called for a ceasefire, and most important announced that Georgia was an independent, democratic state that had the right to join NATO if its people wanted. Germany, a civilian power, took sides, essentially articulating EU foreign policy. No doubt important as well was Merkel's own background as a child of the GDR, where she had learned Russian and studied Soviet culture and politics, and even visited Moscow as an exchange student. This certainly made her unique among the world's leaders: she understood Putin's native tongue and could even claim some sense of a shared past. But already in the first years of her chancellorship, Merkel started to distrust Putin. For Germany, however, international politics was not just about military issues, it was about economic relations. And Russia was important for Germany's economy.

Geopolitics, economics, and morality in German foreign policy

Germany's economic strength lay in its export trade. With only about 80 million people, a bit over 1 percent of the total world population, it was the world's leading exporter before 2008 and by 2016 the third largest exporter of goods in the world, behind the powerhouses China and the United States. An increasing amount of that trade since 2000 was with countries like China and Russia. Russia became an ever more important source for energy raw materials needed by German firms to manufacture the goods that they exported. Chancellor Schröder had worked closely with the Russians to ensure a steady supply of natural gas to Germany. To this end, he promoted a new company called Nord Stream, 51 percent of which was owned by the Russian energy giant Gazprom, which Putin was in the process of putting under state control at the time. Nord Stream aimed to build a direct pipeline to Germany through the Baltic Sea, bypassing countries like Poland and

Ukraine. The new pipeline would provide more energy security to Germany and western European states—without strengthening Russia's ability to control energy supplies into Poland and Ukraine. Schröder strongly supported the project and convinced his own government to underwrite the Nord Stream venture during his last weeks as chancellor. In the process, he appeared to become a close friend of Putin. Only a few weeks after resigning as chancellor, Schröder accepted a position as chair of Nord Stream, a decision met with harsh criticism and allegations of corruption across party lines in Germany.

Whatever the public reaction, Schröder represented one important strand of Germany's foreign policy as a civilian power, namely its search for markets and reliable raw materials in countries that did not necessarily adhere to Germany's self-proclaimed democratic ideals or military alliances. Russia and China, both authoritarian nations, were leading trading partners with Germany, helping to keep its own economy booming as domestic demand remained stifled. Under both Merkel and Schröder, furthermore, German firms supplied states that had bad human rights records and potentially destabilizing regional policies with materials that could be used to help their militaries: chemicals capable of producing poison gases to Syria, nuclear materials to Iran, and under Chancellor Merkel a number of advanced armaments to Saudi Arabia. All of these deals contributed to Germany's trade surplus and its booming economy.

Germany was hardly alone; US, British, and French firms were also heavily involved in the arms industry. Arms, energy, and other trading areas play a role in all these countries' foreign policies. No doubt German interests in Russian raw materials played some role in Germany's resistance to the Second Gulf War and NATO expansion. But they do not explain the policies completely. Germany was interested both in maintaining the stability necessary for production and trade and, as a post-fascist power, in rejecting militarism and war. Both interests and values shaped German diplomacy.

Growing critique of Putin's authoritarianism in Germany

After the resolution of the Russian-Georgian war, German trade with Russia expanded further. It became even more important for the German economy after Merkel's 2011 decision to abandon nuclear energy. Alternative energy could not provide for all of Germany's needs. Russian natural gas was necessary. And yet, Germany found itself forced to take a position against the increasing authoritarianism of the Russian state.

In 2012, Putin ran for president after having promised to not seek the presidency again. The elections were managed by the state, which Putin and Putin loyalists controlled. Putin therefore had no serious challengers and his message dominated the airwaves. He won the election, but

European observers noted many irregularities, including reports of people who voted multiple times. During the election, the state cracked down on protesters, including the punk protest band Pussy Riot, which engaged in a spontaneous anti-Putin protest in a church. Two of their leading members received long prison sentences for having undermined public morality. After the election, Putin and his strong majority in parliament enacted new laws against "extremism" and "foreign agents" that allowed the state to monitor, detain, or jail or expel critical journalists and members of nongovernmental organizations like Human Rights Watch and Amnesty International. In 2012 as well, the Russian parliament enacted a law that allowed the state to monitor and filter out content from the internet. And in 2013, the parliament approved legislation, almost unanimously, to protect children against information that would undermine "family values"; the law's target was the gay, lesbian, and transgender community, and an upsurge in antigay violence followed the legislation's approval.

The German government reacted strongly to these developments. Foreign Minister Guido Westerwelle of the Free Democrats, himself openly gay, criticized the anti-LGBQ legislation. Both Christian Democrats and Social Democratic politicians reacted with displeasure when Russian officials searched the Russian offices of their political foundations in early 2013, as part of an intimidation campaign against human rights organizations. Chancellor Merkel complained to Putin directly. Although both sides sought to smooth relations over, distance and distrust between Russia and Germany grew, despite their close economic ties.

Underlying the tension was another issue, this one related to the European Union. The European Union, just like NATO, had also expanded into eastern Europe. And just as eastern European states wanted NATO for its security, they wanted the European Union for its connection to the wealth and development models of western Europe. But Russia under Putin viewed the European Union just as it viewed NATO: as both anti-Russian and an encroachment into its area of influence. In response, Putin proposed a Eurasian Economic Union (EEU) in 2011, essentially a Russia-centered version of the European Union that would recreate some of the close ties of the Soviet era while promoting free trade and the movement of commodities. Membership in the EEU precluded membership in the European Union. It was, in other words, a way to keep countries from falling into the EU/NATO orbit. One such country was Ukraine.

The Ukraine crisis, EU sanctions, and Germany

In 2004, the so-called Orange Revolution brought an end to a corrupt, pro-Russian government in Ukraine. The opposition won the election that followed, but fell victim to internal fights. In new elections in 2010, the pro-Russian candidate Viktor Yanukovych won with the strong support of ethnic Russians in Ukraine's eastern provinces. Yanukovych followed the Putin model of centralizing power; his chief rival, Yulia Tymoshenko, was arrested and jailed for alleged abuse of power. In 2013, Yanukovych rejected an association agreement with the European Union, opting to join Russia's EEU instead. Street protests followed, demanding an association with the European Union and criticizing Yanukovych for corruption. Yanukovych fled to Russia in February 2014. The new leadership announced its intent to join the European Union. Putin and the state-dominated Russian media presented these events as an illegal coup orchestrated by the West and supported by Ukrainian nationalist fascists, though they could offer no real evidence.

In February, citizens' militias of ethnic Russians supported by Russian troops in unmarked uniforms claimed the Crimean Peninsula, a part of Ukraine historically dominated by ethnic Russians that housed a significant Russian naval base. On March 18, 2014, an illegal referendum was held in Crimea. According to the official results, 95 percent of the voters called to secede from Ukraine. Foreign observers condemned the vote as fraudulent. On the basis of the vote, Russia formally annexed the Crimean Peninsula. Soon thereafter, Russian ethnic agitation began in the Donbass region of Ukraine bordering Russia, once again supported by unmarked Russian troops and Russian equipment. On July 17, 2014, a Malaysian Airlines jet flying overhead was shot down, almost certainly by pro-Russian insurgents with Russian armaments, killing hundreds of EU citizens on board. The Russian government blamed Ukraine, despite evidence to the contrary.

The annexation of Crimea was a shock for the European Union and for Merkel. Putin's Russia had flagrantly violated international law, supported a civil war, and taken land from a sovereign power, risking wider military confrontation. Merkel referred to the action as "criminal," while her finance minister Schäuble compared it with the Nazi takeover of the Sudetenland in 1938. The shooting down of the airliner, and more importantly Putin's crude lying about it, came as an additional shock. The European Union, as noted, does not have a strong foreign policy presence but in this case it needed one. Merkel, in close contact with President Obama, stepped into that role. Against expectations that Germany might prioritize its trade relations with Russia above all else, Germany stressed the need for a peaceful Europe and, despite opposition from member countries that feared harming their relations with Russia, rallied the EU countries around a coordinated sanctions policy against Russia starting in July 2014, overcoming both the demands of Poland and other eastern European states for a directly arming the Ukrainian state and the lagging interest in the issue in France, Spain, and the Mediterranean states far from the action. Putin had not expected sanctions from the European Union. But they persisted in the face of his occupation of Crimea, and together with the drop in oil prices they led to a dramatic weakening of the Russian economy in 2015.

The Russian crisis overlapped with the financial crisis, however. In the midst of the 2015 conflict with Greece, that country's prime minister, Tsipras, visited with Putin and announced his opposition to the EU sanctions. In return, Putin stressed the valuable economic relationship Russia had with Greece, and how much more Russia could purchase from Greece if the sanctions were lifted. Greece's implied threat of leaving NATO and the European Union indicates just how complicated Germany's leadership role was by 2015–16. And indeed, the Greeks and French, but also the Social Democrats within Germany, began to call for an end to sanctions in summer 2016. The economic and diplomatic interests of a civilian power were in tension.

The refugee crisis of 2015

The refugee crisis of 2015 highlighted again the tension between a Europe made up of sovereign states and the European Union. At issue was a massive influx of immigrants, many of them victims of war, which affected some European states more than others. To avoid potential chaos and to equalize burdens across Europe, some unified policy was necessary. Again, Germany took the lead and was then blamed for the outcome. Anti-immigrant parties strengthened across Europe.

Underlying the refugee crisis, in other words, was another deep issue facing especially western European states: how to come to terms with immigration. Immigration has arguably always been a central part of German culture, society, and economy, but only with the Red-Green coalition did the political system catch up with the fact that Germany is an immigration country. Continuing what the Red-Green government began, a 2005 immigration act made it easier for foreigners to immigrate to Germany, partly as a way to deal with the declining overall population of Germany. And in 2007, the government set up new offices to help refugees integrate into German society. Germany itself remained more protected from migration movements within the European Union than other states; only in 2011 were citizens from countries in eastern Europe like Poland permitted to take jobs and reside freely in Germany. During these years, however, the German economy was booming, and the most visible new immigrants were young professionals from the crisis-riddled economies of southern Europe. Perhaps as a result, German public opinion became far less anti-foreigner than was the case, for example, in Great Britain.

The problem of political refugees and asylum seekers was likewise not new to the European Union. Political and religious strife magnified by interference by outside powers and arms shipments had helped create refugee movements from African civil wars, the Iran–Iraq war of the 1980s and the political despotisms that resulted from it, the Balkan Wars of the 1990s, and the violence engulfing Iraq and Afghanistan after the United States-led invasions in 2002–03. Iraqi, Iranian, Kurdish, Kosovar, Croat, Ethiopian, Eritrean, Somali, Ukrainian, and many more refugees from across the world came to the European Union and to Germany in search of safe haven. The EU countries officially agreed to the international human rights conventions granting refugees the right to seek asylum. In Germany, that right remained embedded in the Basic Law itself.

Asylum policies and practices varied from country to country, as did the level of support given to refugees for their housing needs and for integration. The differences in policy and aid could matter: the Schengen Agreement of 1985 dictated open borders within the European Union, potentially allowing refugees to move to an EU country offering better social services and asylum prospects. To limit this mobility, the Dublin Convention of 1990 declared that an asylum seeker had to seek asylum within the first EU country he or she reached. That policy put a special burden on those states at the borders of the European Union, such as Greece, Hungary, Italy, and Spain, which were the most likely states to receive asylum seekers.

In 2010, the Arab Spring erupted, as young people across the Arab world made use of new technologies to protest against dictatorship and corrupt ruling elites. The main EU governments expressed their sympathies with the protesters, but the European Union as a body did not intervene. In Libya, the French and British led an intervention against the forces of the dictator Muammar Gaddafi under UN auspices, in which Germany refused to participate. Immediately after the collapse of the Gaddafi regime, the coalition ended its military action, and Libya descended into civil war. In Syria, a popular uprising against the dictatorship of the ruling Assad family also descended into civil war as the government beat back civilians with poison gas, chemicals that they possibly received from German business suppliers. Russia, with a naval base in the Syrian city of Tartus, openly supported Bashar al-Assad and delivered arms to the country as Assad's forces carried out attacks on civilians. The ongoing civil violence in Iraq meanwhile took on a new form as disgruntled former security forces of Saddam Hussein teamed up with Muslim extremists to form a new grouping across Iraq, Syria, and Libya known as the Islamic State. The stage was set for humanitarian catastrophe, as hundreds of thousands of people were killed and millions driven from their homes.

The European Union had tried to forestall a flow of refugees, promising billions of Euros to support refugee camps in the small states of Jordan and Lebanon; in Jordan by early 2016, the refugees constituted some 10 percent of the total population, in Lebanon over 20 percent. There and in Turkey, which was home to over 2.5 million Syrian refugees by the end of 2015, living conditions were poor and refugees' right to work restricted. Seeing a return home as unlikely, many of the refugees decided to migrate to the European Union, which offered not only better living conditions but also peace, the rule of law, and the possibility of political asylum.

The sheer number of refugees over the first half of 2015 overwhelmed the existing European system. The countries on the leading edge, including Greece, Italy, and Spain, were still in the midst of their fiscal crises. Hungary, receiving refugees coming up through the Balkans, was likewise inundated. Soon refugees made up almost 2 percent of its total population. By early summer 2015, it was clear that tens of thousands of refugees were leaving the makeshift camps in the EU border states, as the civil war in Syria, exacerbated by Russian military intervention, pushed even more people out of that country. The authorities in Turkey (outside of the European Union) and Greece waved them on, preoccupied as they were with their own problems. Syriza's Greece even refused economic aid from the European Union for the refugees, using the event as a bargaining chip in their own financial crisis. The member states of the European Union faced a dilemma: send the refugees back to Hungary, Greece, and Turkey, countries unable and perhaps unwilling to provide adequate support, or violate the Dublin Regulations, which required asylum applicants to apply in the first EU country they entered? Under these circumstances, a German federal ministry made the decision around August 25, 2015, not to enforce the EU regulations. The news spread through social media before Merkel's government was actually informed.[3] Under these circumstances, and taking advantage of her power as popular head of the main conservative party in Germany in alliance with the Social Democrats, Merkel affirmed the ministry's decision, essentially inviting refugees in. Her decision was a calculated gamble to affirm European solidarity with the beleaguered states on the European Union's southern border. It also seems to have been her heartfelt reaction to the image of refugees with no place to return to and restrained by soldiers and fences, reflecting, perhaps, her experiences as a former citizen of the GDR.

By the end of August 2015, Germans saw ever more images of the refugees, and heard ever higher estimates of how many would actually come to Germany. On August 31, Merkel sought to calm public opinions, with her now famous phrase "we can do it" (*Wir schaffen das*). Some initial reactions were negative. In Saxony, demonstrators denounced Merkel as a "traitor to the people" (*Volksverräterin*), a term with Nazi connotations. Meanwhile, conditions for refugees in Hungary were worsening, as tensions between security forces and refugees grew. By early September, the situation in Hungary was veering out of control, and the flow of refugees increased. At the worst point, Germany was receiving up to 10,000 new arrivals a day. More than a million arrived over the course of 2015.

Overall, German society responded positively. Main newspapers on both sides of the political spectrum endorsed Merkel's challenge, and thousands of citizens volunteered to help and house refugees. For Merkel as for many of the citizens, the crisis had a moral and historical aspect: in light of its own history and the ideals captured by the Basic Law's right to asylum, Germany would not ignore or reject legitimate asylum seekers. The political parties also stood behind the actions, despite criticism from the right wing of the CDU, and especially the Bavarian Christian Social Union, about admitting too many refugees, and criticism from the Greens and the Linke that the government was not doing enough. Communities made sacrifices as well, giving up sports halls and other public spaces so that the refugees could be housed.

Public enthusiasm only sustains politics for a short time. Local budgets became tight, as institutions aimed at integrating refugees were stretched to the limit. Fears that some of these refugees might be involved with terrorism grew, especially after it became clear that some participants in the Islamic State terrorist attack in Paris on November 15, 2015, had slipped into Europe posing as Syrian refugees. The offices in charge of examining asylum claims, which also would have checked on possible terrorist connections, were themselves overwhelmed. One year after the refugee crisis began, in summer 2016, the German government had still not processed hundreds of thousands of asylum applications.

Public discontent with the government grew, and anti-immigration groups began to form. Merkel herself experienced the lowest approval rating of her career, as she slipped down from ratings above 70 percent to 46 percent in early 2016. A month later, however, her ratings began to rise again, despite widespread concerns about how Germany could handle the influx of refugees. The positive response, especially at first, was the result not only of the many years of rejecting the legacy of xenophobia and Nazism. The newspapers were also full of discussions about how immigration, especially of highly skilled workers, would help Germany deal with its own problem of an aging society and a low birthrate.

Merkel, known for her risk aversion and pragmatism, had taken a major risk in her decision to allow the refugees into the country. She had risked losing the support of the German people. Germany's decision furthermore meant that Germany, resented by some countries in the European Union for its wealth, now faced the prospect of bearing an inordinate burden for the European Union's refugee policy as a whole. By 2016, Germany faced other European countries that put their own particular interests ahead of the need for a coherent, Europe-wide policy on refugees. A new conservative government in Poland announced that it would only accept Christian refugees, and then only a few hundred. The conservative right-wing populist government in Hungary built a wall against more refugees and refused to cooperate in an EU plan to spread refugees fairly across the member states. A similar reaction took place in Austria, where an anti-immigration politician of the far right Freedom Party threatened to win that country's presidential election. The rise of the xenophobic National Front in France was also related to the immigration crisis. Last but certainly not least, the British referendum to leave the European Union was fueled by a strong anti-immigrant mood.

The populist challenge

The Great Recession, the Russian crisis, and the refugee crisis all occurred at the same time, all required German leadership, and all put into focus contradictions and weaknesses of the European Union itself. Most important, all were complex and not susceptible to easy answers. The populist movements that challenged political and cultural elites across Europe, from Le Pen's National Front to the movement to leave the European Union in Britain, from the left-wing Syriza Party in Greece to the right-wing Law and Justice Party in Poland, claimed to bring politics closer to the people, to take it out of the hands of "nameless bureaucrats" in the European Union (i.e., experts appointed by democratically elected representatives), to find easy answers to the hard questions the established parties were dealing with. It is not surprising, then, that unified Germany has also had its share of populist groupings that claimed to represent ordinary citizens against the alien authority of "experts."

The PDS played that populist role on the left in the 1990s, until it became too involved with politics at the Land level. In 2000, the judge Ronald Schill formed a right-wing variant, the Party for the Rule of Law (*Partei Rechtsstaatlicher Offensive*; the latter word implies an "offensive" in the military sense), really a law and order party calling for dramatic measures against criminality and drugs that the established parties were allegedly unable to provide. Schill criticized Germany's immigration policy, immigrants, and asylum seekers. The harsh rhetoric about criminals, critique of the established parties, nationalism, and anti-foreigner sentiment connected Schill's party to other parties, such as the Republikaner of the 1980s, and to similar right-wing parties in Austria, Belgium, and the Netherlands. The party established itself for a short time in Hamburg but nowhere else. Conflicts about the content and leadership of the party led to its collapse after 2003. Individual intellectuals like Thilo Sarrazin, once a leading Social Democrat, also brought anti-immigrant, anti-Islam, and anti-Euro arguments to a mass audience; his book sold well despite, or perhaps because, it was denounced by experts. The Social Democrats considered expelling Sarrazin from the party, but never did so in part because of the amount of support he found in the population.

A similar grouping appeared in Dresden, in the heart of Saxony, in former East Germany. Calling themselves PEGIDA, or the Patriotic Europeans against the Islamization of the Occident, a group of citizens founded a Facebook page in fall 2014 to protest the threat that bad immigrants would bring their fights into Germany. PEGIDA also protested against established parties and experts. Instead of presenting a set of leaders, they began to march on Mondays in Dresden, echoing the Monday marches in the fall of 1989. They implied a parallel between the undemocratic SED regime and the democratically elected government in Berlin. The numbers rose from a few hundred in November to around 25,000 on January 12, 2015. Thereafter, the movement seemed to decline, but as the refugee crisis developed over the summer of 2015, PEGIDA resurged. Its demonstrations took on more extreme tones that fall, with open threats to Merkel and other leading politicians and strong anti-Muslim and anti-immigrant slogans.

PEGIDA remained distant from the press, which it referred to as a bunch of liars (*Lügenpresse*, a term also used by the Nazis), so getting a firm idea of what the group stood for was hard. The most detailed such attempt, however, shows it to be a collection of different complaints about the established parties, the refugees, globalization, the European Union, and so on: in other words, a classic right-wing anti-establishment party.[4]

And a party that struck a chord. Just as one part of German society and the majority of the political elite opened its arms to the refugees, another part rejected them. The second half of 2015 saw a dramatic increase of attacks on asylum shelters, such as had not been seen since the early 1990s. The Federal Criminal Office registered over 1,000 attacks in 2015, along with hundreds more attacks on individuals.[5] A militant anti-foreigner protest movement was taking shape. Another right-wing and populist organization offered a voice for the protest movement, one that could unite anti-immigrant and anti-foreigner sentiments with social criticism of globalization and its effects on wages in Germany: the Alternative for Germany.

Following its formation in 2013, the Alternative for Germany broke the 5 percent hurdle as a protest party in Brandenburg and Saxony, as well as in elections to the European Parliament. Over time its platform had become more complex, addressing the right-populist topics of criminality, immigration, and the failure of the "old parties." Over the course of 2014–15, the party was pulled apart by internal squabbles, as it argued over its approach to PEGIDA. The early supporters rejected PEGIDA as too anti-foreigner and anti-Muslim. A new leader from Saxony, the telegenic, successful chemist and businesswoman Frauke Petry, however, welcomed and moderated the PEGIDA rhetoric. In the first months of 2015, the Alternative for Germany crossed the 5 percent threshold in elections in both Hamburg and Bremen, establishing itself as a populist party in both the east and the west, and Petry rode this success to become leader of Alternative for Germany in summer 2015.

It was not Petry but the Syrian refugee crisis that propelled the Alternative for Germany to astounding victories in 2016: over 24 percent of the vote in the eastern Land Saxony-Anhalt and 12.6 percent of the vote in the western Rhineland-Palatinate in March. In the same month, it became the leading opposition party in Baden-Württemberg, gaining more votes than Social Democrats, the Linke, or Free Democrats. Alternative for Germany gained nearly 21 percent of the vote in Merkel's home Land, Mecklenburg-Vorpommern, leaving the Christian Democrats in third place with only 19 percent of the vote. The party drew voters from across the political spectrum: from the Linke in eastern Germany, from Social Democrats and Christian Democrats in the west, from some of the right extremist parties, and a large number of voters from previous nonvoters. Its party program of May 1, 2016, expressed the usual combination of right-wing populist demands:

- Popular referenda and electoral reforms should lower the influence of the traditional parties: the Alternative for Germany rejected the party-oriented political culture of the Federal Republic.
- Support for a "Europe of the Fatherlands," and with that a call for a referendum on the Euro: the AfD was thus the leading critic of combined European financial policies, but also of a European government with its own foreign policy.
- Call for "more children instead of mass immigration": the AfD endorsed pronatalism, and connected this position to a defense of the role of the traditional housewife.
- Demand for a "dominant German culture" in place of multiculturalism, and more specifically for the position that "Islam is not part of Germany": the AfD demanded an end to foreign financing of mosques, denial of official legal status for Islamic organization, and the banning of full-face veils.

The list of demands was long, ranging from educational (cut gender studies programs, ban Koran schools), to financial (lower taxes, less regulation). It read more like a protest list, sometimes sounding more conservative, sometimes more liberal, sometimes more ecological. Underlying the program was a tone, reminiscent of the early years of the Greens or of the PDS, implying the failure of the existing parties.[6] The political content of the Alternative for Germany became, however, ever more clearly far right, as it was awarded at the polls for allying itself with other anti-Islamic and anti-foreigner groups in the European Parliament, such as France's National Front.

Like other right-wing populist groups, the Alternative for Germany consisted of many different factions. Racist, anti-Islamic, and sometimes anti-Semitic statements from some of its leaders, defended as a "breaking of taboos," led to occasional fights within the party, and even splitting the party in Baden-Württemberg in summer 2016. These debates over etiquette did not seem to hurt the party. In the federal elections of September 2017, the Alternative for Germany won 12.6 percent of the votes, becoming the third largest party, in an election that saw dramatic losses for both Social Democrats and Christian Democrats. But immediately after the victory, several leading members, including Frauke Petry, left the party in protest over other members' far right tendencies. The immediate result? A new conservative faction, the Blue Party, still to the right of Christian

FIGURE 13.3 *An Alternative for Deutschland (AfD) supporter holds a poster portraying Chancellor Angela Merkel as "mommy multicultural" at a weekly gathering in the economically depressed city of Erfurt, November 4, 2015. (Getty Images/Jens Schlueter)*

Democracy but more "goal-oriented" than what Petry described as the AfD's "anarchist" opposition.

The rise of the Alternative for Germany was part of a general mood of discontent and right-wing populist protest across Europe and into the United States. Its positions were echoed by the conservative governments of Poland and Hungary, by populist candidates with some likelihood of victory in Austria and France, by the leading voices of the British referendum to leave the European Union, and not least by the US presidential candidate Donald Trump.

The Alternative for Germany leadership greeted Trump's election as a victory against media bias, "establishment" parties, and "political correctness." Merkel, by contrast, congratulated Trump on his victory with the remarkable words: "Germany and America are bound by common values—democracy, freedom, as well as respect for the rule of law and the dignity of each and every person, regardless of their origin, skin color, creed, gender, sexual orientation, or political views. It is based on these values that I wish to offer close cooperation, both with me personally and between our countries' governments." Her statement seemed to set conditions for cooperation between Germany and the United States, revealing her distrust for the person entering the White House, a wariness rooted in Germans' intimate knowledge of fascism and the destruction that one man, claiming that he alone would make the nation great again, could bring.

Conclusion: Germany and Europe/Germany in Europe

The final chapter of this book has stressed foreign policy. But foreign policy was bound up with domestic and economic issues for Germany. The German economic success after 2005 was based on its exports; German foreign policy thus also involved reaching out to its trading partners. Germany's commitment to the European Union found its limits in the willingness of Germans to act in European, not just German, interests. In this regard, however, Chancellor Merkel was a democratically elected politician like any other, and German citizens, like citizens elsewhere, were leery of making sacrifices for other nations. Germany's attempt to deal with the European Union's refugee crisis revealed a basic tension between the interests of the European Union as a whole and those of individual states.

Underlying all of these dilemmas is an uncomfortable fact about modern democracies. Leaders may be elected, but once elected they have to deal with complicated questions in ways that don't always accord with the immediate interests of their constituents. Modern, global democracy necessarily limits national sovereignty: a country's leaders work within international networks organizing and regulating the flow of energy and goods, of arms and aid, of capital and debt. The potential for a populist critique grows with complexity, especially in a time of crises that are not easily understandable by ordinary people—or indeed by experts.

Germany faces challenges similar to other advanced industrialized democracies, then. But several basic principles also shape German policy. First, a rejection of racism and defense of the rule of law remains strong, despite gains on the far right during moments of crisis. An anti-Semitic utterance becomes a topic of national debate today; debates about immigrants become debates about the role of racism in German culture. The worst legacies of German history have not been forgotten, at the same time as immigration, Europeanization, and globalization raise hard questions about what German "identity" really is.

Second, there is no strong voice in Germany for a dramatic expansion of the military and a strong military presence. Germany remains committed to its role as a civilian power, and uses that role to contribute to diplomacy, both economic and political, across the world. Certainly, self-interest is involved in this decision. That self-interest has guided much Social Democratic thinking about Germany's Russian policy since Schröder, for example, and reemerged in summer 2016 when SPD foreign minister Frank-Walter Steinmeier criticized NATO "saber-rattling" in eastern Europe. Germany's role in the European Union and NATO remained disputed: is it a civilian power capable of bridging the gap between big powers and thereby contributing to peace, or an economic powerhouse with a special relationship to Russia?

Third, Germany remains a strong defender of the European Union, even at a time when the union itself is under stress. The explanation lies in part with Germany's own interests. Military hegemony failed in the First World War and the Second World War, at the cost of tens of millions of lives. Economic hegemony has succeeded in central Europe, where German firms like Volkswagen were main economic drivers for Slovakia and other eastern European states and German credit is essential (though controversial) throughout. Europe also remains, for the Christian Democrats and for the Greens in particular, a principled commitment to a world beyond the sovereign state. It is connected to a commitment to the rule of law and clear processes that has left a mark on the European project in general.

Further reading

Amnesty International. "Syria's Refugee Crisis in Numbers." February 3, 2016. Available at https://www.amnesty.org/en/latest/news/2016/02/syrias-refugee-crisis-in-numbers/.

Baldini, Gianfranco, and Silvia Bogherine, "So Similar, Yet So Different: Alternative für Deutschland and the Pirate Party." In *Germany After the 2013 Elections: Breaking the Mold of Postunification Politics?* Edited by Gabriele d'Ottavio and Thomas Saalfeld, 181–202. New York: Routledge, 2016.

Forsberg, Tuomas. "From Ostpolitik to 'Frostpolitik'? Merkel, Putin and German Foreign Policy towards Russia." *International Affairs* 92 (2016), 21–42.

Grimm, Dieter. "Defending Sovereign Statehood against Transforming the Union into a State." *European Constitutional Law Review* 5 (2009), 353–73.

Heckmann, Friedrich. "Understanding the Creation of Public Consensus: Migration and Integration in Germany, 2005 to 2015." June 2016. Migration Policy Institute. Available at: http://www.migrationpolicy.org/research/understanding-creation-public-consensus-migration-and-integration-germany-2005-2015

Hildebrand, Rainer. "Germany and its Eurozone Crisis Policy: The Impact of the Country's Ordoliberal Heritage." *German Politics and Society* 114 (2015), 6–24.

Kramer, Mark, and Mary Elise Sarotte. "No Such Promise." *Foreign Affairs* 6 (2014), 208.

Kundnani, Hans. *The Paradox of German Power.* London: Hurst, 2014.
Latsch, Guther, Fidelius Schmid, and Klaus Wiegrefe. "Decades of Suspicion: Die German Companies Aid Syrian Chemical Weapons Program?" Spiegel Online, January 23, 2015. Access at: http://www.spiegel.de/international/germany/german-companies-suspected-of-aiding-syrian-chemical-weapons-program-a-1014722.html.
Maull, Hanns W. "Germany and Japan: The New Civilian Powers." *Foreign Affairs* 5 (1990), 91–107.
Mushaben, Joyce Marie. *Becoming Madame Chancellor: Angela Merkel and the Berlin Republic*, New York: Cambridge University Press, 2017.
Mushaben. "The Best of Times, the Worst of Times: Angela Merkel, the Grand Coalition, and 'Majority Rule' in Germany." *German Politics and Society* 34 (2016), 1–25.
Sarotte, Mary Elise. "A Broken Promise? What the West Really Told Russia about Nato Expansion." *Foreign Affairs,* 5 (2014), 90–7.
Schäuble, Wolfgang. "German Priorities and European Myths." *International New York Tribune.* April 16, 2015, 8.
Schmitt-Beck, Rüdiger. "The 'Alternative für Deutschland in the Electorate': Between Single-Issue and Right-Wing Populist Party." *German Politics* 25 (2016), 124–48.
Speck, Ulrich. "German Power and the Ukraine Conflict." The Carnegie Endowment for International Peace. April 4, 2015. Available at: http://carnegieeurope.eu/2015/03/26/german-power-and-ukraine-conflict.
Szabo, Stephen F. *Germany, Russia, and the Rise of Geo-Economics.* London: Bloomsbury, 2015.
Yoder, Jennifer A. "From Amity to Enmity: German-Russian Relations in the Post Cold War Period." *German Politics and Society* 33 (2015), 49–69.

NOTES

Introduction: Total defeat

1 Heinrich August Winkler, *Germany: The Long Road West*, trans., Alexander J. Sager (New York: Oxford University Press, 2007).

2 Ulrich Herbert, *Geschichte Deutschlands im 20. Jahrhundert* (Munich: Beck, 2014).

3 Hans-Ulrich Wehler, *Deutsche Gesellschaftsgeschichte. Fünfter Band: Bundesrepublik und DDR, 1949-1990* (Munich: Beck, 2008), 426–27, 437–38.

Chapter 1

1 Leonie Treber, *Mythos Trümmerfrauen. Von der Trümmerbeseitigung in der Kriegs-und Nachkriegszeit und der Entstehung eines deutschen Erinnerungsortes* (Essen 2014).

2 Clemens Vollnhals, *Evangelische Kirche und Entnazifizierung 1945-1949* (Munich: Oldenbourg, 1989), 54–55; Lutz Niethammer, *Entnazifizierung in Bayern: Säuberung und Rehabilitierung unter amerikanischer Besatzung* (Frankfurt am Main: Fischer, 1972), 396.

3 Gerhard Keiderling, "Scheinpluralismus und Blockparteien: Die KPD und die Gründung der Parteien in Berlin 1945," *Vierteljahrshefte für Zeitgeschichte* 45 (1997), 257–96.

4 Ulrich Herbert, *Geschichte Deutschlands im 20. Jahrhundert* (Munich: Beck 2014), 600–01.

Chapter 2

1 For the first election in 1949, the "five percent hurdle" only applied to vote totals in the individual Länder.

2 Wilhelm Grewe, "Das Grundgesetz," *Deutsche Rechts-Zeitschrift* 4 (1949), 314.

3 Ernst Forsthoff, *Rechtsstaat im Wandel* (Stuttgart: Kohlhammer, 1964), 104–05.

4 Werner Weber, *Spannungen und Kräfte im westdeutschen Verfassungssystem*, 3rd ed. (Berlin: Duncker und Humblot, 1970), 29–30.

5 Dolf Sternberger, "Demokratie der Furcht oder Demokratie der Courage?" *Die Wandlung* 4, no. 1 (1949): 8–11, 13.

6 On the question of German standard of living under Nazism, see the argument between Götz Aly, *Hitler's Beneficiaries: Plunder, Racial War, and the Nazi Welfare State* (New York: Metropolitan, 1997) and Adam Tooze, *The Wages of Destruction: The Making and Breaking of the Nazi Economy* (New York: Penguin Books, 2008).

Chapter 3

1 http://www.bib-demografie.de/EN/Facts_Figures/Divorces/Figures/a_05_02_ ehescheidungen_d_ab1888.html;jsessionid=DC6CCF655119E227F9D 3237FD7478D7E.2_cid380?nn=3214408

2 Helge Heidemeyer, *Flucht und Zuwanderung aus der SBZ/DDR 1945/1949-1961: Die Flüchtlingspolitik der Bundesrepublik Deutschland bis zum Bau der Berliner Mauer* (Dusseldorf: Droste, 1993), 43.

Chapter 4

1 Gabriele Metzler, "Am Ende aller Krisen? Politisches Denken und Handeln in der Bundesrepublik der sechziger Jahre," *Historische Zeitschrift* 275 (2002), 57–103.

2 Phillip Felsch, *Der lange Sommer der Theorie: Geschichte einer Revolte 1960-1990* (Munich: Beck, 2015), 32.

3 Wolfgang Kraushaar, ed. *Frankfurter Schule und Studentenbewegung. Von der Flaschenpost zum Moltowcocktail 1946-1995.* Vol. 1–3 (Hamburg: Rogner und Bernhard), 1998.

4 Detlef Siegfried, *Time is on My Side. Konsum und Politik in der westdeutschen Jugendkultur der 60er Jahre* (Göttingen: Wallstein Verlag, 2006).

Chapter 5

1 Falco Werkentin, *Politische Strafjustiz in der Ära Ulbricht: Vom bekennenden Terror zur verdeckten Repression*, Second edition (Berlin: Links, 1997), 248–50.

2 Helmut Müller-Enbergs, *Die inoffiziellen Mitarbeiter (MfS-Handbuch)* (Berlin: Bundesbeauftragter für die Unterlagen der ehemaligen Deutschen Demokratischen Republik, 2008), 36–38.

3 Fulbrook, *The People's State*, 256–63.

4 Roland Jahn, *Wir Angepassten: Überleben in der DDR* (Munich: Piper, 2015).

5 Madlen Schäfer, "Waffen für Syrien," Bundeszentrale fur politische Bildung, February 1, 2017, http://www.bpb.de/geschichte/deutsche-geschichte/ stasi/233561/stasi-in-syrien, *with further references*.

Chapter 6

1 Dierk Hoffmann, "Sicherung bei Alter, Invalidität und für Hintergebliebene, Sonderversorgungssysteme," in *Geschichte der Sozialpolitik in Deutschland seit 1945* (Baden-Baden: Nomos, 2008), X:325–62.

2 Oskar Anweiler, "Bildungspolitik," in *Geschichte der Sozialpolitik in Deutschland seit 1945*. Baden-Baden: Nomos, 2006, V: 709–53.

3 Anweiler, "Bildungspolitik," 750–52.

Chapter 7

1 Robert Jungk, *The Nuclear State*, trans. Eric Mosbacher (London: John Calder, 1979), 30–31, 132–36.

2 Rudolf Augstein, "Atomstaat oder Rechtsstaat?" *Der Spiegel* 31:10 (February 28, 1977), 29–34.

3 Ingrid Matthäus-Maier, speech of April 20, 1978, Protokolle des Deutschen Bundestags, 8. Wahlperiode, 86. Sitzung, p. 6798.

4 Norbert Eimer, speech of November 27, 1986, Protokolle des Deutschen Bundestags, 10. Wahlperiode, 250. Sitzung, p. 19457.

Chapter 8

1 Hermann Wentker, *Aussenpolitik in engeren Grenzen: Die DDR im internationalen System, 1949-1989* (Munich: Oldenbourg, 2007), 402ff., Valentini Zamperini, "Die DDR in den 1970ern und 1980ern: Auf der Suche nach einer eigenen Aussenpolitik im Schatten Moskaus," *Deutschland Archiv*, February 2, 2014, accessed June 20, 2017, available at: http://www.bpb.de/geschichte/zeitgeschichte/deutschlandarchiv/179837/die-ddr-in-den-1970er-und-1980er-jahren-suche-nach-einer-eigenen-aussenpolitik-im-schatten-moskaus.

Chapter 9

1 Marvin Kalb, "Beyond the Missile Crisis," NBC Reports, December 28, 1983; see also Frank Brettschneider, *Öffentliche Meinung und Politik: Eine empirische Studie zur Responsivität des deutschen Bundestags* (Wiesbaden: Springer Fachmedien, 1995), 304, with references to other similar polls.

2 Statistisches Bundesamt, *Bevölkerung und Erwerbstätigkeit* (Wiesbaden: Kohlhammer, 1982).

3 Heinz Friedrich, ed., *Chamissos Enkel* (Munich: dtv, 1986), 29.

4 Sina Fabian, "Massentourismus und Individualität. Pauschalurlaube westdeutscher Reisender in Spanien während der 1970er- und 1980er-Jahre," *Zeithistorische Forschungen* 1 (2016), 61–85.

5 Maren Möhring, *Fremdes Essen. Die Geschichte der ausländischen Gastronomie in der Bundesrepublik* (Munich: Oldenbourg, 2012).

Chapter 10

1 Although the conspirators apparently did not act only with the approval of the Soviet Union, as has occurred in Ulbricht's case: Andreas Malycha and Peter Jochen Winters, *Die SED: Geschichte einer deutschen Partei* (Munich: Beck, 2009), 338.

Chapter 11

1 Quoted in Helmut Schmidt, "Uns Deutsche kann der Teufel holen," *Die Zeit* 21 (May 17, 1991), 3. Reprinted in Dirk Philipsen, *We Were the People*, 329.

2 Marcus Böick, *Die Treuhandanstalt 1990-1994* (Erfurt: Landeszentrale für politische Bildung Thüringen, 2015), 92–94.

3 "Arroganter Wesse und nörgeliger Ossi," *Volksstimme*, October 10, 2014, available at: http://www.volksstimme.de/nachrichten/sonderthemen/25_jahre_mauerfall/1350648_Arroganter-Wessi-und-noergeliger-Ossi.html.

4 *So geht Einheit: Wie weit das einst geteilte Deutschland zusammengewachsen ist,* a report from the Berlin-Institut für Bevölkerung und Entwicklung and the GfK Verein (Berlin: Berlin-Institut für Bevölkerung und Entwicklung, 2015), 44, 56.

5 Susanne Worbs, et al., *(Spät-) Aussiedler in Deutschland: Eine Analyse aktueller Daten und Forschungsergebnisse* (Berlin: Bundesamt für Migration und Flüchtlinge, 2013), 28.

Chapter 12

1 "Grün ist der Wechsel. Programm zur Bundestagswahl 1998." Accessed at: https://www.boell.de/sites/default/files/assets/boell.de/images/download_de/publikationen/1998_Wahlprogramm_Bundestagswahl.pdf

2 According to the Federal Ministry for the Environment: http://www.umweltbundesamt.de/themen/klima-energie/erneuerbare-energien/erneuerbare-energien-in-zahlen

3 "Zwanzig Jahre jüdische Zuwanderung nach Deutschland," Zentralrat der Juden in Deutschland, September 22, 2009, at: www.zentralratderjuden.de/de/article/2646.html

4 Özlem Topçu, Alice Bota, and Khuê Pham, *Wir neuen Deutschen. Wer wir sind, was wir wollen* (Reinbek bei Hamburg: Rowohlt, 2012), 102.

Chapter 13

1 http://www.idea.int/vt/countryview.cfm?id=61

2 On this logic: Andreas Wirsching, *Demokratie und Globalisierung: Europa seit 1789* (Munich: Beck, 2015).

3 Chronology in Tina Hildebrandt and Bernd Ulrich, "Im Auge des Orkans," *Die Zeit*, September 17, 2015, access at http://www.zeit.de/2015/38/angela-merkel-fluechtlinge-krisenkanzlerin.

4 Hans Vorländer, Maik Herold, and Steven Schäller, *PEGIDA: Entwicklung, Zusammensetzung und Deutung einer Empörungsbewegung* (Berlin: Springer, 2015).

5 "Deutlich mehr Anschläge auf Asylbewerberheime," *Tagesschau* January 13, 2016, accessed at: https://www.tagesschau.de/inland/anschlaege-asylunterkuenfte-bka-101.html; "Mehr als 1600 Delikte: Zahl rechter Gewalttaten gegen Flüchtlichen steigt dramatisch," *Spiegel-Online*, Dec. 15, 2015, accessed at: http://www.spiegel.de/politik/deutschland/fluechtlinge-1610-delikte-in-zusammenhang-mit-unterkuenften-a-1067825.html.

6 "Grundsatzprogramm der Alternative für Deutschland" (April 30/May 1, 2016), accessed at: https://www.alternativefuer.de/wp-content/uploads/sites/7/2016/03/Leitantrag-Grundsatzprogramm-AfD.pdf

INDEX